Assessment of Eating Behavior

About the Editor

Adrian Meule, PhD, is a researcher at the University Hospital of the LMU Munich and the Schoen Clinic Roseneck (Prien am Chiemsee, Germany). His major research interests include eating behavior, eating disorders, obesity, and other topics in health and clinical psychology, about which he has published more than 150 scientific articles and book chapters as well as one book. He served as editor for several scientific journals and is currently on the editorial boards of *Mental Health Science* and *Obesity Science and Practice.*

Psychological Assessment – Science and Practice

Each volume in the series *Psychological Assessment - Science and Practice* presents the state-of-the-art of assessment in a particular domain of psychology, with regard to theory, research, and practical applications. Editors and contributors are leading authorities in their respective fields. Each volume discusses, in a reader-friendly manner, critical issues and developments in assessment, as well as well-known and novel assessment tools. The series is an ideal educational resource for researchers, teachers, and students of assessment, as well as practitioners.

Psychological Assessment - Science and Practice is edited with the support of the European Association of Psychological Assessment (EAPA).

Psychological Assessment – Science and Practice, Vol. 6

Assessment of Eating Behavior

Edited by

Adrian Meule

Department of Psychiatry and Psychotherapy,
University Hospital, LMU Munich, Munich, Germany;
Schoen Clinic Roseneck, Prien am Chiemsee, Germany

hogrefe

Library of Congress Cataloging in Publication information for the print version of this book is available via the Library of Congress Marc Database under the LC Control Number 2023935606

Library and Archives Canada Cataloguing in Publication
Title: Assessment of eating behavior / edited by Adrian Meule (Department of Psychiatry and Psychotherapy, University Hospital, LMU Munich, Munich, Germany; Schoen Clinic Roseneck, Prien am Chiemsee, Germany).
Names: Meule, Adrian, editor.
Series: Psychological assessment--science and practice ; v. 6.
Description: Series statement: Psychological assessment--science and practice ; vol. 6 | Includes bibliographical references.
Identifiers: Canadiana (print) 20230178960 | Canadiana (ebook) 20230178987 | ISBN 9780889376168 (softcover) | ISBN 9781616766160 (PDF) | ISBN 9781613346167 (EPUB)
Subjects: LCSH: Eating disorders—Diagnosis. | LCSH: Eating disorders—Patients—Psychological testing.
Classification: LCC RC552.E18 A87 2023 | DDC 616.85/26075—dc23

http://www.hogrefe.com

PUBLISHING OFFICES
USA: Hogrefe Publishing Corporation, 44 Merrimac St., Suite 207, Newburyport, MA 01950
Phone (978) 255 3700; E-mail customersupport@hogrefe.com
EUROPE: Hogrefe Publishing GmbH, Merkelstr. 3, 37085 Göttingen, Germany
Phone +49 551 99950-0, Fax +49 551 99950-111; E-mail publishing@hogrefe.com
SALES & DISTRIBUTION
USA: Hogrefe Publishing, Customer Services Department,
30 Amberwood Parkway, Ashland, OH 44805
Phone (800) 228-3749, Fax (419) 281-6883; E-mail customersupport@hogrefe.com
UK: Hogrefe Publishing, c/o Marston Book Services Ltd., 160 Eastern Ave., Milton Park, Abingdon, OX14 4SB
Phone +44 1235 465577, Fax +44 1235 465556; E-mail direct.orders@marston.co.uk
EUROPE: Hogrefe Publishing, Merkelstr. 3, 37085 Göttingen, Germany
Phone +49 551 99950-0, Fax +49 551 99950-111; E-mail publishing@hogrefe.com
OTHER OFFICES
CANADA: Hogrefe Publishing, 82 Laird Drive, East York, Ontario, M4G 3V1
SWITZERLAND: Hogrefe Publishing, Länggass-Strasse 76, 3012 Bern

Printed and bound in Germany

ISBN 978-0-88937-616-8 (print) • ISBN 978-1-61676-616-0 (PDF) • ISBN 978-1-61334-616-7 (EPUB)
https://doi.org/10.1027/00616-000

Contents

Part I Introduction

Chapter 1 Introduction: Assessment of Eating Behavior 3
Adrian Meule

Part II Eating Behavior Domains

Chapter 2 Assessment of Restrained Eating and Dieting 15
Janet Polivy, C. Peter Herman, and Jennifer S. Mills

Chapter 3 Assessment of Emotional Eating 27
Catharine Evers, Nathalie Michels, Sandra Verbeken, and Caroline Braet

Chapter 4 Assessment of Food Craving and Food "Addiction" 44
Lindzey V. Hoover and Ashley N. Gearhardt

Chapter 5 Assessment of Orthorexia Nervosa 56
Crystal D. Oberle and Natalie A. Noebel

Chapter 6 Assessment of Intuitive Eating and Mindful Eating 71
Melanie J. Zimmer-Gembeck, Harley J. Stansfield, Jessica Kerin, and Caroline Donovan

Chapter 7 Assessment of Grazing 82
Eva M. Conceição, Marta de Lourdes, and Carmen Beatriz Neufeld

Chapter 8 Assessment of Anorexia Nervosa 97
Heather A. Davis, Meredith Kells, and Jennifer E. Wildes

Chapter 9 Assessment of Bulimia Nervosa 109
Sophie R. Abber, Sarrah I. Ali, and Pamela K. Keel

Chapter 10 Assessment of Binge Eating Disorder 124
Amy H. Egbert and Andrea B. Goldschmidt

Chapter 11 Assessment of Other Eating Disorders 140
Kelly C. Allison

Part III Adjacent Domains

Chapter 12 Assessment of Body Image 157
Rike Arkenau-Kathmann, Hannah L. Quittkat, and Silja Vocks

Chapter 13 Assessment of Physical Activity 170
Elizabeth W. Lampe and Sasha Gorrell

Chapter 14 Assessment of Body Composition and Energy Expenditure 190
Nuno Casanova, Ruairi O'Driscoll, Graham Finlayson, R. James Stubbs, and Mark Hopkins

Chapter 15 Assessment of Food Neophobia and Disgust Sensitivity 206
Christina Hartmann and Klazine van der Horst

Chapter 16 Assessment of Weight-Related Stigmatization....................... 218
Megan Lindloff and Angela Meadows

Part IV Assessment Methods and Issues

Chapter 17 Measuring Food Intake in the Laboratory 237
Suzanne Higgs

Chapter 18 Ecological Momentary Assessment of Eating Behavior 250
Diana Zhang, Tyler Mason, and Kathryn Smith

Chapter 19 Behavioral Tasks for Measuring and Changing Reactions to Food.... 260
Sarah Masterton and Andrew Jones

Chapter 20 Psychophysiological Measures in Eating Behavior Research 275
Annika P. C. Lutz, Zoé van Dyck, and Claus Vögele

Contributors 291

Part I

Introduction

Chapter 1

Introduction

Assessment of Eating Behavior

Adrian Meule[1,2]

[1] Department of Psychiatry and Psychotherapy, University Hospital, LMU Munich, Germany
[2] Schoen Clinic Roseneck, Prien am Chiemsee, Germany

Introduction

If not prevented by food shortage, humans typically eat every day. At first glance, eating seems like a very simple behavior: if you feel hungry, you eat something until you are satiated. Yet, it is in fact a very complex behavior. Humans have to make numerous decisions each day, for example, when to eat, what to eat, and how long or how much to eat. According to a study by Wansink and Sobal (2007), people make more than 200 of such food decisions every day – most of them unconsciously. Despite this complexity, it appears that eating works quite well for most people without having to think about it much. Yet, given its complexity, eating can also go awry, potentially resulting in eating and weight disorders.

Some people do not consume enough calories or certain nutrients, leading to underweight or nutritional deficiencies. Such restrictive eating may be intentional (e.g., in persons with anorexia nervosa) but can also be unintentional (e.g., resulting from a physical illness). A much larger group of people, however, consume more energy than their body needs, resulting in them becoming overweight or obese (i.e., an excessive accumulation of body fat). As with restrictive eating, overeating can have different causes and patterns. For example, certain forms of overeating are characterized by a disinhibited eating style (e.g., binge eating episodes that are marked by a loss of control over eating). The majority of persons whose weight increases slowly over time, however, are largely unaware of living in a chronic state of positive energy balance ("passive overeating"; Davis, 2013). Figure 1.1 provides an overview of the different eating styles and eating disorders presented in Chapters 2 to 10 by arranging them according to body weight and on a continuum ranging from restrictive to disinhibited eating.

Following this introductory chapter, this book is organized in three parts. In *Part II: Eating Behavior Domains*, Chapters 2 to 11 describe the assessment of different eating styles and eating disorders. In *Part III: Adjacent Domains*, Chapters 12 to 16 describe the assessment of aspects that may determine or follow from the eating behaviors described in

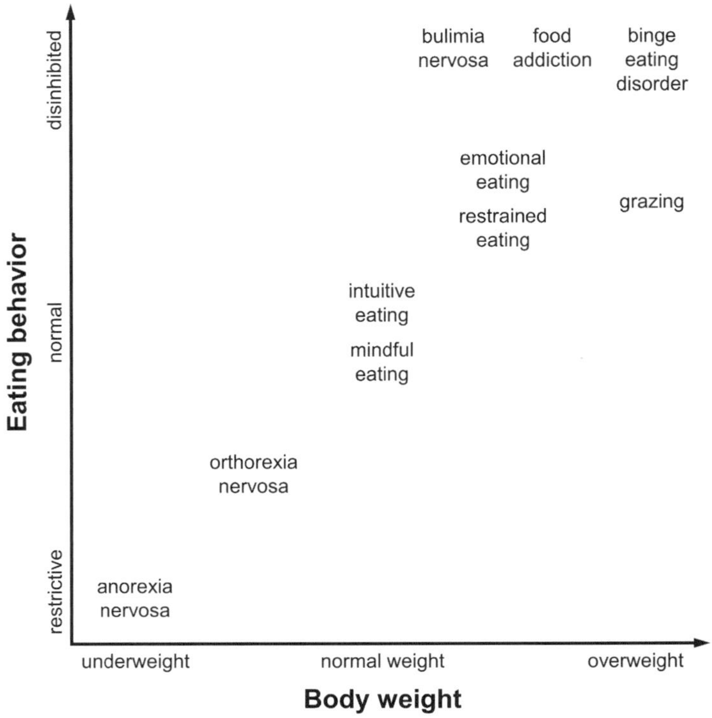

Figure 1.1. Schematic depiction of eating styles and eating disorders arranged according to eating behavior and body weight.

Part II. In *Part IV: Assessment Methods and Issues*, Chapters 17 to 20 examine methodological issues in the assessment of eating behavior and its related aspects.

Eating Behavior Domains

In Chapter 2, Polivy, Herman, and Mills describe the assessment of restrained eating and dieting. Research on restrained eating was heavily influenced – in fact, was started off – by a now classic experiment by Herman and Mack (1975). When participants had to consume a so-called preload (one or two milkshakes), unrestrained (i.e., "normal") eaters adjusted their subsequent food intake (here, ice cream) while restrained eaters (who were trying to limit their food intake) actually increased their food intake (Figure 1.2). As later research confirmed that such and other experimental manipulations can lead to a "disinhibited" food intake in restrained eaters and as restrained eating measures are usually positively correlated with body mass index (BMI), restrained eating is located somewhat in the upper right corner in Figure 1.1. However, as will be demonstrated in Chapter 2, the assessment of restrained eating and dieting is much more complex as these terms are not synonymous and it appears that there is also a subgroup of successful restrained eaters who do not show disinhibited eating or an elevated body weight (Figure 1.3).

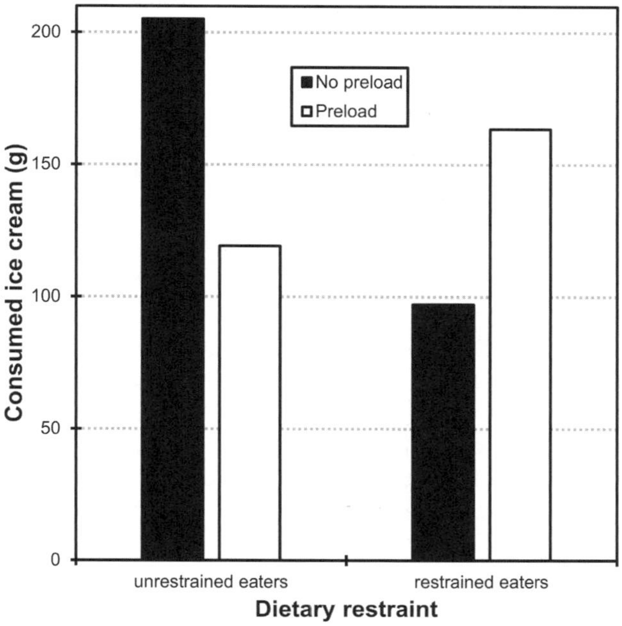

Figure 1.2. Mean consumed ice cream in grams as a function of dietary restraint and experimental condition in the classic study by Herman and Mack (1975). Note that there were actually two preload conditions (consumption of one or two milkshakes), the numbers of which are collapsed in this depiction.

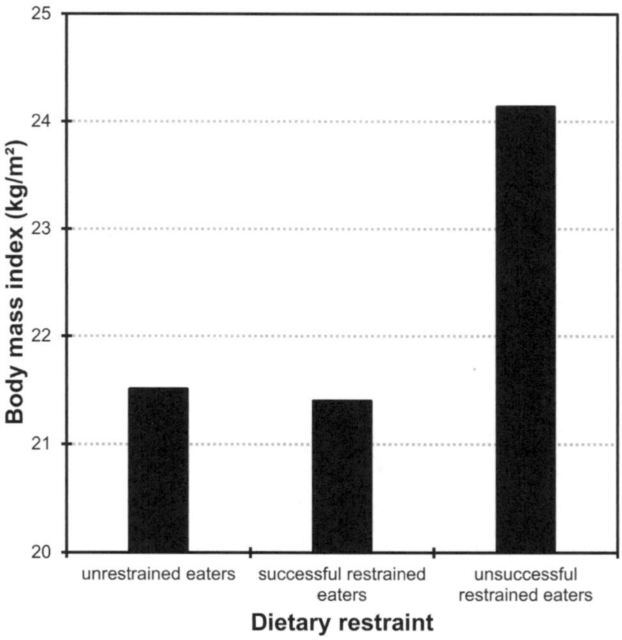

Figure 1.3. Mean body mass index in kg/m² as a function of dietary restraint. The data are based on a study reported in Meule et al. (2012), in which 499 participants were not only classified as unrestrained and restrained eaters but restrained eaters were additionally categorized as successful and unsuccessful based on their perceived self-regulatory success in weight regulation.

In Chapter 3, Evers, Michels, Verbeken, and Braet describe the assessment of emotional eating. Research on this eating style has largely focused on negative emotional states that trigger food intake and – similar to measures of restrained eating – measures of emotional eating are usually weakly, positively correlated with BMI (Frayn & Knäuper, 2018). This is why emotional eating is also located somewhat in the upper right corner in Figure 1.1, close to restrained eating. Yet again, as will be demonstrated in Chapter 3, the concept and assessment of emotional eating is much more complex than this, as it appears that certain affective states can also lead to a decrease in food intake and that self-report measures of emotional eating are not always congruent with other assessment methods.

In Chapter 4, Hoover and Gearhardt describe the assessment of food craving and food "addiction." Both concepts are strongly related, with the latter term being controversially discussed among scientists and practitioners. Food craving can refer to a transient state of a current, strong desire to consume a specific food but also to a more trait-like eating style (i.e., individuals who often experience and give into such cravings). As such, the experience of food craving is an essential component of conceptualizing certain forms of overeating as an addiction. It appears that current assessment approaches of addiction-like eating strongly overlap with established eating disorders such as bulimia nervosa and binge eating disorder (Meule & Gearhardt, 2019), which is why food addiction is located between the two in the upper right corner in Figure 1.1.

In Chapter 5, Oberle and Noebel describe the assessment of so-called orthorexia nervosa – another concept that has been controversially discussed in the literature. It was proposed by Bratman (1997) who argued that some people are so obsessed with eating healthily that this can even be considered as a new type of disordered eating. While persons who show orthorexic eating tendencies are not trying to limit the quantity of food intake (i.e., the amount of food or calories consumed), they are more concerned about the quality of foods. As such, however, they do exhibit a form of restriction and it appears that there is a large overlap with anorexic eating behavior (at least with currently used measures of orthorexia nervosa; Meule & Voderholzer, 2021). Because of this, orthorexia nervosa is located somewhat in the lower left corner in Figure 1.1.

In Chapter 6, Zimmer-Gembeck, Stansfield, Kerin, and Donovan describe the assessment of intuitive eating and mindful eating. Both concepts are strongly related and their definitions somewhat overlap: Intuitive eating can be defined as a tendency to follow physical hunger and satiety cues when determining when, what, and how much to eat (Tylka & Kroon Van Diest, 2013) and mindful eating can be defined as a nonjudgmental awareness of physical and emotional sensations associated with eating (Framson et al., 2009). As both intuitive and mindful eating represent functional, adaptive, and healthy eating styles that promote having a normal weight in the absence of intentional food restriction or loss-of-control eating, they are located in the center of Figure 1.1.

In Chapter 7, Conceição, de Lourdes, and Neufeld describe the assessment of grazing. Grazing is characterized by repetitive eating of small amounts of food in an unplanned manner. Although measures of grazing usually correlate only weakly with BMI, grazing appears to be a highly prevalent eating style in persons with obesity (Heriseanu et al., 2017), which is why it is located on the right-hand side in Figure 1.1. While it is a form of overeating, it is not necessarily characterized by a distinct loss of control over eating like during binge eating episodes, which is why it is located between normal and disinhibited eating in Figure 1.1.

In Chapter 8, Davis, Kells, and Wildes describe the assessment of anorexia nervosa. Although one of the first descriptions in the psychiatric literature is often attributed to Gull in 1873 (reprinted in Gull, 1997), there are also earlier reports about its symptomatology (cf. Bemporad, 1996). Anorexia nervosa is an eating disorder that is characterized by restriction of energy intake relative to requirements, leading to a significantly low body weight. Therefore, it is located in the lower left corner in Figure 1.1. However, two subtypes are commonly differentiated. The restricting type describes presentations in which weight loss is accomplished primarily through dieting, fasting, and/or excessive exercise. The binge/purge type describes presentations in which individuals engage in recurrent episodes of binge eating and purging behavior (e.g., self-induced vomiting). Thus, a subgroup of persons with anorexia nervosa do indeed show recurring disinhibited eating. Yet, it appears that at the same time they have similar levels of dietary restraint to those with restricting type anorexia nervosa (Uniacke et al., 2020), which is why this subtype is not separately depicted in Figure 1.1.

In Chapter 9, Abber, Ali, and Keel describe the assessment of bulimia nervosa. The term bulimia nervosa was coined by Russell (1979) but there are also earlier reports about its symptomatology (cf. Vandereycken, 1994). Bulimia nervosa is an eating disorder that is characterized by recurrent episodes of binge eating and inappropriate compensatory behaviors in order to prevent weight gain (e.g., self-induced vomiting). In contrast to persons with binge/purge type anorexia nervosa, however, persons with bulimia nervosa typically have normal weight or are slightly overweight. Therefore, bulimia nervosa is located at the top in Figure 1.1 and somewhat at the border from normal weight to overweight.

In Chapter 10, Egbert and Goldschmidt describe the assessment of binge eating disorder. Binge eating was first described as an eating pattern among obese persons by Stunkard (1959) although it appears that earlier case reports even date back to the 1930s (Stunkard, 1990; Wulff, 1932). Binge eating disorder is an eating disorder that is characterized by recurrent episodes of binge eating. Unlike persons with bulimia nervosa, however, persons with binge eating disorder do not engage in inappropriate compensatory behaviors to prevent weight gain. Accordingly, the majority of persons with binge eating disorder are overweight or obese. Therefore, binge eating disorder is located in the upper right corner in Figure 1.1.

In Chapter 11, Allison describes the assessment of other eating disorders, namely night eating syndrome, avoidant/restrictive food intake disorder (ARFID), rumination disorder, and pica. Night eating syndrome is characterized by recurrent episodes of night eating, as manifested by eating after awakening from sleep or by excessive food consumption after the evening meal. Similar to binge eating disorder, night eating syndrome was first described by Stunkard as early as the 1950s (Stunkard et al., 1955) but has not been included in diagnostic classification systems until 2013 (American Psychiatric Association, 2013). ARFID can be defined as an eating or feeding disturbance that is manifested by persistent failure to meet appropriate nutritional or energy needs. Rumination disorder is marked by repeated regurgitation of food that may be rechewed, reswallowed, or spit out. Pica is characterized by persistent eating of nonnutritive, nonfood substances. Locating these eating disorders on a spectrum from underweight to overweight and from restrictive to disinhibited eating is not straightforward. For example, although night eating syndrome has originally been conceptualized as an eating behavior among persons with obesity, its relationship with body weight is ambiguous (Meule et al., 2014). While ARFID is often associated with a low body weight, this is not the result of an intentional food restriction driven by weight and shape concerns (i.e., unlike in persons with anorexia nervosa). Similarly, regurgitation of food in rumination disorder is not driven by an intention to lose weight or prevent weight gain (i.e., unlike self-induced vomiting in persons with bulimia nervosa). Finally, the essential feature of pica refers to the nature of consumed substances. Therefore, these eating disorders are not represented in Figure 1.1.

Adjacent Domains

In Chapter 12, Arkenau -Kathmann, Quittkat, and Vocks describe the assessment of body image. Body image refers to a person's perception of their body and shape as well as attitudes and feelings toward their body. There is also a behavioral component, that is, body-related behaviors (e.g., body checking) that result from – and in turn can influence (Shafran et al., 2007) – a person's body image. Marked weight and shape concerns and a disturbed body image are key features of eating disorders such as anorexia nervosa and bulimia nervosa and drive intentions to restrict eating. However, the relationship between body image and eating behavior is bidirectional. For example, weight and shape concerns can also be the result of weight gain after a longer period of excess energy intake.

In Chapter 13, Lampe and Gorrell describe the assessment of physical activity. Although not included as a diagnostic criterion, excessive or compulsive exercise can often be observed in persons with eating disorders such as anorexia nervosa and bulimia nervosa. The relationship between physical activity and eating behavior, however, is not restricted to persons with eating disorders and, similar to body image, is bidirectional. For example, eating behavior (e.g., carbohydrate intake) influences exercise performance. Vice versa, physical activity also influences eating behavior as it seems that acute exercise is associated with a short-term suppression of hunger and energy intake and exercising regularly appears to be associated with better appetite control (Drenowatz et al., 2019).

In Chapter 14, Casanova, O'Driscoll, Finlayson, Stubbs, and Hopkins describe the assessment of body composition and energy expenditure. By taking a person's height into account, BMI is a fairly good estimator of a person's percent body fat, at least in certain groups of individuals (e.g., young adult women; Meule & Platte, 2018). However, it is less precise in others, particularly athletes with a large amount of muscle mass, children and adolescents, pregnant or breastfeeding women, and elderly persons. As will be described in this chapter, there are several methods to measure body composition more precisely, for example, by differentiating fat and fat-free mass. Besides physical activity, body composition (particularly fat-free mass) is a major determinant of energy expenditure, yet it also relates to appetite and energy intake. Thus, similar to the previous chapters on adjacent domains, there is a bidirectional relationship: eating behavior influences body composition and energy expenditure and vice versa.

In Chapter 15, Hartmann and van der Horst describe the assessment of food neophobia and disgust sensitivity. Food neophobia refers to the fear or reluctance to eat unfamiliar or novel foods. In children, it has been suggested that food neophobia can be considered as lying on the continuum ranging from food neophobia to picky/fussy eating to ARFID (Dovey, 2018). Disgust sensitivity refers to the predisposition for experiencing disgust. At first glance, both concepts seem quite similar: In relation to food, both neophobia and the experience of disgust result in the avoidance of consuming a particular food. However, it seems that they can indeed influence food selection and consumption independently. In one study, for example, food neophobia and disgust sensitivity were uncorrelated with each other and both concepts independently predicted lower intentions to eat insect-based foods (La Barbera et al., 2018).

In Chapter 16, Lindloff and Meadows describe the assessment of weight-related stigmatization. Weight stigmatization refers to negative attitudes, beliefs, and behaviors towards persons who are overweight because of their weight or size. Similar terms include weight discrimination, weight bias, antifat bias, or antifat attitudes. Besides the assessment of stigmatizing attitudes in nonoverweight persons towards persons who are overweight, an important line of research in this field is the self-stigmatization or internalization of weight bias in these persons with overweight. Experiences of weight stigma and higher levels of weight bias internalization have been linked to a range of adverse outcomes, including physical, psychological, and social detriments (Pearl, 2018).

Assessment Methods and Issues

In Chapter 17, Higgs describes how food intake can be measured in the laboratory. The majority of measures described in Parts II and III of this book are self-report questionnaires. While such measures are widely used, they are susceptible to be biased (e.g., due to social desirability or recall bias). Measuring food intake in the laboratory may, therefore, be a more "objective" approach in eating behavior research. For example, it allows for examining not only amount, calories, or macronutrients of consumed food but also food choice (if several foods are offered) and eating microstructure (e.g., eating rate, duration). Measuring food intake in the laboratory is often disguised as a taste test in an attempt to avoid that participants feel that their eating is being observed. While there is support that such bogus taste tests can validly be used as a measure of food intake, there are numerous aspects that need to be considered when planning and conducting such studies (Best et al., 2018; Buckland & Dalton, 2018; Hetherington & Rolls, 2018; Meule, 2018; Robinson et al., 2018; Stubbs & Finlayson, 2018).

In Chapter 18, Zhang, Mason, and Smith describe ecological momentary assessment of eating behavior. Similar to measuring food intake in the laboratory, ecological momentary assessment can avoid biases inherent in self-report questionnaires. Here, participants answer questions about their food intake and other information (e.g., hunger, mood) usually several times a day. Thus, ecological momentary assessment allows the capturing of this information almost in real time, thus avoiding recall biases. In contrast to measuring food intake in the laboratory, it also allows for capturing dynamic changes in eating and associated aspects and – as eating is assessed in daily life – avoids the artificial situation inherent in laboratory studies. Yet, although it solves many issues compared with other assessment methods, there are also caveats as ecological momentary assessment may itself change eating behavior. For example, it has been found that keeping a daily snack diary suffices to decrease unhealthy snacking (Verhoeven et al., 2014).

In Chapter 19, Masterton and Jones describe behavioral tasks for measuring and changing reactions to food. Reactions to food that are often automatic, implicit, and unconscious are a strong force that drives eating behavior. In this chapter, the authors focus on three main domains that have been of increased interest in recent years: inhibitory control, approach-avoidance tendencies, and attentional biases. Moreover, research indicates that these reactions to food (or other) stimuli cannot only be measured but can also be modified by adapting reaction time tasks as trainings, which is done by simply altering stimulus-response contingencies (Kemps & Tiggemann, 2021; Tiggemann & Kemps, 2020). As of yet, however, studies have produced inconsistent findings whether this cognitive bias modification also results in changes of real-world consumption behaviors.

In Chapter 20, Lutz, van Dyck, and Vögele describe psychophysiological measures in eating behavior research. Physiology is, obviously, highly relevant to eating behavior. The digestion of food represents an interplay of complex physiological processes. Yet, physiological reactions occur even before food has been ingested. For example, salivary flow increases merely in response to seeing or smelling food, with more salivation being related to a stronger craving for the food (Meule & Hormes, 2015). In addition, there are numerous psychophysiological methods that have been used in eating behavior research that measure physiological responses that are not part of the digestive system. Among others, these include measuring brain activity, facial muscular activity, eye movements, or cardiovascular activity.

Conclusions

This volume treats the assessment of many different eating styles and eating disorders, describes the assessment of domains that are adjacent to eating behavior, and discusses methodological topics. As eating behavior is so multifaceted, however, it cannot fully cover all aspects that might be relevant to eating behavior research. For example, as the focus of this book is more on psychological aspects of eating behavior, it does not include a detailed description of dietary intake assessment - that is, how to assess consumed macro- and micronutrients in daily life - as would be required during nutrition counseling. Other omissions include the assessment of certain forms of nutrition (e.g., vegetarianism, pescetarianism, veganism) and their motivational and attitudinal aspects (e.g., attitudes towards meat consumption and animal welfare). These are just a few examples but there are probably many more aspects that could be mentioned here. Yet, with the topics covered in this book, readers - both researchers and practitioners - will be well-equipped for the assessment of eating behavior and its related aspects.

References

American Psychiatric Association. (2013). *Diagnostic and Statistical Manual of Mental Disorders* (5th ed.). American Psychiatric Association.

Bemporad, J.R. (1996). Self-starvation through the ages: Reflections on the pre-history of anorexia nervosa. *International Journal of Eating Disorders, 19*, 217–237. https://doi.org/10.1002/(SICI)1098-108X(199604)19:3<217::AID-EAT1>3.0.CO;2-P

Best, M., Barsalou, L.W., & Papies, E.K. (2018). Studying human eating behaviour in the laboratory: Theoretical considerations and practical suggestions. *Appetite, 130*, 339–343. https://doi.org/10.1016/j.appet.2018.06.001

Bratman, S. (1997). Health food junkie. *Yoga Journal, September-October*, 42–50.

Buckland, N.J., & Dalton, M. (2018). Commentary: Methodological and reporting practices for laboratory studies assessing food intake using fixed and ad libitum test meals. *Appetite, 130*, 336–338. https://doi.org/10.1016/j.appet.2018.06.007

Davis, C. (2013). From passive overeating to "food addiction": A spectrum of compulsion and severity. *ISRN Obesity, 2013*, 435027. https://doi.org/10.1155/2013/435027

Dovey, T.M. (2018). Avoidant/restrictive food intake disorder: An eating disorder on a spectrum with food neophobia. In S. Reilly (Ed.), *Food Neophobia* (pp. 329–349). Woodhead Publishing. https://doi.org/10.1016/B978-0-08-101931-3.00016-1

Drenowatz, C., Greier, M.d.C., & Greier, K. (2019). Association of exercise with control of eating and energy intake. *Current Addiction Reports, 6*(3), 210–217. https://doi.org/10.1007/s40429-019-00255-1

Framson, C., Kristal, A.R., Schenk, J.M., Littman, A.J., Zeliadt, S., & Benitez, D. (2009). Development and validation of the Mindful Eating Questionnaire. *Journal of the American Dietetic Association, 109*, 1439–1444. https://doi.org/10.1016/j.jada.2009.05.006

Frayn, M., & Knäuper, B. (2018). Emotional eating and weight in adults: A review. *Current Psychology, 37*, 924–933. https://doi.org/10.1007/s12144-017-9577-9

Gull, W.W. (1997). V.-Anorexia Nervosa (Apepsia Hysterica, Anorexia Hysterica). *Obesity Research, 5*, 498–502. https://doi.org/10.1002/j.1550-8528.1997.tb00677.x

Heriseanu, A.I., Hay, P., Corbit, L., & Touyz, S. (2017). Grazing in adults with obesity and eating disorders: A systematic review of associated clinical features and meta-analysis of prevalence. *Clinical Psychology Review, 58*, 16–32. https://doi.org/10.1016/j.cpr.2017.09.004

Herman, C.P., & Mack, D. (1975). Restrained and unrestrained eating. *Journal of Personality, 43*, 647–660. https://doi.org/10.1111/j.1467-6494.1975.tb00727.x

Hetherington, M.M., & Rolls, B.J. (2018). Favouring more rigour when investigating human eating behaviour is like supporting motherhood and apple pie: A response to Robinson, Bevelander, Field, and Jones (2018). *Appetite, 130*, 330–333. https://doi.org/10.1016/j.appet.2018.05.013

Kemps, E., & Tiggemann, M. (2021). Attentional bias modification for chocolate: Sham-n training as a new control group. *PLoS ONE, 16*(11), Article e0260294. https://doi.org/10.1371/journal.pone.0260294

La Barbera, F., Verneau, F., Amato, M., & Grunert, K. (2018). Understanding Westerners' disgust for the eating of insects: The role of food neophobia and implicit associations. *Food Quality and Preference, 64*, 120–125. https://doi.org/10.1016/j.foodqual.2017.10.002

Meule, A. (2018). Standardizing versus measuring food deprivation and hunger. *Appetite, 130*, 328–329. https://doi.org/10.1016/j.appet.2018.05.014

Meule, A., Allison, K.C., Brähler, E., & Zwaan, M. de (2014). The association between night eating and body mass depends on age. *Eating Behaviors, 15*, 683–685. https://doi.org/10.1016/j.eatbeh.2014.10.003

Meule, A., & Gearhardt, A.N. (2019). Ten years of the Yale Food Addiction Scale: A review of version 2.0. *Current Addiction Reports*. https://doi.org/10.1007/s40429-019-00261-3

Meule, A., & Hormes, J.M. (2015). Chocolate versions of the Food Cravings Questionnaires: Associations with chocolate exposure-induced salivary flow and ad libitum chocolate consumption. *Appetite, 91*, 256–265. https://doi.org/10.1016/j.appet.2015.04.054

Meule, A., Lutz, A., Vögele, C., & Kübler, A. (2012). Food cravings discriminate differentially between successful and unsuccessful dieters and non-dieters: Validation of the Food Cravings Questionnaires in German. *Appetite, 58*, 88–97. https://doi.org/10.1016/j.appet.2011.09.010

Meule, A., & Platte, P. (2018). An examination of the "Freshman-15" in Germany: Predictors of weight change in female university students. *European Journal of Health Psychology, 25*, 2–8. https://doi.org/10.1027/2512-8442/a000001

Meule, A., & Voderholzer, U. (2021). Orthorexia nervosa – It is time to think about abandoning the concept of a distinct diagnosis. *Frontiers in Psychiatry, 12*, Article 640401. https://doi.org/10.3389/fpsyt.2021.640401

Pearl, R.L. (2018). Weight bias and stigma: Public health implications and structural solutions. *Social Issues and Policy Review, 12*(1), 146–182. https://doi.org/10.1111/sipr.12043

Robinson, E., Bevelander, K.E., Field, M., & Jones, A. (2018). Comments on methodological and reporting quality in laboratory studies of human eating behaviour. *Appetite, 130*, 344–345. https://doi.org/10.1016/j.appet.2018.07.001

Russell, G. (1979). Bulimia nervosa: An ominous variant of anorexia nervosa. *Psychological Medicine, 9*, 429–448. https://doi.org/10.1017/S0033291700031974

Shafran, R., Lee, M., Payne, E., & Fairburn, C.G. (2007). An experimental analysis of body checking. *Behaviour Research and Therapy, 45*(1), 113–121. https://doi.org/10.1016/j.brat.2006.01.015

Stubbs, R.J., & Finlayson, G.S. (2018). Improving laboratory studies of human eating behaviour: Energy balance and real-world considerations. *Appetite, 130*, 334–335. https://doi.org/10.1016/j.appet.2018.05.009

Stunkard, A. (1990). A description of eating disorders in 1932. *American Journal of Psychiatry, 147*, 263–268. https://doi.org/10.1176/ajp.147.3.263

Stunkard, A.J. (1959). Eating patterns and obesity. *Psychiatric Quarterly, 33*, 284–295. https://doi.org/10.1007/bf01575455

Stunkard, A.J., Grace, W.J., & Wolff, H.G. (1955). The night-eating syndrome: A pattern of food intake among certain obese patients. *American Journal of Medicine, 19*, 78–86. https://doi.org/10.1016/0002-9343(55)90276-X

Tiggemann, M., & Kemps, E. (2020). Is sham training still training? An alternative control group for attentional bias modification. *Frontiers in Psychology, 11*, Article 583518. https://doi.org/10.3389/fpsyg.2020.583518

Tylka, T.L., & Kroon Van Diest, A.M. (2013). The Intuitive Eating Scale–2: Item refinement and psychometric evaluation with college women and men. *Journal of Counseling Psychology, 60*, 137–153. https://doi.org/10.1037/a0030893

Uniacke, B., Slattery, R., Walsh, B.T., Shohamy, D., Foerde, K., & Steinglass, J. (2020). A comparison of food-based decision-making between restricting and binge-eating/purging subtypes of anorexia nervosa. *International Journal of Eating Disorders, 53*(10), 1751–1756. https://doi.org/10.1002/eat.23359

Vandereycken, W. (1994). Emergence of bulimia nervosa as a separate diagnostic entity: Review of the literature from 1960 to 1979. *International Journal of Eating Disorders, 16*, 105–116. https://doi.org/10.1002/1098-108X(199409)16:2<105::AID-EAT2260160202>3.0.CO;2-E

Verhoeven, A.A.C., Adriaanse, M.A., de Vet, E., Fennis, B.M., & de Ridder, D.T.D. (2014). Identifying the "if" for "if-then" plans: Combining implementation intentions with cue-monitoring targeting unhealthy snacking behaviour. *Psychology & Health, 29*, 1476–1492. https://doi.org/10.1080/08870446.2014.950658

Wansink, B., & Sobal, J. (2007). Mindless eating: The 200 daily food decisions we overlook. *Environment and Behavior, 39*, 106–123. https://doi.org/10.1177/0013916506295573

Wulff, M. (1932). Über einen interessanten oralen Symptomenkomplex und seine Beziehungen zur Sucht [On an interesting oral symptom complex and its relationship to addiction]. *Internationale Zeitschrift für Psychoanalyse, 18*, 281–302.

Part II

Eating Behavior Domains

Chapter 2

Assessment of Restrained Eating and Dieting

Janet Polivy,[1] C. Peter Herman,[1] and Jennifer S. Mills[2]

[1] Department of Psychology, University of Toronto, Canada
[2] Department of Psychology, York University, Canada

Introduction

The purpose of this chapter is to describe and discuss the various measures used in the assessment of restrained eating and dieting. We separate these two constructs, despite the fact that restrained eating has often been seen as virtually synonymous with dieting. Indeed, it was originally proposed as a way of capturing chronic dieting attempts. As will become evident, the characteristics associated with long-term, on-again/off-again dieting are not always the same as those associated with single-episode, current dieting. Thus, we will treat restrained eating and dieting as separate constructs requiring different assessment and measurement approaches. Moreover, we will focus the present discussion only on "normal dieting" and normal restrained eating, not on eating disorders and their measurement, which will be addressed in later chapters.

Defining Restrained Eating and Dieting

One cannot assess an attribute without defining it, and with dieting and restrained eating, definitions can be somewhat complex. People have different reasons for dieting and/or restricting their eating. Many people eat or avoid particular foods for ethical, moral, or religious reasons, such as eating only religiously defined halal or kosher foods, or being vegetarian or vegan because of a moral opposition to killing animals for food. Some people follow a healthful food regimen which they regard as a diet. Others eat or avoid particular foods because of allergies, digestive issues, or other health concerns. The goal in these instances is unrelated to weight or appearance, and may not involve any restriction on the number of calories consumed. Many individuals who "diet" do so in order to be healthier by losing weight, and thus they restrict their food intake but are not particularly concerned with their body shape or appearance. Nevertheless, most of the psychological literature on eating behavior, and more specifically restrained eating and dieting, focuses on a different group, namely the large number of people who go on weight-loss diets specifically in order to try to improve their appearance and/or body image. These are the individuals whom researchers consider to be restrained eaters or dieters.

But even defining weight-loss dieters is not a simple matter. Should people who try to restrict their eating in order to lose weight or to look more attractive be considered dieters if they do not succeed in restricting their intake with any consistency? Or should only those who actually succeed at cutting back on their intake be considered dieters? Are people who say that they are dieters actually dieters regardless of whether they are really restricting their food intake? Is being a dieter based on intent, self-identification, or action?

Identifying restrained eaters or weight-loss dieters also leads to some interesting distinctions. Restrained eaters were originally defined by Herman and Polivy (1980) as chronic dieters who make repeated attempts to lose weight by dieting, but who are also inclined to bouts of overeating interspersed among periods of restricting intake. Moreover, these chronic on-again, off-again dieters displayed a set of behaviors (restraining one's eating but then eating excessive amounts), emotional reactions (such as greater responses to emotional provocation), and attentional or cognitive patterns (such as a focus on food cues). Thus, restrained eating is more than simply being on a diet to lose weight at any given moment, and is therefore not the same as being a dieter per se. As Martz, Sturgis, and Gustafson (1996, p. 298) pointed out, "recent literature defined dieting as a set of current behaviors, whereas dietary restraint is defined as a more enduring style of eating behavior including excessive food restriction, dieting, and sometimes binge eating and weight-cycling."

Dieting tends to be defined much more simply in the research literature as simply whether one is attempting to restrict one's intake in order to control one's weight (either losing weight or maintaining an already reduced weight; e.g., Lowe, 1993), but dieting can also be based on restriction of amounts or certain types of food (e.g., following a particular weight-loss diet that eliminates sugar or carbohydrates). Like dieting, restrained eating has been defined and assessed in different ways (e.g., Polivy et al., 2020). In this chapter, we will try to distinguish among different measures of restrained eating and dieting based on the definitions used by those who constructed the assessment devices.

Defining Dieting

Researchers studying dieting (not restrained eating) are usually looking specifically at current dieters, individuals who claim to be on a diet at present. Lowe (1993, p. 100) defines "current dieting" as "a current effort to reduce caloric intake to lose weight" and "a commitment to lose weight by dieting." However, French and Jeffrey (1994, p. 195) reviewed the literature (at that time) on dieting and noted that "current dieting, chronic dieting, desire to lose weight, specific weight control behaviors, and weight changes may have different effects on health and need to be distinguished." When Martz and colleagues (1996) attempted to construct a scale to measure "dieting to lose weight," they suggested operationalizing dieting on the basis of not only specific behaviors, but also on the basis of cognitions and intentions, specifying that actual weight loss may not occur despite the appropriate dieting behaviors and intentions and thus should not be part of the operationalization of the concept. Moreover, simply asking people whether or not they are dieting at that moment forces a dichotomy of dieting versus not dieting to which Martz et al. object. Accordingly, they developed a set of current dieting behaviors rather than a single question to measure dieting. They concluded that dieting should refer only to various current behaviors in a specific episode, whereas the more chronic condition should be seen as restrained eating. Importantly, trends in weight control behaviors change over time, which adds complexity to defining dieting. Any definition of dieting needs to be flexible and may vary according to social trends. Intermittent fasting, as an example, has multiple eating patterns associated with it, depending on how much time elapses between meals and the time of day during which people eat.

Defining Restrained Eating

The original definition of restrained eating was proposed by Herman and Polivy (1975), and reflected not only the attempt to restrict food intake by dieters, but also other attributes seen as part of the construct. Restrained eating was seen as a complex set of behaviors (both food restriction, and a breakdown of that restriction resulting in episodes of excessive consumption), weight fluctuations presumably resulting from these behaviors, plus attitudes about one's weight and eating, cognitions about food and eating, emotional responses to eating, and the motivation to be thinner. In addition, the Restraint Scale (RS) asked about frequency of "dieting" (Herman & Polivy, 1980). The definition of restrained eating as originally presented by Herman and Polivy (1975, 1980) was that it is a complex individual-difference trait consisting of dieting behaviors, episodes of diet abandonment and overeating, and a set of cognitions, attitudes, and a motivation to be thinner or more physically attractive. Finally, self-identification as a dieter was assessed by asking how often one dieted, with possible responses from "never" to "always." Thus, Herman and Polivy saw restrained eating as composed of: individual differences in motivation to be thinner, by means of cognitive efforts to "restrain" one's food intake; behavioral restriction and also overeating in the face of overwhelming temptations; emotional reactions to such eating (e.g., feeling guilty after overeating); and a self-identification as someone who diets to control one's weight. Both restriction and succumbing to temptation were seen as critical to the definition of restrained eating (Herman & Polivy, 1980; Polivy & Herman, 1985, 1987; Williamson et al., 2007).

In 1985, a new measure, the Three Factor Eating Questionnaire (TFEQ), was developed by Stunkard and Messick to capture multiple aspects of eating behavior. The TFEQ had a subscale that the authors named "cognitive restraint" as well as subscales assessing "disinhibition" and "hunger." These authors were primarily interested in identifying successful dieters who managed to restrict their intake consistently enough to lose weight. Unfortunately, using the same term ("restraint") as Herman and Polivy's earlier conceptualization has led to decades of confusion in the literature, if only because Stunkard deliberately separated the disinhibition component from the restriction component in his questionnaire. Thus, "cognitive restraint" (which, naturally, became shortened by those using the questionnaire to "restraint" or "restrained eating") differs from the earlier notion of restraint: The Stunkard and Messick version is meant to describe only successful control over food intake, not caloric restriction combined with episodes of overeating or disinhibition (see Heatherton et al., 1988; or Polivy et al., 2020 for more complete discussions of this issue).

A year later, van Strien and her colleagues presented their eating assessment device, the Dutch Eating Behavior Questionnaire (DEBQ; Strien, Frijters, Berger, & Defares, 1986;

Strien, Frijters, Staveran et al., 1986). This measure also contains a subscale labeled "restrained eating" along with scales assessing "emotional eating" and "external eating." Similar to the TFEQ, van Strien viewed restrained eating as successful restriction of intake without a disinhibitory component (see Heatherton et al., 1988 or Polivy et al., 2020).

The restrained eating described by both the Stunkard group and the van Strien group appears to be successful dietary restriction over a long term (Laessle et al., 1989; Tuschl et al., 1990), and is independent of the other dimensions (e.g., periodic episodes of disinhibited eating and emotional and cognitive responses to food and eating) that were seen as critical components of restrained eating by Herman and Polivy (Heatherton et al., 1988; Polivy et al., 2020). These later conceptions of restrained eating may be seen as purer views of dietary restriction.

Questionnaire Measures of Dieting and Restrained Eating

In order to predict and understand how people behave around foods of various types, we need to identify dieters and restrained eaters. We will examine the main measures that have been developed and used for this purpose.

Dieting Scales

Single Questions: For the most part, researchers have been content to simply ask participants if they are currently on a diet as a yes/no question (e.g., Lowe et al., 1991; Neumark-Sztainer et al., 1997; Rideout & Barr, 2009). Despite the finding that clear, single-item questions asking about whether or not one is currently dieting to lose weight do correlate well with energy intake, several researchers have tried to develop multi-item measures of current dieting.

Cognitive Behavioral Dieting Scale: Martz and colleagues (1996) developed the Cognitive Behavioral Dieting Scale (CBDS), a 14-item scale designed to measure current dieting behaviors and related thoughts during the preceding two weeks. Internal and test-retest reliability were both high ($\alpha = .95$; $r = .95$) and the scale predicted caloric intake. While related to restrained eating, the behaviors measured by the CBDS were deemed to be different from dietary restraint, and to reflect simple dieting. Martz and colleagues concluded that this measure operationalizes dieting and measures it on a continuum. Unfortunately, this measure does not seem to have attracted much research attention.

Dietary Intent Scale: The Dietary Intent Scale (DIS; Stice, 1998a) has been described by its author as "a 9-item measure of dietary behaviors with three sub-scales assessing reduced intake of food, abstaining from eating, and consumption of low-calorie foods" (p. 282). The original paper presenting this scale described it somewhat differently as

> a nine-item measure of restraint ... that was created for the present study because of the questionable validity of the RS. A pilot study ($N = 117$) indicated that the DIS is internally ($\alpha = .94$) and temporally reliable (1-month test-retest $r = .92$). (Stice, 1998b, p. 247)

Because later work by Stice continues to describe the DIS as a measure of dieting rather than restraint (e.g., Stice et al., 2004, 2010), we will include it here. As Stice (1998b) indicated, the scale appears to have good internal and test-retest reliability. The full nine-item questionnaire is available in Stice (1998b).

Perceived Self-Regulatory Success in Dieting Scale: Fishbach and colleagues (2003) developed a measure of self-perceived success at dieting. The Perceived Self-Regulatory Success in Dieting Scale (PSRS) consists of three questions designed to distinguish between successful and unsuccessful dieters. The scale has been found to have reasonable internal reliability ($\alpha = .72–.79$), and validity was determined by its consistent negative correlations with body mass index (BMI) and various measures of dietary concern (Meule et al., 2012).

Current Dieting Questionnaire: A more recent and more streamlined dieting scale was presented by Williamson and his colleagues (2007). The Current Dieting Questionnaire (CDQ) consists of three dichotomous (true/false; yes/no) self-report items with reasonably good internal reliability ($\alpha = .85$). The three items are available in the paper discussing the scale (Williamson et al., 2007).

Restrained Eating Scales

As we mentioned earlier, the various measures of restrained eating were constructed with different goals in mind. The RS (Herman & Polivy, 1980) was intended to measure chronic dieting that consists of cycles of restriction, or at least attempted restriction, and periods of disinhibition or overeating, whereas the TFEQ and DEBQ both have subscales for purely restricted eating and other subscales to measure such constructs as disinhibition (TFEQ) or emotional eating (DEBQ). The Eating Disorder Examination (EDE; Fairburn & Beglin, 1994) was, like the RS, designed to identify more disordered dieting and overeating behaviors. As we will see, these different goals led to somewhat different, although related, measures, with the RS and EDE restrained eating measures combining dietary restriction with episodes of disinhibited overeating, while the TFEQ and DEBQ restraint scales explicitly remove disinhibitory lapses of control, assessing actual restriction of food intake.

Restraint Scale: The construct of restrained eating was originally proposed to account for the self-reported behavior of chronic weight-concerned dieters, who described dieting for long periods (all-day or all-week long) only to eat excessively at night or on the weekend. The RS (Herman & Polivy, 1975, 1980) was thus designed to measure restrictive dieting behaviors and cognitions, bouts of overeating and their consequences, and also attitudes about oneself or one's body, all of which were believed to be part of the broad construct of restrained eating. Weight fluctuations, for example, could result from alternations between restricting one's intake and overeating or splurging when the diet was abandoned. Measurement of such fluctuations was included to assess the extent to which individuals both reduced and increased their food intake. The RS is a 10-item self-report questionnaire that asks about dieting, weight fluctuations, and attitudes toward one's body and eating (e.g., "Do you have feelings of guilt after overeating?" and "Do you eat sensibly in front of others and splurge alone?"). The internal reliability ($\alpha = .79–.86$) and test-retest reliability of the scale have been found over several studies to be good (e.g., Stice et al., 2004), and early concerns about the possibility of the scale being bifactorial have proven not to be an issue (Heatherton et al., 1988; Stice et al., 2004).

Three Factor Eating Questionnaire: The TFEQ (Stunkard & Messick, 1985) was designed (as its name suggests) to measure three aspects of eating behavior, which were derived iteratively from a large number of initial items into cognitive restraint (20 items), disinhibition (20 items), and hunger (15 items). The coefficient alpha internal reliabilities were above .92 for the first two factors and .85 for hunger. The cognitive restraint factor has been shortened to simply being called a measure of restraint (the TFEQ-R). It is described as assessing behaviors designed to reduce or maintain weight, as well as concerns with thinness and physique (e.g., Stice et al., 2004) or "the extent to which one engages in cognitive and behavioral efforts to limit food intake" (French & Jeffrey, 1997, p. 34). Thus, like the RS, the full TFEQ measures both cognitions and behaviors related to weight-loss dieting.

Later work on the TFEQ identified two dimensions of TFEQ-R, flexible and rigid control of eating (Westenhoefer et al., 1999), later called flexible and rigid restraint (e.g., Masheb & Grilo, 2002; Westenhoefer et al., 2013). Flexible restraint appears to be associated with more positive eating behaviors and lower weight, less overeating, and more successful weight loss, whereas rigid restraint is opposite on all these dimensions (Westenhoefer et al., 1999).

Dutch Eating Behavior Questionnaire: The DEBQ measures restrained, emotional, and external eating. The restrained eating subscale contains 10 items, with excellent internal reliability (α=.95; Strien et al., 1986). The intent of the DEBQ-R was to assess "the degree to which an individual eats less than he or she actually would like to eat" (Strien, Frijters, Staveran et al., 1986, p. 747). The focus is thus specifically on actual behavioral reductions in intake rather than the combination of restriction and overconsumption captured by the RS or restriction and body concern captured by the TFEQ-R. The external eating and emotional eating scales look at other influences on eating behavior separately from restrained eating.

Eating Disorder Examination: The EDE began as a structured interview assessing four factors: restraint and food avoidance, eating concern, shape concern, and weight concern (Fairburn & Cooper, 1993). Later, a self-report questionnaire version was developed (EDE-Q; Fairburn & Beglin, 1994). Both versions of the EDE are widely used, mainly in the eating disorder area, as the purpose of the interview and questionnaire versions is to identify people suffering from an anorexia or bulimia nervosa. The agreement between the two versions of the EDE is acceptable for all four subscales, although greater pathology seems to be reported on the EDE-Q than in the interviews (Wilfley et al., 1997).

Successful and Unsuccessful Restraint: It was pointed out decades ago that measures of restraint, particularly the RS, do not discriminate well between successful and unsuccessful restriction of intake (e.g., Laessle et al., 1989; Ogden, 1993). Ogden suggested two items to assess such success. One of the items simply asks about current weight-loss dieting status (answered on a 5-point scale from *never* to *always*), but the other asks how successful one views oneself in this enterprise (answered on the same 5-point scale). She used these questions as additions to the RS and DEBQ-R scales and found that for both questionnaires, the most successful dieters had the lowest scores on restraint, the least successful scored the highest, and moderately successful dieters scored between the other two groups. Those who tried the most to diet and failed most often thus had the highest restraint scores on two of the main measures of restrained eating. Ogden thus sees her measure as one of successful restraint, rather than simply of successful dieting.

Van Strien (1997) found different results using these questions with the DEBQ-R scale, finding higher scores on DEBQ-R for successful than for unsuccessful dieting, and no evidence that attempting to reduce intake was related to unsuccessful dieting nor that actually eating less was associated with successful dieting. Although one could question whether Ogden's measure reflects dieting or restrained eating, it probably does not actually matter how these questions are classified: they help to raise the issue of self-rated success versus failure for both dieting and restrained eating.

Outcomes and Effectiveness of Measures of Dieting and Restrained Eating

In order to decide which assessment measure one should use, it is important to know how the various techniques perform. Obviously, we cannot review all of the evidence here, but we will try to present a general view of how well each measurement instrument achieves its intended goal of predicting how people will behave with respect to eating, and what each measure seems to assess.

Measures of Dieting

The simplest measure, simply asking people whether or not they are dieting to lose weight, has been found to have mixed results in terms of predicting either reduced caloric intake or weight loss. In one study the question predicted reported expenditure of energy through exercising, but not caloric intake (e.g., French et al., 1994), whereas in other studies by the same research team, it was associated not only with decreased energy intake (Neumark-Sztainer et al., 1997) but also with lower intakes of fat and sugar, increased intake of fruits and vegetables, and a greater frequency of weighing oneself (French & Jeffrey, 1997). However, individuals who self-identify as current dieters have also been found to underreport their energy intake when self-reports are compared to actual food diaries (e.g., Rennie et al., 2006) and to have higher BMIs than nondieters (e.g., Rideout & Barr, 2009).

Stice's DIS was also not found to correlate with caloric intake in one study (Stice et al., 2010) but it did correlate negatively with both calories and grams of fat consumed in another (Stice et al., 2004). It did not predict weight loss over time (Stice, 1998a), however. More recently, DIS scores did not correlate with various measures indicating failure of self-regulation (as the RS did), nor did it predict eating behavior, leading the authors of the study to conclude that "it is still unclear what exactly the DIS measures" (Boyce et al., 2015, p. 6).

The PSRS is really an indirect measure of dieting, as it asks not about whether or how much one is dieting, but how successful one has been at it. This may be a problem for it, at least as a measure of dieting, because it is not clear that respondents can indicate if they are actually not dieters. In our own laboratory, we re-examined data from 17 studies wherein we measured both RS and PSRS and we found that individuals who scored as successful dieters did not eat less when tempting food was available, and were actually more likely to be unrestrained eaters and current nondieters (Nguyen & Polivy, 2014). On the other hand, we did find that regardless of restraint level, high scorers on the PSRS did have lower BMIs, indicating that although most of them might not actually be dieting or concerned about their eating at all, the ones who were dieters might be more successful, as they do weigh less. Similarly, Alblas and colleagues (2021) found that regardless of restraint level, those lower on PSRS made more unhealthy food choices on a computerized food-choice measure than those scoring high. Thus, the PSRS may not be a measure of dieting per se, but it does seem to identify more successful dieters.

The CDQ was successful in predicting weight loss during a diet study. In addition, scores on the CDQ did increase during the dietary restriction phase of the study, indicating that the scale does measure current dieting (Williamson et al., 2007).

Measures of Restrained Eating

The RS has consistently been found to measure the combination of (a) dieting/restricting intake and (b) bouts of overeating and abandonment of restrictions or disinhibition (e.g., Boyce et al., 2015; Heatherton et al., 1988; Laessle et al., 1989; Ogden, 1993; Stice et al., 2004, 2010; Williamson et al., 2007). The RS does not predict consistent caloric restriction, or actual dieting behavior on any given occasion involving food, but it is associated with unsuccessful dieting attempts and disinhibited eating. For example, Ogden (1993, p. 75) concluded (looking only at the RS) that "restrained eating represents attempts at restriction followed by compensatory eating," and Laessle et al. (1989) indicated that the RS is related to unsuccessful dieting, disinhibited eating, and weight fluctuations, but not to successful caloric restriction. The TFEQ-R and DEBQ-R scales, on the other hand, seem to be more consistently associated with caloric restriction, or more successful dieting (e.g., French et al., 1994; Laessle et al., 1989; Rideout & Barr, 2009; Rodgers et al., 2018; Strien, 1997; Westenhoefer et al., 2013; Williamson et al., 2007), although some studies do not find a (negative) correlation between these measures of restrained eating and actual caloric consumption over many days (Stice et al., 2004, 2007, 2010). A study comparing self-rated successful versus unsuccessful dieters found that the successful dieters scored lower and the unsuccessful dieters scored higher on both the RS (as would be expected) and the DEBQ-R (more surprisingly; Ogden, 1993). A more recent study concluded that the RS is a better measure than the DEBQ for identifying individuals who struggle the most to control their food intake (Adams et al., 2019).

Conclusions

Dieting Versus Restrained Eating: Are They the Same?

We have separated measures of dieting from measures of restrained eating, arguing that there are important differences between these two concepts. We return to that issue now in an attempt to clarify what each type of measure is assessing. Williamson et al. (2007) argue that their measure of dieting produces results similar to those of the TFEQ-R and DEBQ-R scales. There is consensus across studies and laboratories that RS does seem to be measuring more than just dieting or the intent to diet: scores on the RS also correlated with measures of overeating and binge eating, and RS scores loaded not only on a dieting factor but also on a binge eating factor as well. Laessle et al. (1989) found clear evidence that the TFEQ-R and DEBQ-R were successful at identifying dieters who suppressed their caloric intake, but that RS scores were associated with weight fluctuations and unsuccessful dieting. French et al. (1994) also found lower food and particularly sweet food intake in TFEQ-R restrained eaters but not in those scoring higher on the RS. More recently, Boyce and colleagues (2015) found that despite significant correlations between RS restraint and DIS dieting scores, the RS was more strongly associated with variables indicative of overeating such as expectations that eating will improve mood and poor self-control. They state that "it was already very clear that high RS scores relate to overeating" (p. 6), and that neither RS scores nor DIS scores measure successful dieting.

Ogden (1993) found some evidence that even DEBQ-R scores may be associated with less successful dieting attempts, but she still sees restrained eating as different from dieting per se. Van Strien (1997) identifies two subgroups of restrained eaters, marked by higher or lower tendency toward overeating (or disinhibition) and indicating who will be successful versus failed dieters, with the unsuccessful dieters sounding a lot like high RS scorers. Stice's series of studies argues that none of the restraint scales actually measure successful dieting as indicated by reduced caloric intake over time (Stice et al., 2004, 2007, 2010). Looking at BMI and restrained eating versus dieting, however, Rideout and Barr (2009) found that BMI was higher in dieters than nondieters, but TFEQ-R scores predicted lower BMI. They thus concluded that dieting and dietary restraint are not equivalent constructs. Their work also seems to provide evidence of what van Strien (1997) would call dieters who are prone to overeating, and are thus unsuccessful, who would probably have scored higher on the RS, had it been utilized.

It thus appears that while it is mixed, the evidence generally indicates that restraint and dieting are not equivalent constructs, especially when restrained eating is measured by the RS. The DEBQ and TFEQ may identify those who eat less or weigh less, although this is not always found, and is still not seen as being the same as dieting at the moment. In sum, not all current dieters are restrained eaters, by any measure of restrained eating. And not all restrained eaters are currently on a diet, especially RS restrained eaters.

What Measure Should Be Used When

Given that dieting and restrained eating do not appear to be exactly the same, despite correlating with each other and having some overlap, it is important to be clear about what one is trying to measure. To study the effects of caloric restriction induced by currently following a weight-loss diet, the most appropriate assessment device would appear to be a measure of current dieting such as the CDQ or simply asking if one is currently dieting to lose weight. Either way of measuring current dieting provides reasonable predictive utility in terms of how that person behaves around food, especially food that is high in fat or sugar. Measures of restrained eating do not appear to be ideal for this purpose.

If, however, one is interested in investigating the long-term effects of trying repeatedly to diet to lose weight, the restraint scales are the appropriate measures. Successful restrained eating marked by better, more consistent food restriction is best measured by the TFEQ and DEBQ restraint subscales. Because the evidence suggests that weight-loss dieting is more often unsuccessful than successful, and that attempts to diet are often followed by episodes of disinhibited eating, the RS or EDE restraint scales are the best measures for studying chronic, on-again, off-again dieting attempts (Polivy et al., 2020).

References

Adams, R. C., Chambers, C. D., & Lawrence, N. S. (2019). Do restrained eaters show increased BMI, food craving and disinhibited eating? A comparison of the Restraint Scale and the Restrained Eating Scale of the Dutch Eating Behaviour Questionnaire. *Royal Society Open Science, 6*(6), 190174. https://doi.org/10.1098/rsos.190174

Alblas, M. C., Mollen, S., Fransen, M. L., & Van den Putte, B. (2021). See the cake and have it too? Investigating the effect of watching a cooking show on unhealthy food choices. *Physiology & Behavior, 236,* 113409. https://doi.org/10.1016/j.physbeh.2021.113409

Boyce, J. A., Gleaves, D. H., & Kuijer, R. G. (2015). Measuring dietary restraint status: Comparisons between the Dietary Intent Scale and the Restraint Scale. *Frontiers in Nutrition, 2,* Article 8. https://doi.org/10.3389/fnut.2015.00008

Fairburn, C. G., & Beglin, S. J. (1994). Assessment of eating disorders: Interview or self-report questionnaire? *International Journal of Eating Disorders, 16,* 363–370.

Fairburn, C. G., & Cooper, Z. (1993). The Eating Disorder Examination (12th ed.). In C. G. Fairburn, & G. T. Wilson (Eds). *Binge eating – Nature, assessment, and treatment* (pp. 317–360). Guilford Press.

Fishbach, A., Friedman, R. S., & Kruglanski, A. W. (2003). Leading us not unto temptation: Momentary allurements elicit overriding goal activation. *Journal of Personality and Social Psychology, 84,* 296–309. https://doi.org/10.1037/0022-3514.84.2.296

French, S. A., & Jeffery, R. W. (1994). Consequences of dieting to lose weight: Effects on physical and mental health. *Health Psychology, 13,* 195–212. https://doi.org/10.1037/0278-6133.13.3.195

French, S. A., & Jeffrey, R. W. (1997). Current dieting, weight loss history, and weight suppression: Behavioral correlates of three dimensions of dieting. *Addictive Behaviors, 22,* 31–44. https://doi.org/10.1016/S0306-4603(96)00002-0

French, S., Jeffrey, R., & Wing, R. R. (1994). Food intake and physical activity: A comparison of three measures of dieting. *Addictive Behavior, 19,* 401–409. https://doi.org/10.1016/0306-4603(94)90063-9

Heatherton, T., Herman, C. P., Polivy, J., King, G. A., & McGree, T. (1988). The (mis)measurement of restraint: An analysis of conceptual and psychometric issues. *Journal of Abnormal Psychology, 97,* 19–28.

Herman, C. P., & Polivy, J. (1975). Anxiety, restraint, and eating behavior. *Journal of Abnormal Psychology, 84,* 666–672. https://doi.org/10.1037/0021-843X.84.6.666

Herman, C. P., & Polivy, J. (1980). Experimental and clinical aspects of restrained eating. In A. Stunkard (Ed.), *Obesity: Basic mechanisms and treatment* (pp. 208–225). W. B. Saunders.

Laessle, R. G., Tuschl, R. J., Kotthaus, B. C., & Pirke, K. M. (1989). A comparison of the validity of three scales for the assessment of dietary restraint. *Journal of Abnormal Psychology, 98,* 504–507. https://doi.org/10.1037/0021-843X.98.4.504

Lowe, M. R. (1993). The effects of dieting on eating behavior: A three-factor model. *Psychological Bulletin, 114,* 100–121. https://doi.org/10.1037/0033-2909.114.1.100

Lowe, M. R., Whitlow, J. W., & Bellwoar, V. (1991). Eating regulation: The role of restraint, dieting, and weight. *International Journal of Eating Disorders, 10,* 461–471. https://doi.org/10.1002/1098-108X(199107)10:4<461::AID-EAT2260100411>3.0.CO;2-U

Martz, D. M., Sturfis, E. T., & Gustafson, S. B. (1996). Development and preliminary validation of the cognitive behavioral dieting scale. *International Journal of Eating Disorders, 19,* 297–309. https://doi.org/10.1002/(SICI)1098-108X(199604)19:3<297::AID-EAT9>3.0.CO;2-H

Masheb, R. M., & Grilo, C. M. (2002). On the relation of flexible and rigid control of eating to body mass index and overeating in patients with binge eating disorder. *International Journal of Eating Disorders, 31,* 82–91. https://doi.org/10.1002/eat.10001

Meule, A., Papies, E.K., & Kubler, A. (2012). Differentiating between successful and unsuccessful dieters: Validity and reliability of the Perceived Self-Regulatory Success in Dieting Scale. *Appetite, 58*, 822–826. https://doi.org/10.1016/j.appet.2012.01.028

Neumark-Sztainer, D., Jeffrey, R.W., & French, S.A. (1997). Self-reported dieting: How should we ask? What does it mean? Associations between dieting and reported energy intake. *International Journal of Eating Disorders, 22*, 437–449. https://doi.org/10.1002/(SICI)1098-108X(199712)22:4<437::AID-EAT9>3.0.CO;2-N

Nguyen, C., & Polivy, J. (2014). Eating behavior, restraint status, and BMI of individuals high and low in perceived self-regulatory success. *Appetite, 75*, 49–53.

Ogden, J. (1993). The measurement of restraint: Confounding success and failure? *International Journal of Eating Disorders, 13*, 69–76. https://doi.org/10.1002/1098-108X(199301)13:1<69::AID-EAT226 0130109>3.0.CO;2-Z

Polivy, J., & Herman, C.P. (1985). Dieting and bingeing: A causal analysis. *American Psychologist, 40*, 193–201. https://doi.org/10.1037/0003-066X.40.2.193

Polivy, J., & Herman, C.P. (1987). The diagnosis and treatment of normal eating. *Journal of Consulting and Clinical Psychology, 55*, 635–644. https://doi.org/10.1037/0022-006X.55.5.635

Polivy, J., Herman, C.P., & Mills, J.S. (2020). What is restrained eating and how do we identify it? *Appetite, 155*, 104820. https://doi.org/10.1016/j.appet.2020.104820

Rennie, K.L., Siervo, M., & Jebb, S.A. (2006). Can self-reported dieting and dietary restraint identify underreporters of energy intake in dietary surveys? *Journal of the American Dietetic Association, 106*, 1667–1672. https://doi.org/10.1016/j.jada.2006.07.014

Rideout, C.A., & Barr, S.I. (2009). "Restrained eating" vs "trying to lose weight": How are they associated with body weight and tendency to overeat among postmenopausal women? *Journal of the American Dietetic Association, 109*, 890–893. https://doi.org/10.1016/j.jada.2009.02.009

Rodgers, R.F., Woodward, A.L., Swinburn, B., & Dietz, W.H. (2018). When does behavior follow intent? Relationships between trait level dietary restraint and daily eating behaviors. *Appetite, 120*, 449–455. https://doi.org/10.1016/j.appet.2017.09.030

Stice, E. (1998a). Prospective relation of dieting behaviors to weight change in a community sample of adolescents. *Behavior Therapy, 29*, 277–299. https://doi.org/10.1016/S0005-7894(98)80007-5

Stice, E. (1998b). Relations of restraint and negative affect to bulimic pathology: A longitudinal test of three competing models. *International Journal of Eating Disorders, 23*, 243–260. https://doi.org/10.1002/(SICI)1098-108X(199804)23:3<243::AID-EAT2>3.0.CO;2-J

Stice, E., Cooper, J.A., Schoeller, D.A., Tappe, K., & Lowe, M.R. (2007). Are dietary restraint scales valid measures of moderate- to long-term dietary restriction? Objective biological and behavioral data suggest not. *Psychological Assessment, 19*, 449–458. https://doi.org/10.1037/1040-3590.19.4.449

Stice, E., Fisher, M., & Lowe, M.R. (2004). Are dietary restraint scales valid measures of acute dietary restriction? Unobtrusive observational data suggest not. *Psychological Assessment, 16*, 51–59. https://doi.org/10.1037/1040-3590.16.1.51

Stice, E., Sysko, R., Roberto, C.A., & Allison, S. (2010). Are dietary restraint scales valid measures of dietary restriction? Additional objective behavioral and biological data suggest not. *Appetite, 54*, 331–339. https://doi.org/10.1016/j.appet.2009.12.009

Strien, T. van (1997). Are most dieters unsuccessful? An alternative interpretation of the confounding of success and failure in the measurement of restraint. *European Journal of Psychological Assessment, 13*, 186–194. https://doi.org/10.1027/1015-5759.13.3.186

Strien, T. van, Frijters, J.E., Bergers, G.P., & Defares, P.B. (1986). Dutch Eating Behavior Questionnaire for assessment of restrained, emotional, and external eating behavior. *International Journal of Eating Disorders, 5*, 295–315. https://doi.org/10.1002/1098-108X(198602)5:2<295::AID-EAT22600502 09>3.0.CO;2-T

Strien, T. van, Frijters, J.E., Staveran, W.A. van, Defares, P.B., & Deurenberg, P. (1986). The predictive validity of the Dutch Restrained Eating Scale. *International Journal of Eating Disorders, 5*, 747–755. https://doi.org/10.1002/1098-108X(198605)5:4<747::AID-EAT2260050413>3.0.CO;2-6

Stunkard, A. J., & Messick, S. (1985). The three-factor eating questionnaire to measure restraint, disinhibition, and hunger. *Journal of Psychosomatic Research, 29*, 71–83. https://doi.org/10.1016/0022-3999(85)90010-8

Tuschl, R. J., Platte, P., Laessle, R. G., Stichler, W., & Pirke, K. M. (1990). Energy expenditure and everyday eating behavior in healthy young women. *American Journal of Clinical Nutrition, 52*, 81–86. https://doi.org/10.1093/ajcn/52.1.81

Westenhoefer, J., Engel, D., Holst, C., Lorenz, J., Peacock, M., Stubbs, J., Whybrow, S., & Raats, M. (2013). Cognitive and weight-related correlates of flexible and rigid restrained eating behaviour. *Eating Behaviors, 14*, 69–72. https://doi.org/10.1016/j.eatbeh.2012.10.015

Westenhoefer, J., Pudel, V., & Stunkard, A. J. (1999). Validation of the flexible and rigid control dimensions of dietary restraint. *International Journal of Eating Disorders, 26*, 53–64. https://doi.org/10.1002/(SICI)1098-108X(199907)26:1<53::AID-EAT7>3.0.CO;2-N

Wilfley, D. E., Schwartz, M. B., Spurrell, E. B., & Fairburn, C. G. (1997). Assessing the specific psychopathology of binge eating disorder patients: Interview or self-report? *Behaviour Research and Therapy, 35*, 1151–1159. https://doi.org/10.1016/S0005-7967(97)80010-1

Williamson, D. A., Martin, C. K., York-Crowe, E., Anton, S. D., Redman, L. M., Han, H., & Ravussin, E. (2007). Measurement of dietary restraint: Validity tests of four questionnaires. *Appetite, 48*, 183–192. https://doi.org/10.1016/j.appet.2006.08.066

Chapter 3

Assessment of Emotional Eating

Catharine Evers,[1] Nathalie Michels,[2] Sandra Verbeken,[2] and Caroline Braet[2]

[1] Department of Social, Health, and Organizational Psychology, Utrecht University, The Netherlands
[2] Department of Developmental, Personality and Social Psychology, Ghent University, Belgium

Introduction

Emotional eating is a popular concept reflecting problems with regulating one's eating behavior. However, the concept is difficult to capture. Most often, it refers to subjectively experienced reports (Strien, 2018; Strien et al., 1986). However, according to recent insights this does not always reflect objective observations (Bongers & Jansen, 2016), while others argue that it is a multicomponent construct (Macht, 2008). Therefore, all attempts to measure emotional eating in all its facets should be applauded. The current chapter will explore and evaluate different operationalizations and measures that can contribute to making a deliberate choice how to measure emotional eating.

The phenomenon of emotional eating is often defined as "eating in response to stress or negative/positive affective states" (Bongers & Jansen, 2016). It is seen as problematic behavior because it hinders weight control and it often initiates feelings of shame and guilt. Emotional eating can also be characterized by different facets of food consumption. Examples are: type of food, often so-called comfort food representing high-fat and energy-dense food (Macht, 2008); the amount of food that is problematic; the feeling that leads to craving or overeating (Tomiyama, 2019); or the timing of food consumption, as it mostly occurs in the absence of hunger. In contrast with the many different assumed characteristics related to emotional eating, in the literature more consensus has been reached on explaining why emotional eating occurs. According to the well-researched affect regulation model, people suffering from stress and related negative affective states regulate their affect by eating (Grilo & Shiffman, 1994; Burton et al., 2007). So, emotional eating is seen as a coping mechanism, regulating emotions and/or arousal (Aparicio et al., 2016; Evers et al., 2010; Vandewalle et al., 2017). Of note, the differentiation with emotion regulation is not straightforward and triggers questions like: Do we have to see emotional eating as an emotion regulation strategy or is emotional eating a more automatic process that occurs when feelings are too intense as an escape form self-awareness (Heatherton & Baumeister, 1991)?

At least two other models also claim to explain emotional eating; the models are not conflicting with each other but rather overlapping and additionally explain how emotional eating can become a habit or trait. First, emotional eating is assumed to have a short-term reinforcing effect by reducing stress-related arousal and/or physical signs related with negative affective states, or by increasing positive affect when feeling stressed or sad (Macht, 2008). Consequently, a classical reinforcement learning process is assumed, leading to emotional eating as an established coping strategy (and expectancies of reinforcement from eating).

Finally, a third model refers to emotional eating as a consequence of disinhibited eating (related with loss of control, loss of cognitive resources to control, depletion of self-regulatory resources) due to a burden of negative affect or because of strict dietary restraint intentions (Burton et al., 2007; Strien et al., 1986).

Although the three models are helpful in clinical practice, they are less useful in research as they did not make nuanced differentiations (Bongers & Jansen, 2016; Meule et al., 2018). This results in several unanswered questions that will be discussed below:

- Emotional eating is often measured by self-reports, that is, people report retrospectively that they eat because of stress or sad news. Can these self-reports in laboratory experiments be validated? Do the scales measure what we think they do? And if not, how can these self-reports be interpreted?
- Studies operationalized the characteristics of emotional eating in many ways which makes comparisons between studies difficult (questionnaires, diaries, food-taste buffets, food-choice tasks, reports on snacking, disinhibition, absence of hunger, liking, wanting, or craving for food). What should be recommended?
- Emotional eating is assumed to occur not always in reaction to stress (i.e., evaluation of a specific situation as threatening), but is also related to other negative affective states, aiming to neutralize the emotional experience, such as sadness, frustration, shame, guilt, anxiety, angriness, tension, and boredom. Should we differentiate between all these affective states that can trigger emotional eating in one person? And, should we also measure the effects of the intensity of the affective states or stressors?
- Emotional eating can also occur in the context of positive affective states, enhancing a good mood (e.g., excitement, surprise, amusement). What can we learn from the research involved here?
- Some argue to consider emotional eating as any alteration in food intake: not only eating more but also eating less than usual. How can both of these aspects be measured?
- Is it possible to differentiate between momentary emotional eating and the role of stable traits? Is it possible that emotional eating has become a habit and, therefore, functions as a stable trait, so that the models we have are not sufficient anymore?
- How to differentiate emotional eating from loss of control over eating (related to restraint intentions), leading to an eating disorder? Is it important to make this difference?

In answering these questions, it is insightful to categorize the different emotional eating measures into questionnaires, laboratory paradigms, and ecological momentary assess-

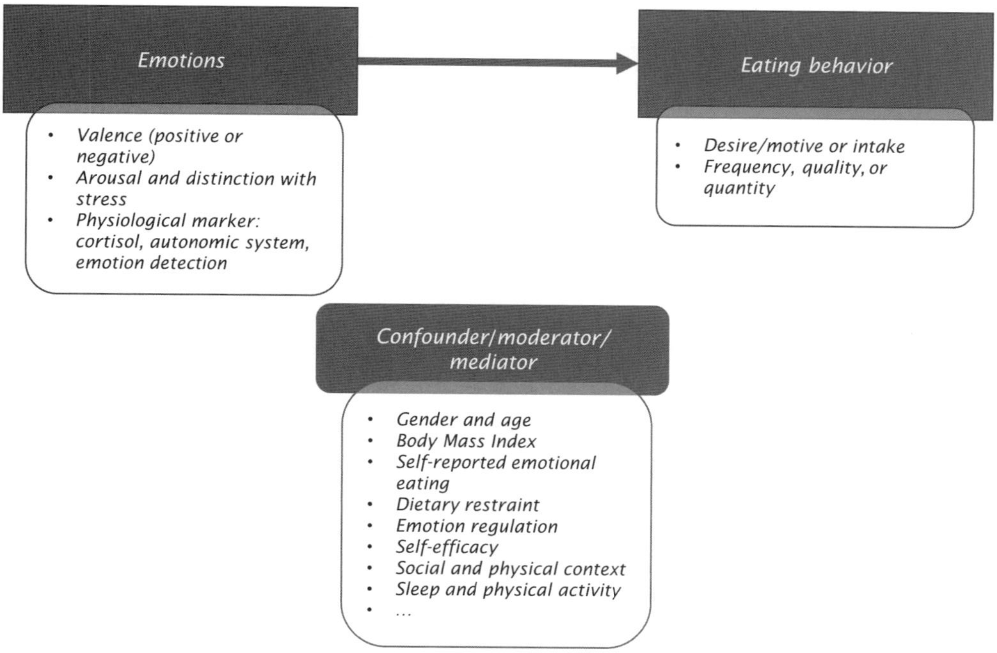

Figure 3.1. Key concepts in assessing the impact of emotions on eating behavior

ments (EMA) and discuss their abilities to assess the many different facets of emotional eating. A summary of the key concepts in emotional eating assessment is shown in Figure 3.1.

Emotional Eating Questionnaires

Several questionnaires have been developed to measure emotional eating. Table 3.1 provides an overview of all currently available emotional eating questionnaires and relevant characteristics, such as number of items, example items, subscales, and internal reliability. They diverge in how emotions and eating behaviors are assessed. Older scales mostly center on negative emotions only, while more recent scales have added positive emotions. Also the type of eating behavior varies, from the extent to which individuals eat when being emotional to the amount of (over)eating and the tendency, desire, or urge to eat when being emotional.

Table 3.1 reveals that the internal reliability of all (sub)scales is satisfactory to good. References to validity information can be found in this table as well. Overall, validity has been tested for most of the emotional eating questionnaires, and the results typically provide (preliminary) support for validity. Noteworthy is that validity has often been claimed based on the finding that the questionnaires successfully predict eating-related indicators, like body mass index (BMI), weight gain, or unsuccessful dieting. A point of concern, however, is that high scores on these questionnaires are not validated in terms of actual eating behavior in response to emotions. The studies that did so typically illustrate that these scales lack predictive validity. For example, a review on emotional eating scales amongst experimental and naturalistic studies (Bongers & Jansen, 2016) re-

Table 3.1. Emotional eating questionnaires

	# Items	Example Item	Response scale	Emotional Valence	Subscales (n = # items), internal Strien (2013) (Cronbach's α)	Reference to validity information	License required?
DEBQ: Dutch Eating Behavior Questionnaire (Strien et al., 1986)	33	"Do you have a desire to eat when you are depressed or discouraged?"	1 (= *never*) to 5 (= *very often*)	Negative	Total emotional eating scale ($n = 13, \alpha = .94$): 1. Clearly labelled emotions ($n = 9, \alpha = .93$) 2. Diffuse emotions ($n = 4, \alpha = .86$)	Strien (2013)	Yes
EES: Emotional Eating Scale (Arnow et al., 1995)	25	"Please indicate the extent to which the following feelings lead you to feel an urge to eat by checking the appropriate box." Followed by 25 feelings.	1 (= *no desire to eat*) to 5 (= *an over-whelming urge to eat*)	Negative	Total scale ($n = 25, \alpha = .81$): 1. Anger/frustration ($n = 11, \alpha = .78$) 2. Anxiety ($n = 9, \alpha = .78$) 3. Depression ($n = 5, \alpha = .72$)	Arnow et al. (1995)	No
EES-II: Emotional Eating Scale-II (Kenardy et al., 2003)	34	"Please indicate the extent to which the following feelings lead you to feel an urge to eat by checking the appropriate box." Followed by 34 feelings.	1 (= *no desire to eat*) to 5 (= *an over-whelming urge to eat*)	Negative & positive	1. Anger ($n = 6, \alpha = .88$) 2. Anxiety ($n = 5$ $\alpha = .86$) 3. Depression ($n = 12, \alpha = .86$) 4. Positive mood ($n = 11, \alpha = .70$)	Not available	No
TFEQ-R18: Three Factor Eating Questionnaire (Karlsson et al., 2000)	18	"When I feel anxious, I find myself eating."	1 (= *definitely false*) to 4 (= *definitely true*)	Negative	Emotional eating subscale ($n = 3, \alpha = .85$)	Karlsson et al. (2000)	No
EMAQ: Emotional Appetite Question-naire (Geliebter & Aversa, 2003)	22	"As compared to usual, do you eat ..." Followed by 14 feelings and eight situations, such as "when you are confident" and "after a heated argument."	1 (= *much less*) to 9 (= *much more*)	Negative & positive	1. Negative emotions ($n = 9, \alpha = .78$) 2. Negative situations ($n = 5, \alpha = .65$) 3. Positive emotions ($n = 5, \alpha = .75$) 4. Positive situations ($n = 3, \alpha = .57$)	Bourdier et al. (2017) Nolan et al. (2010)	No

Table 3.1. continued

	# Items	Example Item	Response scale	Emotional Valence	Subscales (n = # items), internal Strien (2013) (Cronbach's α)	Reference to validity information	License required?
EOQ: Emotional Overeating Questionnaire (Masheb & Grilo, 2006)	6	"On how many days out of the past 28 days have you eaten an unusually large amount of food, given the circumstances, in response to feelings of ..." Followed by six feelings.	0 (= *no days*) to 6 (= *every day*)	Negative & positive	Total emotional eating scale (n = 6, α = .85)	Masheb & Grilo (2006) Masheb et al. (2020)	No
EADES: Eating and Appraisal Due to Emotions and Stress (Ozier et al., 2007)	49	"I am confident I can control my eating when I am frustrated."	1 (= *strongly disagree*) to 5 (= *strongly agree*)	Negative & positive	Total scale (n = 49, α = .95): 1. Emotion & stress-related eating (n = 24, α = .95) 2. Appraisal of ability & resources to cope (n = 20, α = .87) 3. Appraisal of outside influences & stressors (n = 5, α = .65)	Not available	No
EAH: Eating in the Absence of Hunger Questionnaire – Children/Parents version Tanofsky-Kraff et al., 2008/ Shomaker et al., 2013)	14	A prompt referring to a state like "Imagine that you are/your child is eating a snack at home. Imagine that you/your child eat(s) enough and are/is no longer hungry." Followed by questions about whether they/ their child would keep eating "because you are/your child is feeling sad or depressed."	1 (= *never*) to 5 (= *always*)	Negative	1. Negative affect eating (n = 6, α = .88/.92) 2. External eating (n = 4, α = .80/.86) 3. Fatigue/boredom eating (n = 4, α = .83/.79)	Tanofsky-Kraff et al. (2008) Shomaker et al. (2013)	No

Table 3.1. continued

	# Items	Example Item	Response scale	Emotional Valence	Subscales (n = # items), internal Strien (2013) (Cronbach's α)	Reference to validity information	License required?
PNEES: Positive-Negative Emotional Eating Scale (Sultson et al., 2017	19	"I tend to eat when I am grumpy"	0 (= *never*) to 4 (= *very often*)	Negative & positive	Total scale (n = 19, α = .93): 1. Negative emotions (n = 12, α = .95) 2. Positive emotions (n = 7, α = .91)	Sultson et al. (2017)	No
SSES: Salzburg Stress Eating Scale (Meule et al., 2017)	10	"When the things I have to do threaten to crush me ..." Followed by response scales tackling amount of eating (see below).	1 (= *I eat much less*) to 5 (= *a lot more*) than usual	Negative & positive	Total scale (n = 10, α = .90)	Meule et al. (2017)	No
SEES: Salzburg Emotional Eating Scale (Meule et al., 2018)	20	"When I feel depressed." Followed by response scales tackling amount of eating (see below).	1 (= *I eat much less*) to 5 (= *a lot more*) than usual	Negative & positive	1. happiness (n = 5, α = .80) 2. sadness (n = 5, α = .77) 3. anger (n = 5) 4. anxiety (n = 5, α = .71)	Meule et al. (2018)	No

Note: Internal reliability is inferred from the reference corresponding to the questionnaire in the first row except for the EES-II, for which internal reliability values refer to Allen et al. (2012).

sulted in the conclusion that emotional eating questionnaires are not adequate measures of eating behavior in response to emotions. Also, a meta-analysis on the effect of emotions on eating behavior in experimental settings (Evers et al., 2018) revealed that scores on emotional eating scales do not translate to increased eating when being emotional. This raises the question what the value is of these emotional eating questionnaires. The answer to this question is twofold.

On the one hand, using these questionnaires in research settings seems problematic. Based on their limited predictive validity, it is unclear what high scores on these questionnaires precisely portray. For example, it has been argued that they reflect (biased) beliefs of people about the relation between emotions and eating (Adriaanse et al., 2011; Evers et al., 2009). Additionally, it has been claimed that high scores on these scales reflect "uncontrolled" or "concerned" eating – a tendency to attribute overeating to negative affect – or to learned cue reactivity, which is the tendency to overeat in response to many cues, not only emotional ones (see Bongers & Jansen, 2016 for details). In sum, in research settings, the implementation of emotional eating questionnaires should be treated with utmost care and, in any case, scholars should be aware and take into consideration the validity concerns that have been raised.

On the other hand and despite the validity issues, these scales are extensively used worldwide among scholars and professionals. Obviously, there is a clear need to use these noninvasive questionnaires in order to get an indication to what extent individuals believe that their eating behavior is related to emotional eating, or to what extent emotions are self-assessed triggers of overeating. These self-reports do have a value, as they are the reflection of one's internal states and so they have the ability to guide future emotions and behavior as well. As we will outline in the discussion, one strategy we recommend is to enrich this assessment always with other modalities (multimethod-multi-informant assessment).

However, in large cohort studies there is regularly only limited capacity for the inclusion of questions. We see that instead of a multimethod-multi-informant assessment only a few items were included. In that case, we recommend including a reliable subscale, not only two random items of a (sub)scale. Finally, it would be recommendable to consider and add alternative tools to assess emotional eating adequately, like the alternatives discussed below.

Laboratory Paradigms

Emotional eating has also been assessed by means of laboratory paradigms. Such paradigms prototypically consist of two phases. In the first phase, emotions are evoked – for example by autobiographic recall, film clips, or stress-inducing math or speech tasks – and contrasted against control conditions without any emotion induction. In the second phase, eating behavior is measured, mostly in a so-called "unrelated task."

Eating behavior measures vary extensively. In their most basic form, they relate to self-reported eating motives in the laboratory, such as the desire or motivation to eat or snack. Preferably, however, they concern more ecologically valid eating behaviors that involve actual eating, such as snack choice, consumption from buffets, or bogus tasting tasks where consumed energy can be precisely calculated based on the number of calories consumed. Laboratory studies to assess the relation between emotions and eating have been performed since the 1960s. Their heterogeneous outcomes reflect the widely different designs that have been based on the various postulated underlying mechanisms. That is, across decades it has been found that emotions result in decreased, increased, or unaffected eating. Additionally, findings about moderators of these effects (i.e., when or for whom emotions result in different eating behavior) have been heterogeneous.

Findings of Meta-Analyses

The effects of the existing body of laboratory research have recently been combined in three separate meta-analyses (Cardi et al., 2015, Evers et al., 2018; Hill et al., 2021). These meta-analyses all focused on adults that participated in experimental research in the laboratory that contained designs similar to the two phases described above, and measured actual eating behavior.

First, the meta-analyses of Cardi et al. (2015; including 33 studies) and Evers et al. (2018; including 56 studies) related to experiments that paired negative and/or positive emotions to caloric intake. Both meta-analyses revealed that overall, negative emotions did not impact caloric intake, while positive emotions were found to be associated with increased eating. Moreover, both meta-analyses found a moderating impact of restrained eating, such that restrained eaters showed increased eating in response to negative emotions. Other moderators, such as being overweight or obese, did not affect the emotion-eating associations.

The meta-analysis of Hill et al. (2021; including 54 studies) focused on stress. Studies were required to have a discrete stress measure; a noxious event in one's environment that could be appraised as threatening. Consequently, studies were excluded that tackled psychological states such as emotional distress or negative affect, as they were considered to be responses to stressors. Overall, stress was found to be associated with increased food intake. No moderating impacts were found. Thus, in contrast to the other meta-analyses, stress was not associated with increased eating in restrained eaters. Additionally, analyses in Hill et al.'s meta-analysis were run separately for healthy versus unhealthy food intake. Results showed that stress was associated with increased intake of unhealthy food and with decreased intake of healthy food. Dietary restraint was associated with a weakening of the stress–unhealthy eating association. This is contrary to the findings of the other meta-analyses. This specific result was based on only six studies, so in line with the authors we agree that undue emphasis should not be placed on these findings.

To comprehend the contrasting findings on restraint, it is relevant to note that there are roughly two restrained eating types. The so-called "successful dieters" seem effective in establishing restrained eating behavior, but the remaining group of restrained eaters score high on disinhibition of control, which makes them vulnerable to overeat in response to cues that trigger disinhibition, including emotional stimuli (Westenhoefer, 1991). When we inspect the studies with restraint measures that were included in the meta-analyses, it can be observed that the majority of the studies in the meta-analysis by Hill et al. (2021), the one without a moderating impact of restraint status, used restraint scales that do not load on disinhibition of control (e.g., DEBQ-restraint, Strien et al., 1986, and TFEQ-restraint, Stunkard & Messick, 1985). In contrast, the majority of the studies in the meta-analyses revealing that negative emotions were associated with increased eating in restrained eaters, used restraint scales loading on disinhibition (e.g.,

Restraint Scale; Herman & Polivy, 1975). While more systematic research is needed, such observation triggers the speculation that the type of restraint measure is relevant in explaining the contrasting findings between the meta-analyses. Obviously also other variations may explain some of the contrasting results, including the focus on specifically stress versus the wide spectrum of the affective realm. On a more general level, all meta-analyses found considerable heterogeneity in their results, and as such, findings should be interpreted carefully.

Together, these meta-analyses enable some alignment in the different findings about emotional eating assessed by means of laboratory paradigms, and the following conclusions could be drawn cautiously. First, negative emotions in general do not seem to affect eating behavior directly. It has been assumed that a "normal" response to negative emotions would be decreased eating, but this was not observed. Discretely, stressful events appraised as threatening, risky, or harmful, seem to relate to increased eating of unhealthy foods and decreased eating of healthy foods, but this effect was small. This indicates the need to clearly define what is meant by emotions when a phenomenon like emotional eating is discussed. Next, positive emotions in general seem to relate to increased eating. Although positive emotions were originally not part of the definition of emotional eating, individuals in general seem vulnerable to increased eating in response to positively valenced encounters. Another compelling conclusion is that it is hard to detect moderating impacts. Thus far hardly any moderating variables have been detected, with dietary restraint as exception. Particularly restrained eaters that are vulnerable to disinhibition of control seem likely to overeat in response to negative emotions.

Recommendations for Laboratory Paradigms

To start, it is important to clearly define and operationalize the emotion-part within the phenomenon of "emotional eating" that is assessed. For example, emotional eating has also been labeled as "comfort eating" or "stress-induced eating" (e.g., Greeno & Wing, 1994). Although these synonyms for emotional eating may ultimately point towards similar affective states as triggers for eating, the findings of the different meta-analyses illustrate that it is important to differentiate between affective concepts like specific stressors and negative emotions. Moreover, there may be individual differences in what type of emotions trigger eating behaviors. To this end, it may be important to tackle several different stressors and emotional encounters, including idiosyncratic ones. Further, it is important to carefully consider the type of eating measure. Most laboratory studies focus on only one eating-related feature (e.g., snack choice) or have been limited to artificial laboratory environments to assess food intake (e.g., crisps and cookies in bogus taste tests). Future work should try to resemble the complex daily food environment, for example by considering different and more varied aspects of eating behavior (e.g., snack purchase, food choice in buffet, eating under pressure). Next, as restrained eating has been the only consistent moderator of the negative emotion-eating link, it seems highly recommendable to always include measures of dietary restraint, particularly one that loads on disinhibition (e.g., the Restraint Scale, Herman & Polivy, 1975). Finally, it remains important to keep an eye on other potential moderators that have not been identified yet.

Disadvantages

While laboratory paradigms have the advantageous ability to assess causality between emotions and eating, a disadvantage is that they do not allow assessing to what extent an individual is an emotional eater. Another disadvantage is that laboratory settings remain unnaturalistic settings to experience emotions and to consume foods. Therefore, it may remain difficult to fully grasp and assess a complex phenomenon like emotional eating in the laboratory. A compelling example is the German lay term "grief bacon" referring to increased body fat in response to unhappiness and sorrow (Reichenberger et al., 2020). Going through a period of grief, for example, is difficult to tackle in laboratory settings. For this reason, EMA have become increasingly popular to assess emotional eating.

Ecological Momentary Assessments

Despite many design and analytical challenges, EMA give valuable insights in emotional eating via its real-life approach. Specific for emotions, the main advantage is the ecologically valid and dynamic reflection of emotional state. Indeed, EMA are ideal to sample the highly dynamic state of emotions and to assess temporality/directionality. Still, results can be biased due to awareness of one's own emotional eating behavior by logging it.

Methodological Decisions in EMA of Emotional Eating

Timing

In addition to the key concepts portrayed in Figure 3.1, the timing issue is very specific for EMA in relation to the eating, emotional, and moderating parameters. Two main timing prompting strategies exist in EMA: event-contingent versus time/signal-contingent. As both eating and emotions have to be reported, an event-contingent approach can be based on eating occasions or emotions/stressors. The eating occasion is the most often used one since eating is a more distinct event, but this approach loses information on emotional moments that have not led to eating. A signal-contingent approach or even automatic event detection (see the subsections "Measuring the eating parameter" and "Measuring the emotional parameter") might prevent underreporting of events. Studies often use a combination of both approaches or a summary approach within signal/time-contingent recordings to report on emotions and eating over the past several hours but exact timing of eating then remains unknown (Mason et al., 2020; Schembre et al., 2018).

The statistical analysis approach can test an immediate effect or a prolonged/cumulative effect of emotions/stress on next eating occasions (e.g., as done in Reichenberger et al., 2021). After all, emotional eating might be due to factors like availability of food or the breakdown of self-control at the end of the day with high-calorie foods being more popular during the afternoon and evening (Carnell et al., 2018; Haynes et al., 2016; Reichenberger, Richard et al., 2018). Hence, the EMA design should consider that the emotion–food relation might only arise in the afternoon (Huh et al., 2015). This time-lagged approach is also relevant to distinguish the cause–effect direction as there may also be a reversed causality of effects such as "being emotional about eating" (Adriaanse et al., 2011). Due to the highly dynamic states of craving and emotions, even repeated assessments across minutes might be necessary (Intille et al., 2016). Sometimes, data are aggregated on day-level but then this time information is lost. Next to time of the day, timing in the week (ideally workdays and weekend) or the person's schedule should be well-considered to detect snacking moments and to allow the study of different daily life settings.

Measuring the Eating Parameter

The distinction should be made between actual food intake and the desire to eat (i.e., food craving or hedonic eating) or other eating motives like hunger eating (i.e., homeostatic eating). After all, food craving does not always lead to food intake (Richard et al., 2017). EMA might allow the distinction with other forms of dysregulated eating like clinical binge eating episodes.

In measuring actual food intake, the frequency or timing (e.g., snacking) can be easily reported but ideally also the quality and quantity is reported. A report of the specific food item enables the distinction between healthy and unhealthy food intake, such as fat/sweet snacks versus fiber-rich snacks. Although seldomly applied in emotional eating EMA, a reported quantity (i.e., portion size) further allows caloric calculation and the distinction in total healthy versus unhealthy nutrient intake. The choice in food report methodology should balance time and data quality/detail. Food reports range from open question reports or choosing from a list to taking pictures. Despite not giving quality information, passive monitors like swallowing detectors or bite counters can prevent underreporting of snack frequency (Schembre et al., 2018).

Measuring the Emotional Parameter

Similar as in questionnaire studies, the intensity and valence of the emotion/stressor should be inquired. Indeed, some EMA studies reported a larger role for positive compared to negative emotions in eliciting eating behavior (Boh et al., 2016; Evers et al., 2013; Macht et al., 2004) or differential directions depending on the stress intensity (Stone & Brownell, 1994). Hence, it is important to make a distinction between stress and several types of emotions here as well, albeit with a limited amount of question items to decrease burden (e.g., Reichenberger, Kuppens, et al., 2018). Although EMA allow further distinction in different types of negative/positive emotions, this has not been explored yet. After all, unique patterns may exist between specific emotional triggers of emotional eating (depression, boredom, anxiety, anger) and psychological outcomes (Braden et al., 2018). Due to the potential bidirectionality in the emotion–eating relationship, the question should specify that the emotion present before eating should be reported.

EMA has the advantage that psychophysiological markers can be integrated. It allows repeated sampling of salivary cortisol, continuous measuring of the autonomic nervous system amongst others via heart rate variability and even automatic emotion detection (Wilhelm & Grossman, 2010). For cortisol, often between five to 10 assessments per day have been executed while taking into account circadian rhythms (Schlotz, 2019). However, compliance can be an issue and high frequency changes in cortisol might need automated continuous measures in interstitial fluid or sweat (Bhake et al., 2020; Kaushik et al., 2014). In fact, both cortisol and autonomic nervous system activity can reflect variation in emotion regulation or self-regulation. Indeed, lower heart rate variability prior to eating predicted higher loss of control over eating (Ranzenhofer et al., 2016) and high cortisol reactivity to stress promoted food intake in response to real-life stressors (Newman et al., 2007). The use of such biomarkers of course necessitates the measurement of relevant covariates. Finally, automatic emotion detection systems like facial electromyography or speech recognition often need more development to be feasible in daily life settings (Schlotz, 2019).

Relevant Moderators to Consider in Emotional Eating EMA

Moderators can be person-specific (i.e., a trait) or moment-specific (i.e., a state). Concerning person-specific parameters, sociodemographics, BMI and trait eating behavior like self-reported emotional eating and dietary restraint are among the most examined ones. Indeed, several results support an individual difference model and not modelling these inter-individual differences might completely obscure any effect of momentary emotions/stress on eating (Debeuf et al., 2018). In children, the developmental context should be considered (Hill et al., 2021). The advantage of EMA is that moment-specific parameters can also be explored as moderators (Wilhelm & Grossman, 2010). An important parameter set includes situational context like the social context (e.g., emotional eating mainly in absence of other people), physical context (e.g., at home comfort food is within reach), and other activities (e.g., sleep and physical activity). Finally, studying the role of reactivity to the emotion/stressor is also important. Trait cortisol reactivity as measured in a laboratory study has already been shown to be a moderator in EMA stress-eating associations (Newman et al., 2007). This indicates an added value of combining laboratory and EMA studies. However, state/momentary emotion regulation is dynamic and can be even more informative as the success of emotion regulation might depend on contextual factors (Svaldi et al., 2019) or emotional regulation flexibility (Dougherty et al., 2020). The ability of EMA to let people report their coping in real time is crucial since a retrospective recall of coping corresponded poorly with EMA reported coping (Stone et al., 1998).

General Results on Emotional Eating in EMA Designs

Systematic reviews of the above described EMA designs reveal that in adults positive stress–eating associations are often seen (Hill et al., 2021), but also a negative association was detected mainly in persons with high stress severity and men (Stone & Brownell, 1994). In children, the findings were mixed with several null findings (Mason et al., 2020). Due to the high diversity in the EMA approach, meta-analyses are difficult to execute, but would be welcome in light of the need for further insights.

Conclusions

Despite the rich amount of studies on emotional eating, the discussed findings show that there are often more questions than answers yet, and above all, they illustrate the need for additional multimethod future research on the assessment of emotional eating and its underlying mechanisms.

We can conclude that it is worth considering both retrospective and momentary measurement approaches reflecting valid yet distinct components of emotional eating, in line with results reported by Chwyl et al. (2021). Consequently, not one measure will be sufficient when studying emotional eating. Depending on one's aim, a multimodal assessment of emotional eating should be considered integrating both emotional eating behavior as well as the perception of oneself as an emotional eater.

For the clinical practice, we recommend to focus not only on the assessment of emotional eating, but also on emotion regulation. As outlined above, research suggests that the way people regulate their emotions may be the underlying problem and not necessarily the emotion per se. This may indicate that we need more instruments when estimating emotional eating, for example by measuring one's coping with emotions. In line with this idea, results of network models, based on EMA data, showed that the regulation of stress and affect predicts eating behavior, while the experience of a stressor and related affect was unrelated to eating behavior (Reichenberger et al., 2021). When emotion regulation is indeed a key concept within emotion regulation, it would be worthwhile to investigate if it is possible to intervene on emotional eating by manipulating emotion regulation, for example by applying self-compassion, reappraisal, or rumination.

As the presence of direct associations between affect and emotional eating behavior is questioned, the role of intermediate variables is suggested (Evers et al., 2010; Reichenberger et al., 2021). For example, self-efficacy, the confidence in the own regulatory abilities, seems more likely involved in problematic eating attitudes and behaviors, regardless the level of daily stress or affect (Reichenberger et al., 2021; MacNeil et al., 2012). Therefore, the belief in one's own capabilities to cope with stress or affect will shape one's appraisal about the potential impact of these affective factors. This indicates that we may need additional instruments, like measuring self-efficacy or other intermediate variables. Manifold other possibilities are worthwhile to explore as moderators, such as age, gender, sleep, one's learned emotional eating style, BMI, dietary restraint, and dispositional cortisol reactivity (see Figure 3.1).

Besides these recommendations, it can be questioned to what extent emotional eating is good or bad. Although in general it is assumed that emotional eating leads to overeating and thus is health-wise undesirable, it can be questioned to what extent it is an effective emotion regulation strategy. In other words, can emotional eating neutralize negative affective states, reduce physiological affect-related signals, or even enhance positive feelings? Related to the question if emotional eating is good or bad, there is hardly any research on the downstream consequences of emotional eating. That is, most likely emotional eating does not solve the origins of the primary stress source, but if secondary negative affective states arise due to emotional eating, like guilt, shame or regret, then vicious circles may arise. Alternatively, in the long term people may also compensate for eating after emotions. For example, intake may be increased immediately after the emotion. Such single act would imply that the emotion results in more eating, but if the individual would compensate this single act of increased eating by not eating the remainder of the day, the secondary effects resulting from the emotional eating may be overlooked. On the other hand, one single act of emotional eating may also trigger disinhibition and result in even more eating. How emotional eating is precisely related with overeating and overweight remains to be assessed.

Acknowledgment

This work was supported by the Ghent University funding: IOP - BOF24J2016.000701 and GOA01G00217.

References

Adriaanse, M.A., Ridder, D.T. de, & Evers, C. (2011). Emotional eating: Eating when emotional or emotional about eating? *Psychology and Health, 26*(1), 23–39. https://doi.org/10.1080/08870440903207627

Allen, K.L., McLean, N.J., & Byrne, S.M. (2012). Evaluation of a new measure of mood intolerance, the Tolerance of Mood States Scale (TOMS): Psychometric properties and associations with eating disorder symptoms. *Eating Behaviors, 13*(4), 326–334. https://doi.org/10.1016/j.eatbeh.2012.05.005

Aparicio, E., Canals, J., Arija, V., De Henauw, S., & Michels, N. (2016). The role of emotion regulation in childhood obesity: Implications for prevention and treatment. *Nutrition Research Reviews, 29*, 17–29. https://doi.org/10.1017/S0954422415000153

Arnow, B., Kenardy, J., & Agras, W.S. (1995). The Emotional Eating Scale: The development of a measure to assess coping with negative affect by eating. *International Journal of Eating Disorders, 18*(1), 79–90. https://doi.org/10.1002/1098-108X(199507)18:1<79::AID-EAT2260180109>3.0.CO;2-V

Bhake, R., Russell, G.M., Kershaw, Y., Stevens, K., Zaccardi, F., Warburton, V.E.C., Linthorst, A.C.E., & Lightman, S.L. (2020). Continuous free cortisol profiles in healthy men: Validation of microdialysis method. *The Journal of Clinical Endocrinology & Metabolism, 105*(4), e1749–e1761.

Boh, B., Jansen, A., Clijsters, I., Nederkoorn, C., Lemmens, L.H., Spanakis, G., & Roefs, A. (2016). Indulgent thinking? Ecological momentary assessment of overweight and healthy-weight participants' cognitions and emotions. *Behaviour Research and Therapy, 87*, 196–206. https://doi.org/10.1016/j.brat.2016.10.001

Bongers, P., & Jansen, A. (2016). Emotional eating is not what you think it is and emotional eating scales do not measure what you think they measure. *Frontiers in Psychology, 7*, Article 1932. https://doi.org/10.3389/fpsyg.2016.01932

Bourdier, L., Lalanne, C., Morvan, Y., Kern, L., Romo, L., & Berthoz, S. (2017). Validation and factor structure of the French-language version of the Emotional Appetite Questionnaire (EMAQ). *Frontiers in Psychology, 8*, Article 442. https://doi.org/10.3389/fpsyg.2017.00442

Braden, A., Musher-Eizenman, D., Watford, T., & Emley, E. (2018). Eating when depressed, anxious, bored, or happy: Are emotional eating types associated with unique psychological and physical health correlates? *Appetite, 125*, 410–417. https://doi.org/10.1016/j.appet.2018.02.022

Burton, E., Stice, E., Bearman, S.K., & Rohde, P. (2007). Experimental test of the affect-regulation theory of bulimic symptoms and substance use: A randomized trial. *International Journal of Eating Disorders, 40*(1), 27–36. https://doi.org/10.1002/eat.20292

Cardi, V., Leppanen, J., & Treasure, J. (2015). The effects of negative and positive mood induction on eating behaviour: A meta-analysis of laboratory studies in the healthy population and eating and weight disorders. *Neuroscience & Biobehavioral Reviews, 57*, 299–309. https://doi.org/10.1016/j.neubiorev.2015.08.011

Carnell, S., Grillot, C., Ungredda, T., Ellis, S., Mehta, N., Holst, J., & Geliebter, A. (2018). Morning and afternoon appetite and gut hormone responses to meal and stress challenges in obese individuals with and without binge eating disorder. *International Journal of Obesity, 42*(4), 841–849. https://doi.org/10.1038/ijo.2017.307

Chwyl, C., Berry, M. P., Manasse, S. M., & Forman, E. M. (2021). Rethinking emotional eating: Retrospective and momentary indices of emotional eating represent distinct constructs. *Appetite, 167*, 105604. https://doi.org/10.1016/j.appet.2021.105604

Debeuf, T., Verbeken, S., Van Beveren, M. L., Michels, N., & Braet, C. (2018). Stress and eating behavior: A daily diary study in youngsters. *Frontiers in Psychology, 9*, Article 2657. https://doi.org/10.3389/fpsyg.2018.02657

Dougherty, E. N., Murphy, J., Hamlett, S., George, R., Badillo, K., Johnson, N. K., & Haedt-Matt, A. A. (2020). Emotion regulation flexibility and disordered eating. *Eating Behaviors, 39*, 101428. https://doi.org/10.1016/j.eatbeh.2020.101428

Evers, C., Adriaanse, M., Ridder, D. T. de, & Witt Huberts, J. C. de (2013). Good mood food. Positive emotion as a neglected trigger for food intake. *Appetite, 68*, 1–7.

Evers, C., Ridder, D. T. de, & Adriaanse, M. A. (2009). Assessing yourself as an emotional eater: Mission impossible? *Health Psychology, 28*(6), 717–725. https://doi.org/10.1037/a0016700

Evers, C., Dingemans, A., Junghans, A. F., & Boevé, A. (2018). Feeling bad or feeling good, does emotion affect your consumption of food? A meta-analysis of the experimental evidence. *Neuroscience & Biobehavioral Reviews, 92*, 195–208. https://doi.org/10.1016/j.neubiorev.2018.05.028

Evers, C., Stok, M., & Ridder, D. T. de (2010). Feeding your feelings: Emotion regulation strategies and emotional eating. *Personality & Social Psychology Bulletin, 36*(6), 792–804. https://doi.org/10.1177/0146167210371383

Geliebter, A., & Aversa, A. (2003). Emotional eating in overweight, normal weight, and underweight individuals. *Eating Behaviors, 3*(4), 341–347. https://doi.org/10.1016/S1471-0153(02)00100-9

Greeno, C. G., & Wing, R. R. (1994). Stress-induced eating. *Psychological Bulletin, 115*(3), 444–464. https://doi.org/10.1037/0033-2909.115.3.444

Grilo, C. M., & Shiffman, S. (1994). Longitudinal investigation of the abstinence violation effect in binge eaters. *Journal of Consulting and Clinical Psychology, 62*(3), 611. https://doi.org/10.1037/0022-006X.62.3.611

Haynes, A., Kemps, E., & Moffitt, R. (2016). Is cake more appealing in the afternoon? Time of day is associated with control over automatic positive responses to unhealthy food. *Food Quality and Preference, 54*, 67–74. https://doi.org/10.1016/j.foodqual.2016.07.004

Heatherton, T. F., & Baumeister, R. F. (1991). Binge eating as escape from self-awareness. *Psychological Bulletin, 110*(1), 86. https://doi.org/10.1037/0033-2909.110.1.86

Herman, C. P., & Polivy, J. (1975). Anxiety, restraint, and eating behavior. *Journal of Abnormal Psychology, 84*(6), 666. https://doi.org/10.1037/0021-843X.84.6.666

Hill, D., Conner, M., Clancy, F., Moss, R., Wilding, S., Bristow, M., & O'Connor, D. B. (2021). Stress and eating behaviours in healthy adults: A systematic review and meta-analysis. *Health Psychology Review, 16*, 280–304.

Huh, J., Shiyko, M., Keller, S., Dunton, G., & Schembre, S. M. (2015). The time-varying association between perceived stress and hunger within and between days. *Appetite, 89*, 145–151. https://doi.org/10.1016/j.appet.2015.02.001

Intille, S., Haynes, C., Maniar, D., Ponnada, A., & Manjourides, J. (2016, September). μEMA: Microinteraction-based ecological momentary assessment (EMA) using a smartwatch. In ACM (Ed.), *Proceedings of the 2016 ACM International Joint Conference on Pervasive and Ubiquitous Computing* (pp. 1124–1128). ACM.

Karlsson, J., Persson, L. O., Sjöström, L., & Sullivan, M. (2000). Psychometric properties and factor structure of the Three-Factor Eating Questionnaire (TFEQ) in obese men and women: Results from the Swedish Obese Subjects (SOS) study. *International Journal of Obesity, 24*(12), 1715–1725. https://doi.org/10.1038/sj.ijo.0801442

Kaushik, A., Vasudev, A., Arya, S.K., Pasha, S.K., & Bhansali, S. (2014). Recent advances in cortisol sensing technologies for point-of-care application. *Biosensors and Bioelectronics, 53*, 499–512. https://doi.org/10.1016/j.bios.2013.09.060

Kenardy, J., Butler, A., Carter, C., & Moor, S. (2003). Eating, mood, and gender in a noneating disorder population. *Eating Behaviors, 4*(2), 149–158. https://doi.org/10.1016/S1471-0153(03)00019-9

Macht, M. (2008). How emotions affect eating: A five-way model. *Appetite, 50*, 1–11. https://doi.org/10.1016/j.appet.2007.07.002

Macht, M., Haupt, C., & Salewsky, A. (2004). Emotions and eating in everyday life: Application of the experience-sampling method. *Ecology of Food and Nutrition, 43*(4), 11–21. https://doi.org/10.1080/03670240490454723

MacNeil, L., Esposito-Smythers, C., Mehlenbeck, R., & Weismoore, J. (2012). The effects of avoidance coping and coping self-efficacy on eating disorder attitudes and behaviors: A stress-diathesis model. *Eating Behaviors, 13*(4), 293–296. https://doi.org/10.1016/j.eatbeh.2012.06.005

Masheb, R.M., Douglas, M.E., Kutz, A.M., Marsh, A.G., & Driscoll, M. (2020). Pain and emotional eating: Further investigation of the Yale Emotional Overeating Questionnaire in weight loss seeking patients. *Journal of Behavioral Medicine, 43*(3), 479–486. https://doi.org/10.1007/s10865-020-00143-4

Masheb, R.M., & Grilo, C.M. (2006). Emotional overeating and its associations with eating disorder psychopathology among overweight patients with binge eating disorder. *International Journal of Eating Disorders, 39*(2), 141–146. https://doi.org/10.1002/eat.20221

Mason, T.B., Do, B., Wang, S., & Dunton, G.F. (2020). Ecological momentary assessment of eating and dietary intake behaviors in children and adolescents: A systematic review of the literature. *Appetite, 144*, 104465. https://doi.org/10.1016/j.appet.2019.104465

Meule, A., Reichenberger, J., & Blechert, J. (2017). Development and preliminary validation of the Salzburg Stress Eating Scale. *Appetite, 120*, 442–448. https://doi.org/10.1016/j.appet.2017.10.003

Meule, A., Reichenberger, J., & Blechert, J. (2018). Development and preliminary validation of the Salzburg Emotional Eating Scale. *Frontiers in Psychology, 9*, Article 88. https://doi.org/10.3389/fpsyg.2018.00088

Newman, E., O'Connor, D.B., & Conner, M. (2007). Daily hassles and eating behaviour: The role of cortisol reactivity status. *Psychoneuroendocrinology, 32*(2), 125–132. https://doi.org/10.1016/j.psyneuen.2006.11.006

Nolan, L.J., Halperin, L.B., & Geliebter, A. (2010). Emotional Appetite Questionnaire : Construct validity and relationship with BMI. *Appetite, 54*(2), 314–319. https://doi.org/10.1016/j.appet.2009.12.004

Ozier, A.D., Kendrick, O.W., Knol, L.L., Leeper, J.D., Perko, M., & Burnham, J. (2007). The eating and appraisal due to emotions and stress (EADES) questionnaire: Development and validation. *Journal of the American Dietetic Association, 107*(4), 619–628. https://doi.org/10.1016/j.jada.2007.01.004

Ranzenhofer, L.M., Engel, S.G., Crosby, R.D., Haigney, M., Anderson, M., McCaffery, J.M., & Tanofsky-Kraff, M. (2016). Real-time assessment of heart rate variability and loss of control eating in adolescent girls: A pilot study. *International Journal of Eating Disorders, 49*(2), 197–201. https://doi.org/10.1002/eat.22464

Reichenberger, J., Kuppens, P., Liedlgruber, M., Wilhelm, F.H., Tiefengrabner, M., Ginzinger, S., & Blechert, J. (2018). No haste, more taste: An EMA study of the effects of stress, negative and positive emotions on eating behavior. *Biological Psychology, 131*, 54–62. https://doi.org/10.1016/j.biopsycho.2016.09.002

Reichenberger, J., Pannicke, B., Arend, A.K., Petrowski, K., & Blechert, J. (2021). Does stress eat away at you or make you eat? EMA measures of stress predict day to day food craving and perceived food intake as a function of trait stress-eating. *Psychology & Health, 36*(2), 129–147. https://doi.org/10.1080/08870446.2020.1781122

Reichenberger, J., Richard, A., Smyth, J.M., Fischer, D., Pollatos, O., & Blechert, J. (2018). It's craving time: Time of day effects on momentary hunger and food craving in daily life. *Nutrition, 55*, 15–20. https://doi.org/10.1016/j.nut.2018.03.048

Reichenberger, J., Schnepper, R., Arend, A.K., & Blechert, J. (2020). Emotional eating in healthy individuals and patients with an eating disorder: Evidence from psychometric, experimental and naturalistic studies. *Proceedings of the Nutrition Society, 79*(3), 290–299. https://doi.org/10.1017/S0029665120007004

Richard, A., Meule, A., Reichenberger, J., & Blechert, J. (2017). Food cravings in everyday life: An EMA study on snack-related thoughts, cravings, and consumption. *Appetite, 113*, 215–223. https://doi.org/10.1016/j.appet.2017.02.037

Schembre, S.M., Liao, Y., O'Connor, S.G., Hingle, M.D., Shen, S., Hamoy, K.G., Huh, J., Dunton, G.F., Weiss, R., Thomson, C., & Boushey, C.J. (2018). Mobile ecological momentary diet assessment methods for behavioral research: Systematic review. *JMIR mHealth and uHealth, 6*(11), e11170.

Schlotz, W. (2019). Investigating associations between momentary stress and cortisol in daily life: What have we learned so far? *Psychoneuroendocrinology, 105*, 105–116. https://doi.org/10.1016/j.psyneuen.2018.11.038

Shomaker, L.B., Tanofsky-Kraff, M., Mooreville, M., Reina, S.A., Courville, A.B., Field, S.E., Matheson, B.E., Brady, S.M., Yanovski, S.Z., & Yanovski, J.A. (2013). Links of adolescent-and parent-reported eating in the absence of hunger with observed eating in the absence of hunger. *Obesity, 21*(6), 1243–1250.

Stone, A.A., & Brownell, K.D. (1994). The stress-eating paradox: Multiple daily measurements in adult males and females. *Psychology and Health, 9*(6), 425–436. https://doi.org/10.1080/08870449408407469

Stone, A.A., Schwartz, J.E., Neale, J.M., Shiffman, S., Marco, C.A., Hickcox, M., Paty, J., Porter, L.S., & Cruise, L.J. (1998). A comparison of coping assessed by ecological momentary assessment and retrospective recall. *Journal of Personality and Social Psychology, 74*(6), 1670.

Strien, T. van (2013). *NVE Nederlandse Vragenlijst voor Eetgedrag Handleiding en Verantwoording* [Dutch Eating Behaviour Questionnaire. Manual]. Boom test uitgevers.

Strien, T. van (2018). Causes of emotional eating and matched treatment of obesity. *Current Diabetes Reports, 18*(6), 1–8. https://doi.org/10.1007/s11892-018-1000-x

Strien, T. van, Frijters, J.E., Bergers, G.P., & Defares, P.B. (1986). The Dutch Eating Behavior Questionnaire (DEBQ) for assessment of restrained, emotional, and external eating behavior. *International Journal of Eating Disorders, 5*(2), 295–315. https://doi.org/10.1002/1098-108X(198602)5:2<295::AID-EAT2260050209>3.0.CO;2-T

Stunkard, A.J., & Messick, S. (1985). The three-factor eating questionnaire to measure dietary restraint, disinhibition and hunger. *Journal of Psychosomatic Research, 29*(1), 71–83. https://doi.org/10.1016/0022-3999(85)90010-8

Sultson, H., Kukk, K., & Akkermann, K. (2017). Positive and negative emotional eating have different associations with overeating and binge eating: Construction and validation of the Positive-Negative Emotional Eating Scale. *Appetite, 116*, 423–430. https://doi.org/10.1016/j.appet.2017.05.035

Svaldi, J., Werle, D., Naumann, E., Eichler, E., & Berking, M. (2019). Prospective associations of negative mood and emotion regulation in the occurrence of binge eating in binge eating disorder. *Journal of Psychiatric Research, 115*, 61–68. https://doi.org/10.1016/j.jpsychires.2019.05.005

Tanofsky-Kraff, M., Ranzenhofer, L.M., Yanovski, S.Z., Schvey, N.A., Faith, M., Gustafson, J., & Yanovski, J.A. (2008). Psychometric properties of a new questionnaire to assess eating in the absence of hunger in children and adolescents. *Appetite, 51*(1), 148–155. https://doi.org/10.1016/j.appet.2008.01.001

Tomiyama, A.J. (2019). Stress and obesity. *Annual Review of Psychology, 70*(1), 703–718. https://doi.org/10.1146/annurev-psych-010418-102936

Vandewalle, J., Mabbe, E., Debeuf, T., Braet, C., & Moens, E. (2017). The daily relation between parental rejection and emotional eating in youngsters: A diary study. *Frontiers in Psychology, 8,* Article 691. https://doi.org/10.3389/fpsyg.2017.00691

Westenhoefer, J. (1991). Dietary restraint and disinhibition: Is restraint a homogeneous construct? *Appetite, 16*(1), 45–55. https://doi.org/10.1016/0195-6663(91)90110-E

Wilhelm, F.H., & Grossman, P. (2010). Emotions beyond the laboratory: Theoretical fundaments, study design, and analytic strategies for advanced ambulatory assessment. *Biological Psychology, 84*(3), 552–569. https://doi.org/10.1016/j.biopsycho.2010.01.017

Chapter 4

Assessment of Food Craving and Food "Addiction"

Lindzey V. Hoover and Ashley N. Gearhardt

Department of Psychology, University of Michigan, Ann Arbor, MI, USA

Introduction

Cravings, which are often defined as an intense desire to consume a specific substance (Meule, 2017), have been identified as a key factor that can drive eating behavior. The scientific study of craving has long been a central focus in the science behind what compels individuals to consume addictive drugs (even in the face of stark negative consequences). In 2013, the experience of intense cravings (i.e., a strong desire or urge to use a substance; American Psychiatric Association, 2013) was added to the diagnostic criteria for substance use disorders. A concerted effort into understanding food craving, and its role in problematic patterns of eating, has increased greatly in the past 20 years (Meule, 2017, 2020; Taylor, 2019). Numerous assessment approaches exist to capture food craving and reviews of these assessment options have recently been published (Meule, 2017; Taylor, 2019). Based on the current science, the general consensus is that food craving, particularly for highly processed foods (i.e., foods high in refined carbohydrates and/or added fat), contributes to excessive food intake, obesity, and diet-related disease (Nijs et al., 2007; Taetzsch et al., 2020).

The centrality of craving as a factor contributing to problematic patterns of eating highlights similarities between pathological eating and addictive disorders. This is consistent with the theory that highly processed foods may be capable of triggering addictive processes and that some individuals may exhibit an addictive pattern of food intake (Gearhardt & Schulte, 2021). This construct is commonly referred to as food addiction and is typically measured by assessing whether the *Diagnostic and Statistical Manual of Mental Disorders* (5th ed.; DSM-5) substance use disorder diagnostic criteria are occurring in the consumption of highly processed food (American Psychiatric Association, 2013; Gearhardt et al., 2016). There is evidence that this food addiction phenotype is associated with heightened craving and other mechanisms implicated in addiction (e.g., reward dysfunction, impulsivity; Gearhardt & Schulte, 2021; Hardy et al., 2018; Minhas et al., 2021). In this chapter, we aim to (a) highlight approaches to assessing food craving, (b) discuss methodological consideration when assessing food craving, (c) review literature on the most common approach to assess food addiction, (d) discuss controversies in the assessment of food addiction, and (e) outline future directions in the assessment of both food craving and food addiction.

Approaches to Assessing Food Craving

Food craving can be defined as an intense desire to consume a specific type of food (Gendall et al., 1997; Weingarten & Elston, 1991). These foods tend to be highly palatable and are often highly processed with heightened levels of refined carbohydrates and fats (Schulte et al., 2015). Food craving is multifaceted and includes cognitive (e.g., thinking about food), behavioral (e.g., seek and consume food), emotional (e.g., desire to eat, changes in mood), and physiological (e.g., salivation) components (Rodríguez-Martín & Meule, 2015). Several recent publications have provided in-depth reviews of food craving and the available assessment tools (Meule, 2017; Taylor, 2019), including one that provides a tool to aid in choosing a food craving measure (Taylor, 2019). Thus, we do not aim to replicate these reviews, but instead will discuss some of the most frequently used tools to assess food craving in the literature and highlight important methodological considerations when assessing food craving.

Subjective Reports

State Food Craving

The most commonly used method for assessing food craving is subjective self-report measures. There are a wide variety of subjective self-report measures available, including measures that capture the transient experience of food cravings (i.e., state food craving) and measures assessing stable individual variations in the frequency and intensity of food cravings (i.e., trait food craving; Taylor, 2019). A frequently used measure of state food craving is the Food Craving Questionnaire-State (FCQ-S), a 15-item self-report measure of momentary food craving. Response categories on the FCQ-S range from 1 = *strongly disagree* to 5 = *strongly agree* (Cepeda-Benito et al., 2000) and responses on the FCQ-S can be summed for a total score (where higher scores indicate more intense momentary food cravings). There are five subscales (desire, anticipation positive reinforcement, anticipation negative, lack of control, and hunger/physiological) that can also be calculated for the FCQ-S. However, support for the factorial validity of the FCQ-S is limited as the five-factor structure of the FCQ-S has only been partially replicated in prior cross-national studies (Meule, 2020; Taylor, 2019).

A recent review covering the past 20 years of research found support for the internal reliability ($\alpha > .90$), construct validity, predictive validity, and discriminant validity of the FCQ-S and, as expected of a state measure of food craving, the test–retest reliability of the FCQ-S is typically low (r typically $< .60$; Meule, 2020). The FCQ-S is a brief, easy to administer, multi-item assessment of state food craving that has been translated into multiple languages including Spanish, German, Italian, Portuguese, and Korean (Meule,

2020) allowing for the assessment of food craving across subcultures of the United States and in cross-national studies. Higher scores on the FCQ-S have been associated with a number of factors including increased eating disorder pathology, longer durations of food deprivation, and higher subsequent food intake in the laboratory (Meule, 2020; Moreno et al., 2008). Thus, the FCQ-S is a useful, well-studied measure of state food craving. However, the FCQ-S is a multi-item assessment. Therefore, it may not be the most appropriate assessment in situations where time constraints or participant burden are a significant concern.

One option for assessing self-report state food craving with minimal participant burden is through a Visual Analogue Scale (VAS). VAS are single-item measures where participants place a mark on a, for example, 100mm line anchored at each end by descriptors. For example, prior research has had participants rate their food craving intensity on a 100mm line ranging from *no desire or urge to eat* to *extremely strong desire or urge to eat* (Tiggemann et al., 2004). VAS measures are often the quickest and most straightforward approach to assessing state food craving. They are also easily adaptable (e.g., to ask about a specific food type) and can be administered in a variety of formats (e.g., paper, computer, phone) and settings (e.g., laboratory, home). However, there can be significant variability in the wording (e.g., intensity of cravings, desire to consume food) and response options used between studies for VAS measures of food craving (Flint et al., 2000; Tiggemann et al., 2004). This represents a challenge to study the validity and reliability of this assessment approach. Further, food craving is a multifaceted experience, and it is unlikely that a single response can accurately summarize this complexity. Thus, multi-item measures like the FCQ-S may be a more appropriate tool for accurately capturing state food craving unless time constraints or participant burden are a significant concern.

Trait Food Craving

In addition to state measures of food craving, there are several measures available to assess general frequency and intensity of food craving (i.e., trait food craving). For example, the Food Craving Questionnaire-Trait (FCQ-T; Cepeda-Benito et al., 2000), is a widely used 39-item measure of the frequency and intensity of food craving. The response categories on the FCQ-T range from 1 = *never* to 6 = *always* and responses on the FCQ-T can be summed to create a total score (where higher scores represent more frequent and intense food cravings) and used to calculate nine subscales (intent, positive anticipation, negative anticipation, control, thoughts, hunger/physiological, emotions/negative affect, cues/environment, and guilt). Similar to the FCQ-S, there is limited support for the factorial validity of the FCQ-T due to inconsistencies in replicating the nine-factor structure in prior research, particularly in other cultures or languages and in specific populations (e.g., persons with obesity; Meule, 2020; Taylor, 2019). Evidence suggests that the total score for the FCQ-T has excellent internal reliability ($\alpha > .90$) and test–retest reliability ($r > .80$) while the internal reliability and test–retest reliability of the subscales tends to be lower (Meule, 2020). A recent review of the past 20 years of literature also found support for the construct validity, predictive validity, and discriminant validity of the FCQ-T (Meule, 2020). Like the FCQ-S, the FCQ-T is a straightforward assessment of food craving available in multiple languages (e.g., Spanish, German, Portuguese, Persian, Turkish, Chinese; Meule, 2020) allowing for the assessment of food craving in cross-national studies and across subcultures of the United States. A shortened 15-item version of the FCQ-T (FCQ-T-reduced; Meule et al., 2014) is also available, which provides a briefer alternative to assess trait food craving. Higher trait food craving on the FCQ-T has been associated with a number of relevant factors including eating disorder pathology, uncontrolled eating, and obesity (Meule, 2018, 2020; Moreno et al., 2008; Reents & Pedersen, 2021). Thus, the FCQ-T is an appropriate measure when interested in the frequency and intensity of food craving in general. However, the FCQ-T is not food specific so an alternative measure should be selected when interested in assessing food cravings towards specific types of foods.

The Food Craving Inventory (FCI; White et al., 2002) is a widely used measure of trait food craving that can assess food cravings for specific foods. Specifically, the FCI measures the frequency of cravings for a list of 28 specific foods over the past month. Foods on the FCI are divided into a four-factor structure (high-fat foods, sweets, carbohydrates/starches, fast-food fats) and cravings for each type of food are rated on a scale from 1 = *never* to 5 = *always/almost every day*. Compared to the FCQ-T, significantly less research has been dedicated to the validity and reliability of the FCI. However, a recent review of the literature did find evidence to support the test–retest reliability ($r = .79$–$.91$), criterion validity, and predictive validity of the FCI (Taylor, 2019) and higher food cravings on the FCI have been associated with higher levels of hunger, loss of control overeating, and disordered eating (Taylor, 2019). A unique strength of the FCI is that there are several versions available that have been adapted to reflect culturally relevant typical food cravings of specific countries including Spain, Brazil, Germany, the United Kingdom, and Japan (Taylor, 2019). Additionally, the FCI allows for the assessment of food cravings for specific types of foods, which may be particularly useful for studies that are interested in a more nuanced assessment of food types. Thus, the decision whether to use the FCQ-T or the FCI should be guided by study specific research questions as each of these scales assesses different aspects of trait food craving (i.e., general cravings versus specific foods).

Behavioral and Physiological Measures

A common criticism of subjective self-report measures of food craving is the notion that an enhanced motivational drive to consume food might not always be within an individual's conscious awareness (Berridge, 1996). Thus, it is possible that subjective self-report measures do not fully capture the multifaceted experience of food craving due to the inability to accurately report on subconscious experiences. Multiple physiological and behavioral variables have been identified that correlate with subjectively reported craving (e.g., heart rate, blood pressure, salivation, attention allocation, consumption; Meule, 2017). Therefore, objective physiological and behavioral indicators of food craving may be one option for assessing food craving in a way that also captures food craving outside conscious awareness. However, currently available techniques for measuring objective indicators of craving are often lacking in specificity, not adequately validated, or unreliable (Shiffman, 2000). Functional magnetic resonance imaging (fMRI) is another technique that has become increasingly popular in the past decade that could be considered for an objective measure of food craving. Prior research has found associations between craving relevant brain regions (e.g., striatum) and self-report measures of food craving (Kahathuduwa et al., 2018; Ravichandran et al., 2021). However, recent research has called into question the test–retest reliability of fMRI paradigms across multiple research domains (Elliott et al., 2020; Noble et al., 2019) including eating and obesity

(Yokum, Bohon, et al., 2021; Yokum, Gearhardt, et al., 2021) highlighting potential concerns with the reproducibility of fMRI-based techniques for assessing food craving. Thus, based on the current evidence base, there is not sufficient evidence to suggest that behavioral and physiological indicators of craving are more valid or have greater utility than subjective self-reports of food craving.

Methodological Considerations for Food Craving

Careful consideration should be given to the potential influence of hunger on assessments of food craving. Hunger and food craving are sometimes mistaken as being synonymous, but there are important distinctions between these terms. While hunger is the general drive for caloric intake, food craving is a more specific desire for a food or taste (usually for highly palatable, highly processed foods with heightened levels of refined carbohydrates and fats; Schulte et al., 2015; Weingarten & Elston, 1991) and is not typically satisfied by the caloric intake of other, noncraved foods. Thus, it is the intensity and specificity towards specific foods that differentiates food cravings from feelings of hunger (Hill, 2007). However, food craving and hunger are also interconnected by shared biological systems. For example, being in an environment rich in palatable food cues while satiated can lead to increased levels of gut peptides implicated in the experience of hunger (Joyner et al., 2017). Thus, a feeling of "hunger" endorsed in these environments may actually reflect an increase in cue-induced food craving. Hunger may also moderate the effects of environmental cues, whereby hunger amplified cue-induced food cravings and satiety dampens them (Joyner et al., 2017). Thus, accounting for hunger is an important consideration for the assessment of food craving.

Similarly, it is important to consider the potential impact of both affect and stress on the measurements of food craving. Negative affect and increased stress have both been found to induce cravings (Sinha & Jastreboff, 2013) meaning that stress and affect induced by unrelated secondary factors (e.g., work stress, bad news, recent argument) prior to the assessment of food craving may influence food craving. Likewise, individual differences in sensitivity to negative affect and stress could contribute to differences in craving detected by food craving assessments. In an experimental design, the paradigm being employed may also elicit individual differences in affective reaction that could impact food craving. For example, there may be significant variability in the level of stress and affect elicited by having one's weight measured in a study protocol. Thus, researchers should consider the inclusion of measures of affect and stress in their studies and consider the potential impact of these factors on measures of food craving in study designs.

Finally, a significant challenge to accurately assessing food craving is the reliance on retrospective recall (which is known to introduce bias) to complete self-report measures of food craving (Shiffman, 2000). When possible, real-time assessments of food craving can be utilized to eliminate such concerns. For example, ecological momentary assessment (EMA) can be used as one strategy, which allows for repeated, in-the-moment assessments of food craving. EMA also allows for data collection while a participant is in their normal environment, which may increase the generalizability of findings. Researchers conducting laboratory-based studies should similarly strive to minimize or eliminate the need for participants to engage in retrospective recall to ensure the accuracy of self-report measures of food craving.

Assessment of Food Addiction

Yale Food Addiction Scale

Evidence from both animals and humans suggests that highly processed foods stimulate reward systems in the brain and are often consumed compulsively (Gearhardt & Schulte, 2021). This has contributed to the theory that some foods – particularly highly processed foods – are capable of triggering an addictive process for at least some individuals. The Yale Food Addiction Scale (YFAS), initially published in 2009, operationalizes this addictive response by applying substance-related diagnostic criteria to the intake of highly processed foods (i.e., food addiction; Gearhardt et al., 2009). While the validity of the food addiction construct is a focus of intense scientific debate (Gearhardt & Hebebrand, 2021), the YFAS provides an assessment tool to support research in this area.

Versions of the YFAS

The original version of the YFAS assesses the seven DSM-IV diagnostic criteria for substance dependence (e.g., loss of control over intake, continued use despite negative consequences, withdrawal, tolerance; Gearhardt et al., 2009). Of note, craving was not a diagnostic criterion for substance dependence at this time and was not included in the original YFAS. The YFAS primes participants to think about their intake of highly processed foods (e.g., chocolate, pizza) and to report on the frequency that they experience behaviors that reflect the symptoms of substance dependence in the past 12 months. The scale has a total of 25 questions and each question has a clinically relevant threshold of endorsement. If a participant indicates a response at or above the threshold for any question relevant to a specific symptom, then the criterion for that symptom is met. The YFAS provides two scoring options: a symptom count that reflects the number of symptom criteria met (ranges from 0 to 7) and a "diagnostic" threshold that represents whether a participant meets the criteria for food addiction (yes/no) based on the criteria for substance dependence (i.e., three or more symptoms plus clinically significant impairment/distress). The YFAS has been translated and validated in over a dozen different languages, including German, Spanish, Korean, and Turkish (Meule & Gearhardt, 2014). Thus, the YFAS is well-situated for international comparisons of food addiction.

Other versions of the YFAS have been created, including an abbreviated modified version of the YFAS (mYFAS) which has only one question for each symptom (Flint et al., 2014). The mYFAS is most useful in situations where participant burden is high, and a briefer measure may be needed. A children's version (the YFAS-C) was also developed to allow for assessment of food addiction in younger samples based on developmentally appropriate criteria, a lower reading level, and simpler response options (Gearhardt et al., 2013). The ability to assess food addiction across the lifespan is particularly important, as children are exposed to high levels of highly processed foods very early in development (Herrick et al., 2020; Wang et al., 2021). These versions of the scale are also available in a number of different languages (e.g., Persian, Korean, Hungarian, French; Meule & Gearhardt, 2014).

In 2016, an updated version of the YFAS was published (YFAS 2.0) that reflects the DSM-5 substance use disorder criteria. This 35-item version includes all seven symptoms previously in the YFAS, but to reflect the DSM-5, also includes craving and three problem-focused symptoms (e.g., use in hazardous situations, failure to fulfill role obligations due to use, interpersonal difficulties due to use; Gearhardt et al., 2016). The scoring approach to the YFAS 2.0 is the same as the original YFAS, except the symptom count ranges from 0 to 11, the "diagnostic" threshold lowered to two symptoms plus clinically significant impairment/distress, and a severity threshold of mild (two to three symptoms), moderate (four to five symptoms) or severe (six or more symptoms) is available. The YFAS 2.0 has also been translated into a number of different languages, including German, Spanish, Japanese, and Arabic (Meule & Gearhardt, 2019).

An abbreviated version of the YFAS 2.0 also exists (mYFAS 2.0; Schulte & Gearhardt, 2017) and has been validated in other languages (e.g., Italian, Chinese, Czech; Meule & Gearhardt, 2019). A dimensional version of the scale has been developed (dYFAS-C 2.0) that aims to pick up subclinical variability in food addiction in adolescent community samples (Schiestl & Gearhardt, 2018). The dYFAS-C 2.0 provides a summary score of question endorsement (but does not provide a symptom count or "diagnosis"). This scale has been evaluated in samples from the USA and Denmark (Horsager et al., 2021; Schiestl & Gearhardt, 2018). A full version of the YFAS-C 2.0 is currently under development in adolescents and future evaluation in younger children is needed.

Psychometric Properties of the YFAS

There has been extensive research investigating the psychometric properties of versions of the YFAS, particularly the original YFAS and the YFAS 2.0 (see Meule & Gearhardt, 2014, 2019 for reviews). Overall, prior research has found support for high internal reliability, appropriate test-retest reliability, and a one-factor structure across multiple versions of the scale (Meule & Gearhardt, 2014, 2019). Associations between versions of the YFAS and constructs like obesity, binge eating, emotional eating, and craving, have also been consistently found (Meule & Gearhardt, 2014, 2019). Although the content of the YFAS exhibits overlap with eating disorder diagnoses, the majority of individuals who meet the food addiction threshold do not currently meet for an existing eating disorder, thus, providing support for discriminant validity (Gearhardt et al., 2016). Evidence for predictive validity includes the ability of the YFAS to predict response to treatment for bulimia nervosa (Hilker et al., 2016), traditional weight loss treatments (Fielding-Singh et al., 2019), and long-term bariatric surgery response (Martin-Fernandez et al., 2022). In sum, the existing literature supports the utility of the YFAS as a measure to operationalize an addictive response to highly processed foods in a psychometrically valid way.

Limitations and Future Directions for Food Addiction Research

There are important limitations and future directions to consider with the YFAS. First, a clinical interview version of the self-report scale is an important next step. There is evidence that individuals over-endorse binge behavior on self-report measures (relative to clinical interviews; Everett et al., 2021), which may also apply to food addiction. Second, there are relatively high levels of endorsement of food addiction for individuals with restrictive eating disorders (e.g., anorexia nervosa; Tran et al., 2020). In the cases of binge eating, there are objective binges (marked by an objectively large amount of food being consumed) and subjective binges (where a large amount of food is not consumed, but the individual experiences a subjective sense of loss of control; Fairburn & Cooper, 1993). Both subjective and objective binge eating are clinically meaningful (Dalle Grave et al., 2012). It is plausible that the food addiction endorsed in the context of anorexia may reflect a subjective version of food addiction (similar to subjective binge eating episodes), but more research is needed. Third, there are some questions about the utility of the impairment/distress criterion required for the food addiction diagnosis. Some individuals report high levels of food addiction symptoms but deny experiencing clinically significant impairment/distress. Some research has found that high symptom levels (even without impairment/distress) are associated with clinically meaningful outcomes (Carr et al., 2021; Ouellette et al., 2018). Thus, future research is needed on the utility of the impairment/distress criterion and the underlying factors that lead individuals who are experiencing high levels of food addiction symptoms to report little impairment/distress. Finally, the Addiction-Like Eating Behavior Scale (AEBS) has been recently developed as an alternative to the YFAS (Ruddock et al., 2017). This scale focuses on addictive eating as a behavioral addiction unrelated to a specific type of food. However, it is not based on diagnostic criteria reflective of other addictive disorders, thus questions arise about whether it is truly capturing an addictive phenotype (Schulte et al., 2018). Others have questioned whether the AEBS is capturing the same construct as the YFAS and other eating measures and that the incremental validity of the scale needs to be examined to prevent a jangle fallacy epidemic in obesity research (Vainik & Meule, 2018).

Conclusions

In the domain of craving, evidence suggests that multi-item self-report measures are currently the most valid and reliable way to assess food craving. While behavioral and physiological measures may be a promising approach to objectively assess food craving in the future, available techniques are currently under evaluated for the assessment of food craving. Thus, those interested in utilizing objective measures of food craving should only do so in combination with empirically supported self-report measures. Considering the wide variety of self-report assessments available (e.g., state, trait, specific foods), significant thought should be given to which measure is the best match for the overall goal or research question. The potential influence of secondary factors (e.g., hunger, affect, stress) and limitations of retrospective recall should also be considered in study designs. EMA may be a particularly useful approach to allow for real-time assessments of food craving without the limitations of retrospective recall in future research. Regarding food addiction, the YFAS is the most commonly used measure to operationalize food addiction to highly processed foods. Multiple versions of the YFAS have been found to be psychometrically valid and it is available in a number of languages and for different developmental stages. Important future directions include the development of a clinical interview assessment of food addiction, investigation of subjective versions of food addiction and consideration of alternative approaches to conceptualizing addictive-like eating behavior.

References

American Psychiatric Association. (2013). Substance-related and addictive disorders. In American Psychiatric Association (Ed.), *Diagnostic and Statistical Manual of Mental Disorders* (5th ed., pp. 481–590). APA. https://doi.org/10.1176/appi.books.9780890425596.dsm16

Berridge, K.C. (1996). Food reward: Brain substrates of wanting and liking. *Neuroscience & Biobehavioral Reviews, 20*(1), 1–25. https://doi.org/10.1016/0149-7634(95)00033-B

Carr, M.M., Lawson, J.L., Wiedemann, A.A., & Barnes, R.D. (2021). Examining impairment and distress from food addiction across demographic and weight groups. *Eating Behaviors, 43*, 101574. https://doi.org/10.1016/j.eatbeh.2021.101574

Cepeda-Benito, A., Gleaves, D.H., Williams, T.L., & Erath, S.A. (2000). The development and validation of the state and trait food-cravings questionnaires. *Behavior Therapy, 21*(1), 151–173. https://doi.org/10.1016/S0005-7894(00)80009-X

Dalle Grave, R., Calugi, S., & Marchesini, G. (2012). Objective and subjective binge eating in underweight eating disorders: Associated features and treatment outcome. *International Journal of Eating Disorders, 45*(3), 370–376. https://doi.org/10.1002/eat.20943

Elliott, M.L., Knodt, A.R., Ireland, D., Morris, M.L., Poulton, R., Ramrakha, S., Sison, M.L., Moffitt, T.E., Caspi, A., & Hariri, A.R. (2020). What is the test-retest reliability of common task-functional MRI measures? New empirical evidence and a meta-analysis. *Psychological Science, 31*(7), 792–806. https://doi.org/10.1177/0956797620916786

Everett, V.S., Crochiere, R.J., Dallal, D.H., Martin, G.J., Manasse, S.M., & Forman, E.M. (2021). Self-report versus clinical interview: Discordance among measures of binge eating in a weight-loss seeking sample. *Eating and Weight Disorders-Studies on Anorexia, Bulimia and Obesity, 26*(4), 1259–1263. https://doi.org/10.1007/s40519-020-01002-6

Fairburn, C.G., & Cooper, Z. (1993). The eating disorder examination. In C.G. Fairburn & G.T. Wilson (Eds.), *Binge eating: Nature, assessment, and treatment* (12th ed., pp. 317–360). Guilford Press.

Fielding-Singh, P., Patel, M.L., King, A.C., & Gardner, C.D. (2019). Baseline psychosocial and demographic factors associated with study attrition and 12-month weight gain in the DIETFITS trial. *Obesity, 27*(12), 1997–2004. https://doi.org/10.1002/oby.22650

Flint, A., Raben, A., Blundell, J.E., & Astrup, A. (2000). Reproducibility, power and validity of visual analogue scales in assessment of appetite sensations in single test meal studies. *International Journal of Obesity, 24*, 38–48. https://doi.org/10.1038/sj.ijo.0801083

Flint, A.J., Gearhardt, A.N., Corbin, W.R., Brownell, K.D., Field, A.E., & Rimm, E.B. (2014). Food-addiction scale measurement in 2 cohorts of middle-aged and older women. *The American Journal of Clinical Nutrition, 99*(3), 578–586. https://doi.org/10.3945/ajcn.113.068965

Gearhardt, A.N., Corbin, W.R., & Brownell, K.D. (2016). Development of the Yale Food Addiction Scale Version 2.0. *Psychology of Addictive Behaviors, 30*(1), 113–121. https://doi.org/10.1037/adb0000136

Gearhardt, A.N., Corbin, W.R., & Brownell, K.D. (2009). Preliminary validation of the Yale Food Addiction Scale. *Appetite, 52*, 430–436. https://doi.org/10.1016/j.appet.2008.12.003

Gearhardt, A.N., & Hebebrand, J. (2021). The concept of "food addiction" helps inform the understanding of overeating and obesity: Debate consensus. *The American Journal of Clinical Nutrition, 113*(2), 274–276. https://doi.org/10.1093/ajcn/nqaa345

Gearhardt, A.N., Roberto, C.A., Seamans, M.J., Corbin, W.R., & Brownell, K.D. (2013). Preliminary validation of the Yale Food Addiction Scale for children. *Eating Behaviors, 14*(4), 508–512. https://doi.org/10.1016/j.eatbeh.2013.07.002

Gearhardt, A.N., & Schulte, E.M. (2021). Is food addictive? A review of the science [review-article]. *Annual Reviews, 41*, 11.11–11.24. https://doi.org/10.1146/annurev-nutr-110420-111710

Gendall, K.A., Joyce, P.R., & Sullivan, P.F. (1997). Impact of definition on prevalence of food cravings in a random sample of young women. *Appetite, 28*(1), 63–72. https://doi.org/0.1006/appe.1996.0060

Hardy, R., Fani, N., Jovanovic, T., & Michopoulos, V. (2018). Food addiction and substance addiction in women: Common clinical characteristics. *Appetite, 120*, 367–373. https://doi.org/10.1016/j.appet.2017.09.026

Herrick, K.A., Fryar, C.D., Hamner, H.C., Park, S., & Ogden, C.L. (2020). Added sugars intake among US infants and toddlers. *Journal of the Academy of Nutrition and Dietetics, 120*(1), 23–32. https://doi.org/10.1016/j.jand.2019.09.007

Hilker, I., Sánchez, I., Steward, T., Jiménez-Murcia, S., Granero, R., Gearhardt, A.N., Rodríguez-Muñoz, R.C., Dieguez, C., Crujeiras, A.B., Tolosa-Sola, I., Casanueva, F.F., Menchón, J.M., & Fernández-Aranda, F. (2016). Food addiction in bulimia nervosa: Clinical correlates and association with response to a brief psychoeducational intervention. *European Eating Disorders Review, 24*(6), 482–488.

Hill, A.J. (2007). The psychology of food craving. *The Proceedings of the Nutrition Society, 66*(2), 277–285. https://doi.org/https://doi.org/10.1017/S0029665107005502

Horsager, C., Færk, E., Gearhardt, A.N., Østergaard, S.D., & Lauritsen, M.B. (2021). Validation of the dimensional Yale Food Addiction Scale for Children 2.0 and estimation of the weighted food addiction score in a sample of adolescents from the general population. *Eating and Weight Disorders-Studies on Anorexia, Bulimia and Obesity, 28*(8), 2563–2576. https://doi.org/10.1037/t84127-000

Joyner, M.A., Kim, S., & Gearhardt, A.G. (2017). Investigating an incentive-sensitization model of eating behavior: Impact of a simulated fast-food laboratory. *Clinical Psychological Science, 5*(6), 1014–1026. https://doi.org/10.1177/2167702617718828

Kahathuduwa, C.N., Davis, T., O'Boyle, M., & Binks, M. (2018). Do scores on the Food Craving Inventory and Three-Factor Eating Questionnaire correlate with expected brain regions of interest in people with obesity? *Physiology & Behavior, 188*, 1–10. https://doi.org/10.1016/j.physbeh.2018.01.018

Martin-Fernandez, K.W., Creel, D.B., & Schuh, L.M. (2022). Psychosocial and behavioral correlates of weight loss 12 to 15 years after bariatric surgery. *Journal of Behavioral Medicine, 45*(2), 252–259. https://doi.org/10.1007/s10865-021-00263-5

Meule, A. (2017). Assessment of food cravings. In J. Ifland, M.T. Marcus, & H.G. Preuss (Eds.), *Processed food addiction: Foundations, assessment, and recovery* (1st ed., pp. 137–146). CRC Press. https://doi.org/10.1201/9781315119922-11

Meule, A. (2018). Food cravings in food addiction: Exploring a potential cut-off value of the Food Cravings Questionnaire-Trait-reduced. *Eating and Weight Disorders - Studies on Anorexia, Bulimia and Obesity, 23*, 39–43. https://doi.org/10.1007/s40519-017-0452-3

Meule, A. (2020). Twenty years of the Food Cravings Questionnaires: A comprehensive review. *Current Addiction Reports, 7*, 30–43. https://doi.org/10.1007/s40429-020-00294-z

Meule, A., & Gearhardt, A.N. (2014). Five years of the Yale Food Addiction Scale: Taking stock and moving forward. *Current Addiction Reports, 1*(3), 193–205. https://doi.org/10.1007/s40429-014-0021-z

Meule, A., & Gearhardt, A.N. (2019). Ten years of the Yale Food Addiction Scale: A review of Version 2.0. *Current Addiction Reports, 6*(3), 218–228. https://doi.org/10.1007/s40429-019-00261-3

Meule, A., Hermann, T., & Kübler, A. (2014). A short version of the Food Cravings Questionnaire—Trait: The FCQ-T-reduced. *Frontiers in Psychology, 5*, Article 190. https://doi.org/10.3389/fpsyg.2014.00190

Minhas, M., Murphy, C.M., Balodis, I.M., Samokhvalov, A.V., & MacKillop, J. (2021). Food addiction in a large community sample of Canadian adults: Prevalence and relationship with obesity, body composition, quality of life and impulsivity. *Addiction, 116*(10), 2870–2879. https://doi.org/10.1111/add.15446

Moreno, S., Rodríguez, S., Fernandez, M.C., Tamez, J., & Cepeda-Benito, A. (2008). Clinical validation of the trait and state versions of the Food Craving Questionnaire. *Assessment, 15*(3), 375–387. https://doi.org/10.1177/1073191107312651

Nijs, I.M.T., Franken, I.H.A., & Muris, P. (2007). The modified Trait and State Food-Cravings Questionnaires: Development and validation of a general index of food craving. *Appetite, 49*(1), 38–46. https://doi.org/10.1016/j.appet.2006.11.001

Noble, S., Scheinost, D., & Constable, R.T. (2019). A decade of test-retest reliability of functional connectivity: A systematic review and meta-analysis. *NeuroImage, 203*, 116157. https://doi.org/10.1016/j.neuroimage.2019.116157

Ouellette, A.-S., Rodrigue, C., Lemieux, S., Tchernof, A., Biertho, L., & Bégin, C. (2018). Establishing a food addiction diagnosis using the Yale Food Addiction Scale: A closer look at the clinically significant distress/functional impairment criterion. *Appetite, 129*, 55–61. https://doi.org/10.1016/j.appet.2018.06.031

Ravichandran, S., Bhatt, R.R., Pandit, B., Osadchiy, V., Alaverdyan, A., Vora, P., Stains, J., Naliboff, B., Mayer, E.A., & Gupta, A. (2021). Alterations in reward network functional connectivity are associated with increased food addiction in obese individuals. *Scientific Reports, 11*, 3386. https://doi.org/10.1038/s41598-021-83116-0

Reents, J., & Pedersen, A. (2021). Differences in food craving in individuals with obesity with and without binge eating disorder. *Frontiers in Psychology, 12*, Article 660880. https://doi.org/10.3389/fpsyg.2021.660880

Rodríguez-Martín, B.C., & Meule, A. (2015). Food craving: New contributions on its assessment, moderators, and consequences. *Frontiers in Psychology, 6*, Article 21. https://doi.org/10.3389/fpsyg.2015.00021

Ruddock, H.K., Christiansen, P., Halford, J.C., & Hardman, C.A. (2017). The development and validation of the Addiction-like Eating Behaviour Scale. *International Journal of Obesity, 41*(11), 1710–1717. https://doi.org/10.1037/t68001-000

Schiestl, E.T., & Gearhardt, A.N. (2018). Preliminary validation of the Yale Food Addiction Scale for Children 2.0: A dimensional approach to scoring. *European Eating Disorders Review, 26*(6), 605–617.

Schulte, E.M., Avena, N.M., & Gearhardt, A.N. (2015). Which foods may be addictive? The roles of processing, fat content, and glycemic load. *PloS One, 10*(2). https://doi.org/10.1371/journal.pone.0117959

Schulte, E.M., & Gearhardt, A.N. (2017). Development of the modified Yale Food Addiction Scale version 2.0. *European Eating Disorders Review, 25*(4), 302–308. https://doi.org/10.1002/erv.2515

Schulte, E.M., Potenza, M.N., & Gearhardt, A.N. (2018). How much does the Addiction-Like Eating Behavior Scale add to the debate regarding food versus eating addictions? *International Journal of Obesity, 42*(4), 946. https://doi.org/10.1038/ijo.2017.265

Shiffman, S. (2000). Comments on craving. *Addiction, 95*, S171–S175. https://doi.org/10.1080/09652140050111744

Sinha, R., & Jastreboff, A.M. (2013). Stress as a common risk factor for obesity and addiction. *Biological Psychiatry, 73*(9), 827–835. https://doi.org/10.1016/j.biopsych.2013.01.032

Taetzsch, A., Roberts, S.B., Gilhooly, C.H., Lichtenstein, A.H., Krauss, A.J., Bukhari, A., Martin, E., Hatch-McChesney, A., & Das, S.K. (2020). Food cravings: Associations with dietary intake and metabolic health. *Appetite, 152*, 104711. https://doi.org/10.1016/j.appet.2020.104711

Taylor, M. (2019). A review of food craving measures. *Eating Behaviors, 32*, 101–110. https://doi.org/10.1016/j.eatbeh.2019.01.005

Tiggemann, M., Woods, D., & Soekov, B. (2004). Reduction of food cravings through concurrent visuospatial processing. *International Journal of Eating Disorders, 36*(1), 31–40. https://doi.org/10.1002/eat.20005

Tran, H., Poinsot, P., Guillaume, S., Delaunay, D., Bernetiere, M., Bégin, C., Fourneret, P., Peretti, N., & Iceta, S. (2020). Food addiction as a proxy for anorexia nervosa severity: New data based on the Yale Food Addiction Scale 2.0. *Psychiatry Research, 293*, 113472. https://doi.org/10.1016/j.psychres.2020.113472

Vainik, U., & Meule, A. (2018). Jangle fallacy epidemic in obesity research: A comment on Ruddock et al. (2017). *International Journal of Obesity, 42*(3), 585–586. https://doi.org/10.1038/ijo.2017.264

Wang, L., Martínez Steele, E., Du, M., Pomeranz, J.L., O'Connor, L.E., Herrick, K.A., Luo, H., Zhang, X., Mozaffarian, D., & Fang Zhang, F. (2021). Trends in consumption of ultraprocessed foods among US youths aged 2–19 years, 1999–2018. *JAMA, 326*(6), 519–530. https://doi.org/10.1001/jama.2021.10238

Weingarten, H.P., & Elston, D. (1991). Food cravings in a college population. *Appetite, 17*(3), 167–175. https://doi.org/10.1016/0195-6663(91)90019-O

White, M.A., Whisenhunt, B.L., Williamson, D.A., Greenway, F.L., & Netermeyer, R.G. (2002). Development and validation of the food-craving inventory. *Obesity Research, 10*(2), 107–114. https://doi.org/10.1038/oby.2002.17

Yokum, S., Bohon, C., Berkman, E., & Stice, E. (2021). Test-retest reliability of functional MRI food receipt, anticipated receipt, and picture tasks. *The American Journal of Clinical Nutrition, 114*(2), 764–779. https://doi.org/10.1093/ajcn/nqab096

Yokum, S., Gearhardt, A. N., & Stice, E. (2021). In search of the most reproducible neural vulnerability factors that predict future weight gain: Analyses of data from six prospective studies. *Social Cognitive and Affective Neuroscience*, Article nsab013. https://doi.org/10.1093/scan/nsab013

Chapter 5

Assessment of Orthorexia Nervosa

Crystal D. Oberle[1] and Natalie A. Noebel[2]

[1]Department of Psychology, Texas State University, San Marcos, TX, USA
[2]Department of Psychiatry, University of Texas, Dallas, TX, USA

Introduction

Orthorexia nervosa (ON) is a condition characterized by compulsive behaviors and obsessive thoughts concerning healthy eating and nutrition (Bratman & Knight, 2000). Though ON has not yet been included as a distinct psychiatric disorder in the *Diagnostic and Statistical Manual of Mental Disorders* (5th ed.; DSM-5; American Psychiatric Association, 2013), there are consistencies among the diagnostic criteria proposed by multiple clinicians and researchers (Barthels et al., 2015; Dunn & Bratman, 2016; Moroze et al., 2015; Setnick, 2013). These consistent diagnostic criteria are as follows: (a) obsessive-compulsive behaviors and preoccupation with healthy eating and nutrition that includes rigidly following an overly restrictive diet that the individual believes to be as healthy and pure as possible; (b) violations of their restrictive dietary rules causing extreme emotional distress with feelings of guilt, shame, and anxiety; (c) physical impairments, whereby nutritional deficiencies may result in significant weight loss, malnutrition, and accompanying physical health complications; and (d) psychosocial impairments in social and vocational/academic functioning due to the other diagnostic criteria.

A comprehensive review of risk factors revealed that ON symptomatology has been consistently associated with a vegetarian or vegan diet, as well as greater levels of exercise or sport activity, disordered eating, obsessive-compulsive tendencies, and emotional issues that include depression and anxiety (McComb & Mills, 2019). The associations with a vegetarian diet and exercise activity make sense given that people with ON are motivated by their pursuit of perfect physical health. Regarding the association with obsessive-compulsive tendencies, the obsessions and compulsions concerning both eating and exercise may at least partly be attributed to a more general neuropsychological personality profile. As for the association with disordered eating, excessive calorie restriction and weight preoccupation may be the result of the person's heightened fear about the negative health risks of being overweight. Finally, the associations with depression and anxiety are not surprising when considering that the proposed diagnostic criteria for ON include both emotional distress and psychosocial impairments. Interestingly, the comprehensive literature review (McComb & Mills, 2019) revealed that researchers generally failed to find gender differences in ON symptomatology, suggesting that ON is distinct from anorexia nervosa, for which prevalence is much greater in women than in men.

Table 5.1. Summary of psychometric properties for ON assessments

	BOT	ORTO-15	EHQ	DOS	TOS	ONI
Reliability	Mean reliability values across multiple studies					
Cronbach's α	.73	.61	.90	.85	.87	.93
Test–retest *r*	untested	untested	.78	.79	.78	.91
Content validity	Number of assessment items relevant to the diagnostic criteria for ON					
Behaviors/preoccupation	4	8	13	6	9	9
Emotional distress	4	5	3	2	5	5
Physical impairments	0	0	0	0	0	6
Social/work impairments	2	2	5	2	3	4
Criterion validity	Correlations with the other ON assessments?					
Correlations	yes	yes	yes	yes	yes	untested
Convergent validity	Percent of studies finding associations with the related constructs					
Vegetarian/vegan diet	0%	75%	100%	86%	untested	100%
Exercise/sport activity	100%	80%	100%	67%	untested	100%
Disordered eating	100%	100%	100%	100%	100%	100%
Obsessive-compulsiveness	50%	100%	100%	67%	100%	100%
Depression/anxiety	100%	100%	50%	86%	100%	100%
Discriminant validity	Percent of studies finding no gender differences in ON					
Gender	100%	67%	100%	50%	100%	100%

Note. ON = orthorexia nervosa; BOT = Bratman Orthorexia Test (Bratman & Knight, 2000); ORTO-15 (Donini et al., 2005); EHQ = Eating Habits Questionnaire (Gleaves et al., 2013); DOS = Düsseldorf Orthorexia Scale (Barthels et al., 2015); TOS = Teruel Orthorexia Scale (Barrada & Roncero, 2018), ONI = Orthorexia Nervosa Inventory (Oberle et al., 2021).

Several measures have been created and used in multiple studies to assess ON: the Bratman Orthorexia Test (BOT; Bratman & Knight, 2000), the ORTO-15 (Donini et al., 2005), the Eating Habits Questionnaire (EHQ; Gleaves et al., 2013), the Düsseldorf Orthorexia Scale (DOS; Barthels et al., 2015), the Teruel Orthorexia Scale (TOS; Barrada & Roncero, 2018), and the Orthorexia Nervosa Inventory (ONI; Oberle et al., 2021). This chapter will provide the following psychometric information for each of these assessment tools: internal reliability (i.e., Cronbach's α), test–retest reliability, content validity (i.e., items assessing each diagnostic criterion for ON), criterion validity, convergent validity (i.e., associations with a vegetarian or vegan diet, exercise or sport activity, disordered eating, obsessive-compulsive tendencies, and depression or anxiety), and discriminant validity (i.e., no gender differences). Table 5.1 presents a summary of the psychometric properties for these measures.

Bratman Orthorexia Test

The BOT (Bratman & Knight, 2000) was developed by Steven Bratman, who first coined the "orthorexia nervosa" phrase. This test was developed in English as an informal self-test, and it has been translated into German (Kinzl et al., 2005), Swedish (Eriksson et al., 2008), and Greek (Grammatikopoulou et al., 2018). It includes 10 questions, to which the respondents answer either "yes" (1) or "no" (0) for a total possible sum score of 0–10. Higher scores represent higher levels of ON symptomatology, and the maximum score of 10 is considered to be representative of the ON condition (Bratman & Knight, 2000). Using this criterion in a study with 430 college students, researchers found the prevalence of ON to be less than 1% (Dittfeld et al., 2017). The internal reliability among this measure's items has been low to acceptable, with Kuder-Richardson α values of .67 and .79 (M=0.73; Andreas et al., 2018; Bundros et al., 2016) for the measure using the original "yes" or "no" dichotomous response options, and with a Cronbach's α value of .79 (Meule et al., 2020) for a version of the measure using a 4-point scale for the purpose of increasing comparability of this measure with other ON measures. The test-retest reliability for this measure has not yet been explored.

Pertaining to validity, four of the 10 questions relate to the behaviors and preoccupation diagnostic criterion for ON (e.g., "Do you spend more than three hours a day thinking about healthy food?"), four relate to the emotional distress diagnostic criterion (e.g., "Do you feel guilt or self-loathing when you stray from your diet?"), two relate to the psychosocial impairments diagnostic criterion (e.g., "Does your diet socially isolate you?"), and none relate to the physical impairments diagnostic criterion. Regarding criterion validity, BOT scores have been significantly correlated with scores on the ORTO-15 (r=–.47; Meule et al., 2020), the EHQ (r=.72; Meule et al., 2020), and the DOS (r=.78–.86; Barthels, Meyer, Amrhein, et al., 2018; Meule et al., 2020). Regarding convergent validity, researchers have consistently found greater BOT scores to be significantly associated with greater levels of exercise activity (Eriksson et al., 2008), disordered eating (Andreas et al., 2018; Bundros et al., 2016), and depression and anxiety (Andreas et al., 2018). Although greater BOT scores were also significantly associated with greater levels of obsessive-compulsive tendencies in one study (Bundros et al., 2016), another study found no relationship (Andreas et al., 2018). In addition, vegetarians and meat eaters have unexpectedly not differed on BOT scores (Dittfeld et al., 2017). Finally, regarding discriminant validity, men and women have not differed on BOT scores (Bundros et al., 2016; Grammatikopoulou et al., 2018), consistent with most other studies finding no gender differences in ON symptomatology (McComb & Mills, 2019).

ORTO-15

The ORTO-15 (Donini et al., 2005) has been one of the most frequently used measures of ON. Developed in Italian and published in an English journal, it has been translated into Turkish (Arusoğlu et al., 2008), Portuguese (Alvarenga et al., 2012), Polish (Brytek-Matera et al., 2014), Hungarian (Varga et al., 2014), Spanish (Parra-Fernandez et al., 2018; Roncero et al., 2017), Arabic (Haddad et al., 2019), French (Babeau et al., 2020), and German (Meule et al., 2020). The Italian, English, Arabic, and German variations include 15 questions, to which the respondents answer using a 4-point scale ranging from 1 = *always* to 4 = *never* for a total possible sum score of 15–60. Lower scores represent higher levels of ON symptomatology, and a score below 40 is considered to be representative of the ON condition (Donini et al., 2005). Using this criterion, the prevalence rates among general samples of college students and other adults recruited from the community have ranged from as low as 4% in the original validation study to as high as 77% (Donini et al., 2005; Dunn et al., 2017; Malmborg et al., 2017; Ramacciotti et al., 2011; Varga et al., 2014). These wide variations may partially be related to problems concerning internal reliability, with Cronbach's α values ranging from as low as .20 to as high as .83 (M = 0.61; Alvarenga et al., 2012; Arusoğlu et al., 2008; Barnett et al., 2016; Farchakh et al., 2019; Haddad et al., 2019; Koven & Senbonmatsu, 2013; Meule et al., 2020; Parra-Fernandez et al., 2018; Roncero et al., 2017; Segura-García et al., 2012, 2015; Varga et al., 2014). Because of poor internal reliability, the researchers translating the original measure into Turkish, Portuguese, Polish, Hungarian, Spanish, and French removed three to six items for these translated versions of the scale. However, wide variations in internal reliability were also found for these reduced-item versions of the scale, with Cronbach's α values ranging from as low as .39 to as high as .83 (M = 0.68; Alvarenga et al., 2012; Arusoğlu et al., 2008; Brytek-Matera et al., 2014; Parra-Fernandez et al., 2018; Roncero et al., 2017; Varga et al., 2014).

Pertaining to validity, eight of the 15 questions relate to the behaviors and preoccupation diagnostic criterion for ON (e.g., "Are you willing to spend more money to have healthier food?"), five relate to the emotional distress diagnostic criterion (e.g., "Do you feel guilty when transgressing?"), two relate to the psychosocial impairments diagnostic criterion (e.g., "Do you think that eating healthy food changes your lifestyle [frequency of eating out, friends, ...]?"), and none relate to the physical impairments diagnostic criterion. Regarding criterion validity, ORTO-15 scores have been significantly correlated with scores on the BOT (r = –.47; Meule et al., 2020), the EHQ (r = –.51; Meule et al., 2020), the DOS (r = –.45; Meule et al., 2020), and the TOS (r = –.45; Barrada & Roncero, 2018). Regarding convergent validity, researchers have consistently found lower ORTO-15 scores (i.e., greater ON symptomatology) to be significantly associated with greater levels of disordered eating (Agopyan et al., 2019; Arusoğlu et al., 2008; Brytek-Matera et al., 2014; Farchakh et al., 2019; Fidan et al., 2010; Gramaglia et al., 2019; Haddad et al., 2019; Koven & Senbonmatsu, 2013; Reynolds, 2018), obsessive-compulsive tendencies (Arusoğlu et al., 2008; Çiçekoğlu & Tunçay, 2018; Koven & Senbonmatsu, 2013), and depression (Çiçekoğlu & Tunçay, 2018). Lower ORTO-15 scores (i.e., greater ON symptomatology) were also significantly associated with greater levels of exercise activity (Almeida et al., 2018; Clifford & Blyth, 2019; Hyrnik et al., 2016; Varga et al., 2014) and with a vegetarian diet (Dell'Osso et al., 2016, 2018; Herranz Valera et al., 2014) in multiple studies, although two studies found no relationship between ON and these variables (Çiçekoğlu & Tunçay, 2018 – vegetarian diet; Dunn et al., 2017 – exercise activity). Finally, regarding discriminant validity, whereas most studies have found that men and women do not differ on ORTO-15 scores (Aksoydan & Camci, 2009; Almeida et al., 2018; Babeau et al., 2020; Bağci Bosi et al., 2007; Brytek-Matera et al., 2014, 2017; Dunn et al., 2017; Farchakh et al., 2019; Herranz Valera et al., 2014; Koven & Senbonmatsu, 2013; Malmborg et al., 2017; Plichta & Jezewska-Zychowicz, 2019; Reynolds, 2018; Varga et al.,

2014), some studies found ORTO-15 scores to be greater in women than in men (Arusoğlu et al., 2008; Dell'Osso et al., 2016, 2018; Gramaglia et al., 2019; Haddad et al., 2019; Kiss-Leizer & Rigó, 2019) and one study even found ORTO-15 scores to be greater in men than in women (Fidan et al., 2010).

Eating Habits Questionnaire

The EHQ (Gleaves et al., 2013), another frequently used measure of ON, was developed in English and has been translated into Italian (Novara et al., 2017), Polish (Brytek-Matera et al., 2019), Arabic (Brytek-Matera, Sacre, et al., 2020), German (Meule et al., 2020), French (Yakin et al., 2021), and Spanish (Parra-Fernández et al., 2021). It includes 21 statements, for which respondents indicate how true the statement is for them using a 4-point scale ranging from 1 = *not at all true* to 4 = *very true* for a total possible sum score of 21–84. Higher scores represent higher levels of ON symptomatology; the developers of the EHQ did not include a recommended criterion for diagnosis or risk of ON. Moreover, this measure includes three subscales: Knowledge (about healthy eating), Problems (associated with their eating behaviors), and Feelings (associated with their eating behaviors). Factor analyses in other studies have confirmed this three-factor structure (Brytek-Matera, Sacre, et al., 2020; Meule et al., 2020; Novara et al., 2017; Parra-Fernández et al., 2021; Yakin et al., 2021; Zickgraf et al., 2019). The internal reliability among all 21 items has been good to excellent with Cronbach's α values of either .89 or .90 (Brytek-Matera, Sacre, et al., 2020; Meule et al., 2020; Mohamed Halim et al., 2020; Oberle et al., 2017; Parra-Fernández et al., 2021; Yakin et al., 2021), and the internal reliability for the individual scales has been acceptable to excellent with Cronbach's α values ranging from .78 to .92 (Gleaves et al., 2013; Parra-Fernández et al., 2021; Zickgraf et al., 2019). Finally, in the original validation study, test–retest reliability (with 2–4 weeks between the two measurements) was .78 for the total EHQ score and ranged from .72 to .81 for the individual scales (Gleaves et al., 2013), demonstrating the stability of these scores.

Pertaining to validity, 13 of the 21 items relate to the behaviors and preoccupation diagnostic criterion for ON (e.g., "My eating habits are superior to others"), three relate to the emotional distress diagnostic criterion (e.g., "I feel in control when I eat healthily" with an assumption that they feel out of control when they transgress), five relate to the psychosocial impairments diagnostic criterion (e.g., "My healthy eating is a significant source of stress in my relationships"), and none relate to the physical impairments diagnostic criterion. Regarding criterion validity, EHQ scores have been significantly correlated with scores on the BOT ($r = .72$; Meule et al., 2020), the ORTO-15 ($r = -.51$; Meule et al., 2020), and the DOS ($r = .74$–$.79$; Brytek-Matera, Sacre, et al., 2020; Chard et al., 2019; Lasson et al., 2021; Meule et al., 2020). Regarding convergent validity, researchers have consistently found greater EHQ scores to be significantly associated with a vegetarian or vegan diet (Brytek-Matera, 2020; Brytek-Matera et al., 2019) and with greater levels of exercise activity (Bert et al., 2019; Oberle et al., 2018), disordered eating (Gleaves et al., 2013; Novara et al., 2017; Parra-Fernández et al., 2021; Zickgraf et al., 2019), and obsessive-compulsive tendencies (Gleaves et al., 2013; Zickgraf et al., 2019). Although greater EHQ scores were also significantly associated with greater levels of negative affect in one study (Gleaves et al., 2013), another study found no relationship between EHQ scores and either depression or anxiety (Novara et al., 2017). Finally, regarding discriminant validity, men and women have not differed on EHQ scores (Brytek-Matera, Sacre, et al., 2020; Gleaves et al., 2013; Hayatbini & Oberle, 2019; Oberle et al., 2017, 2019; Zickgraf et al., 2019).

Düsseldorf Orthorexia Scale

The DOS (Barthels et al., 2015), another widely used measure, was developed in German and has been translated into English (Chard et al., 2019), Chinese (He et al., 2019), Spanish (Parra-Fernández et al., 2019), Arabic (Brytek-Matera, Sacre, et al., 2020), Polish (Brytek-Matera, 2021), Portuguese (Ferreira & Coimbra, 2021), French (Lasson et al., 2021), and Italian (Cerolini et al., 2021). It includes 10 statements, for which respondents indicate how true the statement is for them using a 4-point scale ranging from 1 = *this does not apply to me* to 4 = *this applies to me* for a total possible sum score of 10–40. Higher scores represent higher levels of ON symptomatology, and a score of 30 or greater is considered to be representative of the ON condition (Barthels et al., 2015). Using this criterion, the prevalence rates among general samples of college students and other adults recruited from the community have ranged from 2% to 11% (Brytek-Matera, 2021; Brytek-Matera, Sacre, et al., 2020; Brytek-Matera, Onieva-Zafra, et al., 2020; Cerolini et al., 2021; Chard et al., 2019; Depa et al., 2017; Ferreira & Coimbra, 2021; Greetfeld et al., 2021; He et al., 2019; Lasson et al., 2021; Luck-Sikorski et al., 2019; Strahler et al., 2018). The internal reliability among this measure's 10 items has been good to excellent, with Cronbach's α values ranging from .80 to .90 ($M = 0.85$; Barthels et al., 2015; Barthels, Horn, et al., 2021; Barthels, Kisser, et al., 2021; Brytek-Matera, 2021; Brytek-Matera, Sacre, et al., 2020; Cerolini et al., 2021; Chard et al., 2019; Ferreira & Coimbra, 2021; He et al., 2019, 2021; Luck-Sikorski et al., 2019; Meule et al., 2020; Parra-Fernández et al., 2019; Strahler et al., 2018, 2020). Furthermore, the original validation study demonstrated the stability of the DOS scores with test–retest reliability (with 2 weeks between the two measurements) at .79 (Barthels et al., 2015).

Pertaining to validity, six of the 10 items relate to the behaviors and preoccupation diagnostic criterion for ON (e.g., "I have certain nutritional rules I adhere to"), two relate to the emotional distress diagnostic criterion (e.g., "If I eat something I consider unhealthy, I feel really bad"), two relate to the psychosocial impairments diagnostic criterion (e.g., "I try to avoid getting invited over to friends for dinner if I know that they do not pay attention to healthy nutrition"), and none relate to the physical impairments diagnostic criterion. Regarding criterion validity, DOS scores have been significantly correlated with scores on the BOT ($r = .78$–$.86$; Barthels, Meyer, Amrhein, et al., 2018; Meule et al., 2020), the ORTO-15 ($r = -.45$ and $-.57$; Cerolini et al., 2021; Meule et al., 2020), the EHQ ($r = .74$–$.79$; Brytek-Matera, 2021; Brytek-Matera, Sacre, et al., 2020; Chard et al., 2019; Lasson et al., 2021; Meule et al., 2020), and the TOS ($r = .69$–$.73$; Barrada & Roncero, 2018; Strahler et al., 2020). Regarding convergent validity, researchers have consistently found greater DOS scores to be significantly associated with greater levels of disordered eating (Chard et al., 2019; Barthels, Kisser, et al., 2021; Brytek-Matera, 2021; Brytek-Matera, Onieva-Zafra, et al., 2020; Cerolini et al., 2021; Ferreira & Coimbra, 2021; Greetfeld et al., 2021; Lasson et al., 2021; Parra-Fernández et al., 2019; Strahler et al., 2018). In multiple studies, higher DOS scores were also significantly associated with a vegetarian or vegan diet (Barthels, Meyer, & Pietrowsky, 2018; Ferreira & Coimbra, 2021; Hessler-Kaufmann et al., 2021; Luck-Sikorski et al., 2019) and with greater levels of exercise activity (He et al., 2021; Rudolph, 2017), obsessive-compulsive tendencies (Cerolini et al., 2021; Strahler et al., 2018), depression (Cerolini et al., 2021; Ferreira & Coimbra, 2021; Greetfeld et al., 2021; Hessler-Kaufmann et al., 2021; Luck-Sikorski et al., 2019; Strahler et al., 2018), and anxiety (Ferreira & Coimbra, 2021; Strahler et al., 2018). However, two studies found no relationship between ON and these variables (Lasson et al., 2021 – obsessive-compulsive tendencies, depression, or anxiety; Strahler et al., 2018 – vegetarian/vegan diet or exercise activity). Finally, regarding discriminant validity, whereas most studies have found that men and women do not differ on DOS scores (Barthels, Meyer, & Pietrowsky, 2018; Brytek-Matera, Onieva-Zafra, et al., 2020; Brytek-Matera, Sacre, et al., 2020; He et al., 2021; Luck-Sikorski et al., 2019; Strahler et al., 2020), some studies found DOS scores to be greater in women than in men (Ferreira & Coimbra, 2021; Greetfeld et al., 2021; Hessler-Kaufmann et al., 2021; Rudolph, 2017; Strahler et al., 2018), and one study even found DOS scores to be greater in men than in women (He et al., 2019).

Teruel Orthorexia Scale

The TOS (Barrada & Roncero, 2018) was developed in Spanish and has been translated into Arabic (Awad et al., 2021; Strahler et al., 2020) and German (Strahler et al., 2021). It includes 17 statements, for which respondents indicate how much they agree with the statement using a 4-point scale ranging from 1 = *completely disagree* to 4 = *completely agree* for a total possible sum score of 17–68. Higher scores represent higher levels of ON symptomatology; the developers of the TOS did not include a recommended criterion for diagnosis or risk of ON. Additionally, this measure includes two subscales: Healthy Orthorexia (HO; healthy eating behaviors) and Orthorexia Nervosa (ON; problems associated with healthy eating). Factor analyses in other studies have confirmed this two-factor structure (Barthels et al., 2019; Awad et al., 2021). On a side note, we disagree with the Healthy Orthorexia label of the HO scale, because it implies that orthorexia can be healthy as opposed to being a disorder that negatively impacts one's life, and because greater HO scores have been significantly associated with greater levels of disordered eating, which is obviously not healthy (Barrada & Roncero, 2018). Regarding reliability, although the internal reliability among all 17 items has not been reported, the internal reliability for the individual scales has been good with Cronbach's α values ranging from .84 to .87 ($M = 0.86$) for the HO scale and ranging from .83 to .90 ($M = 0.87$) for the ON scale (Awad et al., 2021; Barrada & Roncero, 2018; Barthels et al., 2019; Strahler et al., 2020). Finally, in the original validation study, test–retest reliability (with 18 weeks between the two measurements) was not reported for the total TOS, but was .73 for the HO scale and .82 for the ON scale (Barrada & Roncero, 2018), demonstrating the stability of the individual scale scores.

Pertaining to validity, nine of the 17 items relate to the behaviors and preoccupation diagnostic criterion for ON (e.g., "I spend a lot of time buying, planning and/or preparing food so my diet will be as healthy as possible"), five relate to the emotional distress diagnostic criterion (e.g., "I feel overwhelmed or sad if I eat food that I consider unhealthy"), three relate to the psychosocial impairments diagnostic criterion (e.g., "My social relations have been negatively affected by my concern about eating healthy food"), and none relate to the physical impairments diagnostic criterion. Regarding criterion validity, scores on both scales of the TOS have been significantly correlated with scores on the OTRO-15 (r=–.48 for the HO scale; r=–.41 for the ON scale; Barrada & Roncero, 2018) and the DOS (r=.70 for the HO scale; r=.76 for the ON scale; Barrada & Roncero, 2018). Regarding convergent validity, researchers have found greater scores on both scales of the TOS to be significantly associated with greater levels of disordered eating (Barrada & Roncero, 2018). Additionally, greater scores on the ON scale were significantly associated with greater levels of obsessive-compulsive tendencies (Barrada & Roncero, 2018) and negative affect or depression (Barrada & Roncero, 2018; Barthels et al., 2019; Strahler, 2020; Strahler et al., 2020), whereas scores on the HO scale were unrelated to these variables in those studies. Associations of the two TOS scales with exercise activity and vegetarianism have yet to be tested. Finally, regarding discriminant validity, men and women have not differed on TOS scores (Barthels et al., 2019; Depa et al., 2019; Domingues & Carmo, 2021; Strahler, 2020).

Orthorexia Nervosa Inventory

The ONI (Oberle et al., 2021), one of the most recently published measures of ON, was developed in English and has been translated into Turkish (Kaya et al., 2021). Translations into Hungarian, Croatian, Italian, Spanish, and Polish are currently in development. It includes 24 statements, for which respondents indicate how true the statement is for them using a 4-point scale ranging from 1=*not at all true* to 4=*very true* for a total possible sum score of 24–96. Higher scores represent higher levels of ON symptomatology, and a score of 72 or greater is considered to be representative of the ON condition (Oberle et al., 2021). Moreover, this measure includes three subscales: Behaviors (behaviors and preoccupation with healthy eating), Impairments (physical and psychosocial impairments associated with their eating habits), and Emotions (emotional distress associated with their eating habits). A factor analysis in another study has confirmed this three-factor structure (Kaya et al., 2021). Using the criterion of a total score of 72 or more, the prevalence rate among a general sample of college students and other adults recruited from the community was 5% (Oberle et al., 2021). The internal reliability among all 24 items of this measure has been excellent, with Cronbach's α values ranging from .91 to .94 (M=0.93; Kaya et al., 2021; Oberle et al., 2021), and the internal reliability for the individual scales has been good, with Cronbach's α values ranging from .82 to .89 (M=0.86) for the Behaviors scale, .84 to .90 (M=0.87) for the Impairments scale, and .81 to .88 (M=0.85) for the Emotions scale (Kaya et al., 2021; Oberle et al., 2021). Finally, in the original validation study, test–retest reliability (with 2 weeks between the two measurements) was .91 for the total ONI and ranged from .86 to .87 for the individual scales (Oberle et al., 2021), demonstrating the stability of these scores.

Pertaining to validity, nine of the 24 items relate to the behaviors and preoccupation diagnostic criterion for ON (e.g., "I follow a health-food diet rigidly, only eating what my diet allows and not allowing myself any deviations from this diet"), five relate to the emotional distress diagnostic criterion (e.g., "I feel much guilt or self-loathing when I stray from my healthy diet"), four relate to the psychosocial impairments diagnostic criterion (e.g., "As a result of the amount of time I devote to my healthy diet, I have spent less time than I used to with my family or friends"), and six relate to the physical impairments diagnostic criterion (e.g., "Even though I have eaten much healthier over time, my physical health has actually declined"). Criterion validity of the ONI has not yet been assessed. Regarding convergent validity, two studies have found higher ONI scores to be significantly associated with greater disordered eating (Kaya et al., 2021; Oberle et al., 2021). Higher ONI scores were also significantly associated with a vegetarian or vegan diet and with greater levels of exercise activity, obsessive-compulsive tendencies, and depression (Oberle et al., 2021). Finally, regarding discriminant validity, men and women have not differed on ONI scores (Kaya et al., 2021; Oberle et al., 2021), consistent with most other studies showing no gender differences in ON symptomatology (McComb & Mills, 2019).

Conclusions

Regarding reliability, internal reliability has generally been good to excellent for the EHQ, the DOS, the TOS, and the ONI, with average Cronbach's α values of .85–.93 (see Table 5.1). Further, the scores for each of these four measures have been shown to be stable over time, with test–retest coefficients of .78–.91. In contrast, the internal reliability of the BOT and the ORTO-15 is questionable, with average Cronbach's α values of .73 and .61, respectively, and the test–retest reliability has not been assessed for either measure. For these reasons, we recommend against using either the BOT or the ORTO-15 for assessing ON symptomatology for either research or clinical purposes.

Of the four reliable measures identified above, the EHQ and the DOS have been the most frequently used tests. Both measures have established criterion validity, having been correlated with multiple measures of ON symptomatology. Regarding content validity, the majority of items for both measures (62 % for the EHQ, 60 % for the DOS) relate to the behaviors and preoccupation diagnostic criterion for ON, with the remaining items relating to the emotional distress diagnostic criterion (14 % for the EHQ, 20 % for the DOS) or to the psychosocial impairments diagnostic criterion (24 % for the EHQ, 20 % for the DOS); none of the items relate to the physical impairments diagnostic criterion. Regarding convergent validity, greater scores on both measures have been significantly associated with greater levels of disordered eating. With the EHQ, 100 % of the studies also reveal consistent relationships with a vegetarian/vegan diet, exercise activity, and obsessive-compulsive tendencies, and 50 % reveal a relationship with depression. With the DOS, 67–86 % of the studies reveal relationships with these variables. Regarding discriminant validity, 100 % of the studies with the EHQ and 50 % of the studies with the DOS reveal no gender differences in ON symptomatology. Given the slightly better convergent and discriminant validity, as well as slightly higher reliability values, we recommend using the EHQ over the DOS.

The two most recently published measures of ON are the TOS (published in 2018) and the ONI (published in 2021). TOS scores have been correlated with the ORTO-15 and with the DOS, whereas no research has assessed the criterion validity of the ONI to date. Regarding content validity, many items for both measures relate to the behaviors and preoccupation diagnostic criterion for ON (53 % for the TOS, 38 % for the ONI), the emotional distress diagnostic criterion (29 % for the TOS, 21 % for the ONI), and the psychosocial impairments diagnostic criterion (18 % for the TOS, 17 % for the ONI). However, the ONI is the only measure that includes items that relate to the physical impairments diagnostic criterion (25 % of the ONI items). Regarding convergent validity, greater scores on both measures have been significantly associated with greater levels of disordered eating, obsessive-compulsive tendencies, and depression. In addition, greater ONI scores have also been significantly associated with a vegetarian/vegan diet and with exercise activity, whereas no research has assessed these relationships using the TOS to date. Given that the ONI is the only measure to assess the physical impairments diagnostic criterion of ON, as well as the misleading Healthy Orthorexia label of the TOS-HO scale that has been significantly associated with disordered eating, we recommend using the ONI over the TOS, with acknowledgment that more research is needed to further validate this new measure.

References

Agopyan, A., Kenger, E.B., Kermen, S., Ulker, M.T., Uzsoy, M.A., & Yetgin, M.K. (2019). The relationship between orthorexia nervosa and body composition in female students of the nutrition and dietetics department. *Eating and Weight Disorders, 24*(2), 257–266. https://doi.org/10.1007/s40519-018-0565-3

Aksoydan, E., & Camci, N. (2009). Prevalence of orthorexia nervosa among Turkish performance artists. *Eating and Weight Disorders, 14*(1), 33–37. https://doi.org/10.1007/BF03327792

Almeida, C., Vieira Borba, V., & Santos, L. (2018). Orthorexia nervosa in a sample of Portuguese fitness participants. *Eating and Weight Disorders, 23*(4), 443–451. https://doi.org/10.1007/s40519-018-0517-y

Alvarenga, M.S., Martins, M.C.T., Sato, K.S.C.J., Vargas, S.V.A., Philippi, S.T., & Scagliusi, F.B. (2012). Orthorexia nervosa behavior in a sample of Brazilian dietitians assessed by the Portuguese version of ORTO-15. *Eating and Weight Disorders, 17*(1), 29–35. https://doi.org/10.1007/BF03325325

American Psychiatric Association. (2013). *Diagnostic and statistical manual of mental disorders* (5th ed.). https://doi.org/10.1176/appi.books.9780890425596

Andreas, S., Schedler, K., Schulz, H., & Nutzinger, D.O. (2018). Evaluation of a German version of a brief diagnosis questionnaire of symptoms of orthorexia nervosa in patients with mental disorders (Ortho-10). *Eating and Weight Disorders, 23*(1), 75–85. https://doi.org/10.1007/s40519-017-0473-y

Arusoğlu, G., Kabakçi, E., Köksal, G., & Kutluay Merdol, T. (2008). Orthorexia nervosa and adaptation of ORTO-11 into Turkish. *Turkish Journal of Psychiatry, 19*(3), 283–291.

Awad, E., Obeid, S., Sacre, H., Salameh, P., Strahler, J., & Hallit, S. (2021). Association between impulsivity and orthorexia nervosa: Any moderating role of maladaptive personality traits? *Eating and Weight Disorders, 27*, 483–493. https://doi.org/10.1007/s40519-021-01186-5

Babeau, C., Le Chevanton, T., Julien-Sweerts, S., Brochenin, A., Donini, L.M., & Fouques, D. (2020). Structural validation of the ORTO-12-FR questionnaire among a French sample as a first attempt to assess orthorexia nervosa in France. *Eating and Weight Disorders, 25*(6), 1771–1778. https://doi.org/10.1007/s40519-019-00835-0

Bağci Bosi, A.T., Gamur, D., & Guler, G. (2007). Prevalence of orthorexia nervosa in resident medical doctors in the faculty of medicine. *Appetite, 49*, 661–666. https://doi.org/10.1016/j.appet.2007.04.007

Barnett, M.J., Dripps, W.R., & Blomquist, K.K. (2016). Organivore or organorexic? Examining the relationship between alternative food network engagement, disordered eating, and special diets. *Appetite, 105*, 713–720. https://doi.org/10.1016/j.appet.2016.07.008

Barrada, J.R., & Roncero, M. (2018). Bidimensional structure of orthorexia: Development and initial validation of a new instrument. *Annals of Psychology, 34*, 283–291. https://doi.org/10.6018/analesps.34.2.299671

Barthels, F., Barrada, J.R., & Roncero, M. (2019). Orthorexia nervosa and healthy orthorexia as new eating styles. *PloS One, 14*(7), Article e0219609. https://doi.org/10.1371/journal.pone.0219609

Barthels, F., Horn, S., & Pietrowsky, R. (2021). Orthorexic eating behaviour, illness anxiety and dysfunctional cognitions characteristic of somatic symptom disorders in a non-clinical sample. *Eating and Weight Disorders, 26*, 2387–2391. https://doi.org/10.1007/s40519-020-01091-3

Barthels, F., Kisser, J., & Pietrowsky, R. (2021). Orthorexic eating behavior and body dissatisfaction in a sample of young females. *Eating and Weight Disorders, 26*, 2059–2063. https://doi.org/10.1007/s40519-020-00986-5

Barthels, F., Meyer, F., Amrhein, J., Scharmach, K., & Pietrowsky, R. (2018). Concurrent construct validity of the Düsseldorf Orthorexia Scale: Correlations with diet quality and specific dimensions of disordered eating behavior. *Zeitschrift für Klinische Psychologie und Psychotherapie, 47*(2), 109–118. https://doi.org/10.1026/1616-3443/a000479

Barthels, F., Meyer, F., & Pietrowsky, R. (2015). Duesseldorf orthorexia scale: Construction and evaluation of a questionnaire measuring orthorexic eating behavior. *Zeitschrift für Klinische Psychologie und Psychotherapie, 44*(2), 97–105. https://doi.org/10.1026/1616-3443/a000310

Barthels, F., Meyer, F., & Pietrowsky, R. (2018). Orthorexic and restrained eating behaviour in vegans, vegetarians, and individuals on a diet. *Eating and Weight Disorders, 23*, 159–166. https://doi.org/10.1007/s40519-018-0479-0

Bert, F., Gualano, M.R., Voglino, G., Rossello, P., Perret, J.P., & Siliquini, R. (2019). Orthorexia nervosa: A cross-sectional study among athletes competing in endurance sports in Northern Italy. *PloS One, 14*(8), Article e0221399. https://doi.org/10.1371/journal.pone.0221399

Bratman, S., & Knight, D. (2000). *Health food junkies: Overcoming the obsession with healthful eating*. Broadway Books.

Brytek-Matera, A. (2020). Restrained eating and vegan, vegetarian and omnivore dietary intakes. *Nutrients, 12*(7), Article 2133. https://doi.org/10.3390/nu12072133

Brytek-Matera, A. (2021). The Polish version of the Düsseldorf Orthorexia Scale (PL-DOS) and its comparison with the English version of the DOS (E-DOS). *Eating and Weight Disorders, 26*(4), 1223–1232. https://doi.org/10.1007/s40519-020-01025-z

Brytek-Matera, A., Czepczor-Bernat, K., Jurzak, H., Kornacka, M., & Kołodziejczyk, N. (2019). Strict health-oriented eating patterns (orthorexic eating behaviours) and their connection with a vegetarian and vegan diet. *Eating and Weight Disorders, 24*(3), 441–452. https://doi.org/10.1007/s40519-018-0563-5

Brytek-Matera, A., Fonte, M.L., Poggiogalle, E., Donini, L.M., & Cena, H. (2017). Orthorexia nervosa: Relationship with obsessive-compulsive symptoms, disordered eating patterns and body uneasiness among Italian university students. *Eating and Weight Disorders, 22*(4), 609–617. https://doi.org/10.1007/s40519-017-0427-4

Brytek-Matera, A., Krupa, M., Poggiogalle, E., & Donini, L.M. (2014). Adaptation of the ORTHO-15 test to Polish women and men. *Eating and Weight Disorders, 19*(1), 69–76. https://doi.org/10.1007/s40519-014-0100-0

Brytek-Matera, A., Onieva-Zafra, M.D., Parra-Fernández, M.L., Staniszewska, A., Modrzejewska, J., & Fernández-Martínez, E. (2020). Evaluation of orthorexia nervosa and symptomatology associated with eating disorders among European university students: A multicentre cross-sectional study. *Nutrients, 12*(12), Article 3716. https://doi.org/10.3390/nu12123716

Brytek-Matera, A., Sacre, H., Staniszewska, A., & Hallit, S. (2020). The prevalence of orthorexia nervosa in Polish and Lebanese adults and its relationship with sociodemographic variables and BMI ranges: A cross-cultural perspective. *Nutrients, 12*(12), Article 3865. https://doi.org/10.3390/nu12123865

Bundros, J., Clifford, D., Silliman, K., & Neyman Morris, M. (2016). Prevalence of orthorexia nervosa among college students based on Bratman's test and associated tendencies. *Appetite, 101*, 86–94. https://doi.org/10.1016/j.appet.2016.02.144

Cerolini, S., Vacca, M., Zagaria, A., Donini, L.M., Barbaranelli, C., & Lombardo, C. (2021). Italian adaptation of the Düsseldorf Orthorexia Scale (I-DOS): Psychometric properties and prevalence of orthorexia nervosa among an Italian sample. *Eating and Weight Disorders, 27*, 1405–1413. https://doi.org/10.1007/s40519-021-01278-2

Chard, C.A., Hilzendegen, C., Barthels, F., & Stroebele-Benschop, N. (2019). Psychometric evaluation of the English version of the Düsseldorf Orthorexie Scale (DOS) and the prevalence of orthorexia nervosa among a U.S. student sample. *Eating and Weight Disorders, 24*(2), 275–281. https://doi.org/10.1007/s40519-018-0570-6

Çiçekoğlu, P., & Tunçay, G.Y. (2018). A comparison of eating attitudes between vegans/vegetarians and nonvegans/nonvegetarians in terms of orthorexia nervosa. *Archives of Psychiatric Nursing, 32*(2), 200–205. https://doi.org/10.1016/j.apnu.2017.11.002

Clifford, T., & Blyth, C. (2019). A pilot study comparing the prevalence of orthorexia nervosa in regular students and those in university sports teams. *Eating and Weight Disorders, 24*(3), 473–480. https://doi.org/10.1007/s40519-018-0584-0

Dell'Osso, L., Abelli, M., Carpita, B., Massimetti, G., Pini, S., Rivetti, L., Gorrasi, F., Tognetti, R., Ricca, V., & Carmassi, C. (2016). Orthorexia nervosa in a sample of Italian university population. *Rivista Di Psichiatria, 51*(5), 190–196. https://doi.org/10.1708/2476.25888

Dell'Osso, L., Carpita, B., Muti, D., Cremone, I.M., Massimetti, G., Diadema, E., Gesi, C., & Carmassi, C. (2018). Prevalence and characteristics of orthorexia nervosa in a sample of university students in Italy. *Eating and Weight Disorders, 23*(1), 55–65. https://doi.org/10.1007/s40519-017-0460-3

Depa, J., Barrada, J.R., & Roncero, M. (2019). Are the motives for food choices different in orthorexia nervosa and healthy orthorexia? *Nutrients, 11*(3), Article 697. https://doi.org/10.3390/nu11030697

Depa, J., Schweizer, J., Bekers, S.-K., Hilzendegen, C., & Stroebele-Benschop, N. (2017). Prevalence and predictors of orthorexia nervosa among German students using the 21-item-DOS. *Eating and Weight Disorders, 22*(1), 193–199. https://doi.org/10.1007/s40519-016-0334-0

Dittfeld, A., Gwizdek, K., Jagielski, P., Brzęk, A., & Ziora, K. (2017). A study on the relationship between orthorexia and vegetarianism using the BOT (Bratman Test for Orthorexia). *Psychiatria Polska, 51*(6), 1133–1144. https://doi.org/10.12740/PP/75739

Domingues, R.B., & Carmo, C. (2021). Orthorexia nervosa in yoga practitioners: Relationship with personality, attitudes about appearance, and yoga engagement. *Eating and Weight Disorders, 26*(3), 789–795. https://doi.org/10.1007/s40519-020-00911-w

Donini, L.M., Marsili, D., Graziani, M.P., Imbriale, M., & Cannella, C. (2005). Orthorexia nervosa: Validation of a diagnosis questionnaire. *Eating and Weight Disorders, 10*(3), 28–32. https://doi.org/10.1007/BF03327537

Dunn, T.M., & Bratman, S. (2016). On orthorexia nervosa: A review of the literature and proposed diagnostic criteria. *Eating Behaviors, 21*, 11–17. https://doi.org/10.1016/j.eatbeh.2015.12.006

Dunn, T.M., Gibbs, J., Whitney, N., & Starosta, A. (2017). Prevalence of orthorexia nervosa is less than 1%: Data from a US sample. *Eating and Weight Disorders, 22*(1), 185–192. https://doi.org/10.1007/s40519-016-0258-8

Eriksson, L., Baigi, A., Marklund, B., & Lindgren, E.C. (2008). Social physique anxiety and sociocultural attitudes toward appearance impact on orthorexia test in fitness participants. *Scandinavian Journal of Medicine & Science in Sports, 18*(3), 389–394. https://doi.org/10.1111/j.1600-0838.2007.00723.x

Farchakh, Y., Hallit, S., & Soufia, M. (2019). Association between orthorexia nervosa, eating attitudes and anxiety among medical students in Lebanese universities: Results of a cross-sectional study. *Eating and Weight Disorders, 24*(4), 683–691. https://doi.org/10.1007/s40519-019-00724-6

Ferreira, C., & Coimbra, M. (2021). To further understand orthorexia nervosa: DOS validity for the Portuguese population and its relationship with psychological indicators, sex, BMI and dietary pattern. *Eating and Weight Disorders, 26*, 2127–2134. https://doi.org/10.1007/s40519-020-01058-4

Fidan, T., Ertekin, V., Isikay, S., & Kirpinar, I. (2010). Prevalence of orthorexia among medical students in Erzurum, Turkey. *Comprehensive Psychiatry, 51*, 49–54. https://doi.org/10.1016/j.comppsych.2009.03.001

Gleaves, D.H., Graham, E.C., & Ambwani, S. (2013). Measuring "orthorexia:" Development of the Eating Habits Questionnaire. *The International Journal of Educational and Psychological Assessment, 12*(2), 1–18.

Gramaglia, C., Gambaro, E., Delicato, C., Marchetti, M., Sarchiapone, M., Ferrante, D., Roncero, M., Perpiñá, C., Brytek-Matera, A., Wojtyna, E., & Zeppegno, P. (2019). Orthorexia nervosa, eating patterns and personality traits: A cross-cultural comparison of Italian, Polish and Spanish university students. *BMC Psychiatry, 19*, Article 235. https://doi.org/10.1186/s12888-019-2208-2

Grammatikopoulou, M.G., Gkiouras, K., Markaki, A., Theodoridis, X., Tsakiri, V., Mavridis, P., Dardavessis, T., & Chourdakis, M. (2018). Food addiction, orthorexia, and food-related stress among dietetics students. *Eating and Weight Disorders, 23*(4), 459–467. https://doi.org/10.1007/s40519-018-0514-1

Greetfeld, M., Hessler-Kaufmann, J.B., Brandl, B., Skurk, T., Holzapfel, C., Quadflieg, N., Schlegl, S., Hauner, H., & Voderholzer, U. (2021). Orthorexic tendencies in the general population: Association with demographic data, psychiatric symptoms, and utilization of mental health services. *Eating and Weight Disorders, 26*, 1511–1519. https://doi.org/10.1007/s40519-020-00961-0

Haddad, C., Obeid, S., Akel, M., Honein, K., Akiki, M., Azar, J., & Hallit, S. (2019). Correlates of orthorexia nervosa among a representative sample of the Lebanese population. *Eating and Weight Disorders, 24*(3), 481–493. https://doi.org/10.1007/s40519-018-0631-x

Hayatbini, N., & Oberle, C.D. (2019). Are orthorexia nervosa symptoms associated with cognitive inflexibility? *Psychiatry Research, 271*, 464–468. https://doi.org/10.1016/j.psychres.2018.12.017

He, J., Ma, H., Barthels, F., & Fan, X. (2019). Psychometric properties of the Chinese version of the Düsseldorf Orthorexia Scale: Prevalence and demographic correlates of orthorexia nervosa among Chinese university students. *Eating and Weight Disorders, 24*(3), 453–463. https://doi.org/10.1007/s40519-019-00656-1

He, J., Zhao, Y., Zhang, H., & Lin, Z. (2021). Orthorexia nervosa is associated with positive body image and life satisfaction in Chinese elderly: Evidence for a positive psychology perspective. *International Journal of Eating Disorders, 54*(2), 212–221. https://doi.org/10.1002/eat.23400

Herranz Valera, J., Acuña Ruiz, P., Romero Valdespino, B., & Visioli, F. (2014). Prevalence of orthorexia nervosa among ashtanga yoga practitioners: A pilot study. *Eating and Weight Disorders, 19*(4), 469–472. https://doi.org/10.1007/s40519-014-0131-6

Hessler-Kaufmann, J.B., Meule, A., Holzapfel, C., Brandl, B., Greetfeld, M., Skurk, T., Schlegl, S., Hauner, H., & Voderholzer, U. (2021). Orthorexic tendencies moderate the relationship between semi-vegetarianism and depressive symptoms. *Eating and Weight Disorders, 26*(2), 623–628. https://doi.org/10.1007/s40519-020-00901-y

Hyrnik, J., Janas-Kozik, M., Stochel, M., Jelonek, I., Siwiec, A., & Rybakowski, J.K. (2016). The assessment of orthorexia nervosa among 1899 Polish adolescents using the ORTO-15 questionnaire. *International Journal of Psychiatry in Clinical Practice, 20*(3), 199–203. https://doi.org/10.1080/13651501.2016.1197271

Kaya, S., Uzdil, Z., & Çakıroğlu, F.P. (2021). Validation of the Turkish version of the Orthorexia Nervosa Inventory (ONI) in an adult population: Its association with psychometric properties. *Eating and Weight Disorders, 27*, 729–735. https://doi.org/10.1007/s40519-021-01199-0

Kinzl, J.F., Hauer, K., Traweger, C., & Kiefer, I. (2005). Orthorexia nervosa: A frequent eating disorder in dieticians? *Ernährungs-Umschau, 52*(11), 436–439.

Kiss-Leizer, M., & Rigó, A. (2019). People behind unhealthy obsession to healthy food: The personality profile of tendency to orthorexia nervosa. *Eating and Weight Disorders, 24*(1), 29–35. https://doi.org/10.1007/s40519-018-0527-9

Koven, N.S., & Senbonmatsu, R. (2013). A neuropsychological evaluation of orthorexia nervosa. *Open Journal of Psychiatry, 3*, 214–222. https://doi.org/10.4236/ojpsych.2013.32019

Lasson, C., Barthels, F., & Raynal, P. (2021). Psychometric evaluation of the French version of the Düsseldorfer Orthorexie Skala (DOS) and prevalence of orthorexia nervosa among university students. *Eating and Weight Disorders, 26*(8), 2589–2596. https://doi.org/10.1007/s40519-021-01123-6

Luck-Sikorski, C., Jung, F., Schlosser, K., & Riedel-Heller, S.G. (2019). Is orthorexic behavior common in the general public? A large representative study in Germany. *Eating and Weight Disorders, 24*(2), 267–273. https://doi.org/10.1007/s40519-018-0502-5

Malmborg, J., Bremander, A., Olsson, M.C., & Bergman, S. (2017). Health status, physical activity, and orthorexia nervosa: A comparison between exercise science students and business students. *Appetite, 109*, 137–143. https://doi.org/10.1016/j.appet.2016.11.028

McComb, S.E., & Mills, J.S. (2019). Orthorexia nervosa: A review of psychosocial risk factors. *Appetite, 140*, 50–75. https://doi.org/10.1016/j.appet.2019.05.005

Meule, A., Holzapfel, C., Brandl, B., Greetfeld, M., Hessler-Kaufmann, J.B., Skurk, T., Quadflieg, N., Schlegl, S., Hauner, H., & Voderholzer, U. (2020). Measuring orthorexia nervosa: A comparison of four self-report questionnaires. *Appetite, 146*, Article 104512. https://doi.org/10.1016/j.appet.2019.104512

Mohamed Halim, Z., Dickinson, K.M., Kemps, E., & Prichard, I. (2020). Orthorexia nervosa: Examining the Eating Habits Questionnaire's reliability and validity, and its links to dietary adequacy among

adult women. *Public Health Nutrition, 23*(10), 1684–1692. https://doi.org/10.1017/S1368980019004282
Moroze, R. M., Dunn, T. M., Holland, J. C., Yager, J., & Weintraub, P. (2015). Microthinking about micronutrients: A case of transition from obsessions about health eating to near-fatal "orthorexia nervosa" and proposed diagnostic criteria. *Psychosomatics, 56*(4), 397–403. https://doi.org/10.1016/j.psym.2014.03.003
Novara, C., Pardini, S., Pastore, M., & Mulatti, C. (2017). Orthorexia Nervosa: An investigation of the construct and psychometric properties of the Italian version of the Eating Habits Questionnaire-21 (EHQ-21). *Psicoterapia Cognitiva e Comportamentale, 23*(3), 291–316.
Oberle, C. D., De Nadai, A. S., & Madrid, A. L. (2021). Orthorexia Nervosa Inventory (ONI): development and validation of a new measure of orthorexic symptomatology. *Eating and Weight Disorders, 26*(2), 609–622. https://doi.org/10.1007/s40519-020-00896-6
Oberle, C. D., Klare, D. L., & Patyk, K. (2019). Health beliefs, behaviors, and symptoms associated with orthorexia nervosa. *Eating and Weight Disorders, 24*(3), 495–506. https://doi.org/10.1007/s40519-019-00657-0
Oberle, C. D., Samaghabadi, R. O., & Hughes, E. M. (2017). Orthorexia nervosa: Assessment and correlates with gender, BMI, and personality. *Appetite, 108*, 303–310. https://doi.org/10.1016/j.appet.2016.10.021
Oberle, C. D., Watkins, R. S., & Burkot, A. J. (2018). Orthorexic eating behaviors related to exercise addiction and internal motivations in a sample of university students. *Eating and Weight Disorders, 23*(1), 67–74. https://doi.org/10.1007/s40519-017-0470-1
Parra-Fernández, M. L., Onieva-Zafra, M. D., Fernández-Muñoz, J. J., & Fernández-Martínez, E. (2019). Adaptation and validation of the Spanish version of the DOS questionnaire for the detection of orthorexic nervosa behavior. *PloS One, 14*(5), Article e0216583. https://doi.org/10.1371/journal.pone.0216583
Parra-Fernández, M. L., Onieva-Zafra, M. D., Fernández-Muñoz, J. J., Głębocka, A., Fernández-Martínez, E., & Brytek-Matera, A. (2021). The Spanish Version of the Eating Habits Questionnaire (EHQ-ES) and its links to symptoms and concerns characteristic of eating disorders among young adults. *Nutrients, 13*(6). https://doi.org/10.3390/nu13061993
Parra-Fernandez, M. L., Rodriguez-Cano, T., Onieva-Zafra, M. D., Perez-Haro, M. J., Casero-Alonso, V., Camargo, J. C. M., & Notario-Pacheco, B. (2018). Adaptation and validation of the Spanish version of the ORTO-15 questionnaire for the diagnosis of orthorexia nervosa. *PLoS One, 13*(1), Article E0190722. https://doi.org/10.1371/journal.pone.0190722
Plichta, M., & Jezewska-Zychowicz, M. (2019). Eating behaviors, attitudes toward health and eating, and symptoms of orthorexia nervosa among students. *Appetite, 137*, 114–123. https://doi.org/10.1016/j.appet.2019.02.022
Ramacciotti, C. E., Perrone, P., Coli, E., Burgalassi, A., Conversano, C., Massimetti, G., & Dell'Osso, L. (2011). Orthorexia nervosa in the general population: A preliminary screening using a self-administered questionnaire (ORTO-15). *Eating and Weight Disorders, 16*(2), 127–130. https://doi.org/10.1007/BF03325318
Reynolds, R. (2018). Is the prevalence of orthorexia nervosa in an Australian university population 65 %? *Eating and Weight Disorders, 23*(4), 453–458. https://doi.org/10.1007/s40519-018-0535-9
Roncero, M., Barrada, J. R., & Perpiñá, C. (2017). Measuring orthorexia nervosa: Psychometric limitations of the ORTO-15. *The Spanish Journal of Psychology, 20*, Article E41. https://doi.org/10.1017/sjp.2017.36
Rudolph, S. (2017). The connection between exercise addiction and orthorexia nervosa in German fitness sports. *Eating and Weight Disorders, 23*(4), 581–586. https://doi.org/10.1007/s40519-017-0437-2
Segura-García, C., Papaianni, M. C., Caglioti, F., Procopio, L., Nisticò, C. G., Bombardiere, L., Ammendolia, A., Rizza, P., De Fazio, P., & Capranica, L. (2012). Orthorexia nervosa: A frequent eating disordered behavior in athletes. *Eating and Weight Disorders, 17*(4), 223–233. https://doi.org/10.3275/8272

Segura-García, C., Ramacciotti, C., Rania, M., Aloi, M., Caroleo, M., Bruni, A., Gazzarrini, D., Sinopoli, F., & De Fazio, P. (2015). The prevalence of orthorexia nervosa among eating disorder patients after treatment. *Eating and Weight Disorders, 20*(2), 161–166. https://doi.org/10.1007/s40519-014-0171-y

Setnick, J. (2013). *The eating disorders clinical pocket guide: Quick reference for healthcare providers* (2nd ed.). Understanding Nutrition.

Strahler, J. (2020). The dark side of healthy eating: Links between orthorexic eating and mental health. *Nutrients, 12*(12), Article 3662. https://doi.org/10.3390/nu12123662

Strahler, J. (2021). Trait mindfulness differentiates the interest in healthy diet from orthorexia nervosa. *Eating and Weight Disorders, 26*(3), 993–998. https://doi.org/10.1007/s40519-020-00927-2

Strahler, J., Haddad, C., Salameh, P., Sacre, H., Obeid, S., & Hallit, S. (2020). Cross-cultural differences in orthorexic eating behaviors: Associations with personality traits. *Nutrition, 77*, Article 110811. https://doi.org/10.1016/j.nut.2020.110811

Strahler, J., Hermann, A., Walter, B., & Stark, R. (2018). Orthorexia nervosa: A behavioral complex or psychological condition? *Journal of Behavioral Addictions, 7*(4), 1143–1156. https://doi.org/10.1556/2006.7.2018.129

Varga, M., Thege, B.K., Dukay-Szabo, S., Tury, F., & Furth, E.F. van (2014). When eating healthy is not healthy: Orthorexia nervosa and its measurement with the ORTO-15 in Hungary. *BMC Psychiatry, 14*, Article 59. https://doi.org/10.1186/1471-244X-14-59

Yakın, E., Raynal, P., & Chabrol, H. (2021). Distinguishing orthorexic behaviors from eating disordered and obsessive-compulsive behaviors: A typological study. *Eating and Weight Disorders, 26*, 2011–2019. https://doi.org/10.1007/s40519-020-01037-9

Zickgraf, H.F., Ellis, J.M., & Essayli, J.H. (2019). Disentangling orthorexia nervosa from healthy eating and other eating disorder symptoms: Relationships with clinical impairment, comorbidity, and self-reported food choices. *Appetite, 134*, 40–49. https://doi.org/10.1016/j.appet.2018.12.006

Chapter 6

Assessment of Intuitive Eating and Mindful Eating

Melanie J. Zimmer-Gembeck,[1,2] Harley J. Stansfield,[1] Jessica Kerin,[1,2] and Caroline Donovan[1]

[1] Griffith University, School of Applied Psychology, Australia
[2] Griffith University, Menzies Health Institute of Queensland, Australia

Introduction

Dieting has been under intense scrutiny in terms of both its safety and efficacy as a weight loss strategy, with research revealing that dieting can have adverse physical consequences (Dulloo et al., 2015; Herman et al., 2008; Logel et al., 2015; Montani et al., 2015; Neumark-Sztainer et al., 2012; Stroebe et al., 2017; Tomiyama et al., 2013; Vink et al., 2016). Partly as an outgrowth of this research, attention has shifted to understanding adaptive self-regulation of eating, which is based on concepts introduced decades ago as part of the anti-dieting movement (e.g., Orbach, 1978; Roth, 1993). Proponents of adaptive eating focus on health and well-being rather than body weight and shape. They promote the respect of satiety cues and eating only when hungry, the intuitive craving and selection of more nutritious foods, and the enhancement of body awareness and appreciation (Herman et al., 2008; Mathieu, 2009; Tylka, 2006; Van Dyke & Drinkwater, 2014). These tendencies are encapsulated within various views of adaptive eating, with theories and research on intuitive and mindful eating two of the most prominent (Herman et al., 2008; Van Dyke & Drinkwater, 2014).

Intuitive eating is defined as eating according to internal physiological cues of hunger and satiety (Tribole & Resch, 1995). It is founded on a philosophy that encourages a positive relationship with food, mind, and the body, rather than attempting to cognitively restrict, control, manage, or limit food and eating choices. Shifting the focus to intuitive eating is also an attempt to de-emphasize body weight when developing new eating habits. In fact, monitoring weight or attempting to lose weight while improving intuitive eating are contraindicated because intuitive eating is considered an internal interoceptive process to monitor health and well-being, while weight-control and even weight monitoring are viewed as external processes that undermine one's ability to engage in internal bodily awareness.

Mindful eating is defined as "being aware in the present moment while eating; intentionally paying attention, nonjudgmentally, to the senses, including physical and emotional sensations" (Peitz et al., 2021, p. 3). It has been described as incorporating a range of beliefs, skills, and behaviors: eating slowly without distraction; listening to physical cues of hunger and fullness and only eating until satiated; distinguishing between physical sensations of hunger and non-hunger triggers for eating such as uncomfortable emotions or external stimuli; engaging the senses by noticing colors, smells, sounds, textures, flavors; learning to alternatively cope with uncomfortable emotions; noticing the effects food has on the body and feelings; and appreciating food. Mindful eating has been treated as a skill set that an individual can learn through dedicated mindful practice. Generic mindfulness practice has received considerable research interest and has been applied as a treatment in many clinical contexts (e.g., see Goldberg et al., 2019; Parsons et al., 2017, for reviews) including to reduce disordered eating. A systematic review of the literature (Warren et al., 2017) reported that mindful eating is significantly related to fewer binge eating symptoms, emotional eating symptoms, and food cravings, but also highlighted the need for more evidence supporting mindful eating programs for weight loss.

Given the similarities between intuitive and mindful eating, there has been discussion about whether one may be the superordinate construct of the other (Van Dyke & Drinkwater, 2014). For example, some researchers propose that intuitive eating is a broader philosophy that incorporates mindful eating plus changing cognitive distortions around body image and eating, reducing emotional eating, and encouraging body respect and physical activity (Peitz et al., 2021; Tribole, 2010). Conversely, others have described mindful eating as including most, if not all, components of intuitive eating, in addition to broader aspects related to food and nutrition (e.g., food quality and quantity, and consumption speed), and a general non-judgmental awareness of one's physical and emotional signals when food is present (Framson et al., 2009; Fung et al., 2016; Schaefer & Magnuson, 2014). The parallels between intuitive and mindful eating are further reflected in researchers' use of these terms somewhat interchangeably or in concert with each other (Tribole, 2010). Moreover, studies have found that self-reported intuitive eating moderately to strongly correlates with self-reported mindful eating, with correlations as high as $r = .70$ (e.g., Kerin et al., 2019; Van Dyke & Drinkwater, 2014). However, in a study that sought to identify the components that explained covariation between three subscales from a measure of intuitive eating (Tylka, 2006), six subscales from a measure of mindful eating (Hulburt-Williams et al., 2014), as well as measures of overeating dysregulation, dietary restraint, emotional eating, and external eating, core components emerged indicating a complex structure to these measures (Kerin et al., 2019). In the first exploratory factor analysis, three subscales loaded positively on a component called attuned eating (Intuitive Eating for Physical Other Than Emotion Reason, Mindful Acting With Awareness, and Mindful Presence While Eating), and others loaded positively on the other three components called unrestrained eating (two subscales of Intuitive Unconditional Permission to Eating, Mindful Acceptance), eating and hunger awareness (mindful awareness) and casual eating attitudes (two subscales of Mindful Nonreactivity and Flexibility).

Measurement of Intuitive and Mindful Eating

Intuitive Eating

We could not locate any behavioral, clinical interviews, or observational measures of intuitive eating. However, three self-report measures have been developed, all called the Intuitive Eating Scale (IES). These are the IES-H (Hawks et al., 2004), the IES-T (Tylka, 2006), and the IES-2 (Tylka & Kroon Van Diest, 2013). The IES-H was the first available measure of intuitive eating, but this measure had low internal and test-retest reliability across multiple subscales and the overall scale had weak criterion validity. Consequently, the IES-T (Tylka, 2006) and its revision – the IES-2 (Tylka & Kroon Van Diest, 2013) – improved on the IES-H, with the first designed to measure three components, but the IES-2 designed to measure four components of intuitive eating: (1) eating for physical rather than emotional reasons; (2) permitting oneself to eat unconditionally (i.e., no food restriction or elimination); (3) relying on internal hunger and satiety cues to guide food intake; and (4) making food choices that enhance body functioning (body-food choice congruence).

The newer 23-item (seven negatively and 16 positively worded items) IES-2 is the currently preferred measure containing eight items to measure eating for physical rather than emotional reasons (e.g., "I find myself eating when I am stressed out, even when I'm not physically hungry," reversed); six items to measure unconditional permission to eat ("I have forbidden foods that I don't allow myself to eat," reversed); six items to measure reliance on internal hunger/satiety cues (e.g., "I trust my body to tell me how much to eat"); and three items to measure body-food choice congruence (e.g., "I mostly eat foods that make my body perform efficiently [well]"). Respondents rate their agreement with each item on a scale from 1 = *strongly disagree* to 5 = *strongly agree*. After reversing the seven negatively worded items, items are averaged or summed to produce four subscale scores, with higher scores indicating more intuitive eating. These four subscales may then be averaged or summed to form an overall intuitive eating composite score.

In a series of three studies (Tylka & Kroon Van Diest, 2013), the IES-2 demonstrated good internal reliability in both women and men. The original exploratory development sample consisted of 1,405 women and 1,195 men attending a Midwestern USA university (aged 18 to 56 years, $M_{age} = 20.4$, $SD = 5.2$; 76 % were in their first year of university), revealing Cronbach's αs for all 23 items of .87 for women and .89 for men. Additional studies have also reported similar internal reliability across adult and university student populations and reported adequate test-retest reliability, and good criterion validity through positive correlations with positive affect, well-being, and life satisfaction and inverse correlations with eating disorder symptomology and body dissatisfaction (Duarte et al., 2016; Madanat et al., 2020; Saunders et al., 2018; Strodl et al., 2020). The IES-T and the IES-2 have been translated to, and the factor structure replicated in, for example, French (Camilleri et al., 2015), Hungarian (Román et al., 2021), Malay (Swami et al., 2020), Romanian (Vintilă et al., 2020), Turkish (Bas et al., 2017), and German (Ruzanska & Warschburger, 2017; Van Dyck et al., 2016).

Mindful Eating

We could not locate any behavioral, clinical interviews, or observational measures of mindful eating. Although a plethora of self-report measures have been developed to measure general trait or state mindfulness (e.g., Mindful Attention Awareness Scale, MAAS; Brown & Ryan, 2003; Five Facet Mindfulness Questionnaire; Baer et al., 2008), only four have been designed to assess mindful eating: the Mindful Eating Questionnaire (MEQ; Framson et al., 2009), the Mindful Eating Scale (MES; Hulbert-Williams et al., 2014), the Mindful Eating Inventory (MEI; Peitz et al., 2021), and the Mindful Eating Behavior Scale (MEBS; Winkens et al., 2018). Table 6.1 provides a summary of the sampling and final measures from these mindful eating measurement development studies.

Mindful Eating Questionnaire

The MEQ was influential in moving forward research on mindful eating and was designed to align with "nonjudgmental awareness of physical and emotional sensations associated with eating" (Framson et al., 2009, p. 1439). Initial development and validation were completed with a sample of 303 individuals, and after exploratory factor analysis, five factors (28 items) were identified as described in Table 6.1. Respondents rate the frequency with which each item applies to them on a 4-point scale from 1 = *never/rarely* to 4 = *usually/always*. A *not applicable* response is also an option and is excluded from total score calculations. Total scores for each subscale are computed by averaging items on each subscale, and the five subscale scores can also be averaged to produce a total MEQ score. However, Framson et al. (2009) reported a Cronbach's α for the full MEQ of .64 suggesting some measurement improvements may be needed, but the proposed divergence of dieting from mindful eating was supported by a negative association between cognitive restraint and MEQ score. The MEQ has been used in many studies since its development (e.g., Beshara et al. 2013; Bryan, 2016; Mantzios & Egan, 2018; see Peitz et al., 2021 for more information) and a short 20-item version with two subscales (Awareness, Cronbach's α = .75; Recognition of Hunger and Satiety Cues, Cronbach's α = .83) has been developed (Clementi et al., 2017).

Mindful Eating Scale

In developing the MES (Hulbert-Williams et al., 2014) items from general mindfulness measures, which were pooled and revised to be specific to eating, were completed by 127 university students using response options from 1 = *never* to 4 = *usually*. Exploratory factor analysis was applied to narrow the items to a final set of 28 (22 are reverse scored), with items loading highly on six factors, as described in Table 6.1: acceptance, awareness, non-reactivity, routine, act with awareness, and unstructured eating. Five of the six Cronbach's αs for the subscales were .75 or higher, and α ranged from .60 (Unstructured Eating) to .89 (Acceptance). In Kerin et al. (2019), Cronbach αs were .72 or higher across all subscales in a sample of $N = 2018$ Australian females ($M_{age} = 23.1$ years, $SD = 8.7$). Total scores for each subscale are calculated by summing the items. Although a total MES score can be calculated, the Cronbach's α for all 28 items was not reported in Hulbert-Williams et al. (2014) and the procedure for forming this composite was not described. In the de-

Table 6.1. Measures of mindful eating (in order of publication date)

Title of measure	Lead author/ year	Sample	Correlates	# items; components measured and reliability
Mindful Eating Questionnaire (MEQ)	Framson et al., 2009	313 adults. 81 % female. Age 18–80 years; $M_{age} = 42$, $SD_{age} = 14.4$.	MEQ total score and most subscales had significant positive associations with yoga practice and age, and significant negative associations with body mass index. All MEQ subscales had significant negative associations with cognitive restraint. MEQ total score was not significantly associated with sex or race.	28 items, 5 subscales 1. Disinhibition (8 items; e.g., *"I stop eating when I'm full even when eating something I love"*) 2. Awareness (7 items; e.g., *"I notice when there are subtle flavors in the foods I eat"*) 3. External Cues (6 items; e.g., *"I recognize when food advertisements make me want to eat"*) 4. Emotional Response (4 items; e.g., *"When I'm sad I eat to feel better"*) 5. Distraction (3 items; e.g., *"My thoughts tend to wander while I am eating"*) Internal reliability ranged from .64 for distraction to .83 for disinhibition. Cronbach's α for the full 28 items was .64.
Mindful Eating Scale (MES)	Hulbert-Williams et al., 2014	127 university students. 77 % female. $M_{age} = 22.7$, $SD_{age} = 8.9$.	MES total score and all subscales except routine had significant positive associations with generic mindfulness. The MES total scores and the subscales of acceptance, routine, and act with awareness had significant negative associations with disordered eating. MES total score was not significantly associated with body mass index, but the MES subscale of acceptance had a significant negative association and the MES subscale of awareness had a positive association.	28 items, 6 subscales 1. Acceptance (6 items; e.g., *"I criticize myself for the way I eat,"* reversed) 2. Awareness (5 items; e.g., *"I notice flavours and textures when I'm eating my food"*) 3. Non-reactivity (5 items; e.g., *"I can tolerate being hungry for a while"*) 4. Routine (4 items; e.g., *"I have a routine for what I eat,"* reversed) 5. Act with Awareness (4 items; e.g., *"I snack without being aware that I'm eating,"* reversed) 6. Unstructured Eating (4 items; e.g., *"I multi-task whilst eating,"* reversed) 5 of the 6 Cronbach's αs for the subscales were .75 or higher, and α ranged from .60 (Unstructured Eating) to .89 (Acceptance). Can exclude the 6th factor given low reliability.

Table 6.1. continued

Title of measure	Lead author/ year	Sample	Correlates	# items; components measured and reliability
Mindful Eating Behavior Scale (MEBS)	Winkens et al., 2018.	1,227 adults. 52 % female. Age 55 years or over; $M_{age} = 68.8$, $SD_{age} = 8.1$.	All subscales except hunger and satiety cues had significant positive associations with life satisfaction, general self-regulation, and self-esteem. All subscales except hunger and satiety cues had significant negative associations with depressive symptoms, difficulty identifying feelings, and body mass index. There were mixed associations of MEBS subscales with external eating and restrained eating. Measurement invariance was supported for sex, age, and body mass index.	17 items selected from the MES, MEQ & IES-2. Narrowed items to focus on attention only, 4 subscales 1. Focused Eating (5 items; e.g., *"I notice how my food looks"*) 2. Hunger and Satiety Cues (5 items; e.g., *"I trust my body to tell me how much to eat"*) 3. Eating With Awareness (3 items; *"I eat automatically without being aware of what I eat,"* reversed) 4. Eating Without Distraction (4 items; *"I think about things I need to do while I am eating,"* reversed) Cronbach's α was.85 for Focused Eating, .89 for Hunger and Satiety Cues, .81 for Eating With Awareness, and .70 for Eating Without Distraction.
Mindful Eating Inventory (MEI)	Peitz et al., 2021	Study 2: 837 adults. 79 % female. Age 18–77 years; $M_{age} = 34.6$, $SD_{age} = 11.5$. Study 3: 612 adults. 79 % female. Age 18–75 years; $M_{age} = 35.5$, $SD_{age} = 11.6$.	Study 2: All subscale scores were significantly negatively associated with loss of control eating. Meditators had a significantly higher MEI total score than nonmeditators. Men had a significantly higher MEI total score than women. Study 3: MEI total score had significant positive associations with generic mindfulness, intuitive eating, weight-related self-efficacy, eating motives of "need and hunger" and "health," and mental well-being. MEI total score had significant negative associations with food cravings and psychological distress. Meditators had a significantly higher MEI total score than nonmeditators. Men had a significantly higher MEI total score than women. Measurement invariance was supported for sex.	30 items, 7 subscales 1. Accepting and Non-attached Attitude Towards One's Own Eating Experience (5 items; e.g., "I feel guilty after eating something 'unhealthy,' 'forbidden,' or 'high-caloric,'" reversed) 2. Awareness of Senses While Eating (5 items; *"I'm fully aware of the smells and aromas of my food"*) 3. Eating in Response to Awareness of Fullness (5 items; *"I stop eating when I'm full, even if my plate is not empty yet"*) 4. Awareness of Eating Triggers and Motives (4 items; e.g., *"I'm able to notice if I'm physically hungry or if I want to eat for other reasons [e.g., boredom, habit, availability, etc.]"*) 5. Connectedness (3 items; e.g., *"While I'm eating, I make myself aware of who and what were part of the origin and the production of this food [e.g., rain, sun, living beings, harvest, etc.]"*) 6. Non-reactive Stance (4 items; e.g., *"When I see or smell something tasty, I have to eat it,"* reversed) 7. Focused Attention on Eating (4 items; e.g., *"While I eat, I keep my whole attention focused on my food"*) Cronbach's α ranged from .73 to .92 for the subscales and was .92 for all 30 items; good test–retest reliability.

velopment study, good criterion validity was demonstrated with moderate positive correlations of most MES subscales and the MES total score with mindful awareness (measured with the MAAS). Criterion validity of MES subscales and the total score was also supported through significant inverse correlations with perfectionism, body dissatisfaction, and eating disorder symptoms.

Mindful Eating Inventory

In their rigorous approach to developing the MEI, Peitz et al. (2021) described using expert opinion, focus groups, layperson opinion, think aloud protocols, and two large survey studies involving 828 and 612 participants. In this development study, the MEI was produced in German and translated to English for publication. Following a thorough assessment of items and multiple steps (Study 1), a final set of 30 items was retained, with items loading highly (>.40) on seven factors (Study 2 N=828). As described in more detail in Table 6.1, the factors were (1) accepting and nonattached attitude towards one's own eating experience, (2) awareness of senses while eating, (3) eating in response to awareness of fullness, (4) awareness of eating triggers and motives, (5) connectedness, (6) non-reactive stance, and (7) focused attention on eating. Twelve of the 30 items are reversed scores and are spread across the majority of the factors. Respondents rate the degree to which each item applies to them on a 6-point scale from 1=*almost never* to 6=*almost always*. Subscale scores are derived by averaging the items on each subscale, and a total score may be calculated by averaging the scores on all 30 items. As described in Table 6.1, Cronbach's α ranged from .73 to .92 for the subscales and was .92 for all 30 items. In the third study reported in Peitz et al. (2021, N=612), criterion validity was established with most MEI subscales and the total score demonstrating moderate to strong positive correlations with, for example, measures of intuitive eating (ranging from r=.25 for connectedness to r=.72 for the total MEI score), eating-related self-efficacy, and well-being. Further supporting criterion validity, most MEI subscales and the total score had strong negative correlations with, for example, loss of control over eating and food cravings, and moderate negative correlations with psychological distress.

Mindful Eating Behavior Scale

The MEBS (Winkens et al., 2018) was derived from 20 items selected from the MEQ, MES, and the IES-2 to focus specifically on the "attention" component of mindfulness and to better differentiate mindful eating from external and emotional eating. Using exploratory and confirmatory structural equation modeling, four factors (17 items), as described in Table 6.1, were maintained including focused eating, hunger and satiety cues, eating with awareness, and eating without distraction. Respondents rate the degree to which each item applies to them on a 6-point scale from 1=*never* to 6=*very often*. Seven of the 17 items are reversed scored and are located on the eating with awareness and eating without distraction subscales. Subscale scores are derived by summing the items on each subscale. Cronbach's α of .85 for focused eating, .89 for hunger and satiety cues, .81 for eating with awareness, and .70 for eating without distraction were reported. In Winkens et al. (2018), scores on the MEBS subscales tended to have the expected associations with multiple measures of general stress and well-being, as well as having the expected associations with participants' reports of their difficulties identifying and describing feelings and with their reports on other eating measures. However, unanticipated positive associations of some MEBS mindful eating subscales with eating problems were reported, which does not support validity. Specifically, a positive association was found between the MEBS subscale of Focused Eating and a measure of restrained eating; and between the MEBS subscale of Hunger and Satiety Cues and a measure of external eating.

Conclusions

Three self-report questionnaire measures of intuitive eating (IES-H, Hawks et al., 2004; IES-T, Tylka, 2006; and IES-2, Tylka & Kroon Van Diest, 2013) and four measures of mindful eating (MEQ, Framson et al., 2009; MES, Hulbert-Williams et al., 2014; MEI, Peitz et al., 2021; and MEBS, Winkens et al., 2018) can be found in the research literature. Fortunately, the most recently developed measures appear to all align with definitions and have good breadth of content. In addition, the most recently developed measures and improvements on other measures are using rigorous methodological approaches to development. At this point in time, we recommend using the IES-2 (Tylka & Kroon Van Diest, 2013) to measure intuitive eating and the MEI (Peitz et al., 2021) to measure mindful eating. However, more research is certainly needed to consider covariation and incremental validity of measures within a single study, and the MEI, in particular, awaits additional use in research to understand health impact, individual differences and correlates, development, and relevance to studying intervention outcomes. Regardless, most of the identified measures (or published refinements of these measures) are supported by good psychometric data and the selection of a measure will always depend on research aims. Overall, also, intuitive and mindful eating do share conceptual space, and future research would be welcome that highlights similarities and differences, especially to further delineate differences between attuned versus disinhibited or restrained eating patterns and dieting. This could be done by considering other potentially related (sometimes inversely) concepts such as overeating regulation (Kerin et al., 2018, 2019) and emotional eating (Strien et al., 1986, 2012).

References

Baer, R.A., Smith, G.T., Lykins, E., Button, D., Krietemeyer, J., Sauer, S., Walsh, E., Duggan, D., & Williams, J.M.G. (2008). Construct validity of the Five Facet Mindfulness Questionnaire in meditating and nonmeditating samples. *Assessment, 15*(3), 329–342. https://doi.org/10.1177/1073191107313003

Bas, M., Karaca, K.E., Saglam, D., Arıtıcı, G., Cengiz, E., Köksal, S., & Buyukkaragoz, A.H. (2017). Turkish version of the Intuitive Eating Scale-2: Validity and reliability among university students. *Appetite, 114*, 391–397. https://doi.org/10.1016/j.appet.2017.04.017

Beshara, M., Hutchinson, A.D., & Wilson, C. (2013). Does mindfulness matter? Everyday mindfulness, mindful eating and self-reported serving size of energy dense foods among a sample of South Australian adults. *Appetite, 67*, 25–29. https://doi.org/10.1016/j.appet.2013.03.012

Brown, K.W., & Ryan, R.M. (2003). The benefits of being present: Mindfulness and its role in psychological well-being. *Journal of Personality and Social Psychology, 84*(4), 822. https://doi.org/10.1037/0022-3514.84.4.822

Bryan, S. (2016). Mindfulness and nutrition in college age students. *Journal of Basic & Applied Science, 12*, 68–74. https://doi.org/10.6000/1927-5129.2016.12.11

Camilleri, G. M., Méjean, C., Bellisle, F., Andreeva, V. A., Sautron, V., Hercberg, S., & Péneau, S. (2015). Cross-cultural validity of the Intuitive Eating Scale-2: Psychometric evaluation in a sample of the general French population. *Appetite, 84*, 34–42. https://doi.org/10.1016/j.appet.2014.09.009

Clementi, C., Casu, G., & Gremigni, P. (2017). An abbreviated version of Mindful Eating Questionnaire (MEQ). *Journal of Nutrition Education and Behavior, 49*(4), P352–356.e1. https://doi.org/10.1016/j.jneb.2017.01.016

Duarte, C., Pinto Gouveia, J., & Mendes, A. (2016). Psychometric properties of the Intuitive Eating Scale-2 and association with binge eating symptoms in a Portuguese community sample. *International Journal of Psychology and Psychological Therapy, 16*(3), 329–341.

Dulloo, A. G., Jacquet, J., Montani, J. P., & Schutz, Y. (2015). How dieting makes the lean fatter: From a perspective of body composition autoregulation through adipostats and proteinstats awaiting discovery: Dieting, weight cycling and predisposition to obesity. *Obesity Reviews, 16*, 25–35. https://doi.org/10.1111/obr.12253

Framson, C., Kristal, A. R., Schenk, J. M., Littman, A. J., Zeliadt, S., & Benitez, D. (2009). Development and validation of the mindful eating questionnaire. *Journal of the American Dietetic Association, 109*(8), 1439–1444. https://doi.org/10.1016/j.jada.2009.05.006

Fung, T. T., Long, M. W., Hung, P., & Cheung, L. W. Y. (2016). An expanded model for mindful eating for health promotion and sustainability: Issues and challenges for dietetics practice. *Journal of the Academy of Nutrition and Dietetics, 116*(7), 1081–1086. https://doi.org/10.1016/j.jand.2016.03.013

Goldberg, S. B., Tucker, R. P., Greene, P. A., Davidson, R. J., Wampold, B. E., Kearney, D. J., & Simpson, T. L. (2019). Mindfulness-based interventions for psychiatric disorders: A systematic review and meta-analysis. *Clinical Psychology Review, 59*, 52–60. https://doi.org/10.1016/j.cpr.2017.10.011

Hawks, S., Merrill, R. M., & Madanat, H. N. (2004). The intuitive Eating Scale: Development and preliminary validation. *American Journal of Health Education, 35*(2), 90–99. https://doi.org/10.1080/19325037.2004.10603615

Herman, C. P., Strien, T. van, & Polivy, J. (2008). Undereating or eliminating overeating? *The American Psychologist, 63*(3), 202–203. https://doi.org/10.1037/0003-066X.63.3.202

Hulbert-Williams, L., Nicholls, W., Joy, J., & Hulbert-Williams, N. (2014). Initial validation of the Mindful Eating Scale. *Mindfulness, 5*(6), 719–729. https://doi.org/10.1007/s12671-013-0227-5

Kerin, J. L., Webb, H. J., & Zimmer-Gembeck, M. J. (2019). Intuitive, mindful, emotional, external and regulatory eating behaviors and beliefs: An investigation of the core components. *Appetite, 132*, 139–146. https://doi.org/10.1016/j.appet.2018.10.011

Kerin, J. L., Webb, H. J., Zimmer-Gembeck, M. J., & Mastro, S. (2018). Resisting the temptation of food: A new measure of regulating overeating and associations with emotion regulation and mindfulness. *Australian Journal of Psychology, 70*, 167–178. https://doi.org/10.1111/ajpy.12169.

Logel, C., Stinson, D. A., & Brochu, P. M. (2015). Weight loss is not the answer: A well-being solution to the "obesity problem." *Social and Personality Psychology Compass, 9*(12), 678–695. https://doi.org/10.1111/spc3.12223

Madanat, H., Hawks, K., Gonzales, A., Miranda, E., Walsh-Buhi, E. R., Takemoto, M., Gaida, E. (2020). Assessing evidence of validity for the Intuitive Eating Scale-2 among adult Latina women. *Health, 12*(4), Article ID 99310. https://doi.org/10.4236/health.2020.124024

Mantzios, M., & Egan, H. (2018). An exploratory examination of mindfulness, self-compassion, and mindful eating in relation to motivations to eat palatable foods and BMI. *Health Psychology Report, 6*(3), 207–215. https://doi.org/10.5114/hpr.2018.73052

Mathieu, J. (2009). What should you know about mindful and intuitive eating? *Journal of the American Dietetic Association, 109*(12), 1982–1987. https://doi.org/10.1016/j.jada.2009.10.023

Montani, J. P., Schutz, Y., & Dulloo, A. G. (2015). Dieting and weight cycling as risk factors for cardiometabolic diseases: Who is really at risk? *Obesity Reviews, 16*(S1), 7–18. https://doi.org/10.1111/obr.12251

Neumark-Sztainer, D., Wall, M., Story, M., & Standish, A. (2012). Dieting and unhealthy weight control behaviors during adolescence: Associations with 10-year changes in body mass index. *Journal of Adolescent Health, 50*(1), 80–86. https://doi.org/10.1016/j.jadohealth.2011.05.010

Orbach, S. (1978). *Fat is a feminist issue*. Berkeley Books.

Parsons, C.E., Crane, C., Parsons, L.J., Fjorback, L.O., & Kuyken, W. (2017). Home practice in mindfulness-based cognitive therapy and mindfulness-based stress reduction: A systematic review and meta-analysis of participants' mindfulness practice and its association with outcomes. *Behaviour Research and Therapy, 95*, 29–41. https://doi.org/10.1016/j.brat.2017.05.004

Peitz, D., Schulze, J., & Warschburger, P. (2021). Getting a deeper understanding of mindfulness in the context of eating behavior: Development and validation of the Mindful Eating Inventory. *Appetite, 159*, 105039. https://doi.org/10.1016/j.appet.2020.105039

Román, N., Rigó, A., Gajdos, P., Tóth-Király, I., & Urbán, R. (2021). Intuitive eating in light of other eating styles and motives: Experiences with construct validity and the Hungarian adaptation of the Intuitive Eating Scale-2. *Body Image, 39*(December), 30–39. https://doi.org/10.1016/j.bodyim.2021.05.012

Roth, G. (1993). *Feeding the hungry heart. The experience of compulsive eating*. Penguin.

Ruzanska, U.A., & Warschburger, P. (2017). Psychometric evaluation of the German version of the Intuitive Eating Scale-2 in a community sample. *Appetite, 117*, 126–134. https://doi.org/10.1016/j.appet.2017.06.018

Saunders, J., Nichols-Lopez, K.A., & Frazier, L. (2018). Psychometric properties of the Intuitive Eating Scale-2 (IES-2) in a culturally diverse Hispanic American sample. *Eating Behaviors, 28*, 1–7. https://doi.org/10.1016/j.eatbeh.2017.11.003

Schaefer, J.T., & Magnuson, A.B. (2014). A review of interventions that promote eating by internal cues. *Journal of the Academy of Nutrition and Dietetics, 114*(5), 734–760. https://doi.org/10.1016/j.jand.2013.12.024

Strien, T. van, Frijters, J.E., Bergers, G., & Defares, P.B. (1986). The Dutch Eating Behavior Questionnaire (DEBQ) for assessment of restrained, emotional, and external eating behavior. *International Journal of Eating Disorders, 5*(2), 295–315. https://doi.org/10.1002/1098-108X(198602)5:2<295::AID-EAT2260050209>3.0.CO;2-T

Strien, T. van, Herman, C.P., & Verheijden, M.W. (2012). Eating style, overeating and weight gain: A prospective 2-year follow-up study in a representative Dutch sample. *Appetite, 59*(3), 782–789. https://doi.org/10.1016/j.appet.2012.08.009

Strodl, E., Markey, C., Aime, A., Rodgers, R.F., Dion, J., Lo Coco, G., Gullo, S., McCabe, M., Mellor, D., Graneo-Gallegos, A., Sicilia, A., Castelnuovo, G., Probst, M., Maiano, C., Mauro Manzoni, G., Begin, C., Blackburn, M., Petrabissa, G., ... & Fuller-Tyszkiewicz, M. (2020). A cross-country examination of emotional eating, restrained eating and intuitive eating: Measurement invariance across eight countries. *Body Image, 35*, 245–254. https://doi.org/10.1016/j.bodyim.2020.09.013

Stroebe, W., Van Koningsbruggen, G.M., Papies, E.K., & Aarts, H. (2017). Why most dieters fail but some succeed: A goal conflict model of eating behavior. *Psychological Review, 120*(1), 110–138. https://doi.org/10.1037/a0030849

Swami, V., Todd, J., Zahari, H.S., Khatib, N.A.M., Toh, E.K.L., & Barron, D. (2020). Dimensional structure, psychometric properties, and sex and ethnic invariance of a Bahasa Malaysia (Malay) translation of the Intuitive Eating Scale-2 (IES-2). *Body Image, 32*, 167–179. https://doi.org/10.1016/j.bodyim.2020.01.003

Tomiyama, A.J., Ahlstrom, B., & Mann, T. (2013). Long-term effects of dieting: Is weight loss related to health? *Social and Personality Psychology Compass, 7*(12), 861–877. https://doi.org/10.1111/spc3.12076

Tribole, E. (2010, November 17). *The difference between intuitive eating and mindful eating*. http://www.intuitiveeating.org/the-difference-between-intuitive-eating-and-mindful-eating/

Tribole, E., & Resch, E. (1995). *Intuitive eating*. St Martin's Griffin.

Tylka, T.L. (2006). Development and psychometric evaluation of a measure of intuitive eating. *Journal of Counseling Psychology, 53*, 226–240. https://doi.org/10.1037//0022-0167.53.2.226

Tylka, T.L., & Kroon Van Diest, A.M. (2013). The Intuitive Eating Scale–2: Item refinement and psychometric evaluation with college women and men. *Journal of Counseling Psychology, 60*(1), 137–153. https://doi.org/10.1037/a0030893

Van Dyke, N., & Drinkwater, E. J. (2014). Review article relationships between intuitive eating and health indicators: Literature review. *Public Health Nutrition, 17*(8), 1757–1766. https://doi.org/10.1017/S1368980013002139

Van Dyck, Z., Herbert, B. M., Happ, C., Kleveman, G. V., & Vögele, C. (2016). German version of the intuitive eating scale: Psychometric evaluation and application to an eating disordered population. *Appetite, 105*, 798–807. https://doi.org/10.1016/j.appet.2016.07.019

Vink, R. G., Roumans, N. J., Arkenbosch, L. A., Mariman, E. C., & van Baak, M. A. (2016). The effect of rate of weight loss on long-term weight regain in adults with overweight and obesity. *Obesity, 24*(2), 321–327. https://doi.org/10.1002/oby.21346

Vintilă, M., Todd, J., Goian, C., Tudorel, O., Barbat, C. A., & Swami, V. (2020). The Romanian version of the Intuitive Eating Scale-2: Assessment of its psychometric properties and gender invariance in Romanian adults. *Body Image, 35*, 225–236. https://doi.org/10.1016/j.bodyim.2020.09.009

Warren, J. M., Smith, N., & Ashwell, M. (2017). A structured literature review on the role of mindfulness, mindful eating and intuitive eating in changing eating behaviours: Effectiveness and associated potential mechanisms. *Nutrition Research Reviews, 30*(2), 272–283. https://doi.org/10.1017/S0954422417000154

Winkens, L. H. H., van Strien, T., Barrada, J. R., Brouwer, I. A., Penninx, B. W. J. H., & Visser, M. (2018). The Mindful Eating Behavior Scale: Development and psychometric properties in a sample of Dutch adults aged 55 years and older. *Journal of the Academy of Nutrition and Dietetics, 118*(7), 1277–1290. https://doi.org/10.1016/j.jand.2018.01.015

Chapter 7

Assessment of Grazing

Eva M. Conceição,[1] Marta de Lourdes,[1] and Carmen Beatriz Neufeld[2]

[1] School of Psychology, University of Minho, Portugal
[2] Department of Psychology, Faculty of Philosophy, Sciences and Languages, Ribeirão Preto of University of São Paulo, Brazil

Introduction

Grazing: Definition and Nomenclature

Over the past two decades, different authors have described and investigated an eating pattern generally characterized by eating repetitively. Being an understudied clinical entity, a variety of nomenclatures, defining criteria, and assessment tools have been published in the literature (Conceição et al., 2014; Heriseanu et al., 2017). Terms such as grazing, picking or nibbling, or snacking have been used with little consensus or research supporting them (Teodoro et al., 2021).

Given the rising clinical interest in this eating behavior, Conceição et al. (2014) surveyed different experts in the field to propose a nomenclature/definition for this behavior. They proposed that grazing is defined as *repetitively* eating small/modest amounts of food in an *unplanned* manner throughout a rather extended period of time (e.g., morning, late afternoon, day). Grazing does not occur in response to hunger or satiety. Two subtypes were proposed: compulsive grazing – when it is associated with the feeling that one cannot resist going back to eat even if trying not to eat – and noncompulsive grazing – characterized by mindless eating without paying attention to what and how much one is eating (Conceição et al., 2014). An example of compulsive grazing would be eating a piece of cake and not resisting going back several times for yet another piece (usually ending up eating more than wanted). An example of noncompulsive grazing would be repetitively eating whatever food is available without paying attention to how much one is eating or what one is doing.

The key aspects of grazing are being unplanned and happening repetitively. Accordingly, grazing should be distinguished from other eating patterns, for instance, when following a diet with plans to eat small meals several times during the day. Grazing is also different from binge eating episodes, which are described as eating in a setting or relatively circumscribed period of time (e.g., 2 hours) and what the individual feels to be a large amount of food. In some cases, extremely large amounts of food are ingested during a binge eating episode. Table 7.1 distinguishes grazing from other eating patterns and provides examples for each problematic eating behavior.

Table 7.1. Grazing and other maladaptive eating episodes in relation to the degree of loss-of-control eating (LOC) according to Conceição et al. (2015)

Eating episode	Degree LOC	Description
None	0	Plan to repeatedly have small amounts of food throughout the day.
Deliberate Overeating	0	Plan to repeatedly have small amounts of food to be able to accommodate large amounts of food in total.
Grazing, Noncompulsive Subtype	1	"Mindless" eating; eating in distracted way repetitively; eating whatever is available "on the spur of the moment." Not planned/anticipated.
Grazing, Compulsive Subtype	2	Trying to resist but repetitively going back and eating small/modest amounts of food. Not planned/anticipated.
(Subjective) Binge Eating Episode	3	Feeling that one cannot stop eating after starting, or cannot control the amount eaten. Eating episode occurs in a circumscribed period of time rather than repeatedly over time.
(Objective) Binge Eating Episode	4	Feeling that one cannot stop eating after starting, or cannot control the amount being eaten. Eating extremely large amounts of food in a short period of time.

Prevalence and Clinical Features

Despite the different definitions and the varied methods used to assess grazing or grazing-like behaviors, the literature points to a high frequency of this eating behavior across different populations (Heriseanu et al., 2017), with prevalence rates ranging from 12% to 47%, and 14% to 86% in clinical and nonclinical samples, respectively (Teodoro et al., 2021).

With cumulative evidence supporting its association with loss of control over eating, eating disorder core psychopathology, and psychological distress, recent research has put grazing in the spectrum of eating disorders (Conceição et al., 2018; Heriseanu et al., 2017; Lourdes et al., 2021). Specifically, Conceição et al. (2018) showed that compulsive grazing is comparable in terms of the degree of loss-of-control eating and eating disorder psychopathology to that of subjective binge eating episodes. In contrast, objective binge eating episodes and noncompulsive grazing seem to be associated with the highest and lowest degree of loss-of-control eating and eating disorder psychopathology, respectively. Table 7.1 also shows grazing and other problematic eating behaviors in relation to the degree of loss of control, which parallels the degree of psychological distress and psychopathology of eating disorders (Conceição et al., 2018).

Grazing has received increased attention in recent years, particularly for its association with attenuated weight loss after bariatric surgery for the treatment of severe obesity.

Grazing has been consistently linked to poor weight-loss outcomes and even weight regain in this population (Conceição et al., 2014; Teodoro et al., 2021). In nonclinical populations, the severity of grazing predicted an increase in body mass index (BMI; Heriseanu et al., 2019). Of note, it seems that when grazing is defined in association with loss of control, these associations with BMI are stronger (Teodoro et al., 2021).

The literature is scarce in the population of children and adolescents. However, the literature suggests that higher snack eating behavior seems to be common among children (Conceição et al., 2020), and associated with loss of control and overweight (Salvy et al., 2008). The limited literature published on psychological aspects of grazing behaviors shows that grazing in children is associated with psychological distress, inappropriate children eating habits, and restrictive parental feeding practices, specifically for children with higher sex-and-age-standardized BMI and with parents concerned with their weight (Conceição et al., 2020).

Why Do We Need to Assess Grazing?

The Clinical Relevance of Assessing Grazing

The clinical relevance of grazing seems to rely on the association detailed above with the psychopathology of eating disorders, loss-of-control eating, and with BMI or weight-loss outcomes (Heriseanu et al., 2017). A recent systematic review highlighted that this association is stronger in clinical samples than in community samples, probably due to the increased degree of psychological distress and psychopathology (Teodoro et al., 2021). Some authors suggested that – similar to binge eating (Colles et al., 2008; Saunders, 2004) – grazing may serve an emotion regulatory function, that is, reducing feelings of discomfort and anxiety (Goodpaster et al., 2016; Kofman et al., 2010; Niego et al., 2007), which is particularly relevant in clinical populations. Despite being frequently reported among individuals across different samples, its association with BMI and psychopathology are weak to nonsignificant in nonclinical populations. Hence, grazing seems to be a form of overconsumption clinically relevant among individuals undergoing weight-loss interventions (Teodoro et al., 2021), or for those at risk for the development of compulsive eating or obesity.

Assessing grazing is a step forward in identifying problematic eating behaviors, besides binge eating, that can be targeted clinically in individuals presenting for bariatric surgery or other weight-loss treatments. After treatment, a systematic screening of grazing could be used as a preventive strategy for weight regain. The assessment of grazing could work as early detection of subclinical compulsive eating behaviors that may progress to the onset of binge eating. This is particularly important for individuals undergoing bariatric surgery as their ability to eat large amounts of food is limited by the surgical procedure, but their experience of loss-of-control eating is still present. Indeed, grazing-like behaviors are known to be reported right after surgery while binge eating episodes tend to be reported in the long term.

Moving the Field Forward

Considering the research showing that grazing is associated with a clinically relevant degree of loss-of-control eating (Conceição et al., 2018; Heriseanu et al., 2017), assessing grazing could also bring light into how this problematic eating behavior may longitudinally precede the onset of binge eating episodes and, ultimately, an eating disorder (particularly, bulimia nervosa or binge eating disorder). This might be of particular interest for populations known to be at risk for compulsive eating and weight gain (e.g., college students; Barrack et al., 2019; Nicoteri & Miskovsky, 2014). Grazing is an eating behavior frequently reported among college students (Heriseanu et al., 2019; Reas et al., 2012), but no study investigated the prospective association between grazing (specifically compulsive grazing) and the onset of binge eating episodes or binge eating disorders. Longitudinal research should also inform to what extent grazing precedes the increase in body weight for this population. Moreover, given that "snack eating" is frequent among children (Conceição et al., 2020), longitudinal research should explore if grazing in the youth is prospectively associated with the onset of binge eating episodes in adolescence or young adulthood, which is also an age of risk for the development of eating disorders and disordered eating behaviors (Volpe et al., 2016).

Being a newly studied eating behavior, the assessment of grazing is frequently neglected by clinicians, and its role in nonsurgical weight loss treatments is still unclear. We expect that assessing and treating grazing as a problematic eating behavior would offer novel strategies for clinicians and patients to identify and deal with overeating behaviors. The assessment of grazing could also serve as a good indicator of regulation of eating behavior and eating patterns for individuals seeking weight loss.

There also is preliminary evidence that a grazing-like behavior (picking or nibbling) is also reported among individuals with eating disorders, including anorexia nervosa and bulimia nervosa (Conceição et al., 2013). Future research should explore the associations with the occurrence of binge eating episodes in the context of these disorders. For example, anecdotal reports suggest that a binge eating episode – during which one eats an extremely large amount of food in a relatively short amount of time, accompanied by the sense of loss of control eating, begins with grazing on a "forbidden food" and not resisting to repetitively going back to eat again and again. However, no study investigated grazing as a risk behavior for the occurrence of binge eating episodes in individuals with compulsive eating disorders. Ecological momentary assessment studies could provide novel insight into the temporal occurrence of these eating behaviors.

The research on children is still scarce and preliminary evidence seems to point to an association between grazing and parental feeding practices. Considering the important role of parents in the eating patterns of their children, research is needed to better explore the parental variables associated with grazing in children, and how the family eating dynamics contribute to grazing eating patterns in children (Conceição et al., 2020). Moreover, the eating behavior of parents seems to be associated with their children's eating behavior (Ramalho et al., 2020) and research is still limited regarding grazing and parental eating patterns. Finally, further research is also required to investigate if parents are good reporters of their children's grazing behavior, and if questionnaires regarding grazing in children can be reliably responded to by their parents (Conceição et al., 2020).

How to Assess Grazing

The variety of measures presented in this chapter reflect the inconsistencies in the literature regarding the definition of grazing behavior and in the terminology used. The initial definitions were based on anecdotal reports of single researchers and clinicians of an eating pattern characterized by repetitive eating. Different authors used more or less lenient criteria to define grazing, and the measures developed reflect these inconsistencies. For instance, while some authors consider the component of loss-of-control eating in association with grazing (e.g., Lane and Szabó, 2013; Conceição et al., 2014), others do not mention this aspect and seem to separate it from loss-of-control eating behaviors (Fairburn et al., 2008). As a result, content validity, which refers to the extent to which the items of a test are representative of the entire construct domain, is limited because the construct has not been properly and consistently defined.

Table 7.2 summarizes the measures used in the literature, describing their factor structure, use in different populations, and availability information. Generally, this table shows that past studies have assessed grazing via clinical interview and/or self-report. Of note, the authors proposing each of these measures used a variety of definitions and conceptualizations of grazing to support the generation of items or questions.

Clinical Interviews

Regarding clinical interviews, we were able to identify five different instruments used in the literature, but no study provided psychometric evidence for their use to assess grazing. Two of these measures, the Eating Disorder Examination (EDE) interview (Fairburn et al., 2008) and the Repetitive Eating (Rep(eat)) interview (Conceição et al., 2014) merit special attention for its use in varied studies or for its ability to assess clinical features of grazing.

The EDE includes one question to access the frequency of picking or nibbling (a grazing-like behavior) and has been used in several studies and with different populations (eating disorders and bariatric surgery patients). Of note, the EDE assesses picking or nibbling conceptualized as a grazing-type behavior, not in association with loss of control. This sets picking or nibbling apart from the definitions of grazing proposed by several other authors who include the sense of loss-of-control eating (e.g., Lane and Szabó, 2013; Conceição et al., 2014; Heriseanu et al., 2019). Hence, the EDE should be used carefully as it lacks content validity for the assessment of grazing.

The Rep(eat) interview was developed based on the proposed definition by Conceição et al. (2014) and allows for the identification of compulsive and noncompulsive grazing. Besides assessing its frequency, this interview is the only one that also includes several questions to characterize clinical aspects in association with grazing such as type and amount of food ingested, type of associated emotions, frequency of eating, attention while eating.

Table 7.2. Self-report measures and clinical interviews used in the literature to assess grazing behavior

Measure/authors	Description and interpretation	Nomenclature/definition	Populations studied	Availability/translation
Interviews				
Repetitive Eating Interview (Conceição et al., 2014)	Semistructured interview that allows the distinction between grazing compulsive grazing (in association with a considerable sense of loss of control) and noncompulsive grazing; it assesses the frequency and clinical features of grazing.	Grazing – definition proposed by Conceição et al., 2014	Bariatric surgery (Conceição et al., 2018; Pinto-Bastos et al., 2018)	European (Portuguese)
n.a. (Goodpaster et al., 2016)	Patients were asked whether they ever constantly snack, pick or nibble throughout the day. If yes, patients were asked whether they feel out of control when graze eating and the number of grazing episodes per week.	Grazing – definition proposed by Saunders, 2004	Bariatric surgery	English (United States)
n.a. (Conceição, Gomes, et al., 2017)	One short question with yes/no responses: (1) "In the past month, did you eat small amounts of food in a repetitive and unplanned manner?"	Picking/nibbling	Elderly community population	European (Portuguese)
Eating Disorder Examination (Fairburn et al., 2008)	One question: "... have you picked at (or nibbled) food between meals and snacks? By 'picking' I mean eating in an unplanned and repetitious way."	Picking/nibbling – the episode should have been unplanned, the amount eaten uncertain, and the eating should have had a repetitious element to it. The total amount eaten should not have been trivial.	Bariatric surgery patients	English (United States)
n.a. (Nicolau et al., 2015)	Structured interview included the assessment of grazing based on the definition of Saunders (2004).	Grazing – definition proposed by Saunders, 2004	Bariatric surgery patients (post-surgery)	Spanish

Table 7.2. continued

Measure/authors	Description and interpretation	Nomenclature/definition	Populations studied	Availability/translation
Self-report measures				
Repetitive Eating Questionnaire (Conceição, Mitchell, et al., 2017)	• 12 items; • 2 subscales: Compulsive Grazing and Repetitive Eating; • Respondents rated the frequency of the behavior in the previous month using a 7-point scale ranging from 0 = *never* to 6 = *every day*; • Higher scores represent a more pronounced grazing eating pattern.	Grazing – definition proposed by Conceição et al., 2014	Community, college students, individuals undergoing bariatric surgery (Conceição, Mitchell, et al., 2017) Adolescents (Ramalho et al., 2018) Primary school students (reported by parents) (Conceição et al., 2020)	European Portuguese (Conceição, Mitchell, et al., 2017); Norwegian (Reas et al., 2019). Ongoing works: Brazilian Portuguese (Conceição et al., 2023); Turkish (Anafarta-Sendag, Tigrak, & Ozbek-Simsek, ongoing work)
Short Inventory of Grazing (Heriseanu et al., 2019)	• 2 items: one assessing grazing in general, and the other assessing a compulsive subtype of grazing including a sense of loss-of-control eating; • Frequency is rated for both items on a 7-point scale from 0 = *none at all* to 6 = *eight or more times per week*; • Higher scores represent a more pronounced grazing eating pattern.	Grazing	General community and university students	English (Australia)
Grazing Questionnaire (Lane & Szabó, 2013)	• 7 items; • 2 factors: a behavioral component relating to "grazing" itself that represents continuous eating behaviors, and a second factor that reflects a cognitive appraisal component relating to perceived control overeating; • Higher scores represent a more pronounced grazing eating pattern.	Grazing – definition proposed by Saunders, 2004	Undergraduate psychology students	English (Australia)

Table 7.2. continued

Measure/authors	Description and interpretation	Nomenclature/definition	Populations studied	Availability/translation
n.a. (Robinson et al., 2014)	1 item in self-report measure: "How often do you graze (defined as nibbling, snacking, or eating small amounts of food in an unplanned and repetitious way over an extended period of time)?"	Grazing	Bariatric surgery (post-surgery)	English (United States)
n.a. (Kofman et al., 2010)	2 items: (1) "During the past 6 months, did you often eat or nibble continuously ('graze') over an extended period of time?"; (2) "During the times when you ate this way, did you often feel you couldn't stop eating or control how much you were eating?"	Grazing – definition proposed by Saunders, 2004	Internet users who had undergone bariatric surgery between 3 and 10 years ago	English (United States)

Self-Report Measures

As for self-report assessment, psychometric properties are only available for three self-report measures: the Grazing Questionnaire (GQ; Lane & Szabó, 2013), the Short Inventory of Grazing (SIG; Heriseanu et al., 2019), and the Repetitive Eating Questionnaire (Rep(eat)-Q; Conceição, Mitchell, et al., 2017). All these questionnaires are relatively short, with the number of items ranging from three to 12 (Table 7.2). Table 7.3 shows a summary of the psychometric properties for each of these measures. Overall, the psychometric testing of these three measures has shown support for acceptable to excellent internal reliability, good test–retest reliability, and indications for construct validity. Exploratory factor analyses available for the Rep(eat)-Q and GQ, and confirmatory factor analyses available for the Rep(eat)-Q, have supported their two-factor structure and, thus, provide further support of their construct validity. Both the Rep(eat)-Q and the SIG were also capable of distinguishing between two clinical groups, suggesting discriminative (or known-groups) validity. Finally, both the Rep(eat)-Q and SIG have available estimates of criterion validity: the Rep(eat)-Q has a good (84.5%) ability to correctly classify patients with and without grazing as assessed by clinical interview, and the SIG showed large ($r > .5$) correlations with the GQ. Of note, considering that the SIG and the GQ are both measuring the same construct based on a similar definition of grazing, we would expect this correlation to be considerably higher (e.g., $r > .8$). Hence, the extent to which this association can be interpreted in terms of supporting criterion validity should be seen with caution. Two other studies used one (Robinson et al., 2014) or two (Kofman et al., 2010) self-report items to assess grazing but did not report psychometric properties.

Conclusions

Research of the construct of grazing and its assessment is still in its infancy and has been hindered by the lack of consensus as to the definition of grazing (Heriseanu et al., 2017). Notwithstanding, a consistent body of research brings support for its association with the experience of loss-of-control eating, the psychopathology of eating disorders, and psychological distress (Teodoro et al., 2021). Additionally, grazing has been consistently associated with poor weight outcomes for individuals seeking surgical weight-loss treatment. Given its clinical relevance, different measures have been developed to assess grazing and there is growing evidence supporting their sound psychometric properties.

We found that grazing, or grazing-like behaviors, has been assessed through clinical interviews and self-report measures. Unfortunately, no study presents psychometric properties of the assessment of grazing through clinical interviews. The Rep(eat) is a semistructured interview and is the only one specially designed to assess the frequency of grazing and its associated clinical features. It is based on the definition of grazing proposed by several experts in the field (Conceição et al., 2014) and it allows the distinction between grazing compulsive grazing (in association with a considerable sense of loss of control) and noncompulsive grazing. Hence, the Rep(eat) might be the best option to further investigate the frequency of the varied presentation of grazing and its construct. It also allows the assessment of aspects that might be of clinical interest to target grazing behavior. The EDE has been widely used to assess the frequency of picking or nibbling, a grazing-like behavior, but caution should be made in interpreting its outputs as grazing behavior.

Table 7.3. Psychometric properties of the Grazing Questionnaire (GQ), the Short Inventory of Grazing (SIG), and the Repetitive Eating Questionnaire (Rep(eat)-Q)

Measure/ authors	Construct validity	Internal reliability	Test–retest reliability	Criterion validity	Discriminative validity (nongroups validity)	Means/(SD); N(%); cut-off points
Rep(eat)-Q (Conceição, Mitchell, et al., 2017)	**Factor structure:** *EFA (community sample):* 2 factors that explained 70.57 % of the variance *CFA (bariatric population):* RMSEA = 0.073, CFI = 0.970, and TLI = 0.947; CMIN = 85.982; DF = 43; $p < .001$; CMIN/df = 2.00; HOELTER.05 = 132; SRMR = 0.048; PCLOSE = 0.050; NFI = 0.942; AIC = 155.982 **Convergent validity:** Positive correlations ($r > .4$) with disordered eating, psychological distress, and negative urgency **Discriminant/divergent validity:** nonsignificant correlations with sociodemographic measures	**Community sample:** Cronbach's $\alpha_{\_Total\text{-}score} = .912$; Cronbach's $\alpha_{\_CG} = .912$; Cronbach's $\alpha_{\_RE} = .867$ **Bariatric population:** Cronbach's $\alpha_{\_Total\text{-}score} = .92$; Cronbach's $\alpha_{\_CG} = .92$, Cronbach's $\alpha_{\_RE} = .85$ **Adolescents** (Ramalho et al., 2018): Cronbach's $\alpha_{\_Total\text{-}score} = .94$ **Parents about children** (Conceição et al., 2020): Cronbach's $\alpha_{\_Total\text{-}score} = .91$ Cronbach's $\alpha_{\_CG} = .80$ Cronbach's $\alpha_{\_RE} = .87$	$r_{sp} = .824$, $p < .001$, across 1 week	ROC curve showed an area under the curve of 0.845, 95 % CI = 0.79–0.89 (S.E. = 0.026; $p < .001$). Based on the total score, a patient randomly selected has an 84.5 % likelihood to be correctly classified with/without grazing by an expert through a face-to-face clinical interview.	Patients reporting grazing scored significantly higher (M = 2.23; SD = 1.12) than those not reporting grazing (M = 0.88; SD = 1.02; $t(236) = -7.764$, $p < .001$)	Cut-off point = 1.25 **Community samples:** $M(SD)_{\_Totalscore} = 1.59\ (1.22)$ $M(SD)_{\_CG} = 1.46\ (1.39)$ $M(SD)_{\_RE} = 1.73\ (1.36)$ **Pre-bariatric surgery patients:** $M(SD)_{\_Totalscore} = 1.27\ (1.18)$ $M(SD)_{\_CG} = 1.38\ (1.34)$ $M(SD)_{\_RE} = 1.17\ (1.15)$ **Post-bariatric surgery patients:** $M(SD)_{\_Totalscore} = 0.88\ (1.07)$ $M(SD)_{\_CG} = 0.92\ (1.26)$ $M(SD)_{\_RE} = 0.83\ (1.03)$ **Adolescents (total score)** (Ramalho et al., 2018): $M(SD)_{\_Overall} = 1.53\ (1.35)$ $M(SD)_{\_Girls} = 1.66\ (1.42)$ $M(SD)_{\_Boys} = 1.33\ (1.21)$ **Parents about children** (Conceição et al., 2020): $M(SD)_{\_Totalscore} = 0.64\ (0.91)$ $M(SD)_{\_CG} = 0.45\ (0.87)$ $M(SD)_{\_RE} = 0.83\ (1.12)$

Table 7.3. continued

Measure/ authors	Construct validity	Internal reliability	Test–retest reliability	Criterion validity	Discriminative validity (nongroups validity)	Means/(SD); N(%); cut-off points
SIG (Heriseanu et al., 2019)	**Factor structure:** not applicable **Convergent validity:** Positive correlations (r > .4) with eating disorder symptoms **Discriminant/divergent validity:** GRLOC significantly and positively associated with psychological distress; GRLOC significantly and negatively associated with mental health-related quality of life and social desirability; no associations between SIG items and quality of life	Spearman-Brown Coefficient = .73; Cronbach's α = .72	GRLOC: Kendall's tau-b = .68, p < .001; GRG: Kendall's tau-b = .82, p < .001, across 2 weeks	Positive associations (r > .5) between SIG and GQ	SIG items could differentiate between groups of participants who were classified as ED cases/noncases (GRG: 3.76 (±1.62) vs. 3.10 (±1.78), F(1, 221) = 6.45, p = .012, omega-sq. = 0.025; GRLOC: 2.71 (±1.64) vs. 1.06 (±1.37), Welch statistic (1, 95.20) = 49.59, p < .001, omega-sq. = 0.180)	**Total sample:** $N(\%)_{GRG}$ = 210 (92.5) $N(\%)_{GRLOC}$ = 137 (60.4) **University sample:** $N(\%)_{GRG}$ = 143 (6.5) $N(\%)_{GRLOC}$ = 86 (56.3) **Community sample:** $N(\%)_{GRG}$ = 67 (98690.6) $N(\%)_{GRLOC}$ = 51 (69)

Table 7.3. continued

Measure/ authors	Construct validity	Internal reliability	Test–retest reliability	Criterion validity	Discriminative validity (nongroups validity)	Means/(SD); N(%); cut-off points
GQ (Lane & Szabó, 2013)	**Factor structure:** *EFA:* two factors that explained 64.50 % of the variance **Convergent validity:** Positive correlations ($r > .5$) between GQ and binge eating, night eating, and chaotic eating; positive associations between GQ and depression, anxiety, stress, emotional eating, external eating, restrained eating, body dissatisfaction, drive for thinness **Discriminant/divergent validity:** nonsignificant correlations between QG and BMI	Cronbach's $\alpha = .82$ (total scale)	$r = .62$, $p < .01$, across 3 weeks	n.a.	n.a.	$M(SD)_{\_Total\ sample} = 18.60$ (4.59) $M(SD)_{\_Women} = 19.09$ (4.33) $M(SD)_{\_Men} = 17.25$ (5.04)

Note. CG – Rep(eat) Compulsive Grazing subscale; RE – Rep(eat) Repetitive Eating subscale; BMI – body mass index; GRG – grazing in general; GRLOC – grazing with a sense of loss of control; ED – eating disorders; M – means; SD – standard deviation; EFA – exploratory factor analysis; CFA – confirmatory factor analysis; ROC – receiver operating characteristic; n.a. – not available.

Regarding the self-report assessment of grazing, only three measures have undergone psychometric testing: the Rep(eat)-Q, the SIG, and the GQ. The existent studies seem to support the psychometric properties of the three self-report measures. However, the Rep(eat)-Q is the measure that has been used in a greater variety of populations across different age and body weight spectrums (e.g., children, adults, and persons with normal weight, overweight, and obesity) and has undergone the most stringent psychometric testing. This measure was also developed based on a definition of grazing proposed by a group of experts (Conceição et al., 2014), supporting content validity. The Rep(eat)-Q has also been the most widely used measure as it has been translated into different languages and used in different countries.

More research is needed to increase the evidence for the psychometric properties of these measures, specifically across different samples (Heriseanu et al., 2017; Teodoro et al., 2021). The research on the assessment and definition of grazing creates a headway towards the identification of a problematic eating behavior that has been neglected but seems to have considerable clinical importance.

Acknowledgment

This work was partially conducted at Psychology Research Centre (PSI/01662), University of Minho, through support from the Portuguese Foundation for Science and Technology and the Portuguese Ministry of Science, Technology and Higher Education (UIDB/01662/2020), through the national funds (PIDDAC), and by grant to Eva Conceição (2020.01538.CEECIND) and Marta de Lourdes (SFRH/BD/146470/2019). The funding body had no role in the design, collection, analysis, and interpretation of the data nor in the writing of the manuscript or the decision to submit the manuscript for publication.

References

Barrack, M. T., West, J., Christopher, M., & Pham-Vera, A. M. (2019). Disordered eating among a diverse sample of first-year college students. *Journal of the American College of Nutrition, 38*(2), 141–148. https://doi.org/10.1080/07315724.2018.1487345

Colles, S. L., Dixon, J. B., & O'Brien, P. E. (2008). Grazing and loss of control related to eating: Two high-risk factors following bariatric surgery. *Obesity, 16*(3), 615–622. https://doi.org/10.1038/oby.2007.101

Conceição, E., Gomes, F. V. S., Vaz, A. R., Pinto-Bastos, A., & Machado, P. P. P. (2017). Prevalence of eating disorders and picking/nibbling in elderly women. *International Journal of Eating Disorders, 50*(7), 793–800. https://doi.org/10.1002/eat.22700

Conceição, E. M., Crosby, R., Mitchell, J. E., Engel, S., Wonderlich, S. A., Simonich, H. K., Peterson, C. B., Crow, S. J., & Le Grange, D. (2013). Picking or nibbling: Frequency and associated clinical features in bulimia nervosa, anorexia nervosa, and binge eating disorder. *International Journal of Eating Disorders, 46*(8), 141–148. https://doi.org/10.1002/eat.22167

Conceição, E. M., Lourdes, M., Pinto-Bastos, A. de, Vaz, A. R., Brandão, I., & Ramalho, S. (2018). Problematic eating behaviors and psychopathology in patients undergoing bariatric surgery: The mediating role of loss of control eating. *International Journal of Eating Disorders, 51*(6), 507–517. https://doi.org/10.1002/eat.22862

Conceição, E. M., Mitchell, J. E., Engel, S., Machado, P. P., Lancaster, K. K., & Wonderlich, S. (2014). What is "grazing"? Reviewing its definition, frequency, clinical characteristics, and impact on bariatric sur-

gery outcomes, and proposing a standardized definition. *Surgery for Obesity and Related Diseases, 10*(5), 973–982. https://doi.org/10.1016/j.soard.2014.05.025
Conceição, E.M., Mitchell, J.E., Machado, P.P.P., Vaz, A.R., Pinto-Bastos, A., Ramalho, S., Brandão, I., Simões, J.B., Lourdes, M. de, & Freitas, A.C. (2017). Repetitive eating questionnaire [Rep(eat)-Q]: Enlightening the concept of grazing and psychometric properties in a Portuguese sample. *Appetite, 117*, 351–358. https://doi.org/10.1016/j.appet.2017.07.012
Conceição, E.M., Pinheiro, J., Félix, S., Ramalho, S., & Gonçalves, S. (2020). Grazing in children: Associations with child's characteristics and parental feeding practices. *Eating and Weight Disorders, 26*, 439–447. https://doi.org/10.1007/s40519-020-00866-y
Conceição, E., Teodoro, M., de Lourdes, M., & Neufeld, C.B. (2023). Adaptation, confirmatory factor analysis, and psychometric properties of the Brazilian version of the Repetitive Eating Questionnaire. *International Journal of Eating Disorder*. (manuscript submitted for publication).
Conceição, E.M., Utzinger, L.M., & Pisetsky, E.M. (2015). Eating disorders and problematic eating behaviours before and after bariatric surgery: Characterization, assessment and association with treatment outcomes. *European Eating Disorders Review, 23*(6), 417–425. https://doi.org/10.1002/erv.2397
Fairburn, C.G., Cooper, Z., & O'Connor, M.E. (2008). Eating disorder examination (Edition 16.0D). In C.G. Fairburn (Ed.), *Cognitive behavior therapy and eating disorders* (pp. 265–308). Guilford Press.
Goodpaster, K.P.S., Marek, R.J., Lavery, M.E., Ashton, K., Rish, J.M., & Heinberg, L.J. (2016). Graze eating among bariatric surgery candidates: Prevalence and psychosocial correlates. *Surgery for Obesity and Related Diseases, 12*(5), 1091–1097. https://doi.org/10.1016/j.soard.2016.01.006
Heriseanu, A.I., Hay, P., Corbit, L., & Touyz, S. (2017). Grazing in adults with obesity and eating disorders: A systematic review of associated clinical features and meta-analysis of prevalence. *Clinical Psychology Review, 58*, 16–32. https://doi.org/10.1016/j.cpr.2017.09.004
Heriseanu, A.I., Hay, P., & Touyz, S. (2019). The short inventory of grazing (SIG): Development and validation of a new brief measure of a common eating behaviour with a compulsive dimension. *Journal of Eating Disorders, 7*(1), 1–12. https://doi.org/10.1186/s40337-019-0234-6
Kofman, M.D., Lent, M.R., & Swencionis, C. (2010). Maladaptive eating patterns, quality of life, and weight outcomes following gastric bypass: Results of an Internet survey. *Obesity, 18*(10), 1938–1943. https://doi.org/10.1038/oby.2010.27
Lane, B., & Szabó, M. (2013). Uncontrolled, repetitive eating of small amounts of food or "grazing": Development and evaluation of a new measure of atypical eating. *Behaviour Change, 30*(2), 57–73. https://doi.org/10.1017/bec.2013.6
Lourdes, M., Pinto-bastos, A. de, Machado, P.P.P., & Conceição, E. (2021). Problematic eating behaviors in patients undergoing bariatric surgery: Studying their relationship with psychopathology. *Journal of Health Psychology*, 1359105320986889. https://doi.org/10.1177/1359105320986889
Nicolau, J., Ayala, L., Rivera, R., Speranskaya, A., Sanchís, P., Julian, X., Fortuny, R., & Masmiquel, L. (2015). Postoperative grazing as a risk factor for negative outcomes after bariatric surgery. *Eating Behaviors, 18*, 147–150. https://doi.org/10.1016/j.eatbeh.2015.05.008
Nicoteri, J.A.L., & Miskovsky, M.J. (2014). Revisiting the freshman "15": Assessing body mass index in the first college year and beyond. *Journal of the American Association of Nurse Practitioners, 26*(4), 220–224. https://doi.org/10.1002/2327-6924.12108
Niego, S., Kofman, D., Weiss, J., & Geliebter, A. (2007). Binge eating in the bariatric surgery population: A review of the literature. *International Journal of Eating Disorders, 40*, 349–359. https://doi.org/10.1002/eat.20376
Pinto-Bastos, A., Conceição, E., Lourdes, M., Arrojado, F. de, Brandão, I., & Machado, P.P.P. (2018). Psychological and behavioral aspects of primary and reoperative surgery: A 6-month longitudinal study. *Obesity Surgery, 28*(12), 3984–3991. https://doi.org/10.1007/s11695-018-3452-0
Ramalho, S., Félix, S., Goldschmidt, A.B., Silva, D., Costa, C., Mansilha, H.F., & Conceição, E.M. (2020). Maternal eating behavior and problematic eating behaviors of children undergoing weight loss treatment: A cluster analysis. *Childhood Obesity, 16*(7), 499–509. https://doi.org/10.1089/chi.2020.0094
Ramalho, S., Saint, P.F., Diana, M., Helena, S., Mansilha, F., Silva, C., Gonçalves, S., Machado, P., & Conceição, E. (2018). APOLO-Teens, a web-based intervention for treatment-seeking adolescents with

overweight or obesity: Study protocol and baseline characterization of a Portuguese sample. *Eating and Weight Disorders, 25*, 453–463. https://doi.org/10.1007/s40519-018-0623-x

Reas, D.L., Lindvall Dahlgren, C., Wonderlich, J., Syversen, G., & Lundin Kvalem, I. (2019). Confirmatory factor analysis and psychometric properties of the Norwegian version of the Repetitive Eating Questionnaire: Further evidence for two distinct subtypes of grazing behaviour. *European Eating Disorders Review, 27*(2), 205–211. https://doi.org/10.1002/erv.2631

Reas, D.L., Wisting, L., Kapstad, H., & Lask, B. (2012). Nibbling: Frequency and relationship to BMI, pattern of eating, and shape, weight, and eating concerns among university women. *Eating Behaviors, 13*, 65–66. https://doi.org/10.1016/j.eatbeh.2011.10.005

Robinson, A.H., Adler, S., Stevens, H.B., Darcy, A.M., Morton, J.M., & Safer, D.L. (2014). What variables are associated with successful weight loss outcomes for bariatric surgery after 1 year? *Surgery for Obesity and Related Diseases, 10*(4), 697–704. https://doi.org/10.1016/j.soard.2014.01.030

Salvy, S., Kieffer, E., & Epstein, L.H. (2008). Effects of social context on overweight and normal-weight children's food selection. *Eating Behaviors, 9*, 190–196. https://doi.org/10.1016/j.eatbeh.2007.08.001

Saunders, R. (2004). "Grazing": A high-risk behavior. *Obesity Surgery, 14*(1), 98–102. https://doi.org/10.1381/096089204772787374

Teodoro, M.C., da Conceição, E.M., Lourdes, M. de, Alves, J.R., & Neufeld, C.B. (2021). Grazing's frequency and associations with obesity, psychopathology, and loss of control eating in clinical and community contexts: A systematic review. *Appetite, 167*, 105620. https://doi.org/10.1016/j.appet.2021.105620

Volpe, U., Tortorella, A., Manchia, M., Monteleone, A.M., Albert, U., & Monteleone, P. (2016). Eating disorders: What age at onset? *Psychiatry Research, 238*, 225–227. https://doi.org/10.1016/j.psychres.2016.02.048

Chapter 8

Assessment of Anorexia Nervosa

Heather A. Davis,[1] Meredith Kells,[2] and Jennifer E. Wildes[3]

[1]Department of Psychology, Virginia Tech, Blacksburg, VA, USA
[2]School of Nursing, University of Rochester Medical Center, NY, USA
[3]Department of Psychiatry & Behavioral Neuroscience,
University of Chicago, IL, USA

Introduction

Anorexia nervosa (AN) is a psychiatric disorder defined in the *Diagnostic and Statistical Manual of Mental Disorders* (5th ed.; DSM-5) as energy restriction relative to requirements resulting in a significantly low body weight in the context of age, sex, developmental trajectory, and physical health (American Psychiatric Association, 2013). In AN, energy restriction is associated with intense fear of gaining weight, poor insight into the illness, body image disturbance, and behaviors to prevent weight gain. AN is subclassified into restricting and binge eating/purging subtypes (APA, 2013). Additionally, individuals who present with all of the symptoms of AN except for significantly low body weight are given the diagnosis atypical AN under the category other specified feeding or eating disorders (OSFED). Atypical AN can be associated with the same profile of psychological distress, impairment in social and occupational functioning, and medical consequences as typical AN (APA, 2013). Thus, AN and atypical AN are referred to as AN-spectrum disorders throughout this chapter.

This chapter will review psychological interview assessments and self-report questionnaires, differential diagnoses, clinical presentation, and medical assessment for individuals with AN-spectrum disorders. The combination of psychiatric severity, nutritional impact, and medical consequences found in individuals with AN-spectrum disorders make interdisciplinary assessment imperative for care.

Psychological Interview Assessment

Initial assessment of AN-spectrum disorders should include a thorough clinical interview. Though structured and semistructured interviews, such as the Structured Clinical Interview for DSM-5 (SCID-5; First et al., 2015) and the Eating Disorder Examination (EDE; Fairburn et al., 2008), have the benefit of strong psychometric properties, they can be time-consuming to administer, and require extensive training to accurately administer, score, and interpret. In general, these assessments are most useful for research purposes but can be helpful in clinical settings, particularly in diagnostically complex situations. Below, we describe interview assessments for research and clinical purposes.

Research

Structured Clinical Interview for DSM-5, Research Version

The Structured Clinical Interview for DSM-5, Research Version (SCID-5-RV) is used to assess DSM-5 diagnoses (First et al., 2015). The SCID-5-RV includes an in-depth eating disorder chapter titled "Feeding and Eating Disorders," which can be used to assess current and lifetime diagnoses of AN-spectrum disorders. It should be noted that there is also a SCID-5 clinician version, which includes only screening questions for eating disorders, but no diagnostic items, and therefore cannot be used to diagnose a patient with an eating disorder. Patients are asked about specific symptoms that make up the criteria for each disorder, and research clinicians rate the symptoms as present, absent, or subthreshold. Because AN-spectrum disorders include symptoms that overlap with other eating disorders (e.g., binge eating and purging, as in bulimia nervosa), the SCID-5 is particularly useful for differentiating diagnoses.

Eating Disorder Examination

The Eating Disorder Examination (EDE; Fairburn et al., 2008) is used to assess and diagnose eating disorders in adults. The current version of the EDE is edition 17.0D, which includes 40 items, 21 of which are used to generate four subscales: Eating Concern, Weight Concern, Shape Concern, and Restraint (note: Two items contribute to both the weight concern and shape concern scales). Patients are asked to report on their attitudes and behaviors over the previous 28 days. Frequencies of key behaviors, including binge eating, self-induced vomiting, excessive exercise, and dietary restriction, also are assessed, as well as the severity of other features of AN-spectrum disorders (e.g., fear of weight gain). The EDE also asks detailed questions regarding pattern of eating by obtaining a description of snacks and meals consumed over the past 4 weeks, as well as specific foods avoided and dietary rules followed. The wide range of questions on the EDE allows for a more detailed picture of the eating problem, which can provide rich information for research purposes. The EDE item scores range from 0 to 6, with higher scores indicating greater severity of eating disorder symptoms. All scores can be averaged to obtain a global scale of disordered eating. Scores of 4 or higher indicate likely eating psychopathology (Fairburn et al., 2008). The EDE demonstrated construct validity, discriminant validity, and internal reliability in previous research comparing patients with AN to healthy controls (Cooper et al., 1989).

Eating Disorder Examination, Child Adaptation

The Eating Disorder Examination, Child Adaptation (ChEDE; Watkins et al., 2005) was adapted from the EDE to measure eating disorder psychopathology in children and adolescents aged 8–14 years. Modifications to the language were made, including using terms more comprehensible to younger children, and the addition of a card-sort task to evaluate overvaluation of shape and weight. Like the EDE, the ChEDE allows for clinical diagnosis and generates four subscale scores (Eating Concern, Weight Concern, Shape Concern, and Restraint) and a global score. There is no established clinical cut-off for the ChEDE. The ChEDE demonstrated good internal reliability, adequate inter-rater reliability, and good discriminant validity in a sample of adolescents with AN compared with adolescents with other clinical eating disturbances and adolescents with no eating disturbances (Watkins et al., 2005).

Eating Disorder Assessment for DSM-5

The Eating Disorder Assessment for DSM-5 (EDA-5; Sysko et al., 2015) was developed to address some of the limitations of other clinical interview assessments, including the extensive training required to administer them, which often is impractical in research and clinical settings. The EDA-5 can be administered with limited training and assesses the DSM-5 criteria for feeding and eating disorders, including AN-spectrum disorders. Of note, the EDA-5 is solely an eating disorder diagnostic instrument and does not assess associated psychopathology and comorbid psychiatric problems (Sysko et al., 2015). The EDA-5 is electronically administered, freely available (https://eda5.org), and can be used across the lifespan. EDA-5 items are rated dichotomously (i.e., present or absent). The EDA-5 can be administered in 5–30 minutes, which is about 14 minutes shorter on average than other interview assessments (Sysko et al., 2015). Importantly, diagnostic agreement between the EDA-5 and the EDE, and test–retest reliability of the EDA-5, were high in a transdiagnostic sample of women with eating disorders across 7–14 days (Sysko et al., 2015).

Clinical Practice

Semistructured clinical interview assessments that contain items from the assessments described above, as well as additional items to allow for more comprehensive clinical assessment, are most often used in clinical contexts to obtain a clearer picture of the nature of a patient's current eating problem, history and development of AN-spectrum disorders, and the maintaining factors of the disorder. Interviewers should prioritize assessment of the following domains of the presenting eating disorder.

Current and Past Eating Behaviors

Assessing the current and premorbid eating pattern aids in generating interventions to address problematic eating behaviors. By assessing the patient's premorbid eating pattern, the clinician can better understand the severity of the current behavior and obtain a realistic view of what recovery may look like for the patient, given the ultimate goal of restoring weight and helping the patient to return to healthy eating behavior. Clinicians also should assess dietary rules common in AN, such as the elimination of specific food groups (e.g., carbohydrates, fats), avoidance of feared foods (e.g., processed foods, desserts, restaurant food), and other rigid eating behaviors including not eating at certain times, not eating more than a certain number of calories, or seeking to eat less than others.

Some patients with AN-spectrum disorders may endorse subjective binge eating episodes (e.g., a typical-sized meal or snack accompanied by a feeling of loss of control over eating), while others may endorse objectively large binge eating episodes similar to those seen in bulimia nervosa or binge eating disorder (i.e., substantially more food than a typical meal or snack). Clinicians should be sure to ask patients about the amount of food eaten during the episode, the time it took to eat that amount of food, and the presence of a sense of loss of control, or not being able to stop eating once they have started. The history of this behavior should be assessed to determine if it is increasing in severity over time, as well as the current frequency to evaluate whether it should be a predominant focus of the treatment.

Current and Past Weight Control Behaviors

Current and past weight control behaviors should be assessed, including fasting, or abstaining from food intake for 8 or more waking hours, self-induced vomiting, excessive exercise, diuretic use, and laxative use. Importantly, clinicians should obtain a detailed picture of the current frequency and history of engagement in each of these behaviors to determine targets for AN treatment.

Psychiatric Comorbidity

Given evidence of the high comorbidity between AN and other forms of psychopathology, including mood, anxiety, substance use, and obsessive-compulsive disorders (Himmerich et al., 2019), it is important to assess a patient's current experience and history of comorbid psychiatric symptoms. This can be achieved by asking questions such as those similar to the screening questions from the SCID-5-RV screener for psychiatric disorders. If a patient endorses a comorbid symptom during the screening, the clinician should plan to assess further for the presence of an additional psychiatric disorder, perhaps using questions from the appropriate module of the SCID-5-RV. As eating often occurs in social settings or with other individuals, anxiety and depressive disorders that impact social function or eating in public settings may be of influence. In addition, consideration should be paid to poor appetite, fear of contamination, and phobias associated with anxiety and depressive disorders that may lead to reduced intake. Body dysmorphic disorder, in which individuals exhibit marked preoccupation with appearance, has overlapping symptoms with AN without reduction in food intake. Psychiatric comorbidity is considered a negative prognostic indicator for AN treatment, and comorbid depression in particular appears to have a negative influence on weight gain during treatment (Eskild-Jensen et al., 2020). As such, assessing comorbid symptoms can aid in treatment planning.

Suicidality and Nonsuicidal Self-Injury

Anorexia nervosa has one of the highest mortality rates of any psychiatric diagnosis (Chesney et al., 2014), and one of the highest suicide rates of any mental illness (Himmerich et al., 2019). Therefore, it is essential that clinicians perform a thorough suicidality assessment at intake to determine a patient's individual risk and the level of monitoring that will be necessary throughout their treatment. The general framework for a thorough suicide assessment includes directly asking the patient about previous suicidal behavior, current suicidal thoughts and plans, hopelessness, stressors, access to highly lethal means of suicide (including firearms), and protective factors such as loved ones, valued future plans, and religious beliefs.

Psychosocial History

Clinicians should inquire about the context in which the AN-spectrum illness developed and is currently maintained, the presence of the patient's support system, and the patient's motivation to make changes to their psychosocial environment in an effort to facilitate recovery. Because greater psychosocial support is likely beneficial for AN recovery (Karatzias et al., 2010), clinicians may use this information in treatment planning.

Psychological Self-Report Questionnaire Assessment

Self-report questionnaires often are used in both research and clinical contexts. In research settings, self-report questionnaires allow for efficient, cost-effective assessment of larger numbers of participants, compared with interview assessments. In clinical settings, self-report questionnaires can be used to quickly screen for specific symptoms or combinations of symptoms (such as in primary care settings), and/or as an adjunct to interview assessment when time may be limited. In particular, self-report assessments can be helpful for quickly assessing the degree to which a patient is experiencing symptoms comorbid with AN, and provide scores for dimensional constructs, such as body dissatisfaction or weight/shape overvaluation. Evaluation of these symptoms can aid in the understanding of the severity of certain symptoms and assist in treatment planning. Table 8.1 includes several commonly used self-report questionnaires in AN assessment.

Cultural Considerations in Psychological Assessment Planning and Interpretation

Knowledge of the role of culture in a person's AN presentation can influence the assessment approach and interpretation, thus improving treatment outcome. Despite the historical thinking that AN occurs predominantly in White women, recent data indicate that the incidence of AN is increasing among non-White individuals, and the prevalence of AN is similar across Latino, Asian, and African American groups when compared to non-Latino Whites (Marques et al., 2011). Certain aspects of AN appear to be different for

Table 8.1. Common self-report questionnaires in AN assessment

Measures of AN symptoms and severity				
Questionnaire	**Description of assessment**	**Number of items**	**Approximate time to complete**	**Clinical cut-off**
Eating Disorder Examination–Questionnaire (EDE-Q; Fairburn & Beglin, 1994)	Eating psychopathology in the previous 28 days on 4 subscales: Restraint, Eating Concern, Shape Concern, and Weight Concern.	38	15 minutes	Various cut-off scores have been proposed depending on the type of sample and patient (Meule, 2021)
Eating Pathology Symptoms Inventory (EPSI; Forbush et al., 2013)	Eating pathology over the past month on 8 dimensions: Body Dissatisfaction, Binge Eating, Cognitive Restraint, Excessive Exercise, Restriction, Purging, Muscle Building, and Negative Attitudes Toward Obesity.	45	15 minutes	Norms have not yet been established
Clinical Impairment Assessment (CIA; Bohn & Fairburn, 2008)	Severity of psychosocial impairment due to an eating disorder over the past 28 days.	16	10 minutes	Sum score ≥16
Measures of comorbid psychopathology symptoms				
Questionnaire	**Description of assessment**	**Number of items**	**Approximate time to complete**	**Clinical cut-off (all sum scores)**
Generalized Anxiety Disorder–7 (GAD-7; Spitzer et al., 2006)	Presence and severity of anxiety disorder symptoms over the past 2 weeks.	7	5 minutes	Mild anxiety: 0–5; moderate anxiety: 6–10; severe anxiety: ≥15
Patient Health Questionnaire (PHQ-9; Kroenke & Spitzer, 2002)	Presence and severity of depressive symptoms .	9	5 minutes	Moderate depression: 6–10; moderately severe depression: 11–15; severe depression: 16–20
Obsessive–Compulsive Inventory-Revised (OCI-R; Foa et al., 2002)	Obsessive-compulsive disorder (OCD) symptoms in 6 domains: washing, checking/doubting, obsessing, neutralizing, ordering, and hoarding.	18	10 minutes	Scores ≥21 indicate the likely presence of OCD

White and non-White individuals. For example, fear of becoming fat is central to the presentation of AN in White individuals, but this feature may be minimal or absent among Asian American women with AN (Lee, 1995). A recent investigation reported that individuals with AN from Western societies tend to report similar symptom profiles and comorbid psychopathology (e.g., depression, anxiety), while individuals with AN from Eastern societies tend to deny or underreport comorbid dysfunction (Agüera et al., 2017). Providers should keep these cultural differences in mind to avoid underdiagnosis in non-White individuals or individuals from non-Western cultures.

It is essential to acknowledge that many of the psychological assessments discussed in this chapter were developed using White, young, female samples. As a result, many of these assessments may not capture the nuances of eating disorder presentation among diverse groups. Given evidence that AN-spectrum disorders occur in all racial and ethnic groups, among all genders, and across the lifespan (Marques et al., 2011; Nagata et al., 2020), it is imperative that research begin to test whether existing assessments are reliable and valid in diverse samples, and the development of new, culturally sensitive assessments using diverse samples, take place.

Medical Assessment

Differential Diagnosis

Differential diagnoses for AN-spectrum disorders include medical and psychiatric conditions that may cause weight loss, and must be considered at initial presentation and throughout treatment (Campbell & Peebles, 2014). Undiagnosed, untreated, or undertreated medical diagnoses may induce weight loss, inhibit weight gain, or contribute to symptoms such as post-prandial vomiting that may be attributed to AN. Clinicians should rule out primary gastrointestinal disease (e.g., celiac disease, irritable bowel disease), thyroid disease (e.g., hypothyroidism or hyperthyroidism), adrenal disease, diabetes mellitus, human immunodeficiency virus or acquired immune deficiency syndrome, malignancy, syndromes that present with loss-of-control eating (Prader–Willi or Kleine–Levin syndrome), tobacco, illicit drug, and stimulant abuse (Campbell & Peebles, 2014). Food-related history including intolerances and allergic conditions should be evaluated. Additionally, a thorough review of medications and possible side effects is necessary to uncover any medication-related weight loss or symptoms.

Physical Exam

Initial presentation to a medical setting may be due to symptoms related to malnutrition or weight loss, rather than evaluation for an eating disorder. For example, individuals may seek care for syncopal episodes or pre-syncope, amenorrhea, or gastrointestinal distress (Campbell & Peebles, 2014). Therefore, complete medical history and review of systems is important to identify disordered eating behaviors that contribute to physical complaints (Campbell & Peebles, 2014). Additionally, careful nutritional history including 24-hour dietary recall with attention to changes in intake or patterns and restrictive practices without medical reasoning or recommendation (e.g., ketogenic diet for those without seizure disorder) is important to differentiate between AN-related food practices and underlying medical etiology of weight loss. Menstrual history with age of menarche and timing of loss of menses in conjunction with weight changes may raise red flags for AN. Clinicians should obtain past growth charts for children and adolescents or weight history for adults in establishing patterns of weight trajectory. Notably, effects of malnutrition are seen regardless of absolute weight and/or body mass index; therefore, comprehensive evaluation is essential for individuals with rapid weight loss, failure to gain weight or difficulty gaining weight, and especially for children and adolescents with growth stunting or pubertal delay at any weight or body mass index. Moreover, findings that are unexpected in an otherwise healthy individual (e.g., bradycardia) should be a prompt for providers to investigate for the possibility of the eating disorder.

Cardiovascular findings are common and range from mild to potentially life-threatening (Sachs et al., 2016). The most common cardiovascular findings include bradycardia, hypotension, and orthostasis. Bradycardia, or heart rate below expected norms, is due to increases in vagal activity that in turn reduces cardiac output in an effort to conserve energy. Postural orthostasis, or marked and sustained increased heart rate and/or decreased blood pressure when changing positions, occurs with hypovolemia and autonomic dysfunction (Sachs et al., 2016) and is reversible with nutritional restoration. Pericardial effusion may be found on imaging, is often asymptomatic, and also reversible with refeeding. Loss of left ventricular mass is associated with degree of malnourishment and may lead to poor systolic functioning. Finally, mortality due to cardiac events in AN has been shown in those with QT interval prolongation and QT repolarization variability which results in arrhythmia (Sachs et al., 2016). Cardiac exam including auscultation, vital signs with orthostatic evaluation, and careful attention to signs of cardiac complications (e.g., venous jugular distention, peripheral edema, chest pain) is warranted.

Gastrointestinal (GI) complaints are frequent in individuals with AN and may or may not precede illness (Wildes et al., 2021). Symptoms reported include constipation, abdominal pain and fullness, nausea, epigastric pain, and vomiting, and may negatively impact treatment (Riedlinger et al., 2020). Increasing awareness of overlap in clinical presentation and symptoms between disorders of gut-brain interaction and eating disorders is an emerging area of clinical and research interest (Wildes et al., 2021) and may identify potential new treatment approaches to reduce GI distress in individuals with AN. Constipation due to chronic restrictive eating resulting in slow intestinal transit time and in combination with dehydration, low fiber intake, and thyroid function abnormalities is found in AN (Westmoreland et al., 2016). Constipation and delayed gastric emptying contribute to postprandial fullness, bloating, and dyspepsia. Laxative abuse and vomiting as compensatory behaviors to reduce caloric burden may cause hematemesis, esophagitis, cathartic colon, and erosion of dental enamel (Westmoreland et al., 2016). The loss of protective fat pad in the abdominal cavity with rapid or substantial weight loss can lead to superior mesenteric artery syndrome (Jordaan et al., 2000). Addressing GI symptoms that are caused by AN-related behaviors through symptom management and harm reduction (cessation of vomiting) is important to improve nutrition and engage patients in care (Riedlinger et al., 2020).

Clinicians should examine for dermatologic effects of poor nutrition and dehydration including xerosis, hair loss, lanugo, brittle hair and nails, and subcutaneous fat loss. Additionally, knuckle abrasions (Russells' sign) and parotid gland enlargement due to repeated self-induced vomiting may be seen (Price et al., 2008). Acrocyanosis and Raynaud's syndrome is found in those with more severe malnourishment who have complications of thermogenesis.

Amenorrhea was formerly a criterion in the diagnosis of AN which was removed in the most recent edition of the DSM. However, amenorrhea and oligomenorrhea remain a marker of severity of illness for females. This is due to alterations in the hypothalamic–pituitary–gonadal axis leading to anovulation and subsequent infrequent or lack of menstrual cycles (Chou & Mantzoros, 2018). Hormonal implications of energy deficit contribute to low bone mineral density and may result in osteopenia or osteoporosis and fractures (Chou & Mantzoros, 2018; Mumford et al., 2019)

Laboratory

Laboratory evaluation should occur at presentation as well as routinely throughout treatment depending on patient behaviors (e.g., purging), illness duration and severity, comorbidities, medications, and weight. A comprehensive metabolic panel, complete blood count, and thyroid evaluation are common areas of focus in laboratory assessment.

A comprehensive metabolic panel to evaluate electrolyte disturbances and liver impact should be done on presentation and ongoing basis, especially during periods of nutritional restoration. Laboratory values may provide insight into surreptitious behaviors, such as hypokalemia, elevated bicarbonate, and hypochloremia that indicate vomiting, or abuse of laxatives or diuretics (Campbell & Peebles, 2014). Hyponatremia can also be found in those who abuse diuretics or ingest large amounts of water prior to weight checks. Alternatively, dehydration is associated with hypernatremia, as well as elevations in blood urea nitrogen, creatinine, potassium, calcium, and albumin. Refeeding hypophosphatemia is the most common laboratory derangement during nutritional rehabilitation and is the hallmark sign of impending refeeding syndrome, a potentially fatal constellation of symptoms seen as metabolic processes shift to anabolism after starvation (Kells et al., 2022).

Liver transaminases, specifically aspartate aminotransferase (AST) and alanine aminotransferase (ALT) increase as body weight decreases (Rosen et al., 2016). These findings may also be seen as nutritional restoration occurs and are associated with hepatic steatosis due to deposition of fat and glucose in the liver. Starvation can cause liver injury which is seen with elevated bilirubin, alkaline phosphate, and international normalized ratio (INR), and hypoglycemia. Pre-albumin is an indicator of illness severity and has been shown to be a predictor of refeeding hypophosphatemia and hypoglycemia; however, albumin is likely to be within normal limits (Gaudiani et al., 2014).

All blood cell lines are influenced by starvation seen in AN. Normocytic anemia (low red blood cells) without B12, folic acid, or iron deficiency, is a common finding (Cleary et al., 2010). Elevated red blood cell counts are seen with dehydration. Mild to severe leukopenia and neutropenia (low white blood cells) may be found; however, increased opportunistic infections are unlikely. Thrombocytopenia (low platelets) are also resultant of bone marrow suppression due to energy restriction. Low free T3 and T4 with low to normal thyroid stimulating hormone (TSH) is improved with higher energy availability (Schorr & Miller, 2017). Low androgen and estradiol levels, hypothalamic amenorrhea, low parathyroid hormone (PTH) and insulin-like growth factor-1, and elevated growth hormone and cortisol are seen in nutritional restriction as well (Schorr & Miller, 2017).

Testing

Routine electrocardiogram (EKG) is common to evaluate for conduction abnormalities, with recommendations for close inpatient monitoring should patients exhibit prolonged QT, junctional escape rhythm, or profound bradycardia of less than 40 beats per minute (Sachs et al., 2016). Conduction and repolarization abnormalities due to correctable electrolyte abnormalities should be considered. Echocardiogram is not indicated unless signs of cardiac complications (e.g., jugular venous distention) or EKG abnormalities suggesting valvular disease are present (Sachs, et al., 2016). To address risk of low bone mineral density, dual energy x-ray absorptiometry (DXA) scans are used in those who have amenorrhea and/or chronic AN (Solmi et al., 2016). This is of critical importance during adolescence as bone mass is primarily achieved during this time and is not reversible if the time of peak bone accrual is missed (Chou & Mantzoros, 2018).

Conclusions

AN is a serious and life-threatening eating disorder that requires comprehensive interdisciplinary assessment in advance of treatment. The integration of psychological and medical assessment is essential to understanding the extent of the illness and the level of treatment needed. It is recommended that providers prioritize the use of semi-structured psychological assessments with strong psychometric properties in combination with regular medical monitoring. Given AN's presence across cultures and the lifespan, an important limitation of AN assessment is the lack of measures developed for patients diverse in terms of race, ethnicity, gender, and age. It is essential that future research focus on better understanding features of AN-spectrum disorders in historically underrepresented populations.

Acknowledgment

This work was supported by a grant from the National Institute of Mental Health (T32 MH082761). The authors have no conflicts of interest to declare.

References

Agüera, Z., Brewin, N., Chen, J., Granero, R., Kang, Q., Fernandez-Aranda, F., & Arcelus, J. (2017). Eating symptomatology and general psychopathology in patients with anorexia nervosa from China, UK and Spain: A cross-cultural study examining the role of social attitudes. *PloS one, 12*(3), e0173781. https://doi.org/10.1371/journal.pone.0173781

American Psychiatric Association. (2013). *Diagnostic and statistical manual of mental disorders* (5th ed.). https://doi.org/10.1176/appi.books.9780890425596

Bohn, K., & Fairburn, C.G. (2008). The clinical impairment assessment questionnaire (CIA 3.0). In C.G. Fairburn (Ed.), *Cognitive Behavior Therapy and Eating Disorders* (pp. 315–317). Guilford Press.

Campbell, K., & Peebles, R. (2014). Eating disorders in children and adolescents: State of the art review. *Pediatrics, 134*(3), 582–592. https://doi.org/10.1542/peds.2014-0194

Chesney, E., Goodwin, G.M., & Fazel, S. (2014). Risks of all-cause and suicide mortality in mental disorders: A meta-review. *World Psychiatry, 13*(2), 153–160. https://doi.org/10.1002/wps.20128

Chou, S.H., & Mantzoros, C. (2018). Bone metabolism in anorexia nervosa and hypothalamic amenorrhea. *Metabolism, 80*, 91–104. https://doi.org/10.1016/j.metabol.2017.10.009

Cleary, B.S., Gaudiani, J.L., & Mehler, P.S. (2010). Interpreting the complete blood count in anorexia nervosa. *Eating Disorders, 18*(2), 132–139. https://doi.org/10.1080/10640260903585540

Cooper, Z., Cooper, P.J., & Fairburn, C.G. (1989). The validity of the eating disorder examination and its subscales. *British Journal of Psychiatry, 154*, 807–812. https://doi.org/10.1192/bjp.154.6.807

Eskild-Jensen, M., Støving, R.K., Flindt, C.F., & Sjogren, M. (2020). Comorbid depression as a negative predictor of weight gain during treatment of anorexia nervosa: A systematic scoping review. *European Eating Disorders Review, 28*(6), 605–619. https://doi.org/10.1002/erv.2787

Fairburn, C.G., & Beglin, S.J. (1994). Assessment of eating disorders: Interview or self-report questionnaire? *International Journal of Eating Disorders, 16*(4), 363–370. https://doi.org/10.1002/1098-108X(199412)16:4<363::AID-EAT2260160405>3.0.CO;2-#

Fairburn, C.G., Cooper, Z., & O'Connor, M. (2008). Eating Disorder Examination (16.0D). In C.G. Fairburn (Ed.), *Cognitive Behavior Therapy and Eating Disorders* (pp. 265–308). Guilford Press.

First, M.B., Williams, J.B.W., Karg, R.S., & Spitzer, R.L. (2015). *Structured Clinical Interview for DSM-5-Research Version (SCID-5 for DSM-5, Research Version; SCID-5-RV)*. American Psychiatric Association.

Foa, E.B., Huppert, J.D., Leiberg, S., Langner, R., Kichic, R., Hajcak, G., & Salkovskis, P.M. (2002). The Obsessive-Compulsive Inventory: Development and validation of a short version. *Psychological Assessment, 14*(4), 485. https://doi.org/10.1037/1040-3590.14.4.485

Forbush, K.T., Wildes, J.E., Pollack, L.O., Dunbar, D., Luo, J., Patterson, K., Petruzzi, L., Pollpeter, M., Miller, H., & Stone, A. (2013). Development and validation of the Eating Pathology Symptoms Inventory (EPSI). *Psychological Assessment, 25*(3), 859. https://doi.org/10.1037/a0032639

Gaudiani, J.L., Sabel, A.L., & Mehler, P.S. (2014). Low prealbumin is a significant predictor of medical complications in severe anorexia nervosa. *International Journal of Eating Disorders, 47*(2), 148–156. https://doi.org/10.1002/eat.22233

Himmerich, H., Hotopf, M., Shetty, H., Schmidt, U., Treasure, J., Hayes, R.D., Stewart, R., & Chang, C.-K. (2019). Psychiatric comorbidity as a risk factor for mortality in people with anorexia nervosa. *European Archives of Psychiatry and Clinical Neuroscience, 269*(3), 351–359. https://doi.org/10.1007/s00406-018-0937-8

Jordaan, G.P., Muller, A., Greeff, M., & Stein, D.J. (2000). Eating disorder and superior mesenteric artery syndrome. *Journal of the American Academy of Child and Adolescent Psychiatry, 39*(10), 1211. https://doi.org/10.1097/00004583-200010000-00005

Karatzias, T., Chouliara, Z., Power, K., Collin, P., Yellowlees, A., & Grierson, D. (2010). General psychopathology in anorexia nervosa: The role of psychosocial factors. *Clinical Psychology & Psychotherapy, 17*(6), 519–527. https://doi.org/https://doi.org/10.1002/cpp.701

Kells, M., Gregas, M., Wolfe, B.E., Garber, A.K., & Kelly-Weeder, S. (2022). Factors associated with refeeding hypophosphatemia in adolescents and young adults hospitalized with anorexia nervosa. *Nutrition in Clinical Practice, 37*, 470–478. https://doi.org/10.1002/ncp.10772

Kroenke, K., & Spitzer, R.L. (2002). The PHQ-9: A new depression diagnostic and severity measure. *Psychiatric Annals, 32*(9), 1–7. https://doi.org/10.3928/0048-5713-20020901-06

Lee, S. (1995). Self-starvation in context: Towards a culturally sensitive understanding of anorexia nervosa. *Social Science & Medicine, 41*(1), 25–36. https://doi.org/https://doi.org/10.1016/0277-9536(94)00305-D

Marques, L., Alegria, M., Becker, A.E., Chen, C.-n., Fang, A., Chosak, A., & Diniz, J.B. (2011). Comparative prevalence, correlates of impairment, and service utilization for eating disorders across US ethnic groups: Implications for reducing ethnic disparities in health care access for eating disorders. *International Journal of Eating Disorders, 44*(5), 412–420. https://doi.org/https://doi.org/10.1002/eat.20787

Meule, A. (2021). Reconsidering the use of cut-off scores for the Eating Disorder Examination-Questionnaire. *Eating Disorders, 29*(5), 480–484. https://doi.org/10.1080/10640266.2019.1678981

Mumford, J., Kohn, M., Briody, J., Miskovic-Wheatley, J., Madden, S., Clarke, S., Biggin, A., Schindeler, A., & Munns, C. (2019). Long-term outcomes of adolescent anorexia nervosa on bone. *Journal of Adolescent Health, 64*(3), 305–310. https://doi.org/10.1016/j.jadohealth.2018.07.025

Nagata, J.M., Ganson, K.T., & Austin, S.B. (2020). Emerging trends in eating disorders among sexual and gender minorities. *Current Opinion in Psychiatry, 33*(6), 562–567. https://doi.org/10.1097/yco.0000000000000645

Price, C., Schmidt, M., Adam, E., & Lacey, H. (2008). Parotid gland enlargement in eating disorders: An insensitive sign? *Eating and Weight Disorders – Studies on Anorexia, Bulimia and Obesity, 13*(4), e79–e83. https://doi.org/10.1007/BF03327509

Riedlinger, C., Schmidt, G., Weiland, A., Stengel, A., Giel, K.E., Zipfel, S., Enck, P., & Mack, I. (2020). Which symptoms, complaints and complications of the gastrointestinal tract occur in patients with eating disorders? A systematic review and quantitative analysis. *Frontiers in Psychiatry, 11*, Article 195. https://doi.org/10.3389/fpsyt.2020.00195

Rosen, E., Sabel, A.L., Brinton, J.T., Catanach, B., Gaudiani, J.L., & Mehler, P.S. (2016). Liver dysfunction in patients with severe anorexia nervosa. *International Journal of Eating Disorders, 49*(2), 151–158. https://doi.org/10.1002/eat.22436

Sachs, K.V., Harnke, B., Mehler, P.S., & Krantz, M.J. (2016). Cardiovascular complications of anorexia nervosa: A systematic review. *International Journal of Eating Disorders, 49*(3), 238–248. https://doi.org/10.1002/eat.22481

Schorr, M., & Miller, K.K. (2017). The endocrine manifestations of anorexia nervosa: Mechanisms and management. *Nature Reviews Endocrinology, 13*(3), 174–186. https://doi.org/10.1038/nrendo.2016.175

Solmi, M., Veronese, N., Correll, C., Favaro, A., Santonastaso, P., Caregaro, L., Vancampfort, D., Luchini, C., De Hert, M., & Stubbs, B. (2016). Bone mineral density, osteoporosis, and fractures among people with eating disorders: A systematic review and meta-analysis. *Acta Psychiatrica Scandinavica, 133*(5), 341–351. https://doi.org/10.1111/acps.12556

Spitzer, R.L., Kroenke, K., Williams, J.B., & Löwe, B. (2006). A brief measure for assessing generalized anxiety disorder: The GAD-7. *Archives of Internal Medicine, 166*(10), 1092–1097. https://doi.org/10.1001/archinte.166.10.1092

Sysko, R., Glasofer, D.R., Hildebrandt, T., Klimek, P., Mitchell, J.E., Berg, K.C., Peterson, C.B., Wonderlich, S.A., & Walsh, B.T. (2015). The eating disorder assessment for DSM-5 (EDA-5): Development and validation of a structured interview for feeding and eating disorders. *International Journal of Eating Disorders, 48*(5), 452–463. https://doi.org/10.1002/eat.22388

Watkins, B., Frampton, I., Lask, B., & Bryant-Waugh, R. (2005). Reliability and validity of the child version of the eating disorder examination: A preliminary investigation. *International Journal of Eating Disorders, 38*(2), 183–187. https://doi.org/10.1002/eat.20165

Westmoreland, P., Krantz, M.J., & Mehler, P.S. (2016). Medical complications of anorexia nervosa and bulimia. *The American Journal of Medicine, 129*(1), 30–37. https://doi.org/10.1016/j.amjmed.2015.06.031

Wildes, J.E., Bedell, A., Graham, A.K., & Kells, M. (2021). Brain-gut psychotherapies: Promising tools to address gastrointestinal problems in patients with eating disorders. *International Journal of Eating Disorders, 54*(6), 1063–1067. https://doi.org/10.1002/eat.23555

Chapter 9

Assessment of Bulimia Nervosa

Sophie R. Abber, Sarrah I. Ali, and Pamela K. Keel

Department of Psychology, Florida State University, FL, USA

Introduction

Bulimia nervosa (BN) is an eating disorder (ED) characterized by recurrent binge eating episodes and the use of inappropriate compensatory behaviors to prevent weight gain. In addition, BN is defined by the undue influence of weight or shape on self-evaluation as a cognitive feature. Inappropriate compensatory behaviors include self-induced vomiting, laxative misuse, diuretic misuse, medication misuse, fasting, and driven/compelled exercise. Primary definitions of BN come from the *Diagnostic and Statistical Manual of Mental Disorders* (5th ed.; DSM-5; American Psychiatric Association, 2013) and the *International Statistical Classification of Diseases and Related Health Problems* (11th ed.; ICD-11; World Health Organization, 2019), which vary somewhat. Specifically, the two manuals differ on their definition of binge episodes. DSM-5 requires the amount of food consumed to be objectively larger than what most people would consume under similar circumstances and to be accompanied by a sense of loss of control over eating to be considered a binge episode. In the field of eating disorders, this has also been called an "objective binge episode" (OBE) or "objective bulimic episode" to denote that the amount of food is considered large by the person conducting the assessment. In contrast, the ICD-11 defines binge eating as "eating notably more or differently than usual" while experiencing a loss of control over eating. Given that many patients with BN attempt to restrict the amount and types of food they eat, eating differently than usual may or may not involve an objectively large amount of food. It could also involve consumption of "forbidden" foods. As such, the ICD-11 includes both objective and "subjective" binge episodes (SBEs) in its definition of BN. Secondarily, the DSM-5 requires binge eating and compensatory behaviors to have been present for at least 3 months, while the ICD-11 requires a duration of at least 1 month. These two differences combine to a broader and more inclusive definition of BN in the ICD-11 that combines DSM-5 BN with different forms of DSM-5 other specified feeding or eating disorder (OSFED), including BN of subthreshold duration and some cases of purging disorder (PD).

When conducting assessments, it is important to be able to distinguish BN from other EDs. Using either DSM-5 or ICD-11, BN is distinguished from binge eating disorder (BED) on the basis of regular engagement in inappropriate compensatory behaviors, which are required for a diagnosis of BN and excluded from a diagnosis of BED. BN is differentiated from anorexia nervosa (AN) on the basis of body weight, where individuals with AN are at a significantly low weight and those with BN are not. In research contexts, a body mass index (BMI) of $<18.5\ kg/m^2$ in adults or <5th percentile in children and adolescents is often used as a cut-off for a diagnosis of AN (American Psychiatric Association, 2013), although it should be noted that both DSM-5 and ICD-11 allow for assessor judgment to be used when interpreting whether a given individual is at a significantly low weight. When using DSM-5 criteria, it is also crucial to distinguish BN from PD, which falls under the OSFED category. Individuals with PD engage in purging behaviors, which include specific forms of inappropriate compensatory behaviors that forcibly evacuate matter from the body (e.g., self-induced vomiting, laxative, diuretic, or other medication misuse), in the absence of OBEs, but may present with SBEs. Thus, assessing for size of binge episodes in addition to loss of control is essential for distinguishing between DSM-5 BN and PD as is distinguishing purging behaviors among the forms of inappropriate compensatory behaviors.

Importantly, there is no widely accepted cut-off for a "definitely large" amount of food as described in DSM-5 (American Psychiatric Association, 2013). This may pose a challenge for individuals wishing to assess for DSM-5 BN who are relatively unfamiliar with EDs and thus are less experienced in distinguishing between SBEs and OBEs. Some researchers have used a cut-off of 1,000 or more kcal consumed to indicate an OBE (Kaye et al., 2004; Keel et al., 2007), but this approach is not faultless as modern restaurant (Scourboutakos et al., 2013) and fast-food (Dumanovsky et al., 2009) meals often exceed this amount. Others have used unpublished lists that describe amounts of individual food items (e.g., five bananas) that could be considered "definitely large" and provide general guidelines (e.g., three main courses) for distinguishing OBEs from SBEs (Fairburn & Cooper, 2000). However, these guidelines are not empirically derived (Arikian et al., 2012). Attempts to empirically derive guidelines for a large amount of food have found that both food type and gender should be taken into account (Arikian et al., 2012; Forney et al., 2015) and that 1,000 kcal may be a good specific but not sensitive rule-of-thumb for distinguishing OBEs and SBEs (Forney et al., 2015).

The assessment of BN occurs in both clinical and research contexts. In a clinical setting, the purpose of initial assessment is to gather information from a client to form a case conceptualization that will guide treatment. In a research setting, initial assessment is often used to determine whether an individual meets inclusion criteria for a study or to determine the prevalence of BN in an epidemiological context. In both clinical and research settings, ongoing assessment may also be used to determine whether an individual's eating disorder symptoms have changed over time or after a specific intervention.

BN can be assessed using interviews and self-report measures, and these measures may function primarily as screening tools (i.e., appropriate for identifying individuals who may require further screening for the presence of BN) or as diagnostic tools (i.e., appropriate for assigning a diagnosis of BN). The remainder of this chapter will discuss the various interview and self-report tools that are available to assess BN in both children/adolescent and adult populations, the advantages and disadvantages of interviews versus self-report measures for the assessment of BN generally, and our recommendations for which interview and self-report tools function best in assessing BN.

Interviews for Adults

Adult Interviews for Clinical Settings

There are several available interviews for the assessment of BN in adults (Table 9.1). First, there is the Eating Disorder Examination (EDE), which is one of the most commonly used interviews for BN in research settings (Cooper & Fairburn, 1987). The latest version is EDE 17.0D and is freely available online through the Centre for Research on Eating Disorders at Oxford (CREDO; www.credo-oxford.com). The interview is semistructured and takes 45–75 minutes to complete (Fairburn et al., 2014). The EDE generates an overall global score, subscale scores on levels of Restraint, Eating Concern, Weight Concern, and Shape Concern, and provides data on the frequency of binge eating episodes and compensatory behaviors, distinguishing between OBEs and SBEs and distinguishing among purging and nonpurging compensatory behaviors. To evaluate the influence of weight and shape on self-evaluation, interviewees provided a rank-ordered list of factors that influence how they judge, evaluate, think, or feel about themselves. The EDE includes specific thresholds of where weight and shape should fall on the list to ensure consistency in the assessment of this complex cognitive feature. The EDE demonstrates good inter-rater reliability, internal reliability, discriminant validity, and construct validity for the assessment of BN (Guest, 2000). Additionally, community norms from a sample of young women (Fairburn & Beglin, 1994) and for young and middle adolescent girls (Wade et al., 2008) are available. Despites these strengths, drawbacks of the EDE include that it is time-consuming to administer, requires significant assessor training, has limited assessment of fasting as an inappropriate compensatory behavior, and assesses only current eating pathology.

The Structured Clinical Interview for DSM-5 (SCID) is another semistructured interview option (First et al., 2015). The most recent version is the SCID-5, which was released in 2013. There is a "Clinician Version" and "Research Version" of the SCID-5; however, it is important to note that EDs are screened for but not fully assessed in the clinician version. All versions of the SCID must be purchased through American Psychiatric Association Publishing (www.appi.org). Although the entire SCID-5 Research Version is time-consuming to administer, the ED module takes approximately 15 minutes to complete because it relies more heavily on yes/no responses without follow-up probes and employs skip rules, in which certain questions are skipped on the basis of prior responses. Psychometric data are not currently available for the ED module of the SCID-5 Research Version (Peyser et al., 2020). In the previous version for the DSM-IV, inter-rater reliability for eating disorders was good, but test-retest reliability was inadequate (Zanarini et al., 2000). Importantly, test-retest reliability estimates reflect properties of the assessment instrument, stability of the diagnosis being assessed, and recall required of those being assessed. Advantages of the ED module of the SCID-5 Research Version include its short administration time, its inclusion of separate questions to distinguish both loss of control over eating and size of the episode, inclusion of the full range of compensatory behaviors, and its measurement of both lifetime and current eating pathology. Disadvantages include that it is not freely available and that, like the EDE, it requires significant assessor training.

The Eating Disorders Assessment for DSM-5 (EDA-5) is a newer semistructured interview option for the assessment of BN that was released in 2015 (Sysko et al., 2015). This assessment is freely available online in an electronically administered format through

Table 9.1. Overview of assessments for BN

Format	Instrument	Adult or child/adolescent	Approximate time to administer	Assesses size of binge episodes	Assesses loss of control	Assesses frequency of binge episodes	Compensatory behaviors assessed	Assesses frequency of compensatory behaviors	Assesses Overvaluation of shape/weight	Assesses weight	Freely available
Interview	Alcohol Use Disorder and Associated Disabilities Interview Schedule – Eating Disorder Module	Adult	?	Y	Y	Y	SIV, LAX, DIUR, ENEMA, MEDS, FAST, EX	Y	Y	Y	Y
Interview	Composite International Diagnostic Interview – Eating Disorder Module	Adult and Adolescent	?	Y	N	Y	SIV, LAX, DIUR, ENEMA, EX, FAST, CS	Y	Y	Y	Y
Interview	Eating Disorder Examination	Adult	45–75 minutes	Y	Y	Y	SIV, LAX, DIUR, EX, OEWCB	Y	Y	Y	Y
Interview	Eating Disorder Examination–Questionnaire	Adult	15 minutes	Y	Y	Y	SIV, LAX, EX	Y	Y	Y	Y
Interview	Eating Disorder Examination – Child Version	Child/Adolescent	60 minutes	Y	Y	Y	SIV, LAX, DIUR, EX, OEWCB	Y	Y	Y	Y

Table 9.1. continued

Format	Instrument	Adult or child/adolescent	Approximate time to administer	Assesses size of binge episodes	Assesses loss of control	Assesses frequency of binge episodes	Compensatory behaviors assessed	Assesses frequency of compensatory behaviors	Assesses Overvaluation of shape/weight	Assesses weight	Freely available
Interview	Eating Disorders Assessment for *DSM-5*	Adult	15 minutes	Y	Y	Y	SIV, LAX, DIUR, PILLS, MEDS, EX	Y	Y	Y	Y
Interview	Eating Disorders Assessment for *DSM-5* – Youth	Child/Adolescent	15 minutes	Y	Y	Y	SIV, LAX, DIUR, PILLS, MEDS, EX	Y	Y	Y	Y
Interview	Kiddie Schedule for Affective Disorders and Schizophrenia	Child/Adolescent	?	Y	Y	Y	SIV, LAX, DIUR, PILLS, EX, FAST	Y	N	Y	Y
Interview	Mini International Neuropsychiatric Interview – Eating Disorder Module	Adult	<15 minutes	Y	Y	Y	SIV, LAX, DIUR, ENEMA, MEDS, FAST, EX	Y	Y	Y	N
Interview	Mini International Neuropsychiatric Interview – Kid Version	Child/Adolescent	<15 minutes	Y	Y	Y	SIV, LAX, DIUR, ENEMA, MEDS, FAST, EX	Y	Y	Y	N

Table 9.1. continued

Format	Instrument	Adult or child/adolescent	Approximate time to administer	Assesses size of binge episodes	Assesses loss of control	Assesses frequency of binge episodes	Compensatory behaviors assessed	Assesses frequency of compensatory behaviors	Assesses Overvaluation of shape/weight	Assesses weight	Freely available
Interview	Structured Clinical Interview for *DSM-5* – Eating Disorder Module	Adult	15 minutes	Y	Y	Y	SIV, LAX, DIUR, ENEMA, MEDS, FAST, EX	Y	Y	Y	N
Self-Report	Eating Disorder Diagnostic Scale	Adult	15 minutes	Y	Y	Y	SIV, LAX, DIUR, FAST, EX	Y	Y	Y	Y
Self-Report	Eating Disorder Examination-Adolescent	Child/Adolescent	15 minutes	Y	Y	Y	SIV, LAX, DIUR, EX	Y	Y	N	Y
Self-Report	Questionnaire on Eating and Weight Patterns – Adolescent	Child/Adolescent	15 minutes	Y	Y	Y	SIV, LAX, DIUR, PILLS, FAST, EX	Y	Y	N	Y
Self-Report	Questionnaire on Eating and Weight Patterns-5	Adult	15 minutes	Y	Y	Y	SIV, LAX, DIUR, PILLS, FAST, EX	Y	Y	Y	Y
Self-Report	Youth Eating Disorder Examination-Questionnaire	Child/Adolescent	15 minutes	Y	Y	Y	SIV, LAX, DIUR, EX	Y	Y	Y	Y

Note. Y = Yes, N = No, ? = unknown. SIV = self-induced vomiting, LAX = laxative use, DIUR = diuretic use, PILLS = diet pill use, FAST = fasting, ENEMA = enema use, MEDS = medication misuse, EX = excessive/driven exercise, CS = chewing and spitting, OEWCB = other extreme weight control behaviors the Columbia Center for Eating Disorders and New York State Psychiatric Institute at www.eda5.org (Sysko et al., 2015). The EDA-5 takes approximately 15 minutes to administer and can generate all DSM-5 feeding and eating disorder diagnoses, including BN. Of note, the EDA-5 does probe for SBEs in addition to OBEs, and thus is able to distinguish DSM-5 BN from PD. This assessment shows good test-retest reliability and although it takes significantly less time to administer compared to the EDE, diagnoses made with the EDA-5 show strong agreement with diagnoses made using the EDE (Sysko et al., 2015). Advantages of the EDA-5 include that it was designed to be used by clinicians who have minimal experience with EDs and its short administration time. Given its recent development, a disadvantage of the EDA-5 is that there are less psychometric data available for this assessment compared to others (e.g., the EDE).

The Mini International Neuropsychiatric Interview (MINI) is a very brief, structured interview (Sheehan et al., 1998). The most recent version is the MINI 7.0.2, which was updated for the DSM-5. The MINI can be purchased through the Harm Research Institute (www.harmresearch.org). The entirety of the MINI takes less than 15 minutes to administer. The MINI ED module assesses the presence or absence of AN, BN, and BED; however, data do not yet exist on the psychometric properties of these modules. The primary advantage of the MINI is its very short administration time, while its primary disadvantage is that it does not probe interviewees to describe the size of their binge eating episodes, and thus cannot distinguish between BN and OSFED. Indeed, the MINI does probe for times when one may have eaten "a very large amount of food," but the assessor must rely on the interviewee's judgment as to whether the binge eating episode was large. Several studies suggest that the emotional context of eating and types of foods consumed impact subjective experiences of food intake as excessive when it is not objectively large.

Adult Interviews Used in Epidemiological Studies

There are also three interviews that assess for BN that have been used in epidemiological studies funded by the National Institutes of Health. While these interviews are less commonly used in clinical settings and for ED-specific research studies, they may be useful for researchers looking to conduct epidemiological studies replicating methods from prior research. The first such interview is the Diagnostic Interview Schedule (DIS), which is a structured interview originally developed to diagnose DSM-III disorders for the Epidemiological Catchment Area Survey. The DIS has recently been updated for use making DSM-5 diagnoses by the University of Florida's Department of Epidemiology. The DIS-5 is not freely available but may be purchased through the University of Florida (www.epidemiology.phhp.ufl.edu) and is offered in a computer administered format. Of note, training is required in order to purchase a license for the DIS-5. Information on administration time and psychometrics for the ED module is not available for this version or prior versions, and thus the DIS is not listed in Table 9.1.

Second, the World Health Organization's Composite International Diagnostic Interview (CIDI) is a structured interview developed to generate both DSM and ICD diagnoses that was used in the National Comorbidity Survey, National Comorbidity Study Follow-Up, and the National Comorbidity Survey Replication (Kessler & Üstün, 2004). The World Mental Health CIDI (WMH-CIDI) is the most recent version and is freely available online from www.hcp.med.harvard.edu in computer-assisted and paper-and-pencil formats. While the entire WMH-CIDI takes approximately 2 hours to complete, information is not available on average duration of the ED module alone (Kessler & Üstün, 2004). The WMH-CIDI generates DSM-IV and ICD-10 BN and AN diagnoses only. A prior version of the CIDI, the CIDI 2.1, demonstrated good test-retest reliability and inter-rater reliability (Andrews & Peters, 1998). While the WMH-CIDI is freely available, it does not directly assess for loss of control during episodes. Instead, it asks if the interviewee "gets upset both during and after the binges" because their eating was out of their control.

Finally, the Alcohol Use Disorder and Associated Disabilities Interview Schedule (AUDADIS) is an additional structured interview that may be used in the assessment of BN and was used in the National Epidemiologic Study of Alcohol Related Conditions (NESARC) and its two follow-up studies, NESARC-II and NESARC-III (Grant et al., 2011). The latest version of this assessment is the AUDADIS-5, which was used in NESARC-III and is freely available online through the National Institute on Alcohol Abuse and Alcoholism website (https://www.niaaa.nih.gov/research/nesarc-iii/questionnaire). Information is not available on the average duration of the assessment. The AUDADIS-5 assesses substance use and related disorders including eating pathology according to DSM-5 diagnostic criteria. The AUDADIS shows good test-retest reliability (Grant et al., 2015), though there is no psychometric data available for the ED module specifically. Advantages of the AUDADIS include that it was developed for lay interviewers, is freely availability, and assesses current and lifetime ED diagnoses, including BN. Its primary disadvantage is that it does not ask the interviewee to describe the types and amounts of food eaten during specific binge eating episodes, which may limit its ability to determine presence of DSM-5 BN.

Interviews for Children and Adolescents

There are several interview options for assessing BN in children and adolescents (Table 9.1). First, there is a version of the EDE adapted for use in children and adolescents, the ChEDE Bryant-Waugh et al., 1996). The most recent version, the ChEDE 17.0D/C.1, corresponds to the EDE 17.0D. The ChEDE is freely available through the Enhanced Cognitive Behaviour Therapy website (https://www.cbte.co/). There are no psychometric data on the ChEDE in adolescents with BN, though it showed high internal reliability and inter-rater reliability as well as good discriminant validity in individuals with AN aged 8–14 (Watkins et al., 2005). Further, two studies of the ChEDE in AN samples have shown that adolescents with AN score similarly to adult AN norms on the EDE (Bryant-Waugh et al., 1996; Watkins et al., 2005). The psychometric properties of its German translation have also been examined in a broader sample of adolescents, and the ChEDE was found to have excellent inter-rater reliability, adequate internal reliability, and good discriminant validity (Hilbert et al., 2013). As with the EDE, advantages of the ChEDE include its free availability and detailed assessment of the size of binge eating episodes. Disadvantages include its lack of assessment of fasting behavior, lengthy administration time, and high requirements for assessor training. In addition, some have raised concerns about children's ability to comprehend complex constructs such as the influence of weight or shape on self-evaluation.

Additionally, there is a youth version of the EDA-5, the EDA-5 Youth, developed for ages 8–14. The EDA-5 Youth is freely available through the Columbia Center for Eating Disorders and New York State Psychiatric Institute at www.eda5.org (Sysko et al., 2015). However, there are no psychometric data or norms or cut-offs available for the EDA-5 Youth. Similar to the adult version of the EDA-5, the EDA-5 Youth is brief, requires less assessor training than the ChEDE, and is freely available.

There is also a child version of the MINI, the MINI-KID. The MINI-KID, like the MINI, is a structured interview. It takes roughly 33 minutes to administer (Duncan et al., 2018). The MINI-KID is available for purchase from Dr. David Sheehan, the author, through www.harmresearch.org. The ED module of the MINI-KID shows moderate test–retest reliability (Duncan et al., 2018). No data are available regarding the validity of the MINI-KID ED module. As with the adult version of the MINI, advantages include its short administration time and availability of a parent-report version that may be useful in assessing younger children. Disadvantages include its reliance on participant report of "very large" amounts of food, and its cost.

The Kiddie Schedule for Affective Disorders and Schizophrenia (K-SADS) contains an ED module that may be used to diagnose EDs. The paper version of the K-SADS is freely available for use in institutional review board-approved research protocols and for clinical usage in nonprofit institutions through the University of Pittsburgh's Child and Adolescent Bipolar Spectrum Services (www.pediatricbipolar.pitt.edu/resources/instruments). A computerized version is available for purchase through the Kennedy Krieger Institute (www.kennedykrieger.com). The full K-SADS takes roughly 45–75 minutes to administer, but the duration of the ED module is unknown. The psychometric properties of the EDs module in the updated, DSM-5 version of the K-SADS have been examined in one study with a small sample of participants with an identified ED (Marques et al., 2021). The K-SADS ED module is short, assesses most of the core features of BN, and is freely available. However, there are key drawbacks to the K-SADS that may lead to under-detection of BN. First, there is a high threshold for fasting; the K-SADS probes for periods of at least 1 week during which nothing but zero-calorie liquids were consumed. Additionally, the K-SADS assesses overvaluation of weight, but not shape. There is also a high threshold for overvaluation of weight, as the instrument probes for whether self-worth is "totally" tied to weight.

Self-Report Assessments for Adults

Self-report questionnaires have been employed for the assessment BN in adults (Table 9.1). Self-report surveys can be less time-consuming than diagnostic interviews, can be administered to several individuals simultaneously, and are not influenced by differences in how interviewers administer questions or interpret responses. Often, scores on self-report measures reflect increased eating pathology compared to interview assessments. This may be because individuals tend to over-report definitionally ambiguous or complex symptoms (e.g., binge eating, overvaluation of shape and weight; Fairburn & Beglin, 1994), or a reflection of increased honesty as a result of perceived anonymity (Keel et al., 2002). Formal diagnoses should not be made using self-reports in clinical settings, but they may be used to assign probable diagnoses or to identify individuals who may warrant further evaluations for BN. We will discuss self-report surveys in terms of measures that may be used to assign probable diagnoses.

There are three self-reports that could be used to assign probable diagnoses of BN in adults. First, there is a self-report version of the EDE, the Eating Disorder Examination-

Questionnaire (EDE-Q), comprising 28 questions. The EDE-Q takes about 15 minutes to complete (Peyser et al., 2020). The current version is the EDE-Q 6.0, which is freely available for noncommercial research use through CREDO (www.credo-oxford.com). The psychometric properties of the EDE-Q have been examined in a wide range of samples, including in men and gender and sexual minorities (Kelly et al., 2012; Nagata et al., 2021; Nagata et al., 2020; Schaefer et al., 2018). Norms and cut-offs are available for the EDE-Q, although there is no consensus as to the optimal cut-off score. Proposed cut-offs indicating the possibility of a clinically significant eating disorder include: a global score of ≥ 4 (Mond et al., 2006), a global score of ≥ 2.3 in conjunction with the presence of OBEs and/or problematic exercise (Mond et al., 2004), a global score of ≥ 1.7 in males (Schaefer et al., 2018), 2.62 for individuals with BN (Rø et al., 2015), and 2.80 in young adult women in a primary care setting (Mond et al., 2008). Cut-off scores alone should not be used to assign a probable diagnosis of BN, and the optimal cut-off score for determining the presence of a clinically significant ED may differ between populations (Meule, 2021). The EDE-Q provides a limited assessment of fasting and does not assess diuretic use as compensatory behaviors.

The Eating Disorder Diagnostic Scale (EDDS) is a 23-item self-report questionnaire and takes about 15 minutes to complete (Peyser et al., 2020; Stice et al., 2000). The current version is the EDDS-5 assesses for DSM-5 criteria. The EDDS is freely available through the Oregon Research Institute (www.ori.org). Psychometrics are not available for DSM-5 diagnoses, but prior versions of the EDDS demonstrated good criterion validity, predictive validity, internal reliability, and test-retest reliability for DSM-IV diagnoses (Stice et al., 2004; Stice et al., 2000). An advantage of the EDDS is that it offers an example of a large amount of food ("e.g., a pint of ice cream") in the section assessing binge eating; a disadvantage is that this example does not clearly exceed what most people might eat under similar circumstances.

The Questionnaire on Eating and Weight Patterns (QEWP) contains 26 items and takes about 15 minutes to complete. The current version, the QEWP-5, is freely available (Yanovski et al., 2015). Psychometric data are not available for the QEWP-5, but prior versions showed adequate test-retest reliability and discriminant validity for DSM-IV diagnoses in an adult sample (Nangle et al., 1994). The QEWP asks participants to list what and how much food was consumed during binge episodes, so that scorers can decide whether the episode is objectively large. This increases accuracy of a probable diagnosis, but it also requires training of scorers and increased scoring time compared to other self-report assessments.

Self-Report Assessments for Children and Adolescents

For children and adolescents, there are several self-reports that may be used to assign a probable BN diagnosis (Table 9.1). The EDE-Q was originally validated using 16–35-year-old women and has also shown good internal reliability and test-retest reliability in adolescents ages 11 and older (Penelo et al., 2013). Nevertheless, there are also three variations of the EDE-Q that have been specifically adapted for children and adolescents: the ChEDE-Q, YEDE-Q, and the EDE-A. The ChEDE-Q was developed by Decaluwé and Braet (1999), and was originally written in Dutch. In a sample of 12–18-year-old adolescents, the ChEDE-Q demonstrated good concordance with the ChEDE (Goossens & Braet, 2010), but in a sample of adolescents aged 10–16 with obesity there were higher scores on the ChEDE-Q compared to the ChEDE, suggesting that the ChEDE-Q may not be able to accurately identify individuals with binge eating (Decaluwé & Braet, 2004). Information about the availability of the ChEDE-Q is unknown. A shorter, eight-item version has also been developed, which demonstrated good internal reliability and construct validity in a sample of 7–18-year-old children and adolescents (Kliem et al., 2017). Due to lack of information about the ChEDE-Q, this measure is not listed in Table 9.1.

The YEDE-Q was developed by Goldschmidt et al. (2007) and is available upon request from authors. The YEDE-Q has primarily been used as a screening tool for binge eating among adolescents with overweight and obesity (Goldschmidt et al., 2007; Sheinbein et al., 2019), rather than to directly assess EDs like BN. Despite its limited use in clinical ED samples (Noetel et al., 2016), the YEDE-Q is strengthened by its use of instructional text to explain binges to children and adolescents in terms of size and loss of control. It also contains pictures indicating objectively large versus not objectively large amounts of food. The YEDE-Q has been used in adolescents aged 12–17 (Goldschmidt et al., 2007).

The EDE-A (Carter et al., 2001) not only changed the wording of questions to be more accessible to adolescents, but altered the timeframe of the questions from asking about the past 4 weeks (28 days) to the past 2 weeks (14 days). A main drawback of the EDE-A is that there is no research on its psychometric properties. Community norms are available for adolescents aged 12–14 years (Carter et al., 2001). As there are no norms available for adolescents younger than 12 or older than 14 or for males, it should be used with caution in other samples. The EDE-A is freely available online through Child Outcomes Research Consortium (www.corc.uk.net).

Like the EDE-Q, the QEWP has also been adapted for adolescents (QEWP-A; (Johnson et al., 1999). Psychometrics of the QEWP-A have been examined in both male and female adolescents aged 10–18 (Johnson et al., 1999; Johnson et al., 2001). The QEWP-A has adequate concurrent validity (Johnson et al., 1999). The QEWP-A also has adequate test–retest reliability, but shows less stability in females versus males over a 3-week period (Johnson et al., 2001). Notably, QEWP-A scores are not concordant with the ChEDE (Tanofsky-Kraff et al., 2003).

Conclusions

The EDE emerges as the strongest interview assessment for adults, but drawbacks include significant assessor and participant burden. The EDA-5 may be an adequate alternative that reduces the necessary level of assessor training and time spent interviewing participants, although there is less data available on its psychometric properties. The SCID is also shorter than the EDE, but its cost may preclude its use when adequate funding is not available. For children and adolescents, the ChEDE is likely the strongest interview assessment. However, as with the original EDE, it requires a significant time commitment both in terms of training assessors and in terms of assessing participants.

The EDE-Q and EDDS are likely the strongest self-report tools for assessing adult BN, given more extensive research on their psychometric properties compared to the QEWP. For children and adolescents, the YEDE-Q and QEWP-A may be the strongest self-report assessment tools. Specifically, the YEDE-Q has the advantage of explaining the definition of a binge episode in greater detail than other assessments, but there is less research on its use in clinical ED samples. The QEWP-A is strengthened by its assessment of compensatory behaviors other than vomiting, laxative use, and diuretic use and its assessment of the prior 3 months (versus 1 month for the EDE-Q, YEDE-Q, and 2 weeks for the EDE-A), although scores are not concordant with interview assessments. Efforts should be made to select tools that adequately assess all core symptoms of BN while taking into account cost, assessor burden, and participant burden.

References

American Psychiatric Association. (2013). *Diagnostic and statistical manual of mental disorders* (5th ed.). APA. https://doi.org/10.1176/appi.books.9780890425596

Andrews, G., & Peters, L. (1998). The psychometric properties of the composite international diagnostic interview. *Social Psychiatry and Psychiatric Epidemiology, 33*(2), 80–88. https://doi.org/10.1007/s001270050026

Arikian, A., Peterson, C.B., Swanson, S.A., Berg, K.C., Chartier, L., Durkin, N., & Crow, S.J. (2012). Establishing thresholds for unusually large binge eating episodes. *International Journal of Eating Disorders, 45*(2), 222–226. https://doi.org/10.1002/eat.20930

Bryant-Waugh, R.J., Cooper, P.J., Taylor, C.L., & Lask, B.D. (1996). The use of the eating disorder examination with children: A pilot study. *International Journal of Eating Disorders, 19*(4), 391–397. https://doi.org/10.1002/(SICI)1098-108X(199605)19:4<391::AID-EAT6>3.0.CO;2-G

Carter, J.C., Stewart, D.A., & Fairburn, C.G. (2001). Eating disorder examination questionnaire: Norms for young adolescent girls. *Behaviour Research and Therapy, 39*(5), 625–632. https://doi.org/10.1016/S0005-7967(00)00033-4

Cooper, Z., & Fairburn, C. (1987). The eating disorder examination: A semi-structured interview for the assessment of the specific psychopathology of eating disorders. *International Journal of Eating Disorders, 6*(1), 1–8. https://doi.org/10.1002/1098-108X(198701)6:1<1::AID-EAT2260060102>3.0.CO;2-9

Decaluwé, V., & Braet, C. (1999). *Child eating disorder examination-questionnaire. Dutch translation and adaptation of the eating disorder examination-questionnaire.* [Unpublished manuscript].

Decaluwé, V., & Braet, C. (2004). Assessment of eating disorder psychopathology in obese children and adolescents: Interview versus self-report questionnaire. *Behaviour Research and Therapy, 42*(7), 799–811. https://doi.org/10.1016/j.brat.2003.07.008

Dumanovsky, T., Nonas, C.A., Huang, C.Y., Silver, L.D., & Bassett, M.T. (2009). What people buy from fast-food restaurants: Caloric content and menu item selection, New York City 2007. *Obesity, 17*(7), 1369–1374. https://doi.org/10.1038/oby.2009.90

Duncan, L., Georgiades, K., Wang, L., Van Lieshout, R.J., MacMillan, H.L., Ferro, M.A., Lipman, E.L., Szatmari, P., Bennett, K., & Kata, A. (2018). Psychometric evaluation of the Mini International Neuropsychiatric Interview for Children and Adolescents (MINI-KID). *Psychological Assessment, 30*(7), 916. https://doi.org/10.1037/pas0000541

Fairburn, C.G., & Cooper, Z. (2000). *The EDE supplement.* [Unpublished manuscript].

Fairburn, C., Cooper, Z., & O'Connor, M.E. (2014). *Eating disorder examination.* https://www.credo-oxford.com/7.2.html

Fairburn, C.G., & Beglin, S.J. (1994). Assessment of eating disorders: Interview or self-report questionnaire? *International Journal of Eating Disorders, 16*(4), 363–370. https://doi.org/10.1002/1098-108X(199412)16:4<363::AID-EAT2260160405>3.0.CO;2-#

First, M.B., Williams, J.B.W., Karg, R.S., & Spitzer, R.L. (2015). *Structured Clinical Interview for DSM-5 - Research Version (SCID-5 for DSM-5, Research Version; SCID-5-RV).* American Psychiatric Association.

Forney, K.J., Holland, L.A., Joiner, T.E., & Keel, P.K. (2015). Determining empirical thresholds for "definitely large" amounts of food for defining binge-eating episodes. *Eating Disorders, 23*(1), 15–30. https://doi.org/10.1080/10640266.2014.931763

Goldschmidt, A.B., Doyle, A.C., & Wilfley, D.E. (2007). Assessment of binge eating in overweight youth using a questionnaire version of the child eating disorder examination with instructions. *International Journal of Eating Disorders, 40*(5), 460–467. https://doi.org/10.1002/eat.20387

Goossens, L., & Braet, C. (2010). Screening for eating pathology in the pediatric field. *International Journal of Pediatric Obesity, 5*(6), 483–490. https://doi.org/10.3109/17477160903571995

Grant, B.F., Goldstein, R.B., Chou, S.P., Saha, T.D., Ruan, W.J., Huang, B., Smith, S.M., Zhang, H., Jung, J., Pickering, R.P., Aiyadyan, C., Greenstein, E., & Hasin, D. (2011). *The Alcohol Use Disorder and Associated Disabilities Interview Schedule – Diagnostic and Statistical Manual of Mental Disorders, Fifth Edition Version (AUDADIS-5).* National Institute on Alcohol Abuse and Alcoholism.

Grant, B.F., Goldstein, R.B., Smith, S.M., Jung, J., Zhang, H., Chou, S.P., Pickering, R.P., Ruan, W.J., Huang, B., & Saha, T.D. (2015). The Alcohol Use Disorder and Associated Disabilities Interview Schedule-5 (AUDADIS-5): Reliability of substance use and psychiatric disorder modules in a general population sample. *Drug and Alcohol Dependence, 148*, 27–33.

Guest, T. (2000). Using the eating disorder examination in the assessment of bulimia and anorexia: Issues of reliability and validity. *Social Work in Health Care, 31*(4), 71–83. https://doi.org/10.1300/J010v31n04_05

Hilbert, A., Buerger, A., Hartmann, A.S., Spenner, K., Czaja, J., & Warschburger, P. (2013). Psychometric evaluation of the eating disorder examination adapted for children. *European Eating Disorders Review, 21*(4), 330–339. https://doi.org/10.1002/erv.2221

Johnson, W.G., Grieve, F.G., Adams, C.D., & Sandy, J. (1999). Measuring binge eating in adolescents: Adolescent and parent versions of the questionnaire of eating and weight patterns. *International Journal of Eating Disorders, 26*(3), 301–314. https://doi.org/10.1002/(SICI)1098-108X(199911)26:3<301::AID-EAT8>3.0.CO;2-M

Johnson, W.G., Kirk, A.A., & Reed, A.E. (2001). Adolescent version of the questionnaire of eating and weight patterns: Reliability and gender differences. *International Journal of Eating Disorders, 29*(1), 94–96. https://doi.org/10.1002/1098-108X(200101)29:1<94::AID-EAT16>3.0.CO;2-8

Kaye, W.H., Devlin, B., Barbarich, N., Bulik, C.M., Thornton, L., Bacanu, S.A., Fichter, M.M., Halmi, K.A., Kaplan, A.S., & Strober, M. (2004). Genetic analysis of bulimia nervosa: Methods and sample description. *International Journal of Eating Disorders, 35*(4), 556–570. https://doi.org/10.1002/eat.10271

Keel, P.K., Crow, S., Davis, T.L., & Mitchell, J.E. (2002). Assessment of eating disorders: Comparison of interview and questionnaire data from a long-term follow-up study of bulimia nervosa. *Journal of Psychosomatic Research, 53*(5), 1043–1047. https://doi.org/10.1016/S0022-3999(02)00491-9

Keel, P.K., Wolfe, B.E., Liddle, R.A., De Young, K.P., & Jimerson, D.C. (2007). Clinical features and physiological response to a test meal in purging disorder and bulimia nervosa. *Archives of General Psychiatry, 64*(9), 1058–1066. https://doi.org/10.1001/archpsyc.64.9.1058

Kelly, N.R., Cotter, E.W., & Mazzeo, S.E. (2012). Eating disorder examination questionnaire (EDE-Q): Norms for Black women. *Eating Behaviors, 13*(4), 429–432. https://doi.org/10.1016/j.eatbeh.2012.09.001

Kessler, R.C., & Üstün, T.B. (2004). The world mental health (WMH) survey initiative version of the world health organization (WHO) composite international diagnostic interview (CIDI). *International Journal of Methods in Psychiatric Research, 13*(2), 93–121. https://doi.org/10.1002/mpr.168

Kliem, S., Schmidt, R., Vogel, M., Hiemisch, A., Kiess, W., & Hilbert, A. (2017). An 8-item short form of the Eating Disorder Examination-Questionnaire adapted for children (ChEDE-Q8). *International Journal of Eating Disorders, 50*(6), 679–686. https://doi.org/10.1002/eat.22658

Marques, C.C., Matos, A.P., do Céu Salvador, M., Arnarson, E.Ö., & Craighead, W.E. (2021). Reliability and validity of the schedule for affective disorders and schizophrenia for school-age children – present and lifetime version (K-SADS-PL): Portuguese version. *Child Psychiatry & Human Development, 53*, 119–128. https://doi.org/10.1007/s10578-021-01196-5

Meule, A. (2021). Reconsidering the use of cut-off scores for the Eating Disorder Examination-Questionnaire. *Eating Disorders, 29*(5), 480–484. https://doi.org/10.1080/10640266.2019.1678981

Mond, J.M., Hay, P.J., Rodgers, B., & Owen, C. (2006). Eating Disorder Examination Questionnaire (EDE-Q): Norms for young adult women. *Behaviour Research and Therapy, 44*(1), 53–62. https://doi.org/10.1016/j.brat.2004.12.003

Mond, J.M., Hay, P.J., Rodgers, B., Owen, C., & Beumont, P. (2004). Validity of the Eating Disorder Examination Questionnaire (EDE-Q) in screening for eating disorders in community samples. *Behaviour Research and Therapy, 42*(5), 551–567. https://doi.org/10.1016/S0005-7967(03)00161-X

Mond, J.M., Myers, T.C., Crosby, R.D., Hay, P.J., Rodgers, B., Morgan, J.F., Lacey, J.H., & Mitchell, J.E. (2008). Screening for eating disorders in primary care: EDE-Q versus SCOFF. *Behaviour Research and Therapy, 46*(5), 612–622. https://doi.org/10.1016/j.brat.2008.02.003

Nagata, J.M., Compte, E.J., Murray, S.B., Schauer, R., Pak, E., Flentje, A., Capriotti, M.R., Lubensky, M.E., Lunn, M.R., & Obedin-Maliver, J. (2021). Community norms for the eating disorder examination questionnaire (EDE-Q) among cisgender bisexual plus women and men. *Eating and Weight Disorders – Studies on Anorexia, Bulimia and Obesity, 26*(7), 2227–2239. https://doi.org/10.1016/j.eatbeh.2020.101381

Nagata, J.M., Murray, S.B., Compte, E.J., Pak, E.H., Schauer, R., Flentje, A., Capriotti, M.R., Lubensky, M.E., Lunn, M.R., & Obedin-Maliver, J. (2020). Community norms for the Eating Disorder Examination Questionnaire (EDE-Q) among transgender men and women. *Eating Behaviors, 37*, 101381. https://doi.org/10.1016/j.eatbeh.2020.101381

Nangle, D.W., Johnson, W.G., Carr-Nangle, R.E., & Engler, L.B. (1994). Binge eating disorder and the proposed DSM-IV criteria: Psychometric analysis of the questionnaire of eating and weight patterns. *International Journal of Eating Disorders, 16*(2), 147–157. https://doi.org/10.1002/1098-108X(199409)16:2<147::AID-EAT2260160206>3.0.CO;2-P

Noetel, M., Miskovic-Wheatley, J., Crosby, R.D., Hay, P., Madden, S., & Touyz, S. (2016). A clinical profile of compulsive exercise in adolescent inpatients with anorexia nervosa. *Journal of Eating Disorders, 4*(1), 1–10. https://doi.org/10.1186/s40337-016-0090-6

Penelo, E., Negrete, A., Portell, M., & Raich, R.M. (2013). Psychometric properties of the Eating Disorder Examination Questionnaire (EDE-Q) and norms for rural and urban adolescent males and females in Mexico. *PLoS One, 8*(12), e83245. https://doi.org/10.1371/journal.pone.0083245

Peyser, D., Campbell, M., & Sysko, R. (2020). Binge eating assessment. In G. Frank & L. Berner (Eds.), *Binge eating* (pp. 13–24). Springer. https://doi.org/10.1007/978-3-030-43562-2_2

Rø, Ø., Reas, D.L., & Stedal, K. (2015). Eating disorder examination questionnaire (EDE-Q) in Norwegian adults: Discrimination between female controls and eating disorder patients. *European Eating Disorders Review, 23*(5), 408–412. https://doi.org/10.1002/erv.2372

Schaefer, L.M., Smith, K.E., Leonard, R., Wetterneck, C., Smith, B., Farrell, N., Riemann, B.C., Frederick, D.A., Schaumberg, K., & Klump, K.L. (2018). Identifying a male clinical cutoff on the Eating Disorder Examination-Questionnaire (EDE-Q). *International Journal of Eating Disorders, 51*(12), 1357–1360. https://doi.org/10.1002/eat.22972

Scourboutakos, M.J., Semnani-Azad, Z., & L'Abbe, M.R. (2013). Restaurant meals: Almost a full day's worth of calories, fats, and sodium. *JAMA Internal Medicine, 173*(14), 1373–1374. https://doi.org/10.1001/jamainternmed.2013.6159

Sheehan, D.V., Lecrubier, Y., Sheehan, K.H., Amorim, P., Janavs, J., Weiller, E., Hergueta, T., Baker, R., & Dunbar, G.C. (1998). The Mini-International Neuropsychiatric Interview (MINI): The development and validation of a structured diagnostic psychiatric interview for DSM-IV and ICD-10. *Journal of Clinical Psychiatry, 59*(20), 22–33. https://doi.org/10.1037/t18597-000

Sheinbein, D.H., Stein, R.I., Hayes, J.F., Brown, M.L., Balantekin, K.N., Conlon, R.P.K., Saelens, B.E., Perri, M.G., Welch, R.R., & Schechtman, K.B. (2019). Factors associated with depression and anxiety symptoms among children seeking treatment for obesity: A social-ecological approach. *Pediatric Obesity, 14*(8), e12518.

Stice, E., Fisher, M., & Martinez, E. (2004). Eating disorder diagnostic scale: Additional evidence of reliability and validity. *Psychological Assessment, 16*(1), 60–71. https://doi.org/10.1037/1040-3590.16.1.60

Stice, E., Telch, C.F., & Rizvi, S.L. (2000). Development and validation of the Eating Disorder Diagnostic Scale: A brief self-report measure of anorexia, bulimia, and binge-eating disorder. *Psychological Assessment, 12*(2), 123 -131. https://doi.org/10.1037/1040-3590.12.2.123

Sysko, R., Glasofer, D.R., Hildebrandt, T., Klimek, P., Mitchell, J.E., Berg, K.C., Peterson, C.B., Wonderlich, S.A., & Walsh, B.T. (2015). The Eating Disorder Assessment for DSM-5 (EDA-5): Development and validation of a structured interview for feeding and eating disorders. *International Journal of Eating Disorders, 48*(5), 452–463. https://doi.org/10.1037/t45613-000

Tanofsky-Kraff, M., Morgan, C.M., Yanovski, S.Z., Marmarosh, C., Wilfley, D.E., & Yanovski, J.A. (2003). Comparison of assessments of children's eating-disordered behaviors by interview and questionnaire. *International Journal of Eating Disorders, 33*(2), 213–224. https://doi.org/10.1002/eat.10128

Wade, T.D., Byrne, S., & Bryant-Waugh, R. (2008). The eating disorder examination: Norms and construct validity with young and middle adolescent girls. *International Journal of Eating Disorders, 41*(6), 551–558. https://doi.org/10.1002/eat.20526

Watkins, B., Frampton, I., Lask, B., & Bryant-Waugh, R. (2005). Reliability and validity of the child version of the Eating Disorder Examination: A preliminary investigation. *International Journal of Eating Disorders, 38*(2), 183–187. https://doi.org/10.1002/eat.20165

World Health Organization. (2019). *International statistical classification of diseases and related health problems* (11th ed.). WHO. https://icd.who.int/

Yanovski, S.Z., Marcus, M.D., Wadden, T.A., & Walsh, B.T. (2015). The questionnaire on eating and weight patterns-5 (QEWP-5): An updated screening instrument for binge eating disorder. *The International Journal of Eating Disorders, 48*(3), 259–261. https://doi.org/10.1002/eat.22372

Zanarini, M.C., Skodol, A.E., Bender, D., Dolan, R., Sanislow, C., Schaefer, E., Morey, L.C., Grilo, C.M., Shea, M.T., & McGlashan, T.H. (2000). The collaborative longitudinal personality disorders study: Reliability of axis I and II diagnoses. *Journal of Personality Disorders, 14*(4), 291–299. https://doi.org/10.1521/pedi.2000.14.4.291

Chapter 10

Assessment of Binge Eating Disorder

Amy H. Egbert[1] and Andrea B. Goldschmidt[2]

[1]Department of Psychological Sciences, University of Connecticut, Storrs, CT, USA
[2]Department of Psychiatry, University of Pittsburgh, PA, USA

Introduction

Binge eating disorder (BED) is the most common eating disorder diagnosis, with lifetime prevalence rates ranging from 1.5 % to 2.6 % (Cossrow et al., 2016; Hudson et al., 2007; Kessler et al., 2013). Although binge eating behaviors were first described in the scientific literature by Stunkard (1959), they did not appear in the diagnostic nomenclature until 1980 with the publication of the *Third Edition of the Diagnostic and Statistical Manual of Mental Disorders* (DSM-III). In DSM-III, binge eating appeared as part of the criteria for bulimia nervosa, along with the regular use of compensatory behaviors intended to offset effects of binge eating/prevent weight gain (American Psychiatric Association, 1980). A formal diagnosis of "binge eating disorder," characterized by recurrent binge eating episodes (eating an unusually large amount of food ("overeating") while experiencing a sense of loss of control over eating ("LOC") at least once per week, on average, for 3 months) in the absence of regular compensatory behaviors, was not formally added to the DSM until its fifth edition (American Psychiatric Association, 2013; see Box 10.1 for DSM-5 diagnostic criteria for BED).

Although the prevalence of BED is higher than that of anorexia nervosa or bulimia nervosa, it is often underdiagnosed, and as a result, rates of treatment utilization are low, which may contribute to excess weight gain, persistent distress, and other physical and psychosocial consequences affecting public health (Kornstein, 2017). This chapter will discuss the current state of the literature with respect to measures for the assessment of BED and their strengths and limitations. To facilitate an accurate diagnosis of BED, comprehensive assessment of binge eating symptoms is required. However, this chapter will focus specifically on measures that can be used as either screening or diagnostic tools for full-syndrome BED (Table 10.1) and will not discuss assessments that only capture components of binge eating in isolation, such as those that measure LOC independent of overeating, and vice versa. Because BED is relatively rare in children and adolescents (although subsyndromal behaviors such as LOC independent of overeating are quite common; Marzilli et al., 2018), and there are few established measures designed to diagnose BED specifically in this age group, this chapter will focus exclusively on assessment in adults.

Box 10.1. DSM-5 criteria for BED

Binge eating episodes that occur, on average, at least once a week for 3 months. Episodes include:

1. Eating an amount of food that is considerably larger than what most people would eat in similar circumstances in a similar time frame
2. A sense of loss of control while eating

Binge eating episodes are associated with at least three of the following:

1. Eating much faster than normal
2. Eating until uncomfortably full
3. Eating large amounts of food in the absence of hunger
4. Eating alone because of embarrassment about how much is being eaten
5. Feeling disgusted, guilty, or depressed after eating

Experiencing marked distress about binge eating.

Binge eating not associated with regular use of compensatory behaviors (like in bulimia nervosa) or exclusively in the context of bulimia nervosa or anorexia nervosa.

Table 10.1. List of tools for assessing BED

	Administration type	Length/number of items	BED-specific?	Diagnosis
Binge Eating Scale (Gormally et al., 1982)	Self-report	16 items	yes	no
Eating Disorder Examination (Fairburn & Cooper, 1993)	Semistructured interview	60–90 minutes	no	yes
Eating Disorder Examination-Questionnaire (Fairburn & Beglin, 1994)	Self-report	28 items	no	no
Eating Disorder Diagnostic Scale (Stice et al., 2000)	Self-report	23 items	no	yes
Eating Disorder Assessment for DSM-5 (Sysko et al., 2015)	Semistructured interview	10–20 minutes	no	yes
Questionnaire on Weight and Eating Patterns-5 (Yanovski et al., 2015)	Self-report	28 items	yes	yes
Binge Eating Disorder Screener-7 (Herman et al., 2016)	Self-report	7 items	yes	no

Challenges in the Assessment of BED

Because BED is primarily defined by two features that are prone to measurement biases, overeating and LOC, assessment of the disorder can be difficult. Although overeating in the context of a binge episode is defined as eating "an amount of food that is definitely larger than what most people would eat in a similar period of time under similar circumstances" (American Psychiatric Association, 2013), the threshold over which a normative eating episode becomes overeating may differ from person to person depending on factors such as body weight, age, and dietary rules (Goldschmidt, 2017). For example, according to guidelines included in the Eating Disorder Examination (EDE), "objectively large" can refer to three full plates of salad, or three full servings of lasagna, which may vary significantly in terms of volume, energy composition, and effects on satiety. Compounding these measurement issues, eating behavior may be prone to significant recall biases, particularly when assessed over the past 3 months. In addition, the presence of "subjective binge episodes," which occur when LOC accompanies eating episodes that are not objectively large according to investigator-based standards (but are considered "excessive" by the respondent), make BED assessment even more difficult due to the need to distinguish between what someone believes is a large amount of food and what the clinician or researcher deems to be "objectively large."

In addition to overeating, LOC while eating is a subjective construct that is also difficult to assess. LOC can currently only be measured via self-report. Despite this, there is accumulating evidence that LOC is a salient construct that is uniquely associated with distress and impairment, independent of the amount of food consumed (Wolfe et al., 2009). Nevertheless, it is difficult to disentangle the subjective, internal experience of LOC while eating from the act of eating itself. Previous research has drawn attention to concerns that LOC is confounded by episode size – that is, one's perceptions of having eaten an excessive amount of food (regardless of whether those perceptions match researcher or clinician standards) may inform reporting of LOC (Pollert et al., 2013). As a result, it is unclear whether LOC drives eating behavior, or problematic interpretations of one's eating behavior (e.g., eating more than intended, breaking a dietary rule) drive subjective reports of LOC. It may be that for some individuals, there is an internal or external threshold governing one's eating behavior which, once crossed, is associated with a perceived or objective inability to stop eating (e.g., restraint theory; Polivy & Herman, 1985). For other individuals, the salient aspect driving LOC while eating may be the experience of negative affect, rather than the quantity or quality of food consumed (e.g., affect regulation theory; Haedt-Matt & Keel, 2011).

As BED is characterized by binge eating episodes that occur once per week, on average, for at least 3 months, assessment requires accurate recall of past eating behaviors. Although the challenges inherent in recalling what and how one ate retrospectively over several months are not unique to BED (Peterson et al., 2007), they do complicate its diagnosis. This is compounded by evidence that emotions may influence an individual's assessment of their eating behavior. Criteria for BED also include endorsement of emotional responses, such as feeling guilty for engaging in binge episodes or feeling disgusted with oneself after a binge episode. Research suggests that recall of binge eating may be complicated by one's emotional state during the binge episode, by retrospective perceptions of the emotional state during the binge, or both (Adriaanse et al., 2016).

Despite challenges with defining and conceptualizing BED, several measures have been created over the last two decades to aid in its assessment. These include structured interviews, such as the Structured Clinical Interview for DSM (SCID; Spitzer et al., 1992) and the Mini International Neuropsychiatric Interview (MINI; Lecrubier et al., 1997), which are formatted to allow for comprehensive assessment of DSM-5 psychiatric disorders, including BED. These interviews are often time-intensive and are likely more appropriate when the goal is to screen for a variety of psychiatric disorders, not just BED. Therefore, the following sections focus on measures that assess for eating disorders broadly or for binge eating specifically. We also discuss research on the reliability (i.e., the extent to which measures of a construct are consistent across time, raters, and methods) and validity (i.e., the extent to which a construct reflects what it is theoretically meant to represent) of each measure.

Interview Measures

Eating Disorder Examination

The Eating Disorder Examination (EDE; Fairburn & Cooper, 1993) is a semistructured diagnostic interview that assesses both cognitive and behavioral features of eating disorders and can generate diagnoses of clinical and subthreshold eating disorders. It is comprised of four subscales reflecting Eating Concerns, Shape Concerns, Weight Concerns, and Dietary Restraint, as well as a global score reflecting the overall severity of eating-related psychopathology. Although the EDE subscales were originally designed to capture the clinical features of anorexia and bulimia nervosa (Fairburn & Cooper, 1993), they also can be used to measure general symptoms of eating-related psychopathology. In addition to the questions that make up the four subscales, the EDE also includes specific questions about the diagnostic criteria of BED, including presence of eating episodes characterized by overeating and/or LOC in the past 3 months, as well as secretive eating, guilt over binge episodes, and eating in front of others. These questions do not factor into either the subscale or the global scores but instead are considered diagnostic items.

To assess for BED, the EDE uses a timeline follow-back method, where the interviewer uses a calendar to help orient the participant before asking them about behavior over the past several months. The EDE has specific guidelines for making a diagnosis of anorexia nervosa, bulimia nervosa, or BED and outlines how specific questions map onto the criteria for each. It is also possible to make a diagnosis of an other specified feeding or eating disorder and a feeding or unspecified feeding or eating disorder using the EDE, which may capture subthreshold symptoms of BED, but this requires referencing the specific guidelines for those disorders in DSM and using clinical judgement. The EDE can be accessed online, free of charge (https://www.cbte.co/for-professionals/measures/).

Reliability and Validity

In general, the EDE has been found to have good psychometric properties, including reliability and validity. Despite the rigorous training and calibration involved in its administration (Grilo et al., 2010), the EDE, as previously noted, is an investigator-based interview and ratings of LOC eating may therefore be subject to rater biases and drift (i.e., changes in rater behavior across test administrations; Harik et al., 2009). However, early studies of inter-rater reliability on the EDE found near-perfect agreement for both objective and subjective binge eating episodes ($r>.90$; Cooper & Fairburn, 1987; Grilo et al., 2004; Rizvi et al., 2000). In contrast to these findings, a study comparing clinician EDE ratings of binge eating with individuals' 24-hour dietary recall (for nonoverlapping time periods) found greater convergence between the measures for days on which subjective binge eating occurred ($r=.81$) as compared to days on which objective binge eating occurred ($r=-.29$). Ratings of subjective binge eating days were higher on the 24-hour dietary recall relative to the EDE, but the reverse pattern was found for objective binge eating days (i.e., greater frequency reported on the EDE relative to the 24-hour dietary recall; Bartholome et al., 2006). Inconsistent findings with regards to whether objective binge eating is reported more frequently via the EDE or self-monitoring, make it difficult to infer whether discrepancies are related to recall biases (i.e., reporting on behaviors in "near real time" via self-monitoring versus recalling behaviors over the past 3–6 months via the EDE) or inconsistencies between participants' and investigators' understanding of binge eating constructs.

The EDE appears to have moderate-to-high test-retest reliability. As reviewed by Berg and colleagues (2012), the short-term (2–14 day) test-retest reliability of EDE-measured objective binge eating episode frequency among adults has been in the moderate to high range ($\rho=.69$, range=.52–.85), but is typically lower for subjective binge eating episode frequency ($\rho=.33$, range=.17–.47; Grilo et al., 2004, 2005; Rizvi et al., 2000). Finally, the EDE has been found to have good criterion-oriented validity, representing its ability to detect group differences. Research has demonstrated large effect sizes to distinguish between subscale scores for individuals with BED as compared to normal-weight controls as well as between individuals with BED and individuals with overweight but without BED, as diagnosed by clinical interview (Wilfley et al., 2000).

Strengths and Limitations of the EDE

Strengths of the EDE include its focus on eating pathology, which makes it shorter than more comprehensive psychiatric interviews, its diagnostic capabilities, and its usage in an extensive amount of clinical research which facilitates cross-study comparisons. Additionally, interviewers can be trained to administer the EDE in a standardized way that facilitates improved reliability. At the same time, the EDE also allows for more personalized probes when necessary. Limitations of the EDE include administration time (≈ 60–90 minutes), which may not be feasible in the context of a busy clinical practice (particularly in non-specialized healthcare settings such as primary care) and the need for extensive training/ongoing calibration of administrators, particularly with respect to accurately assessment of complex constructs such as LOC. Additionally, the EDE asks interviewees to recall symptoms that occurred several months prior to administration. Although there is some evidence to suggest that recall for this timeframe is accurate, data are limited (Berg et al., 2012). More research is also needed to examine the validity of the EDE with regard to binge eating behaviors, which are not assessed via the four subscales, and in populations that are not already seeking treatment for eating disorders.

Although the EDE is perhaps the most widely studied of the interview-based assessments of eating disorders, other assessments may also be used to screen for and diagnose BED.

Below we present alternatives to the EDE including any psychometric information that may exist for those measures with respect to symptoms of BED or populations of individuals with binge eating.

Eating Disorder Assessment for DSM-5

The Eating Disorder Assessment for DSM-5 (EDA-5; Sysko et al., 2015) is a semistructured interview designed to assess for DSM-5 eating disorders. In the assessment of binge eating, the EDA-5 first assesses whether binge eating has occurred over the past week, then asks if that behavior is typical of the past 3 months, and, if not, examines the nature and sources of difference over the past 3 months. Questions on binge eating are presented to all participants regardless of the diagnosis. The EDA-5 does not have specific subscale scores, but instead generates eating disorder diagnoses (or absence thereof). An electronic version of the EDA-5, with built in skip logic and adaptive capabilities, can be completed online free of charge (https://eda5.org/).

Reliability and Validity

The very limited existing research on the psychometric properties of the EDA-5 suggests that it has good test–retest reliability across 1 to 2 weeks in a sample of 33 participants (κ=.87 across diagnoses; Sysko et al., 2015). The EDA-5 also has good criterion-oriented validity with near perfect concordance with the EDE (κ=.90), good concordance with clinician interview (κ=.84) in diagnosing BED, and overall 86% sensitivity and 97% specificity (Sysko et al., 2015).

Strengths and Limitations of the EDA-5

In contrast to the EDE, the EDA-5 asks about the frequency of behaviors over a period of time that is more proximal to the administration of the interview, which may help to facilitate recall. Additionally, the EDA-5 can be administered and scored electronically, reducing time and administrator burden. Limitations of the EDA-5 include minimal research on reliability and validity, primary validation on participants evaluated in specialty tertiary care centers, and little data on how the EDA-5 distinguishes between individuals with and without BED.

Self-Report Questionnaires

Aside from semistructured interviews and clinician-administered measures, there are several self-report measures that also assess for BED. We first present general eating disorder measures that include information about BED and then turn to BED-specific measures.

Eating Disorder Examination-Questionnaire

The Eating Disorder Examination-Questionnaire (EDE-Q; Fairburn & Beglin, 1994) is a 28-item measure adapted from the EDE that assesses both cognitive and behavioral eating disorder symptoms. EDE-Q items are worded very similarly to the EDE but refer to the past 28 days only. The EDE-Q is a self-report measure and as such, does not allow the interviewer to request clarification or ask additional questions. Like the EDE, the EDE-Q has four subscale scores, a global score, and includes separate questions to assess binge eating and other features of BED. There are several examples of published norms for subscale scores (e.g., Luce et al., 2008; Mond et al., 2006). The EDE-Q can be downloaded online and is freely available for use (https://www.cbte.co/for-professionals/measures/).

Reliability and Validity

The EDE-Q has adequate test–retest reliability from 1 to 14 days between administration for the four subscales (r=.66–.94) and the behavioral questions regarding binge eating (r=.51–.92; Berg et al., 2012). EDE-Q subscale scores have demonstrated temporal stability over 5–14 months in community samples ranging from r=.57 (Restraint) to r=.77 (Eating Concerns; Mond et al., 2004a). Questions measuring frequency of binge eating episodes demonstrated much lower temporal stability with ϕ=.24–.44 for the presence of these behaviors and τ=.28–.44 for the frequency of the behaviors (Mond et al., 2004a). The internal consistency of the EDE-Q subscales is good, with α ranging from .72 (Eating Concerns) to .89 (Shape Concerns and Weight Concerns) in community samples (Luce et al., 2008; Mond et al., 2004b, 2006). There are no data on the internal consistency of the EDE-Q in individuals with BED.

Although limited, there is also some evidence to suggest that the EDE-Q has good criterion-oriented validity, such that individuals with eating disorders, including "nonpurging bulimia nervosa," diagnosed from clinical interviews tended to score higher on the EDE-Q than those without eating disorders (Mond et al., 2004b). Additionally, studies have found that individuals with obesity who endorsed binge eating on a clinical questionnaire scored higher on the EDE-Q than those with obesity who did not endorse binge eating (Wilson et al., 1993).

The validity of the EDE-Q has also been tested against the EDE. A meta-analysis found no significant difference between subscale scores on the EDE-Q as compared with the EDE, with correlations ranging from r=.68–.76 between the two measures (Berg et al., 2011). Although correlations were smaller between binge eating frequency endorsement on the EDE-Q as compared with the EDE (r=.55), a meta-analysis again found no significant differences (Berg et al., 2011). However, updated research on the validity of EDE-Q in identifying individuals with BED as it is defined in DSM-5 is limited.

Strengths and Limitations of the EDE-Q

Strengths of the EDE-Q include its concordance with the more comprehensive EDE interview, its assessment of both cognitive and behavioral symptoms of eating disorders, and its specific assessment of binge eating behaviors. Limitations include its possible lack of consistency, as some individuals may interpret the often complex questions about eating behaviors and cognitions differently than others. Additionally, to increase generalizability, more research is needed to examine the psychometric properties of the EDE-Q outside of individuals seeking treatment for eating disorders. Furthermore, because the EDE-Q only asks about the past 28 days of behavior, a diagnosis of BED is not possible to make based on EDE-Q administration alone.

Eating Disorder Diagnostic Scale

The Eating Disorder Diagnostic Scale (EDDS; Stice et al., 2000) is a 23-item self-report measure that assesses for eating disorder pathology and the features of a BED diagnosis. It is a brief symptom checklist that has been updated to align with DSM-5 criteria. The EDDS is comprised of questions using ordinal scales, dichotomous questions, and questions about behavioral frequency. The Diagnostic Scale of the EDDS may be used to aid in the diagnosis of anorexia nervosa, bulimia nervosa, or BED, while the Symptom Composite Scale is a general measure of eating pathology. Clinical cut-points for the EDDS Scales may be found in Stice et al., 2000. The EDDS is freely available for download online (https://www.phenxtoolkit.org/protocols/view/120602).

Reliability and Validity

The EDDS has been found to have good internal reliability (α=.89; Stice et al., 2004) and 1-week test-retest reliability (r=.87) for the overall symptom composite, which includes symptoms of BED (Stice et al., 2000). It has also been found to have good criterion-oriented validity (κ=.74), representing consistency between receiving a BED diagnosis on the EDDS as compared with clinical interview (Stice et al., 2000).

Strengths and Limitations of the EDDS

Strengths of the EDDS include its brief length and alignment with DSM-5 criteria, which make it easy to administer and score. One limitation of the EDDS is that research on its psychometric properties was primarily conducted prior to its update for DSM-5, and thus prior to the inclusion of BED as a formal diagnosis.

Questionnaire on Eating and Weight Patterns-5

The Questionnaire on Eating and Weight Patterns-5 (QEWP-5; Yanovski et al., 2015) is a 28-item measure which assesses dieting, weight history, and specific BED criteria. The QEWP was originally created for the assessment of binge eating and other eating disorder symptoms in field trials researching possible BED criteria prior to its inclusion in DSM (Spitzer, Devlin, et al., 1992). It has since been revised to focus specifically on symptoms of BED and to align with the DSM-5 definition of the disorder. It assesses for frequency of behavior in the past 3 months as well as specific rule-out questions for compensatory behaviors to ensure diagnostic clarity between BN and BED. The QEWP is freely available online and includes scoring instructions to detect a possible diagnosis of BED or bulimia nervosa (https://www.phenxtoolkit.org/toolkit_content/PDF/PX651201.pdf).

Reliability and Validity

Over a 3-week period, an older version of the QEWP had moderate temporal stability in diagnosing BED ($\kappa = .58$; Nangle et al., 1994). The same study found that the mean probability for endorsing binge eating was stable from the first administration of the QEWP to the second administration 3 weeks later ($r = .70$; Nangle et al., 1994).

With regard to criterion-oriented validity, the QEWP had sensitivity of 74% and specificity of 35% diagnosing BED as compared with an EDE diagnosis (Celio et al., 2004). It correctly identified the frequency of binge days over the past 6 months in 63% of people but was more effective at identifying high frequency binge eating as compared with low frequency binge eating (Celio et al., 2004). Additionally, the QEWP has resulted in higher scores on behavioral symptoms of BED as well as distress about binge eating as compared with the EDE (Barnes et al., 2011).

Strengths and Limitations of the QEWP

Because the QEWP was designed for use in field trials seeking to understand binge eating, one major strength is that it is highly applicable to community samples and asks specific questions that are pertinent to BED. However, limitations of the QWEP include the small amount of research on its psychometric properties, particularly as it relates to the QWEP-5.

Binge Eating Scale

The Binge Eating Scale (BES; Gormally et al., 1982) is a 16-item measure that assesses for features of binge eating, body dissatisfaction, and patterns of caloric intake. The answers from each question are totaled to form one composite score, with higher scores signifying more severe binge eating problems. It has been used widely to screen for BED in both clinical and nonclinical populations (Duarte et al., 2015). The BES is freely available for download online (https://psychology-tools.com/test/binge-eating-scale).

Reliability and Validity

The BES has been found to have good internal reliability ($\alpha = .88$) and test-retest reliability ($r = .84$) across 1 month in a sample of 1008 participants (Duarte et al., 2015). The criterion-oriented validity of the BES is mixed, with some studies finding that it accurately identified BED (i.e., a cut-off score of 17 on the BES) with sensitivity of 82% and specificity of 98% compared to an EDE diagnosis (Duarte et al., 2015) and others finding similar sensitivity measurements but much lower specificity (20%; Celio et al., 2004).

Strengths and Limitations of the BES

Strengths of the BES include its brevity and easy scoring instructions, which has led to its use in screening for BED in both clinical and nonclinical populations. The primary limitation of the BES is that there is very little research on its psychometric properties in the general population.

Binge Eating Disorder Screener-7

The Binge Eating Disorder Screener-7 (BEDS-7; Herman et al., 2016) is a seven-item measure based directly on DSM-5 criteria for BED. Its questions align with DSM-5 symptoms of BED and its scoring guidelines instruct clinicians to follow up with respondents who answer yes to items related to the presence of binge eating, distress about binge eating, and endorsement of at least one other symptom listed on the screener. The BEDS-7 is freely available for download online (https://assets.takeda.com/content/dam/takeda/imported/nonproduct/pdfs/pro-binge-eating-screener.pdf).

Reliability and Validity

The BEDS-7 appears to have excellent sensitivity (100 %) to detect the presence of BED in individuals who self-report having the disorder, while having low specificity (37.5 %; Herman et al., 2016).

Strengths and Limitations of the BEDS-7

Strengths of the BEDS-7 include its brevity and convenience, meaning that can be administered in a wide variety of settings. However, little is known about its psychometric properties, which reflects a significant limitation.

Limitations of Current Assessment for BED

Although the wide variety of assessment measures has made it possible to screen for and identify individuals with BED across clinical and research settings, there remain improvements that must be made to improve diagnostic clarity across measures. First, outside of the EDE and the EDE-Q, very few measures of BED have been extensively studied. As a result, very little is known about the reliability and validity of other measures, precluding our understanding of their diagnostic specificity and sensitivity. Although many of the measures discussed in sections above are brief and easy to use in clinical practice, more psychometric research is needed to determine which measures should be implemented more broadly.

Aside from validation concerns, one major limitation of all existing measures of BED, and of eating disorders more broadly, is that few studies have examined their use in diverse populations. However, existing research demonstrates a lack of measurement invariance of both the EDE-Q and EDE between White and Hispanic individuals (Serier et al., 2018) and White and Black individuals (Burke et al., 2017). These findings indicate that even the most well-validated measures of BED may capture slightly different constructs in individuals of different races and ethnicities. Additionally, because these measures have been normed on mostly White populations (e.g., Luce et al., 2008; Mond et al., 2006), it is unclear whether established clinical cut-point scores may be appropriate for individuals who are not White. Lack of diversity in assessment goes beyond the measures that currently exist to diagnose BED and has implications for DSM-5 itself. Because many of the earliest validation studies of BED mostly included White participants (Spitzer et al., 1993), it is unclear whether the DSM-5 criteria for BED are culturally sensitive in the first place. For example, there is evidence to suggest that in Black women, binge eating may occur in more collective, social settings (Scott et al., 2019). As such, some of the Criterion B symptoms of BED may not apply to these women (e.g., eating in secret) and instead there may be other symptoms that do apply to this population that are not captured by DSM-5.

In addition to limitations regarding racial inclusivity, current assessment measures may also have difficulty adequately capturing gender differences. These problems are not only reflected in measurement methodologies, but also in the conceptualization of BED. Research suggests that men are less likely to endorse experiencing LOC, which may be related to inconsistencies between masculinity and a lack of control over behaviors or actions (Carey et al., 2017). However, an endorsement of LOC is required for a diagnosis of BED according to DSM-5, with no discussion about populations that may meet all other criteria but be reticent to describe their behavior as lacking in control. As such, researchers and practitioners may fail to identify men who fall into this category. By failing to understand gender norms in the diagnosis of BED, the percentage of men who are diagnosed with BED may be underreported, and this may contribute to overall modest representation of men in clinical and research settings.

There may also be reporting concerns with LGBTQ+ populations. There is evidence that LGBTQ+ individuals endorse higher rates of binge eating than their heterosexual counterparts (Parker & Harriger, 2020). As such, appropriate assessment of BED in these populations is critical. Recent research has begun to establish norms for measures such as the EDE-Q for use in these populations (Klimek et al., 2021; Nagata et al., 2020, 2021). However, more work is needed to understand whether these populations may exhibit unique symptoms of BED that are not captured by current assessment measures. Additionally, LGBTQ+ individuals are not monolithic and have unique and varied experiences, and it will be important to understand how nuanced aspects of gender/sexual identity contributes to identification of BED across settings.

In addition to needing more research and validation of measures of BED in diverse adult populations, very little research has been conducted on the assessment of BED in children and adolescents. Although youth are more likely to endorse experiencing LOC without overeating, thus not meeting full criteria for BED (Tanofsky-Kraff et al., 2020), BED occurs in approximately 1% of youth (Marzilli et al., 2018). Nevertheless, there is a dearth of research on assessment of either BED or subclinical forms of LOC in youth and few measures that have been adapted for use in children.

Finally, one limitation that is inherent in all the measures presented in this chapter is their reliance on self-report. Even carefully crafted, semistructured interviews require significant reliance on retrospective recall, and no objective measures exist upon which to validate self-report of binge eating. As such, it is important to consider the reporting biases that may occur both intentionally and unintentionally.

Other Assessment Considerations

There are several research methods that have been applied to the assessment of BED features that minimize retrospective recall biases inherent in interview- or questionnaire-based methods. These include ecological momentary assessment, which may be used to assess binge eating and related distress in near real time in the natural environment via smartphone or other mobile device; feeding laboratory studies, which facilitate objective measurement of eating behavior via *in vivo* observation, and corresponding subjective self-report ratings of LOC and distress, in the laboratory setting under a variety of conditions (e.g., instructions to binge versus eat normally); and 24-hour dietary recall to ascertain detailed recall of eating behavior in the past 24 hours which may include multiple passes to minimize omission of food or beverage items. Each of these assessment methods has numerous strengths and limitations in the assessment of BED features, including inability to diagnose BED and concerns about feasibility and representativeness of eating episodes; as these methods are reviewed more extensively in other chapters (e.g., see Chapters 17 and 18), we will not cover their psychometric properties here.

Conclusions

A wide variety of measures exist to aid in the assessment and diagnosis of BED. The EDE and EDE-Q are the most widely researched measures and may be best used in research settings with trained staff, but more research is needed to assess their psychometric properties regarding the assessment of binge eating behavior. Several self-report measures can also be used to assess for BED, and these may be more appropriate for clinical and primary care settings where time is limited. However, many self-report measures lack research on reliability and validity, especially in community samples. Finally, there is a lack of research on the inclusivity of existing measures of BED in diverse populations, making it difficult to know whether they are reliable and valid outside of White, female populations. Taken together, BED is a clinically significant eating disorder, and rigorous measurement is needed to understand its features and limit its impact on public health.

References

Adriaanse, M.A., Prinsen, S., Witt Huberts, J.C. de, Ridder, D.T.D. de, & Evers, C. (2016). "I ate too much so I must have been sad": Emotions as a confabulated reason for overeating. *Appetite, 103*, 318–323. https://doi.org/10.1016/j.appet.2016.04.028

American Psychiatric Association. (1980). *Diagnostic and statistical manual of mental disorders (DSM-III)*. American Psychiatric Publishing.

American Psychiatric Association. (2013). *Diagnostic and statistical manual of mental disorders* (5th ed.). American Psychiatric Publishing. https://doi.org/10.1176/appi.books.9780890425596

Barnes, R.D., Masheb, R.M., White, M.A., & Grilo, C.M. (2011). Comparison of methods for identifying and assessing obese patients with binge eating disorder in primary care settings. *International Journal of Eating Disorders, 44*(2), 157–163. https://doi.org/10.1002/eat.20802

Bartholome, L.T., Raymond, N.C., Lee, S.S., Peterson, C.B., & Warren, C.S. (2006). Detailed analysis of binges in obese women with binge eating disorder: Comparisons using multiple methods of data collection. *International Journal of Eating Disorders, 39*(8), 685–693. https://doi.org/10.1002/eat.20289

Berg, K.C., Peterson, C.B., Frazier, P., & Crow, S.J. (2011). Convergence of scores on the interview and questionnaire versions of the Eating Disorder Examination: A meta-analytic review. *Psychological Assessment, 23*(3), 714–724. https://doi.org/10.1037/a0023246

Berg, K.C., Peterson, C.B., Frazier, P., & Crow, S.J. (2012). Psychometric evaluation of the Eating Disorder Examination and Eating Disorder Examination-Questionnaire: A systematic review of the literature. *International Journal of Eating Disorders, 45*(3), 428–438. https://doi.org/10.1002/eat.20931

Burke, N.L., Tanofsky-Kraff, M., Crosby, R., Mehari, R.D., Marwitz, S.E., Broadney, M.M., Shomaker, L.B., Kelly, N.R., Schvey, N.A., Cassidy, O., Yanovski, S.Z., & Yanovski, J.A. (2017). Measurement invariance of the Eating Disorder Examination in Black and White children and adolescents. *International Journal of Eating Disorders, 50*(7), 758–768. https://doi.org/10.1002/eat.22713

Carey, J.B., Saules, K.K., & Carr, M.M. (2017). A qualitative analysis of men's experiences of binge eating. *Appetite, 116*, 184–195. https://doi.org/10.1016/j.appet.2017.04.030

Celio, A.A., Wilfley, D.E., Crow, S.J., Mitchell, J., & Walsh, B.T. (2004). A comparison of the binge eating scale, questionnaire for eating and weight patterns-revised, and eating disorder examination questionnaire with instructions with the eating disorder examination in the assessment of binge eating disorder and its symptoms. *International Journal of Eating Disorders, 36*(4), 434–444. https://doi.org/10.1002/eat.20057

Cooper, Z., & Fairburn, C. (1987). The eating disorder examination: A semi-structured interview for the assessment of the specific psychopathology of eating disorders. *International Journal of Eating Disorders, 6*(1), 1–8. https://doi.org/10.1002/1098-108X(198701)6:1<1::AID-EAT2260060102>3.0.CO;2-9

Cossrow, N., Pawaskar, M., Witt, E.A., Ming, E.E., Victor, T.W., Herman, B.K., Wadden, T.A., & Erder, M.H. (2016). Estimating the prevalence of binge eating disorder in a community sample from the United States: Comparing DSM-IV-TR and DSM-5 criteria. *Journal of Clinical Psychiatry, 77*(8), 15456. https://doi.org/10.4088/JCP.15m10059

Duarte, C., Pinto-Gouveia, J., & Ferreira, C. (2015). Expanding binge eating assessment: Validity and screening value of the Binge Eating Scale in women from the general population. *Eating Behaviors, 18*, 41–47. https://doi.org/10.1016/j.eatbeh.2015.03.007

Fairburn, C.G., & Beglin, S.J. (1994). Assessment of eating disorders: Interview or self-report questionnaire? *International Journal of Eating Disorders, 16*(4), 363–370. https://doi.org/10.1002/1098-108X(199412)16:4<363::AID-EAT2260160405>3.0.CO;2-#

Fairburn, C.G., & Cooper, Z. (1993). *The eating disorder examination* (12th ed.). Guilford.

Goldschmidt, A.B. (2017). Are loss of control while eating and overeating valid constructs? A critical review of the literature. *Obesity Reviews, 18*(4), 412–449. https://doi.org/10.1111/obr.12491

Gormally, J., Black, S., Daston, S., & Rardin, D. (1982). The assessment of binge eating severity among obese persons. *Addictive Behaviors, 7*(1), 47–55. https://doi.org/10.1016/0306-4603(82)90024-7

Grilo, C.M., Crosby, R.D., Peterson, C.B., Masheb, R.M., White, M.A., Crow, S.J., Wonderlich, S.A., & Mitchell, J.E. (2010). Factor structure of the Eating Disorder Examination Interview in patients with binge-eating disorder. *Obesity, 18*(5), 977–981. https://doi.org/10.1038/oby.2009.321

Grilo, C.M., Lozano, C., & Elder, K.A. (2005). Inter-rater and test-retest reliability of the Spanish language version of the Eating Disorder Examination Interview: Clinical and research implications. *Journal of Psychiatric Practice, 11*(4), 231–240. https://doi.org/10.1097/00131746-200507000-00003

Grilo, C.M., Masheb, R.M., Lozano-Blanco, C., & Barry, D.T. (2004). Reliability of the Eating Disorder Examination in patients with binge eating disorder. *International Journal of Eating Disorders, 35*(1), 80–85. https://doi.org/10.1002/eat.10238

Haedt-Matt, A.A., & Keel, P.K. (2011). Revisiting the affect regulation model of binge eating: A meta-analysis of studies using ecological momentary assessment. *Psychological Bulletin, 137*(4), 660–681. https://doi.org/10.1037/a0023660

Harik, P., Clauser, B.E., Grabovsky, I., Nungester, R.J., Swanson, D., & Nandakumar, R. (2009). An examination of rater drift within a generalizability theory framework. *Journal of Educational Measurement, 46*(1), 43–58. https://doi.org/10.1111/j.1745-3984.2009.01068.x

Herman, B.K., Deal, L.S., DiBenedetti, D.B., Nelson, L., Fehnel, S.E., & Brown, T.M. (2016). Development of the 7-Item Binge-Eating Disorder Screener (BEDS-7). *The Primary Care Companion for CNS Disorders, 18*(2), 10. https://doi.org/10.4088/PCC.15m01896

Hudson, J.I., Hiripi, E., Pope, H.G., & Kessler, R.C. (2007). The prevalence and correlates of eating disorders in the National Comorbidity Survey Replication. *Biological Psychiatry, 61*(3), 348–358. https://doi.org/10.1016/j.biopsych.2006.03.040

Kessler, R.C., Berglund, P.A., Chiu, W.T., Deitz, A.C., Hudson, J.I., Shahly, V., Aguilar-Gaxiola, S., Alonso, J., Angermeyer, M.C., Benjet, C., Bruffaerts, R., Girolamo, G. de, Graaf, R. de, Maria Haro, J., Kovess-Masfety, V., O'Neill, S., Posada-Villa, J., Sasu, C., Scott, K., ... Xavier, M. (2013). The prevalence and correlates of binge eating disorder in the World Health Organization World Mental Health surveys. *Biological Psychiatry, 73*(9), 904–914. https://doi.org/10.1016/j.biopsych.2012.11.020

Klimek, P., Convertino, A.D., Pennesi, J.-L., Gonzales IV, M., Roesch, S.C., Nagata, J.M., & Blashill, A.J. (2021). Confirmatory factor and measurement invariance analyses of the Eating Disorder Examination Questionnaire in sexual minority men and women. *International Journal of Eating Disorders, 54*(5), 745–754. https://doi.org/10.1002/eat.23488

Kornstein, S.G. (2017). Epidemiology and recognition of binge-eating disorder in psychiatry and primary care. *The Journal of Clinical Psychiatry, 78*(Suppl. 1), 6543. https://doi.org/10.4088/JCP.sh16003su1c.01

Lecrubier, Y., Sheehan, D., Weiller, E., Amorim, P., Bonora, I., Harnett Sheehan, K., Janavs, J., & Dunbar, G. (1997). The Mini International Neuropsychiatric Interview (MINI). A short diagnostic structured interview: Reliability and validity according to the CIDI. *European Psychiatry, 12*(5), 224–231. https://doi.org/10.1016/S0924-9338(97)83296-8

Luce, K.H., Crowther, J.H., & Pole, M. (2008). Eating Disorder Examination Questionnaire (EDE-Q): Norms for undergraduate women. *International Journal of Eating Disorders, 41*(3), 273–276. https://doi.org/10.1002/eat.20504

Marzilli, E., Cerniglia, L., & Cimino, S. (2018). A narrative review of binge eating disorder in adolescence: Prevalence, impact, and psychological treatment strategies. *Adolescent Health, Medicine and Therapeutics, 9*, 17–30. https://doi.org/10.2147/AHMT.S148050

Mond, J.M., Hay, P.J., Rodgers, B., & Owen, C. (2006). Eating Disorder Examination Questionnaire (EDE-Q): Norms for young adult women. *Behaviour Research and Therapy, 44*(1), 53–62. https://doi.org/10.1016/j.brat.2004.12.003

Mond, J.M., Hay, P.J., Rodgers, B., Owen, C., & Beumont, P.J.V. (2004a). Temporal stability of the Eating Disorder Examination Questionnaire. *International Journal of Eating Disorders, 36*(2), 195–203. https://doi.org/10.1002/eat.20017

Mond, J.M., Hay, P.J., Rodgers, B., Owen, C., & Beumont, P.J.V. (2004b). Validity of the Eating Disorder Examination Questionnaire (EDE-Q) in screening for eating disorders in community samples. *Behaviour Research and Therapy, 42*(5), 551–567. https://doi.org/10.1016/S0005-7967(03)00161-X

Nagata, J.M., Compte, E.J., Murray, S.B., Schauer, R., Pak, E., Flentje, A., Capriotti, M.R., Lubensky, M.E., Lunn, M.R., & Obedin-Maliver, J. (2021). Community norms for the eating disorder examination questionnaire (EDE-Q) among cisgender bisexual plus women and men. *Eating and Weight Disorders - Studies on Anorexia, Bulimia and Obesity, 26*(7), 2227–2239. https://doi.org/10.1007/s40519-020-01070-8

Nagata, J.M., Murray, S.B., Flentje, A., Compte, E.J., Schauer, R., Pak, E., Capriotti, M.R., Lubensky, M.E., Lunn, M.R., & Obedin-Maliver, J. (2020). Eating disorder attitudes and disordered eating behaviors as measured by the Eating Disorder Examination Questionnaire (EDE-Q) among cisgender lesbian women. *Body Image, 34*, 215–220. https://doi.org/10.1016/j.bodyim.2020.06.005

Nangle, D.W., Johnson, W.G., Carr-Nangle, R.E., & Engler, L.B. (1994). Binge eating disorder and the proposed DSM-IV criteria: Psychometric analysis of the Questionnaire of Eating and Weight Patterns.

International Journal of Eating Disorders, 16(2), 147–157. https://doi.org/10.1002/1098-108X(199409)16:2<147::AID-EAT2260160206>3.0.CO;2-P

Parker, L.L., & Harriger, J.A. (2020). Eating disorders and disordered eating behaviors in the LGBT population: A review of the literature. *Journal of Eating Disorders, 8*(1), 51. https://doi.org/10.1186/s40337-020-00327-y

Peterson, C.B., Miller, K.B., Johnson-Lind, J., Crow, S.J., & Thuras, P. (2007). The accuracy of symptom recall in eating disorders. *Comprehensive Psychiatry, 48*(1), 51–56. https://doi.org/10.1016/j.comppsych.2006.03.010

Polivy, J., & Herman, C.P. (1985). Dieting and binging: A causal analysis. *American Psychologist, 40*(2), 193–201. https://doi.org/10.1037/0003-066X.40.2.193

Pollert, G.A., Engel, S.G., Schreiber-Gregory, D.N., Crosby, R.D., Cao, L., Wonderlich, S.A., Tanofsky-Kraff, M., & Mitchell, J.E. (2013). The role of eating and emotion in binge eating disorder and loss of control eating. *International Journal of Eating Disorders, 46*(3), 233–238. https://doi.org/10.1002/eat.22061

Rizvi, S.L., Peterson, C.B., Crow, S.J., & Agras, W.S. (2000). Test-retest reliability of the eating disorder examination. *International Journal of Eating Disorders, 28*(3), 311–316. https://doi.org/10.1002/1098-108X(200011)28:3<311::AID-EAT8>3.0.CO;2-K

Scott, T.N., Gil-Rivas, V., & Cachelin, F.M. (2019). The need for cultural adaptations to health interventions for African American women: A qualitative analysis. *Cultural Diversity and Ethnic Minority Psychology, 25*(3), 331–341. https://doi.org/10.1037/cdp0000228

Serier, K.N., Smith, J.E., & Yeater, E.A. (2018). Confirmatory factor analysis and measurement invariance of the Eating Disorder Examination Questionnaire (EDE-Q) in a non-clinical sample of non-Hispanic White and Hispanic women. *Eating Behaviors, 31*, 53–59. https://doi.org/10.1016/j.eatbeh.2018.08.004

Spitzer, R.L., Devlin, M., Walsh, B.T., Hasin, D., Wing, R., Marcus, M., Stunkard, A., Wadden, T., Yanovski, S., Agras, S., Mitchell, J., & Nonas, C. (1992). Binge eating disorder: A multisite field trial of the diagnostic criteria. *International Journal of Eating Disorders, 11*(3), 191–203. https://doi.org/10.1002/1098-108X(199204)11:3<191::AID-EAT2260110302>3.0.CO;2-S

Spitzer, R.L., Williams, J., Gibbon, M., & First, M. (1992). The Structured Clinical Interview for DSM-III-R (SCID): I: History, rationale, and description. *Archives of General Psychiatry, 49*(8), 624–629. https://doi.org/10.1001/archpsyc.1992.01820080032005

Spitzer, R.L., Yanovski, S., Wadden, T., Wing, R., Marcus, M.D., Stunkard, A., Devlin, M., Mitchell, J., Hasin, D., & Horne, R.L. (1993). Binge eating disorder: Its further validation in a multisite study. *International Journal of Eating Disorders, 13*(2), 137–153. https://doi.org/10.1002/1098-108X(199303)13:2<137::AID-EAT2260130202>3.0.CO;2-#

Stice, E., Fisher, M., & Martinez, E. (2004). Eating Disorder Diagnostic Scale: Additional evidence of reliability and validity. *Psychological Assessment, 16*(1), 60–71. https://doi.org/10.1037/1040-3590.16.1.60

Stice, E., Telch, C.F., & Rizvi, S.L. (2000). Development and validation of the Eating Disorder Diagnostic Scale: A brief self-report measure of anorexia, bulimia, and binge-eating disorder. *Psychological Assessment, 12*(2), 123–131. https://doi.org/10.1037/1040-3590.12.2.123

Stunkard, A.J. (1959). Eating patterns and obesity. *The Psychiatric Quarterly, 33*, 284–295. https://doi.org/10.1007/BF01575455

Sysko, R., Glasofer, D.R., Hildebrandt, T., Klimek, P., Mitchell, J.E., Berg, K.C., Peterson, C.B., Wonderlich, S.A., & Walsh, B.T. (2015). The eating disorder assessment for DSM-5 (EDA-5): Development and validation of a structured interview for feeding and eating disorders. *International Journal of Eating Disorders, 48*(5), 452–463. https://doi.org/10.1002/eat.22388

Tanofsky-Kraff, M., Schvey, N.A., & Grilo, C.M. (2020). A developmental framework of binge-eating disorder based on pediatric loss of control eating. *American Psychologist, 75*(2), 189–203. https://doi.org/10.1037/amp0000592

Wilfley, D.E., Schwartz, M.B., Spurrell, E.B., & Fairburn, C.G. (2000). Using the eating disorder examination to identify the specific psychopathology of binge eating disorder. *International Journal of Eat-*

ing Disorders, 27(3), 259–269. https://doi.org/10.1002/(SICI)1098-108X(200004)27:3<259::AID-EAT2>3.0.CO;2-G

Wilson, G.T., Nonas, C.A., & Rosenblum, G.D. (1993). Assessment of binge eating in obese patients. *International Journal of Eating Disorders, 13*(1), 25–33. https://doi.org/10.1002/1098-108X(199301)13:1<25::AID-EAT2260130104>3.0.CO;2-T

Wolfe, B.E., Baker, C.W., Smith, A.T., & Kelly-Weeder, S. (2009). Validity and utility of the current definition of binge eating. *International Journal of Eating Disorders, 42*(8), 674–686. https://doi.org/10.1002/eat.20728

Yanovski, S.Z., Marcus, M.D., Wadden, T.A., & Walsh, B.T. (2015). The Questionnaire on Eating and Weight Patterns-5 (QEWP-5): An updated screening instrument for binge eating disorder. *International Journal of Eating Disorders, 48*(3), 259–261. https://doi.org/10.1002/eat.22372

Chapter 11

Assessment of Other Eating Disorders

Kelly C. Allison

Department of Psychiatry, Perelman School of Medicine,
University of Pennsylvania, PA, USA

Introduction

There are additional "Feeding and Eating Disorders" that are specified in the *Diagnostic and Statistical Manual of Mental Disorders* (5th ed.; DSM-5; American Psychiatric Association, 2013), as well as the *International Statistical Classification of Diseases and Related Health Problems* (11th ed.; ICD-11; World Health Organization, 2019) that deserve attention in this volume. Night eating syndrome (NES) is considered under the category "Other Specified Feeding and Eating Disorders," while avoidant/restrictive food intake disorder (ARFID), pica, and rumination disorder comprise the "Feeding Disorders." Purging disorder is also listed as an "Other Specified" disorder, but assessment for this is similar to bulimia nervosa and will not be covered in this chapter. The state of the literature for assessment approaches to each of these disorders varies from established, in the case of NES, to moderately established, e.g., ARFID, to minimal, e.g., rumination disorder. Available assessment approaches for each will be reviewed.

Night Eating Syndrome

NES is a shift in the circadian pattern of eating such that at least a quarter of one's daily food intake is consumed after the evening meal and/or an individual is waking up to eat at least twice per week (Allison, Lundgren, O'Reardon, et al., 2010). Those with NES are awake and have awareness of their nighttime eating. They also have to experience at least three of the following symptoms at least half of the time: lack of hunger or omission of breakfast, an urge to eat to fall (back) to sleep, sleep onset or sleep maintenance insomnia, the belief that one must eat to fall (back) asleep, and depressed mood that often worsens in the evening (Allison, Lundgren, O'Reardon, et al., 2010). These symptoms should be present for at least 3 months to establish diagnosis. The DSM-5 defines the symptoms more generally, with "recurrent episodes of night eating, as manifested by eating after awakening from sleep or by excessive food consumption after the evening meal," with awareness (American Psychiatric Association, 2013). The DSM-5 also states that nighttime eating cannot be better explained by binge eating disorder or other mental or physical disorders. Both criteria state that distress or impairment must be present.

There are two screening questionnaires for NES that have been used most widely, the Night Eating Questionnaire (NEQ; Allison et al., 2008) and the Night Eating Diagnostic Questionnaire (NEDQ; Nolan & Geliebter, 2017, 2019). Further, the Night Eating Symptom Scale (NESS; Lundgren et al., 2012) is a self-report questionnaire based on the NEQ but is designed to assess symptoms over the past week in order to monitor symptom change over time, such as during treatment. The Night Eating Syndrome History and Inventory (NESHI; Lundgren et al., 2012) is a semistructured interview that contains the NEQ items and is designed to confirm a diagnosis of NES based on the research criteria. Finally, food and sleep diaries as well as actigraphy or other wearables can be used to assess for the presence of NES.

NES Self-Report Questionnaires

Night Eating Questionnaire (NEQ)

The NEQ was first drafted by Dr. Albert Stunkard and colleagues in the late 1990s, but not published. It was later refined and validated in 2008 across three samples: (1) an Internet-based sample of persons identifying as having night-eating symptoms (n=1980), (2) patients with NES (n=81), and (3) bariatric surgery patients (n=194; Allison et al., 2008). The NEQ originally contained 14 items that map on to the research criteria. These include items on morning hunger and the time of first food intake (two items); proportion of one's daily intake consumed after dinner (one item); presence of food cravings or degree of control over eating before bedtime and during awakenings (four items); presence of initial insomnia (one item), mood and circadian pattern of mood symptoms (two items); frequency of awakenings and nocturnal ingestions (three items); and an item that assesses level of awareness of nocturnal ingestions (this item is included to differentiate NES from sleep related eating disorder and is not included in the total score). Options range from 0 to 3 for each item, generating a total possible score between 0 and 52. Four factors were identified from these items, including (1) Nocturnal Ingestions, (2) Evening Hyperphagia, (3) Morning Anorexia, and (4) Mood/Sleep. Cut-off scores for screening using the total score were established at 25, with a positive predictive value (i.e., the number or participants who screened positive for NES that was later confirmed with a diagnostic interview) of 41%, for those wanting to cast a wide net. A score of 30 is suggested for more stringent screening, with a positive predictive value of 73%. Four additional items have been added to the NEQ by the authors to assess for upset, guilt, shame, and how much symptoms have affected daily living (available from the author). These items are not included in the total score for screening but are used to confirm if distress is associated with the symptoms, which would be required for diagnosis of NES. Finally, the NEQ has been translated and validated in many languages, including German (Meule, Allison, & Platte, 2014), French (Gallant et al., 2012), Spanish (Moizé et al., 2012), Portuguese (Dantas et al., 2012; Harb et al., 2008), Korean (Kim, Kim, & Choi, 2016), Italian (Innamorati et al., 2018), Swedish (Allison et al., 2014), Arabic (Elsadek, Hamid, & Allison, 2014), Hebrew (Latzer et al., 2014), Turkish (Atasoy et al., 2014), and Mandarin (Tu et al., 2017; He et al., 2019).

There are some considerations and limitations associated with using the NEQ. First, individuals, particularly those with poor health literacy, may find it difficult to estimate their percentage of their total daily intake that they consume after dinner. This requires awareness of how large (proportionally speaking) one's daytime meals and snacks are in comparison to their postdinner snacking (both evening and during the nighttime). Second, there are two potential stopping points on the NEQ. If an individual reports that they do not wake during the night, they do not go on to complete Items 10–14 which all pertain to nighttime awakenings and ingestions. Additionally, if an individual does not eat during awakenings, they would stop at Item 12 and not complete the items that describe the degree of awareness and control over nocturnal ingestions. As such, persons who may meet criteria for NES with only evening hyperphagia (those who consume at least 25 % of their intake after dinner but do not wake to eat) would be less likely to score above a 25 during screening and be properly included as a probable case of NES. Finally, the NEQ is a general assessment of symptoms and does not ascertain an exact percentage of intake consumed after dinner or an average number of nocturnal ingestions per week. These key elements of the NES diagnosis would need to be confirmed via interview or other methods.

Night Eating Diagnostic Questionnaire (NEDQ)

The NEDQ was conceived by Drs. Allan Geliebter, Marci Gluck, and colleagues at Columbia University to diagnose NES (in contrast to the NEQ, which is considered a screening tool). It was established as a face-valid assessment of night eating symptoms, as its name suggests, to diagnose NES. The NEDQ contains 22 items assessing usual sleep routine, morning anorexia and breakfast frequency, timing of dinner and percentage of food consumed after dinner and after 7 pm, presence of an urge to eat in the evening or nighttime, insomnia symptoms, number of nocturnal ingestions per week and duration of this behavior, awareness of nocturnal eating, and assessment of impairment in functioning. The item response options vary from open ended responses, to "yes/no," to "not at all," "somewhat," or "extremely." It does not yield a total score, but instead rates whether someone does or does not meet full criteria for NES, or if that person falls on a continuum from normal/no night eating, mild night eating, moderate night eating, or full-syndrome night eating (Lundgren et al., 2012; Nolan & Geliebter, 2017, 2019).

Nolan and Geliebter (2017) established convergent validity with the NEQ among a sample of 254 students and 468 general community members. The measures were correlated at $r=.25$, with 4.6 % of participants meeting the NEQ's cut score of 25 and 6.9 % being identified as having some degree of NES on the NEDQ. Overall, 56 % of those who met criteria for NES on the NEDQ also scored above the cut score of 25 on the NES, with the NEDQ including more individuals who would meet NES criteria by having evening hyperphagia without nocturnal ingestions. Analysis of the NEDQ's factor structure yielded a single factor, suggesting strong cohesion across the items (Nolan & Geliebter, 2019). Further, psychopathology factors, such as sleep and depression, were each related to several NEDQ items. Nolan and Geliebter (2019) conclude that the NEDQ provides a valid diagnostic questionnaire for NES based on the research criteria.

Night Eating Symptom Scale (NESS)

The NESS contains 13 items that are similar in content to the NEQ items but oriented to the rater's experience of these symptoms in the past week (Lundgren et al., 2012). It is designed to serve as a symptom-tracker over time for treatment or longitudinal symptom fluctuations (e.g., Allison, Lundgren, Moore et al., 2010; O'Reardon et al., 2006). Unlike the NEQ, the NESS's items prompt the responder for their specific percentage of intake consumed after dinner and the number of awakenings and nocturnal ingestions in the previous week. It does not contain an assessment of level of awareness, as this is typically established at a baseline assessment of symptoms. There are no validation studies associated with this measure.

NES Interview-Based Assessments

Night Eating Syndrome History and Inventory (NESHI)

The NESHI is a semistructured interview based on the items of the NEQ and the research criteria that can be used to confirm a diagnosis of NES (Lundgren et al., 2012). As a clinician-administered interview, it has the advantage over the NEQ of helping respondents to consider their typical 24-hour eating schedules with a recall of their usual meal and snack intake for the past month (NESHI Section 1). Then, the clinician and respondent can collaboratively arrive at the percentage of energy intake that they are consuming after the evening meal. This section also includes details about what types of foods are consumed in between dinner and bedtime as well as during nocturnal ingestions. Section 1 also reviews the criteria for NES as covered by the NEQ items. Section 2 focuses on items related to distress and impairment in functioning related to night eating, as well as items to assess if compensatory behaviors are ever used in relation to nighttime eating. Section 3 contains items to assess the history and course of NES, including age of onset, potential triggers, the stability of symptoms in different settings and over time, and whether there are any family members who also engage in night eating. Section 3 also asks about treatment history to date. Finally, Section 4 provides guidelines for the clinician-interviewer to score the interview and arrive on diagnosis status as "none," "subthreshold," or "full threshold."

This measure has been used to establish diagnosis in several treatment studies of NES (e.g., Allison, Lundgren, Moore et al., 2010; Allison et al., 2013; O'Reardon et al., 2006) as well as assessment studies to establish the presence or prevalence of NES (e.g., Allison et al., 2014; Lundgren et al., 2006). The NESHI was used to test the validity of the use of two screening items focused on evening hyperphagia and the presence of nocturnal ingestions to test the prevalence of night eating in the Swedish Twin Registry (Allison et al., 2014). Based on the NESHI diagnosis status, the screening questions yielding a positive predictive value of .66 and .67, a negative predictive value of .52 and .45, a sensitivity of .62 and .63, and specificity of .56 and .50 for the evening hyperphagia and nocturnal ingestion screening questions, respectively. As with other disorders, it would be expected that a clinical interview would yield fewer positive cases of NES than a screening questionnaire or diagnostic instrument. However, more validation work is needed across these assessment instruments for NES.

Eating Disorder Examination (EDE)

If the Eating Disorder Examination (EDE, edition 17D; Fairburn et al., 2014) is being used for more general assessment of eating disorders, there are items included that could be used to screen for the presence of night eating. Under the "Pattern of Eating" item, there is a prompt for number of nocturnal eating episodes over the past 28 days, as well as a question regarding how awake and aware respondents are during these episodes. From this same item, the interviewer can ascertain the frequency of skipping breakfast and the typical time or meal when the respondent starts eating for the day. However, the other aspects of night eating are not assessed in the EDE.

Other Assessment Tools for NES

Other forms of assessment, particularly technology-based approaches, could be useful in characterizing the eating and sleep behaviors associated with NES. Food and sleep diaries could be used, either traditional paper and pencil measures, or food and sleep tracking apps. However, for food tracking apps, most do not include a format where the time of each eating episode can be measured. Therefore, in clinical practice, it is helpful for patients to keep notes of the times of their eating episodes in the notes section, if that is available on the program they are using to track their intake. Wrist actigraphy can also confirm sleep onset, offset, and awakenings for research studies, through an objective measure, which is more accurate than keeping sleep diaries. For clinical practice, wearable activity and sleep technologies often include sleep assessments that could be helpful for patients in tracking their pattern of awakenings associated with eating, as well as improvements in their sleep quality and duration over the course of treatment. Finally, the Automated Self-Administered Recall System-24 is a free research-based tool developed by the National Cancer Institute. It provides a guided computer-based recall of all food and beverages consumed over the previous 24-hour period (Subar et al., 2012). This would be preferable to using food diaries for more accuracy in research studies, and it is often assigned on a weekday and weekend day to have a sampling of eating patterns for both.

Avoidant/Restrictive Food Intake Disorder

ARFID is characterized by what is commonly called extremely picky eating or fear of new foods (food neophobia) that can affect the range of foods and the overall amount of food eaten. It differs from anorexia nervosa in that the restrictive eating is not an attempt to lose or maintain a very low weight. It interferes with an individual's ability to meet their nutritional and/or energy needs leading to significant weight loss, or failure to thrive in children, a significant nutritional deficit, reliance on nutritional supplementation orally or through enteral feeding, and/or interference and psychosocial functioning, usually in the form of avoiding situations where eating is expected (American Psychiatric Association, 2013). It is also specified that these issues are not influenced by the availability of food in one's environment or the result of a cultural practice. Finally, other medical and psychological issues should be addressed and ruled out as the cause of the picky eating. There are three common presenting reasons for food avoidance among those with ARFID, including a fear of eating such that one is afraid of choking or vomiting, disgust for food often associated with sensory sensitivities resulting in gagging when trying foods, and/or a general lack of interest in foods (American Psychiatric Association, 2013; Thomas & Eddy, 2018).

The assessment measures published thus far for ARFID include surveys that specifically target the triggers and DSM symptoms of the disorder as well as instruments that assess ARFID, pica, and rumination disorder together (see Dinkler & Bryant-Waugh, 2021 for review). Many of the screening instruments are brief, and there are versions that target children and adults, as well as parent-report questionnaires for younger children.

ARFID Self-Report Questionnaires

There are several self-report surveys for ARFID, some with published validation data and others still under development. There are also surveys that focus on a specific area or driver of ARFID, such as fear or disgust related to eating. This section focuses only on the published instruments and those that provide a comprehensive assessment of ARFID.

Eating Disorders in Youth-Questionnaire

First, the Eating Disorders in Youth-Questionnaire (EDY-Q) is a 14-item survey based on the DSM-5 ARFID criteria (American Psychiatric Association, 2013) intended to screen for early-onset restrictive eating difficulties in middle childhood (8–13 years old; Kurz et al., 2015; Kurz et al., 2016) with more recent validation studies in adults (Hilbert et al., 2021). Ten items cover three common eating disturbances, including food avoidance emotional disorder, selective eating, and functional dysphagia. Two items cover shape and weight concern to differentiate these issues from anorexia nervosa or other eating disorders, and the final two items screen for pica and rumination disorder. The first 10 items are rated on a 0 = *never* to 6 = *always* scale, which yields a total score. However, to screen positive for ARFID, the first four items covering the DSM criteria were required to be present at least *often* (≥ 4) and the weight and shape concern items were to be endorsed less than *sometimes* (< 3).

Point prevalence of ARFID is lower in adults at 0.8 % (Hilbert et al., 2021) as compared to 3.2 % in children (Kurz et al., 2015). However, the prevalence estimates for the separate factors were similar for both groups, ranging from 1.2 % for fear of swallowing up to 31.3 % for selective eating behavior (Hilbert et al., 2021; Schmidt et al., 2018). One limitation of note is that the EDY-Q does not currently include an item to assess the impact of ARFID symptoms on psychosocial impairment.

Nine-Item Avoidant/Restrictive Intake Screen

The Nine-Item Avoidant/Restrictive Intake Screen (NIAS; Zickgraf & Ellis, 2018) was developed based on chart reviews and interviews of ARFID patients presenting for treatment, as well as literature-based reviews of previous assessment approaches. The nine items are anchored on a 6-point scale, with total scores ranging from 0 to 45. Three items load on each of three subscales, including Picky Eating, Appetite, and Fear, each of which have scores ranging from 0 to 15. The NIAS showed convergent validity with the Adult Eating Behavior Questionnaire, a 35-item measure assessing food approach and avoidance (Hunot et al., 2016). Picky Eating correlated with Food Fussiness and Food Neophobia; Appetite was positively associated with four food avoidance subscales and negatively with three food approach subscales; and Fear was positively correlated with Emotional Overeating, Food Responsiveness, and Slowness of Eating.

While the NIAS subscales show convergent validity with factors associated with ARFID as appropriate for a screening tool, it does not directly assess for weight loss, nutritional deficiencies, dependence on nutritional supplementation, or psychosocial impairment, which are needed to make an ARFID diagnosis. One solution has been to combine the NIAS with a 14-item ARFID Symptom Checklist (ARFID-cl) based on ARFID diagnostic items from the Structured Clinical Interview for DSM-5 (First et al., 2015) to be able to map onto the DSM diagnostic criteria (Zickgraf et al., 2022). Further work is needed to provide cut scores for clinical levels of each of these ARFID symptoms and streamlined procedures for administering these measures together.

ARFID-Brief Screener

The ARFID-Brief Screener (ARFID-BS) is a parent-reported screening tool for assessment of ARFID in young children, ages 4 to 7 years (Dinkler et al., 2022). The items were designed to match the DSM-5 criteria, with five items for Criterion A (avoidance or restriction of food intake), one item for Criterion C (eating disturbance not attributable to weight or shape concerns), and one item for Criterion D (eating disturbance not attributable to concurrent medical condition). Criterion B, eating disturbance due to lack of food availability or culturally sanctioned eating behavior was not included as it was judged not likely in the sample being assessed. Finally, three areas, or “drivers” of food difficulties described above were assessed with one item each: sensory sensitivity to characteristics of food, lack of interest in eating, and fear of aversive consequences of eating. Response sets varied depending on the type of question from “Yes, currently,” “Yes, earlier,” or “No, never” to “Yes/No,” or “Never to Always” on a 5-point scale. Going forward, the “Yes, earlier” options are not recommended for use due to difficulty in determining the exact timeframe for past symptoms. The authors provide a scoring algorithm for meeting the ARFID diagnostic criteria. Of note, the presence of at least one of the drivers was not required for diagnosis, but was considered present if endorsed at least “sometimes” (≥3).

Point prevalence for ARFID with this measure was 1.3% (Dinkler et al., 2022). This estimate was most significantly impacted (lowered) by only half of the sample endorsing that their restrictive/avoidant eating behaviors resulted in physical or nutritional consequences. Further, of the drivers, sensory-based food avoidance was the most common, and fear-based avoidance was the least common. The resulting ARFID-BS is included in an appendix by Dinkler and colleagues (2022) and should undergo further validation, as it is slightly different from the version tested. It is intended for children aged 2 years and older.

AFRID Diagnostic Interviews

Pica, AFRID, and Rumination Disorder Interview

The Pica, AFRID, and Rumination Disorder Interview (PARDI) was developed to be validated for individuals across a wide age range (with initial validation in ages 10–22 years) with a multi-informant approach assessing the DSM-5 criteria comprehensively, while also assessing for related psychopathology and related impairment (Bryant-Waugh et al., 2019). Four versions were developed to accommodate the multi-informant approach across age ranges (from age 2 years to adult). The average time of administration was 39 minutes and can range up to 90 minutes.

The PARDI includes a screening section to rule out the presence of other eating disorders, followed by an introduction that assesses the identified patient's growth and development history, as well as physical or mental health conditions that might better explain their presenting feeding or eating issues (Bryant-Waugh et al., 2019). The remaining items assess the presence and severity of specific ARFID symptoms. There is a scoring algorithm included to make a diagnosis with the completion of the interview. The preliminary evaluation of the interview yielded internal reliabilities of .77 or greater and moderate inter-rater reliability ($\kappa = .75$). Further validation work is needed of this measure, specifically focusing on clinical measures for validation and convergence between self- and parent-report, but it seems to be a promising, comprehensive tool. A questionnaire version is also in development.

Eating Disorder Examination-ARFID Module

The Eating Disorder Examination-ARFID Module (EDE-ARFID Module) was developed for use with the Child EDE (ChEDE; Bryant-Waugh et al., 1996) or as stand-alone assessment of ARFID for children and adults (Schmidt et al., 2019). The initial validation study included children ages 8–13 years, with child and parent rating versions, and an adult version is also in development.

As part of the typical EDE or ChEDE, a typical day of food intake is recalled at the beginning of the interview by the parent and child. The presence of avoidant/restrictive food intake during the past 3 months is assessed next, with the interviewer deciding whether there was inadequate food intake on representative days during these months based on volume and/or variety of foods. The number of days of inadequate food intake for each of the last 3 months is also noted. Reasons for inadequate intake related to medical or mental illness, religion, or lack of food are not included in this count. If insufficient food intake was reported more than half of the days on average for these past 3 months, then additional questions addressing the diagnostic items are queried. The final section of the module aims to characterize different ARFID presentations, including lack of interest in eating or food, selective eating, fear of aversive consequences, and/or food avoidance emotional disorder (generally related to the presence of other psychiatric disorders; American Psychiatric Association, 2013; Schmidt et al., 2019).

In this small pilot study, the authors analyzed nutrition data for the representative food intake described, showing that the children diagnosed with ARFID consumed 62%–68% of the recommended daily energy intake based on the parent- and child-reports, respectively, which maps onto the core criteria of restricted food intake (Schmidt et al., 2019). Agreement between the child and parent report was $\kappa = .80$, and inter-rater reliability for child report was .62 and for parent report was .92. The module also differentiated those diagnosed with ARFID as having lower weight and shape concerns and a higher likelihood of having an underweight status than those not meeting criteria. More work is needed to validate this measure in larger groups and wider age ranges.

Medical Screening

Given the significant weight loss and nutritional deficiencies associated with ARFID, it is recommended that persons presenting for care should be assessed by a medical professional (Eddy et al., 2019). This examination should include an assessment of physical parameters, including growth, eating history, and any associated medical or nutritional impacts of their avoidant/restrictive eating. These could include hypogonadism, bone loss, and vitamin insufficiencies. It should be noted that weight loss is not always present, and individuals with ARFID can present with body mass indices from underweight to obese.

Pica

Pica is characterized by the repeated or persistent ingestion of non-nutritive items or substances, such as magnesium chalk or corn starch, for a period of at least one month (American Psychiatric Association, 2013). This eating behavior should not be consistent with an individual's developmental stage or due to another medical condition. One study showed a prevalence estimate of 5% for recurrent pica behavior among 7–14-year-olds (Hartmann et al., 2018).

Pica Self-Report Questionnaires

Currently, the EDY-Q (described above) is the only published screening measure with items assessing pica (Kurz et al., 2015; Kurz et al., 2016). It includes one item for this disorder, although information on its construct validity and utility have not been provided.

Pica Diagnostic Interviews

The PARDI, as described above, includes items that assess the presence and severity ratings for symptoms associated with pica, with algorithms provided for diagnosis of the disorder. However, psychometric data were only presented for ARFID, suggesting a need for data confirming this measure's utility for diagnosing pica.

The Diagnostic Interview Schedule for Children (DISC-IV) also contains items for the assessment of pica (Shaffer et al., 2000). The DISC-IV is a comprehensive structured interview for the assessment of childhood psychiatric disorders. The miscellaneous disorders section includes items on eating disorders, including pica. Symptoms are assessed for both the past year and the past 4 months, as well as a description of the onset of symptoms and any impairment in functioning. The DISC-IV is available for computer-based administration and takes approximately 70 minutes to complete the full interview. Specific psychometric data for pica were not reported (Shaffer et al., 2000).

Rumination Disorder

Rumination disorder is the repeated regurgitation of food for a period of at least 1 month, not primarily due to a medical condition and not occurring exclusively as part of another eating disorder, such as bulimia nervosa (American Psychiatric Association, 2013). The prevalence estimate in a population-based study of 7–14-year-olds was 1.49 % (Hartmann et al., 2018).

Rumination Disorder Self-Report Measures

Similar to pica, there are very limited psychometric data for the surveys that include items related to rumination disorder. The EDY-Q includes one item, but reports no data in relation to its utility. The Screening Tool of Feeding Problems Applied to Children contains 23 items assessing feeding problems in children (Seiverling et al., 2011). Six factors were identified, including a two-item subscale, Vomiting. Items on the Vomiting subscale include "regurgitates or re-swallows food" and "vomits during or right after meals." However, this factor was not correlated with additional measures of eating behaviors administered in this study, and only limited psychometric data describe the factor. No data on clinical utility for the diagnosis of rumination disorder are included.

Rumination Disorder Diagnostic Interviews

As stated above for pica, the PARDI includes items that assess the presence and severity ratings for symptoms associated with rumination disorder, with algorithms provided for diagnosis of the disorder. However, psychometric data were only presented for ARFID, suggesting a need for data confirming this measure's utility for diagnosing rumination disorder.

Conclusions

The psychometric properties of the NEQ are the most widely published and provide the most support for its utility in screening for NES, as demonstrated across many different translations. However, its limitations include general estimates of diagnostic criteria, such that an interview is needed for NES diagnosis. The NEDQ items provide data that map specially on to diagnostic criteria, but more studies are needed to provide cross-cultural validation of this measure. The NESHI is the only comprehensive diagnostic interview available and should also be further validated in a variety of settings.

ARFID has the widest variety of screening instruments, but many of them are still in development. Most studies providing psychometric data are recent, and suggest the need for more information in large samples and a wider variety of settings and populations. Structured interviews, such as the PARDI are also in development and show promise for their utility in diagnosing ARFID, as well as pica and rumination disorder. Very little psychometric data are available for the few questionnaires and interviews that include items assessing these latter two feeding disorders. They are rare disorders, making this work difficult, but it exists as an area of need.

References

Allison, K.C., Lundgren, J.D., Moore, R.H., O'Reardon, J.P., & Stunkard, A.J. (2010). Cognitive behavior therapy for night eating syndrome: A pilot study. *American Journal of Psychotherapy, 64*(1), 91–106. https://doi.org/10.1176/appi.psychotherapy.2010.64.1.91

Allison, K.C., Lundgren, J.D., O'Reardon, J.P., Geliebter, A., Gluck, M.E., Vinai, P., Mitchell, J.E., Schenck, C.H., Howell, M.J., Crow, S.J., Engel, S., Latzer, Y., Tzischinsky, O., Mahowald, M.W., & Stunkard, A.J. (2010). Proposed diagnostic criteria for night eating syndrome. *International Journal of Eating Disorders, 43*(3), 41–47. https://doi.org/10.1002/eat.20693

Allison, K.C., Lundgren, J.D., O'Reardon, J.P., Martino, N.S., Sarwer, D.B., Wadden, T.A., Crosby, R.D., Engel, S.G., & Stunkard, A.J. (2008). The Night Eating Questionnaire (NEQ): Psychometric properties of a measure of severity of the night eating syndrome. *Eating Behaviors, 9*(1), 62–72. https://doi.org/10.1016/j.eatbeh.2007.03.007

Allison, K.C., Lundgren, J.D., Stunkard, A.J., Bulik, C.M., Lindroos, A.K., Thornton, L.M., & Rasmussen, F. (2014). Validation of screening questions and symptom coherence of night eating in the Swedish Twin Registry. *Comprehensive Psychiatry, 55*(3), 579–587. https://doi.org/10.1016/j.comppsych.2013.01.006

Allison, K.C., Studt, S.K., Berkowitz, R.I., Hesson, L.A., Moore, R.H., Dubroff, J.G., Newberg, A., & Stunkard, A.J. (2013). An open-label efficacy trial of escitalopram for night eating syndrome. *Eating Behaviors, 14*(2), 199–203. https://doi.org/10.1016/j.eatbeh.2013.02.001

American Psychiatric Association (2013). *Diagnostic and statistical manual of mental disorders* (5th ed.). American Psychiatric Association. https://doi.org/10.1176/appi.books.9780890425596

Atasoy, N., Saraçlı, Ö., Konuk, N., Ankaralı, H., Güriz, S.O., Akdemir, A., Sevinçer, G.M., & Atik, L. (2014). The reliability and validity of Turkish version of the Night Eating Questionnaire in psychiatric outpatient population. *Alpha Psychiatry, 15*(3), 238–247. https://doi.org/10.5455/apd.39829

Bryant-Waugh, R., Micali, N., Cooke, L., Lawson, E.A., Eddy, K.T., & Thomas, J.J. (2019). Development of the pica, ARFID, and rumination disorder interview, a multi-informant, semi-structured interview of feeding disorders across the lifespan: A pilot study for ages 10–22. *International Journal of Eating Disorders, 52*(4), 378–387. https://doi.org/10.1002/eat.22958

Bryant-Waugh, R.J., Cooper, P.J., Taylor, C.L., & Lask, B.D. (1996). The use of the eating disorder examination with children: A pilot study. *International Journal of Eating Disorders, 19*, 391–397. https://doi.org/10.1002/(SICI)1098-108X(199605)19:4<391::AID-EAT6>3.0.CO;2-G

Dantas, G.M., Pintom, T.F., Pereira, E.D.B., Magalhães Júnior, R.M., de Bruin, V.M.S., & Bruin, P.F.C. de (2012). Validation of a new Brazilian version of the "Night Eating Questionnaire." *Sleep Science, 5*(1), 7–13.

Dinkler, L., & Bryant-Waugh, R. (2021). Assessment of avoidant restrictive food intake disorder, pica and rumination disorder: Interview and questionnaire measures. *Current Opinions in Psychiatry, 34*(6), 532–542. https://doi.org/10.1097/YCO.0000000000000736

Dinkler, L., Yasumitsu-Lovell, K., Eitoku, M., Fujieda, M., Suganuma, N., Hatakenaka, Y., Hadjikhani, N., Bryant-Waugh, R., Råstam, M., & Gillberg, C. (2022). Development of a parent-reported screening tool for avoidant/restrictive food intake disorder (ARFID): Initial validation and prevalence in 4–7-year-old Japanese children. *Appetite, 168*, 105735. https://doi.org/10.1016/j.appet.2021.105735

Eddy, K.T., Harshman, S.G., Becker, K.R., Bern, E., Bryant-Waugh, R., Hilbert, A., Katzman, D.K., Lawson, E.A., Manzo, L.D., Menzel, J., Micali, N., Ornstein, R., Sally, S., Serinsky, S.P., Sharp, W., Stubbs, K., Walsh, B.T., Zickgraf, H., Zucker, N., & Thomas, J J. (2019). Radcliffe ARFID workgroup: Toward operationalization of research diagnostic criteria and directions for the field. *International Journal of Eating Disorders, 52*(4), 361–366. https://doi.org/10.1002/eat.23042

Elsadek, A.M., Hamid, M.S., & Allison, K.C. (2014). Psychometric characteristics of the Night Eating Questionnaire in a Middle East population. *International Journal of Eating Disorders, 47*(6), 660–665. https://doi.org/10.1002/eat.22285

Fairburn, C.G., Cooper, Z., & O'Connor, M. (2014). *Eating disorder examination (Edition 17D)*. https://www.credo-oxford.com/pdfs/EDE_17.0D.pdf

First, M.B., Williams, J.B.W., Karg, R.S., & Spitzer, R.L. (2015). *Structured clinical interview for DSM5-research version (SCID for DSM-5) (Research version; SCID-5-RV)*. American Psychiatric Association.

Gallant, A.R., Lundgren, J., Allison, K., Stunkard, A.J., Lambert, M., O'Loughlin, J., Lemieux, S., Tremblay, A., & Drapeau, V. (2012). Validity of the Night Eating Questionnaire in children. *International Journal of Eating Disorders, 45*(7), 861–585. https://doi.org/10.1002/eat.22021

Harb, A.B., Caumo, W., & Hidalgo, M.P. (2008). Translation and adaptation of the Brazilian version of the Night Eating Questionnaire. *Cadernos Saude Publica, 24*(6), 1368–1376. https://doi.org/10.1590/s0102-311x2008000600017

Hartmann, A.S., Poulain, T., Vogel, M., Hiemisch, A., Kiess, W., & Hilbert, A. (2018). Prevalence of pica and rumination behaviors in German children aged 7–14 and their associations with feeding, eating, and general psychopathology: A population-based study. *European Child and Adolescent Psychiatry, 27*, 1499–1508. https://doi.org/10.1007/s00787-018-1153-9

He, J., Ji, F., Zhang, X., & Fan, X. (2019). Psychometric properties and gender invariance of the simplified Chinese version of Night Eating Questionnaire in a large sample of mainland Chinese college students. *Eating and Weight Disorders, 24*(1), 57–66. https://doi.org/10.1007/s40519-018-0553-7

Hilbert, A., Zenger, M., Eichler, J., & Brähler, E. (2021). Psychometric evaluation of the eating disorders in youth-questionnaire when used in adults: Prevalence estimates for symptoms of avoidant/restrictive food intake disorder and population norms. *International Journal of Eating Disorders, 54*(3), 399–408. https://doi.org/10.1002/eat.23424

Hunot, C., Fildes, A., Croker, H., Llewellyn, C.H., Wardle, J., & Beeken, R.J. (2016). Appetitive traits and relationships with BMI in adults: Development of the adult eating behaviour questionnaire. *Appetite, 105*, 356–363. https://doi.org/10.1016/j.appet.2016.05.024

Innamorati, M., Imperatori, C., Lester, D., Fabbricatore, M., Gaudini, L., Contardi, A., & Balsamo, M. (2018). Preliminary validation of the Italian Night Eating Questionnaire (I-NEQ-16): Item analysis and factor structure. *Frontiers in Psychology, 209*, Article 2628. https://doi.org/10.3389/fpsyg.2018.02628

Kim, B., Kim, I., & Choi, H. (2016). Psychometric properties and item evaluation of Korean version of night eating questionnaire (KNEQ). *Journal of the Korean Academy of Nursing, 46*(1), 109–117. https://doi.org/10.4040/jkan.2016.46.1.109

Kurz, S., Dyck, Z. van, Dremmel, D., Munsch, S., & Hilbert, A. (2015). Early-onset restrictive eating disturbances in primary school boys and girls. *European Child and Adolescent Psychiatry, 24*(7), 779–785. https://doi.org/10.1007/s00787-014-0622-z

Kurz, S., Dyck, Z. van, Dremmel, D., Munsch, S., & Hilbert, A. (2016). Variants of early-onset restrictive eating disturbances in middle childhood. *International Journal of Eating Disorders, 49*(1), 102–106. https://doi.org/10.1002/eat.22461

Latzer, Y., Tzischinsky, O., Hason Rozenstein, M., & Allison, K. (2014). Reliability and cross-validation of the night eating questionnaire (NEQ): Hebrew version. *Israeli Journal of Psychiatry and Related Sciences, 51*(1), 68–73.

Lundgren, J.D., Allison, K.C., Crow, S., O'Reardon, J.P., Berg, K.C., Galbraith, J., Martino, N.S., & Stunkard, A.J. (2006). Prevalence of the night eating syndrome in a psychiatric population. *American Journal of Psychiatry, 163*(1), 156–158. https://doi.org/10.1176/appi.ajp.163.1.156

Lundgren, J.D., Allison, K.C., Vinai, P., & Gluck, M.E. (2012). Assessment instruments for night eating syndrome. In J.D. Lungren, K.C. Allison, & A.J. Stunkard (Eds.), *Night eating syndrome: Research, assessment, and treatment* (pp. 197–217). Guilford.

Meule, A., Allison, K.C., & Platte, P. (2014). A German version of the night eating questionnaire (NEQ): Psychometric properties and correlates in a student sample. *Eating Behaviors, 15*(4), 523–527. https://doi.org/10.1016/j.eatbeh.2014.07.002

Moizé, V., Gluck, M.E., Torres, F., Andreu, A., Vidal, J., & Allison, K. (2012). Transcultural adaptation of the Night Eating Questionnaire (NEQ) for its use in the Spanish population. *Eating Behaviors, 13*(3), 260–263. https://doi.org/10.1016/j.eatbeh.2012.02.005

Nolan, L.J., & Geliebter, A. (2017). Validation of the night eating diagnostic questionnaire (NEDQ) and its relationship with depression, sleep quality, "food addiction," and body mass index. *Appetite, 111*, 86–95. https://doi.org/10.1016/j.appet.2016.12.027

Nolan, L.J., & Geliebter, A. (2019). Factor structure of the night eating diagnostic questionnaire (NEDQ) and an evaluation of the diagnostic criteria of the night eating syndrome. *Journal of Eating Disorders, 7*, 39. https://doi.org/10.1186/s40337-019-0268-9

O'Reardon, J.P., Allison, K.C., Martino, N.S., Lundgren, J.D., Heo, M., & Stunkard, A.J. (2006). A randomized, placebo-controlled trial of sertraline in the treatment of night eating syndrome. *American Journal of Psychiatry, 163*(5), 893–898. https://doi.org/10.1176/ajp.2006.163.5.893

Schmidt, R., Toralf, K., Hiemisch, A., Kiess, W., Hilbert, A. (2019). Interview-based assessment of avoidant/restrictive food intake disorder (ARFID): A pilot study evaluating an ARFID module for the eating disorder examination. *International Journal of Eating Disorders, 52*(4), 388–397. https://doi.org/10.1002/eat.23063

Schmidt, R., Vogel, M., Hiemisch, A., Kiess, W., & Hilbert, A. (2018). Pathological and non-pathological variants of restrictive eating behaviors in middle childhood: A latent class analysis. *Appetite, 127*, 257–265. https://doi.org/10.1016/j.appet.2018.04.030

Seiverling, L., Hendy, H.M., Williams, K. (2011). The screening tool of feeding problems applied to children (STEP-CHILD): Psychometric characteristics and associations with child and parent variables. *Research in Developmental Disabilities, 32*(3), 1122–1129. https://doi.org/10.1016/j.ridd.2011.01.012

Shaffer, D., Fisher, P., Lucas, C.P., Dulcan, M.K., & Schwab-Stone, M.E. (2000). NIMH diagnostic interview schedule for children version IV (NIMH DISC-IV): Description, differences from previous versions, and reliability of some common diagnoses. *Journal of the American Academy of Child and Adolescent Psychiatry, 39*(1), 28–38. https://doi.org/10.1097/00004583-200001000-00014

Subar, A.F., Kirkpatrick, S.I., Mittl, B., Zimmerman, T. P, Thompson, F.E., Bingley, C., Willis, G., Islam, N.G., Baranowski, T., McNutt, S., & Potischman, N. (2012). The automated self-administered 24-hour dietary recall (ASA24): A resource for researchers, clinicians, and educators from the National Cancer Institute. *Journal of the Academy for Nutrition and Dietetics, 112*, 1134–1137. https://doi.org/10.1016/j.jand.2012.04.016

Thomas, J.J., & Eddy, K.T. (2018). *Cognitive behavioral therapy for avoidant/restrictive food intake disorder: Children, adolescents, and adults.* Cambridge University Press. https://doi.org/10.1017/9781108233170

Tu, C.Y., Tseng, M.M., Chang, C.H., & Lin, C.C. (2017). Comparative validity of the Internet and paper-and-pencil versions of the Night Eating Questionnaire. *Comprehensive Psychiatry, 75*, 53–61. https://doi.org/10.1016/j.comppsych.2017.03.001

World Health Organization (2019). *International statistical classification of diseases and related health problems* (11th ed.). WHO. https://icd.who.int/

Zickgraf, H.F., & Ellis, J.M. (2018). Initial validation of the nine item avoidant/restrictive food intake disorder screen (NIAS): A measure of three restrictive eating patterns. *Appetite, 123*, 32–42. https://doi.org/10.1016/j.appet.2017.11.111

Zickgraf, H.F., Loftus, P., Gibbons, B., Cohen, L.C., & Hunt, M.G. (2022). "If I could survive without eating, it would be a huge relief": Development and initial validation of the fear of food questionnaire. *Appetite, 169*, 105808. https://doi.org/10.1016/j.appet.2021.105808

Part III

Adjacent Domains

Chapter 12

Assessment of Body Image

Rike Arkenau-Kathmann, Hannah L. Quittkat, and Silja Vocks

Department of Clinical Psychology and Psychotherapy,
Osnabrück University, Germany

Introduction

People typically have specific thoughts and emotions related to their body, engage in body-related behaviors, and perceive their body in a specific way. The multifaceted combination of these features is defined as body image (Cash, 2004; Thompson et al., 1999). The perceptual component of body image describes body-related sensations and perceptions (e.g., the perception of one's body size and shape), while the behavioral component describes body-related behaviors (e.g., body checking and the avoidance of body-related situations). These two components are complemented by a cognitive component (attitudes and cognitions towards one's body, e.g., "I'm fat," "My thighs are wobbly") and an affective component (emotions towards one's body, e.g., shame, anxiety, sadness; Cash, 2004; Thompson et al., 1999; Vocks et al., 2007). A disturbed body image and its related symptoms emerge, for instance, in anorexia and bulimia nervosa, for which a disturbed body image represents one of the main diagnostic criteria (American Psychiatric Association, 2013). However, specific aspects of body image disturbance can occur in other mental disorders too, such as body checking in body dysmorphic disorder (BDD), its subtype muscle dysmorphia, and illness anxiety (American Psychiatric Association, 2013).

To describe body image and its related aspects, Cordes et al. (2015) proposed a heuristic meta-model, which is based on established theories and models of body image, eating disorders (ED), and BDD (Figure 12.1). The model comprises an S-O-R-structure, encompassing body-related stimuli and situations (S), processes referring to the organism itself (O), and body-related feelings, behaviors, cognitions, and cognitive biases, which together form the reaction variable (R). Moreover, the model incorporates biological and social influences as well as mediating variables, that is, the internalization of a specific body ideal or social comparison tendencies (Cordes et al., 2015).

The current chapter describes various measures for the assessment of body image. Only measures for which previous studies have provided evidence of internal reliability, test-retest reliability, or convergent, concurrent, predictive, discriminant, and/or discriminative validity were selected. The chapter aims to provide an overview of measures that are suitable for examining body image. However, as not all eligible measures could be included in this chapter, the overview should not be considered as exhaustive.

Measures for the Assessment of Body Image

Self-Report Questionnaires Related to Disordered Eating or Body Dysmorphic Symptomatology

To assess an individual's body image, various internationally established self-report questionnaires on disordered eating or body dysmorphic symptomatology can be used. For instance, the subscales Weight Concern (five items) and Shape Concern (eight items) from the Eating Disorder Examination-Questionnaire (EDE-Q; Fairburn & Beglin, 1994) assess body-related concerns that are typically associated with ED pathology, such as a stronger desire to lose weight or a greater dissatisfaction with one's body shape (Fairburn & Beglin, 1994). Various studies have provided evidence of internal and test-retest reliability and of convergent and discriminative validity of the EDE-Q (for a review, see Berg et al., 2012), while there are also studies pointing to a divergent factor structure (e.g., Carey et al., 2019; Rand-Giovannetti et al., 2020). There are different cut-off scores to identify individuals with ED (e.g., Mond et al., 2008) as well as norms for nonclinical mixed-gender samples of adults and adolescents (e.g., Carey et al., 2019; Mond et al., 2014) and for women, men, and adolescents with ED (e.g., Jennings & Phillips, 2017; Smith et al., 2017).

The Drive for Thinness (seven items) and Body Dissatisfaction (nine items) subscales of the Eating Disorder Inventory (EDI; Garner et al., 1983) likewise appear to be suitable for use in this context. Items from these two EDI subscales examine the fear of gaining weight, the preoccupation with one's weight, and thinness-related body dissatisfaction. The EDI has been constantly updated over the years (EDI-2: Garner, 1991; EDI-3: Garner, 2004) and has been employed in various studies with women, men, and adolescents, also including individuals with ED. These studies provided evidence of internal reliability, test-retest reliability, and convergent and discriminative validity of the EDI (e.g., Espelage et al., 2003; Garner et al., 1983; Salbach-Andrae et al., 2010; Smith et al., 2017; Thiel & Paul, 2006). Furthermore, normative data are available for clinical samples of women and men with ED (e.g., Brewin et al., 2014; Smith et al., 2017).

A further suitable self-report measure is the Dysmorphic Concern Questionnaire (DCQ; Oosthuizen et al., 1998). Containing only seven items, the DCQ assesses appearance-related concerns that are characteristic for BDD, for example, the preoccupation that one's body or parts thereof are misshapen (Oosthuizen et al., 1998). Various studies have provided evidence of internal reliability as well as convergent, concurrent, and discriminative validity of the DCQ for nonclinical and clinical mixed-gender adult samples, including participants with BDD (e.g., Jorgensen et al., 2001; Mancuso et al., 2010; Oosthuizen et al., 1998; Schieber et al., 2018; Stangier et al., 2003). Additionally, different cut-off scores to screen for BDD have been suggested (Mancuso et al., 2010; Stangier et al., 2003) and the DCQ has also been used in samples of adolescent females and males (e.g., Enander et al., 2018). Besides the DCQ, the Yale-Brown Obsessive-Compulsive Scale Modified for Body Dysmorphic Disorder (Phillips et al., 1997) and the BDD-5 for adolescents and adults (Möllmann & Buhlmann, 2021a; 2021b) can similarly be used to assess appearance-related concerns, feelings, and behaviors.

Analogously, self-report questionnaires focusing on the BDD subtype muscle dysmorphia may be used. In particular, the application of the Drive for Size (five items) or the

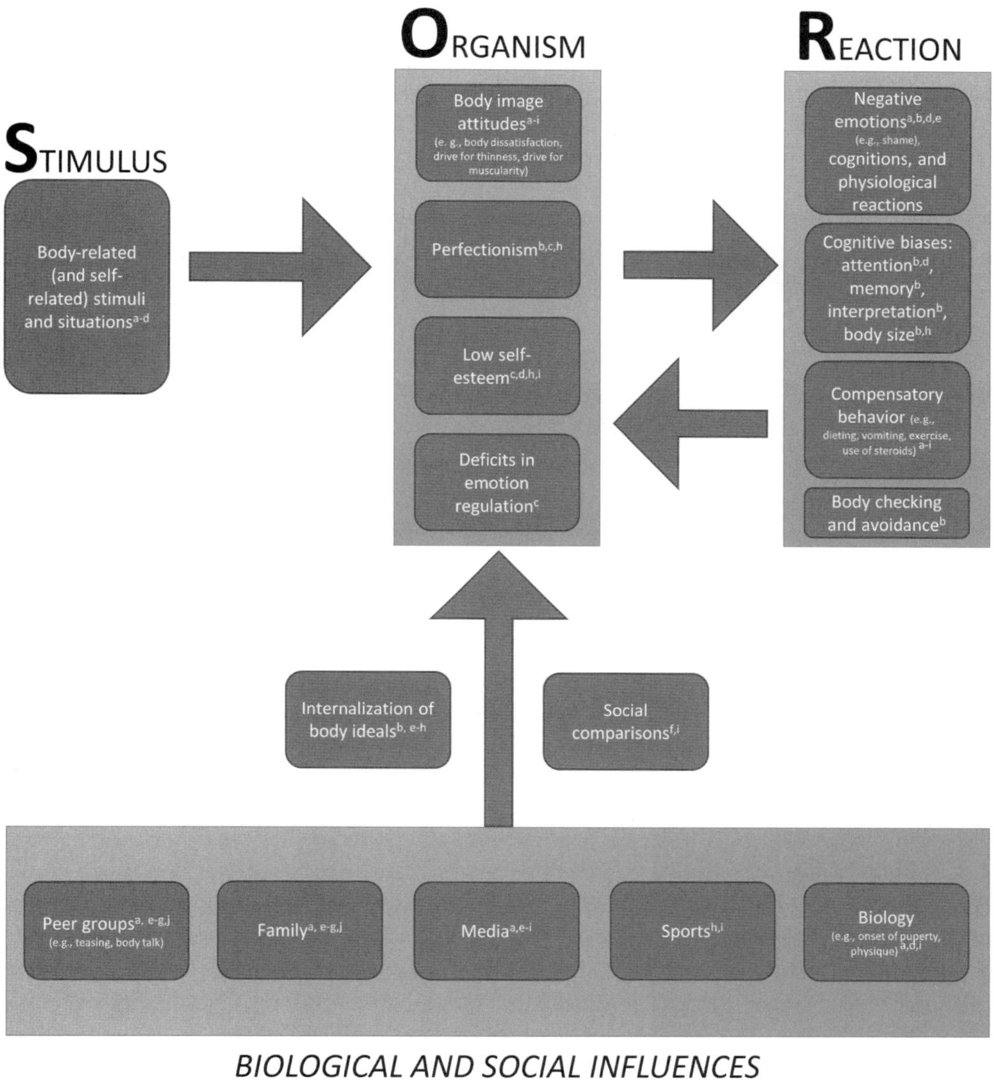

[a] cognitive-behavioral model of body image (Cash, 2011); [b] cognitive-behavioral model of eating disorders (Williamson et al., 2004); [c] transdiagnostic model (Fairburn et al., 2003); [d] integrative attentional-bias model (Aspen et al., 2013); [e] dual-pathway model (Stice, 2001); [f] tripartite influence model (Thompson et al., 1999); [g] quadripartite influence model of male body image (Tylka, 2011); [h] model of muscle dysmorphia (Grieve, 2007); [i] model predicting health risk body change strategies in males (Cafri et al., 2005).

Figure 12.1. Heuristic meta-model of body image disturbance by Cordes et al. (2015). In the presence of specific organism variables, body-related stimuli and situations are assumed to activate specific cognitive-affective, physiological, and behavioral reactions, which then may reinforce the organism variables. The internalization of body ideals and social comparisons are assumed to function as mediators of the association between biological and social influences and the organism variables. © Springer Verlag. Adapted and translated with permission from Cordes, M., Bauer, A., Waldorf, M., & Vocks, S. (2015). Körperbezogene Aufmerksamkeitsverzerrungen bei Frauen und Männern. *Psychotherapeut, 60*(6), 477-487. https://doi.org/10.1007/s00278-015-0058-z

Appearance Intolerance (four items) subscales of the Muscle Dysmorphic Disorder Inventory (MDDI; Hildebrandt et al., 2004) seems to be suitable. These two subscales examine the preoccupation that one's body is too slender as well as associated negative body-related feelings. Previous studies reported evidence of internal reliability, test-retest reliability, and convergent validity of the MDDI for nonclinical samples of women and men (Hildebrandt et al., 2004; Zeeck et al., 2018). A cut-off score was suggested to identify individuals at risk of muscle dysmorphia (Longobardi et al., 2017).

Besides the MDDI, further self-report questionnaires on muscle dysmorphia pathology include the Muscle Dysmorphia Inventory (Rhea et al., 2004) or the Muscle Appearance Satisfaction Scale (Mayville et al., 2002). These measures, which likewise examine, for instance, concerns about losing muscle mass or dissatisfaction with one's muscularity (Mayville et al., 2002; Rhea et al., 2004), can also be used to assess an individual's body image.

Self-Report Questionnaires Related to Body Image

Body-Related Attitudes and Cognitions

In addition to the aforementioned disorder-specific questionnaires, there are various measures that are directly related to the concept of body image, for instance, by focusing specifically on body-related attitudes and cognitions (see Figure 12.1). One such measure is the Multidimensional Body-Self Relations Questionnaire (MBSRQ; Cash, 2000) with its Appearance Scales (MBSRQ-AS). The MBSRQ-AS consist of 34 items that are subdivided into the following five subscales: Appearance Evaluation (seven items; e.g., perceiving oneself to be physically unattractive), Appearance Orientation (12 items; e.g., placing a high importance on one's appearance), Body Areas Satisfaction (nine items; e.g., being satisfied with one's upper body), Overweight Preoccupation (four items; e.g., using restraint eating to lose weight), and Self-Classified Weight (two items; e.g., perceiving oneself to be overweight; Cash, 2000). The psychometric properties of the MBSRQ-AS were tested in samples of adult and adolescent females and males, also including individuals with ED, and evidence of internal reliability, test-retest reliability, and convergent and discriminative validity was found (Cash, 2000; Marco et al., 2017; Vossbeck-Elsebusch et al., 2014).

Another such measure is the Body Image Disturbance Questionnaire (BIDQ; Cash et al., 2004). In contrast to the MBSRQ-AS, the BIDQ consists only of seven items, examining appearance-related concerns, subjective functional impairment, and associated feelings of distress (Cash et al., 2004). The psychometric properties of the BIDQ were examined in female and male adult samples, and evidence of internal reliability, test-retest reliability, and convergent, concurrent, and discriminative validity was reported (Cash & Grasso, 2005; Cash et al., 2004; Collison & Mahlberg, 2018). Additionally, the BIDQ has been used in samples of individuals with ED and BDD, with higher BIDQ scores being found for the index groups as compared to healthy (Hartmann et al., 2015) or clinical comparison groups (Hrabosky et al., 2009).

A further suitable measure is the Drive for Muscularity Scale (DMS; McCreary & Sasse, 2000), which assesses the striving for a more muscular body using 15 items. Previous validation studies included adult and adolescent females and males, and reported internal reliability, test-retest reliability, and concurrent, discriminant, and discriminative validity of the DMS (e.g., McCreary & Sasse, 2000; McCreary et al., 2004; McPherson et al., 2010). For men, but not for women, previous findings further indicated that the DMS could be divided into two separate subscales, with the first examining muscularity-related attitudes (e.g., the desire to be more muscular) and the second examining muscularity-related behaviors (e.g., lifting weights; McCreary et al., 2004). In turn, for both genders, it was recommended to exclude Item 10 ("I think about taking anabolic steroids") when calculating the DMS total score (McCreary et al., 2004).

A related measure is the Drive for Leanness Scale, which aims to assess attitudes associated with the desire for a muscular body with low body fat (DLS; Smolak & Murnen, 2008). The DLS was developed as an unidimensional questionnaire and consists of six items, for example, "It is important to have well-defined abs" (Smolak & Murnen, 2008). The psychometric properties of the DLS were tested in samples of adult women and men, and there is evidence of internal reliability and convergent and concurrent validity (Ryan & Morrison, 2013; Smolak & Murnen, 2008; Tod et al., 2012). Moreover, the DLS has been used in a mixed-gender adolescent sample, although with a slightly different response format (Day et al., 2021). Evidence of internal reliability was reported (Day et al., 2021).

Body-related attitudes can also be assessed using the Male Body Attitudes Scale (MBAS; Tylka et al., 2005). This questionnaire was specifically designed for use in male samples and encompasses 24 items. Following Tylka et al. (2005), the MBAS consists of three subscales, assessing attitudes related to Muscularity (10 items; e.g., the preoccupation that one's body is not muscular enough), Low Body Fat (eight items; e.g., the desire for a leaner body), or Height (two items, e.g., the desire to be taller). While not being subordinated to one of the three subscales, a further set of four items examines attitudes related to the body as a whole (e.g., dissatisfaction related to the overall build of the body). A total score including all 24 items can be calculated (Tylka et al., 2005). The psychometric properties of the MBAS have been examined in male adult and adolescent samples, and there is evidence of internal reliability, test-retest reliability, and convergent, concurrent, and discriminant validity for the total score and the three subscales (Sepúlveda et al., 2017; Tylka et al., 2005). Furthermore, Ryan et al. (2011) proposed a revised version of the MBAS using only 15 items.

To examine cognitions related to body checking, the Body Checking Cognitions Scale can be used (BCCS; Mountford et al., 2006). The BCCS consists of 19 items divided into four subscales, namely, Objective Verification (six items; e.g., thinking that body checking represents an accurate way to evaluate one's appearance), Reassurance (four items; e.g., thinking that body checking will help one to calm down when one feels anxious about one's weight or shape), Safety Beliefs (five items; e.g., thinking that body checking helps one to feel more comfortable when around other people), and Body Control (four items; e.g., thinking that body checking helps to control one's weight). The BCCS was developed and tested in samples of women, also including participants with ED (Mountford et al., 2006), but has also been used in a mixed-gender sample (Meyer et al., 2011). Previous studies indicated evidence of internal reliability and convergent and discriminative validity of the BCCS (Haase et al., 2011; Mountford et al., 2006).

If the aim is to assess body image as a state, for example, to explore the effect of a specific experimental condition, the Body Image States Scale (BISS; Cash et al., 2002) seems to represent a suitable measure. The BISS consists of six items that examine, for instance, current satisfaction with one's overall physical appearance, current feelings of physical attractiveness, or the current evaluation of one's appearance relative to one's usual appearance. The BISS has been examined in mixed-gender samples and there is evidence of internal reliability, test-retest reliability, and convergent validity (Cash et al., 2002).

Further questionnaires assessing body-related attitudes and cognitions include the Body Shape Questionnaire (Cooper et al., 1987), the Thoughts Checklist (Cooper & Fairburn, 1992), and the Weight Concerns Scale (Killen et al., 1993, 1994).

Body-Related Behaviors

While the aforementioned measures primarily examine body-related attitudes and cognitions, there are further measures that directly focus on assessing the engagement in compensatory body-related behaviors (see Figure 12.1). A first scale is the Body Checking Questionnaire (BCQ; Reas et al., 2002). The BCQ consists of 23 items allocated to three subscales, the Overall Appearance Scale (10 items, e.g., trying on special clothes to check if they still fit), the Specific Body Parts Scale (eight items; e.g., pinching one's stomach to check the amount of body fat), and the Idiosyncratic Checking Scale (five items; e.g., measuring the diameter of one's wrist; Reas et al., 2002). The BCQ was developed in samples of adult and adolescent females and there is evidence of internal reliability, test-retest reliability, and convergent and discriminant validity of the three subscales and of the total score (Reas et al., 2002). The BCQ has also been examined in samples of women and female adolescents with ED, and there is further evidence of discriminative validity (Calugi et al., 2006; Steinfeld et al., 2017).

A related measure is the Male Body Checking Questionnaire (MBCQ; Hildebrandt et al., 2010), which was specifically developed for men to account for gender-specific differences (Alfano et al., 2011). The MBCQ encompasses 16 items assigned to four subscales, that is, Global Muscle Checking (six items; e.g., checking one's biceps), Chest and Shoulder Checking (three items; e.g., flexing one's chest muscles in the mirror), Other-Comparative Checking (two items; e.g., comparing one's chest muscles with those of others), and Body Testing (five items, e.g., pinching one's muscles; Hildebrandt et al., 2010). For different samples of adult men, Hildebrandt et al. (2010) reported evidence of internal reliability, test-retest reliability, and convergent validity of the MBCQ subscales and/or the total score.

In addition to the examination of body checking, body-related avoidance behavior can be assessed using the Body Image Avoidance Questionnaire (BIAQ; Rosen et al., 1991). The 19 items of the BIAQ are subdivided into the four subscales of Clothing (nine items; e.g., wearing dark clothes), Social Activities (four items; e.g., avoiding going out with others if it involves eating), Eating Restraint (three items; e.g., fasting), and Grooming and Weighing (three items; e.g., getting dressed up). The BIAQ was developed in female adult samples including healthy women, women with bulimia nervosa, and women with highly negative body image attitudes, and evidence of internal reliability, test-retest reliability, and convergent and discriminative validity was reported (Rosen et al., 1991). Nevertheless, the BIAQ has also been used in male adult samples (e.g., Stapleton et al., 2016). In addition to the BCQ, MBCQ, and BIAQ, the Body Image Coping Strategies Inventory (Cash et al., 2005) can be used to examine body-related coping strategies.

Body-Esteem and Body Appreciation

Beyond this, there are further measures that focus either on body-esteem or positive body-related attitudes, respectively. A first example is the Body-Esteem Scale for Adolescents and Adults (BESAA; Mendelson et al., 2001). The BESAA consists of 23 items that are assigned to the three subscales Body-Esteem Appearance (10 items), Body-Esteem Weight (eight items), and Body-Esteem Attributions (five items). While the first two subscales measure the evaluation of one's appearance and weight-related satisfaction, respectively, the third examines the perceived evaluation of one's appearance by others. The BESAA was empirically examined in a mixed-gender sample of adults and adolescents, and there is evidence of internal and test-retest reliability and convergent and discriminant validity (Mendelson et al., 2001). Furthermore, an adjusted psychometrically tested version for early adolescents aged between 11 and 13 years is available (Cragun et al., 2013).

A second example is the Body Appreciation Scale-2 (BAS-2; Tylka & Wood-Barcalow, 2015). The BAS-2 encompasses 10 items assessing, for instance, feelings of respect towards one's body, positive body-related attitudes, and attentiveness towards body-related needs. Evidence of internal reliability, test-retest reliability, and convergent, concurrent, and discriminant validity of the BAS-2 was reported for a mixed-gender adult sample (Tylka & Wood-Barcalow, 2015). Additionally, there is an adjusted psychometrically tested version for children aged between 9 and 11 years (Halliwell et al., 2017). The BAS-2 has also been used and empirically tested as a state measure (Homan, 2016).

Figure Rating Scales

An alternative method to assess an individual's body image is to use figure rating scales. Typically, these scales consist of a set of bodies that differ in size or shape (e.g., with respect to body mass index, body fat, or muscularity) and individuals are asked to select the body figure which best represents their current, ideal, or desired body (e.g., see Cafri & Thompson, 2004). In this way, body ideals as well as the discrepancy between one's perceived actual and ideal body type can be examined. Furthermore, figure rating scales may be used to examine whether individuals perceive their bodies in a distorted manner, for example, overestimate their body dimensions. Accordingly, an individual's real anthropometric measurements are compared to those of the body figure the individual has chosen to best represent their actual body. Various figure rating scales are available, for both women (e.g., Mölbert et al., 2017; Ralph-Nearman & Filik, 2020; Steinfeld et al., 2020) and men (e.g., Arkenau et al., 2020; Ralph-Nearman & Filik, 2018; Talbot et al., 2019).

Sociocultural Influences on Body Image and Significant Mediators

According to the proposed meta-model (Figure 12.1), an individual's body image may be affected by different sociocultural and biological influences. Furthermore, the association between these variables is assumed to be mediated by the internalization of current body ideals as well as the engagement in appearance-related social comparisons. For the assessment of these additional model components, various psychometrically sound self-report questionnaires are available, for example, the Feedback on Physical Appearance Scale (Tantleff-Dunn et al., 1995), the Perception of Teasing Scale (Thompson et al., 1995), the Sociocultural Attitudes Towards Appearance Questionnaire (Heinberg et al., 1995), or the Upwards and Downward Appearance Comparison Scale (O'Brien et al., 2009).

Conclusions

The present chapter aimed to provide an overview of different measures related to body image. As pointed out by the heuristic meta-model (Cordes et al., 2015), the assessment of body image is transdiagnostic, as it includes thoughts, feelings, behaviors, and perceptions, which are not only distinctive for the assessment of body image but may also indicate a distorted body image co-occurring with mental disorders. In clinical-psychological research and practice, the described measures may be used to examine specific body image facets in a dimensional way or to screen for body image disturbance or associated mental disorders such as ED or BDD. Furthermore, certain measures may also be used to evaluate psychotherapeutic interventions or to examine the effect of an experimental manipulation. As it represents an integrative meta-model, the model by Cordes et al. (2015; Figure 12.1) may help clinical professionals and researchers to select appropriate body image measures.

References

Alfano, L., Hildebrandt, T., Bannon, K., Walker, C., & Walton, K. E. (2011). The impact of gender on the assessment of body checking behavior. *Body Image, 8*(1), 20–25. https://doi.org/10.1016/j.bodyim.2010.09.005

American Psychiatric Association. (2013). *Diagnostic and statistical manual of mental disorders* (5th ed.). American Psychiatric Association. https://doi.org/10.1176/appi.books.9780890425596

Arkenau, R., Vocks, S., Taube, C. O., Waldorf, M., & Hartmann, A. S. (2020). The body image matrix of thinness and muscularity – male bodies: Development and validation of a new figure rating scale for body image in men. *Journal of Clinical Psychology, 76*(7), 1283–1292. https://doi.org/10.1002/jclp.22933

Aspen, V., Darcy, A. M., & Lock, J. (2013). A review of attention biases in women with eating disorders. *Cognition & Emotion, 27*(5), 820–838. https://doi.org/10.1080/02699931.2012.749777

Berg, K. C., Peterson, C. B., Frazier, P., & Crow, S. J. (2012). Psychometric evaluation of the eating disorder examination and eating disorder examination-questionnaire: A systematic review of the literature. *International Journal of Eating Disorders, 45*(3), 428–438. https://doi.org/10.1002/eat.20931

Brewin, N., Baggott, J., Dugard, P., & Arcelus, J. (2014). Clinical normative data for eating disorder examination questionnaire and eating disorder inventory for DSM-5 feeding and eating disorder classifications: A retrospective study of patients formerly diagnosed via DSM-IV. *European Eating Disorders Review, 22*(4), 299–305. https://doi.org/10.1002/erv.2301

Cafri, G., & Thompson, J. K. (2004). Measuring male body image: A review of the current methodology. *Psychology of Men & Masculinity, 5*(1), 18–29. https://doi.org/10.1037/1524-9220.5.1.18

Cafri, G., Thompson, J. K., Ricciardelli, L., McCabe, M., Smolak, L., & Yesalis, C. (2005). Pursuit of the muscular ideal: Physical and psychological consequences and putative risk factors. *Clinical Psychology Review, 25*(2), 215–239. https://doi.org/10.1016/j.cpr.2004.09.003

Calugi, S., Grave, R., Ghisi, M., & Sanavio, E. (2006). Validation of the body checking questionnaire (BCQ) in an eating disorders population. *Behavioural and Cognitive Psychotherapy, 34*(2), 233–242. https://doi.org/10.1017/S1352465805002730

Carey, M., Kupeli, N., Knight, R., Troop, N.A., Jenkinson, P.M., & Preston, C. (2019). Eating disorder examination questionnaire (EDE-Q): Norms and psychometric properties in U.K. females and males. *Psychological Assessment, 31*(7), 839–850. https://doi.org/10.1037/pas0000703

Cash, T.F. (2004). Body image: Past, present, and future. *Body Image, 1*(1), 1–5. https://doi.org/10.1016/S1740-1445(03)00011-1

Cash, T.F. (2011). Cognitive-behavioral perspectives on body image. In T.L. Cash & L. Smolak (Eds.), *Body image: A handbook of science, practice, and prevention* (pp. 39–47). The Guilford Press.

Cash, T.F. (2000). *Users' manual for the multidimensional body-self relations questionnaire* (3rd revision). http://www.body-images.com

Cash, T.F., Fleming, E.C., Alindogan, J., Steadman, L., & Whitehead, A. (2002). Beyond body image as a trait: The development and validation of the body image states scale. *Eating Disorders, 10*(2), 103–113. https://doi.org/10.1080/10640260290081678

Cash, T.F., & Grasso, K. (2005). The norms and stability of new measures of the multidimensional body image construct. *Body Image, 2*(2), 199–203. https://doi.org/10.1016/j.bodyim.2005.03.007

Cash, T.F., Phillips, K.A., Santos, M.T., & Hrabosky, J. (2004). Measuring "negative body image": Validation of the body image disturbance questionnaire in a non-clinical population. *Body Image, 1*(4), 363–372. https://doi.org/10.1016/j.bodyim.2004.10.001

Cash, T.F., Santos, M.T., & Williams, E.F. (2005). Coping with body-image threats and challenges: Validation of the body image coping strategies inventory. *Journal of Psychosomatic Research, 58*(2), 190–199. https://doi.org/10.1016/j.jpsychores.2004.07.008

Collison, J., & Mahlberg, J. (2018). Factor analysis and psychometric validation of the body image disturbance questionnaire in an Australian undergraduate sample. *Australian Psychologist, 53*(3), 195–202. https://doi.org/10.1111/ap.12293

Cooper, M.J., & Fairburn, C.G. (1992). Thoughts about eating, weight and shape in anorexia nervosa and bulimia nervosa. *Behaviour Research and Therapy, 30*(5), 501–511. https://doi.org/10.1016/0005-7967(92)90034-E

Cooper, P.J., Taylor, M.J., Cooper, Z., & Fairburn, C.G. (1987). The development and validation of the body shape questionnaire. *International Journal of Eating Disorders, 6*(4), 485–494. https://doi.org/10.1002/1098-108X(198707)6:4<485::AID-EAT2260060405>3.0.CO;2-O

Cordes, M., Bauer, A., Waldorf, M., & Vocks, S. (2015). Potenzieller Risikofaktor für die Entstehung und Aufrechterhaltung eines gestörten Körperbilds [Body-related attentional bias in women and men. Potential risk factor for the development and maintenance of a distorted body image]. *Psychotherapeut, 60*(6), 477–487. https://doi.org/10.1007/s00278-015-0058-z

Cragun, D., DeBate, R.D., Ata, R.N., & Thompson, J.K. (2013). Psychometric properties of the body esteem scale for adolescents and adults in an early adolescent sample. *Eating and Weight Disorders, 18*(3), 275–282. https://doi.org/10.1007/s40519-013-0031-1

Day, S., Bussey, K., Trompeter, N., Hay, P., Lonergan, A., & Mitchison, D. (2021). Associations of weight- or shape-related bullying with diverse disordered eating behaviors in adolescents. *International Journal of Eating Disorders, 54*(9), 1641–1651. https://doi.org/10.1002/eat.23573

Enander, J., Ivanov, V.Z., Mataix-Cols, D., Kuja-Halkola, R., Ljótsson, B., Lundström, S., Pérez-Vigil, A., Monzani, B., Lichtenstein, P., & Rück, C. (2018). Prevalence and heritability of body dysmorphic symptoms in adolescents and young adults: A population-based nationwide twin study. *Psychological Medicine, 48*(16), 2740–2747. https://doi.org/10.1017/S0033291718000375

Espelage, D.L., Mazzeo, S.E., Aggen, S.H., Quittner, A.L., Sherman, R., & Thompson, R. (2003). Examining the construct validity of the eating disorder inventory. *Psychological Assessment, 15*(1), 71–80. https://doi.org/10.1037/1040-3590.15.1.71

Fairburn, C.G., & Beglin, S.J. (1994). The assessment of eating disorders: Interview or self-report questionnaire? *International Journal of Eating Disorders, 16*(4), 363–370. https://doi.org/10.1002/1098-108X(199412)16:4<363::AID-EAT2260160405>3.0.CO;2-#

Fairburn, C.G., Cooper, Z., & Shafran, R. (2003). Cognitive behaviour therapy for eating disorders: A "transdiagnostic" theory and treatment. *Behaviour Research and Therapy, 41*(5), 509–528. https://doi.org/10.1016/S0005-7967(02)00088-8

Garner, D.M. (1991). *Eating disorder inventory-2: Professional manual.* Psychological Assessment Resources.

Garner, D.M. (2004). *Eating disorder inventory-3: Professional manual.* Psychological Assessment Resources.

Garner, D.M., Olmstead, M.P., & Polivy, J. (1983). Development and validation of a multidimensional eating disorder inventory for anorexia and bulimia. *International Journal of Eating Disorders, 2*(2), 15–34. https://doi.org/10.1002/1098-108X(198321)2:2<15::AID-EAT2260020203>3.0.CO;2-6

Grieve, F.G. (2007). A conceptual model of factors contributing to the development of muscle dysmorphia. *Eating Disorders, 15*(1), 63–80. https://doi.org/10.1080/10640260601044535

Haase, A.M., Mountford, V., & Waller, G. (2011). Associations between body checking and disordered eating behaviors in nonclinical women. *International Journal of Eating Disorders, 44*(5), 465–468. https://doi.org/10.1002/eat.20837

Halliwell, E., Jarman, H., Tylka, T., & Slater, A. (2017). Adapting the body appreciation scale-2 for children: A psychometric analysis of the BAS-2C. *Body Image, 21*, 97–102. https://doi.org/10.1016/j.bodyim.2017.03.005

Hartmann, A.S., Thomas, J.J., Greenberg, J.L., Elliott, C.M., Matheny, N.L., & Wilhelm, S. (2015). Anorexia nervosa and body dysmorphic disorder: A comparison of body image concerns and explicit and implicit attractiveness beliefs. *Body Image, 14*, 77–84. https://doi.org/10.1016/j.bodyim.2015.03.013

Heinberg, L.J., Thompson, J.K., & Stormer, S. (1995). Development and validation of the sociocultural attitudes towards appearance questionnaire. *International Journal of Eating Disorders, 17*(1), 81–89. https://doi.org/10.1002/1098-108X(199501)17:1<81::AID-EAT2260170111>3.0.CO;2-Y

Hildebrandt, T., Langenbucher, J., & Schlundt, D.G. (2004). Muscularity concerns among men: Development of attitudinal and perceptual measures. *Body Image, 1*(2), 169–181. https://doi.org/10.1016/j.bodyim.2004.01.001

Hildebrandt, T., Walker, C.D., Alfano, L., Delinsky, S., & Bannon, K. (2010). Development and validation of a male specific body checking questionnaire. *International Journal of Eating Disorders, 43*(1), 77–87. https://doi.org/10.1002/eat.20669

Homan, K.J. (2016). Factor structure and psychometric properties of a state version of the body appreciation scale-2. *Body Image, 19*, 204–207. https://doi.org/10.1016/j.bodyim.2016.10.004

Hrabosky, J.I., Cash, T.F., Veale, D., Neziroglu, F., Soll, E.A., Garner, D.M., Strachan-Kinser, M., Bakke, B., Clauss, L.J., & Phillips, K.A. (2009). Multidimensional body image comparisons among patients with eating disorders, body dysmorphic disorder, and clinical controls: A multisite study. *Body Image, 6*(3), 155–163. https://doi.org/10.1016/j.bodyim.2009.03.001

Jennings, K.M., & Phillips, K.E. (2017). Eating disorder examination-questionnaire (EDE-Q): Norms for clinical sample of female adolescents with anorexia nervosa. *Archives of Psychiatric Nursing, 31*(6), 578–581. https://doi.org/10.1016/j.apnu.2017.08.002

Jorgensen, L., Castle, D., Roberts, C., & Groth-Marnat, G. (2001). A clinical validation of the dysmorphic concern questionnaire. *Australian & New Zealand Journal of Psychiatry, 35*(1), 124–128. https://doi.org/10.1046/j.1440-1614.2001.00860.x

Killen, J.D., Taylor, C.B., Hammer, L.D., Litt, I., Wilson, D.M., Rich, T., Hayward, C., Simmonds, B., Kraemer, H., & Varady, A. (1993). An attempt to modify unhealthful eating attitudes and weight regulation practices of young adolescent girls. *International Journal of Eating Disorders, 13*(4), 369–384. https://doi.org/10.1002/1098-108X(199305)13:4<369::AID-EAT2260130405>3.0.CO;2-0

Killen, J.D., Taylor, C.B., Hayward, C., Wilson, D.M., Haydel, K.F., Hammer, L.D., Simmonds, B., Robinson, T.N., Litt, I., Varady, A., & Kraemer, H. (1994). Pursuit of thinness and onset of eating disorder symptoms in a community sample of adolescent girls: A three-year prospective analysis. *International Journal of Eating Disorders, 16*(3), 227–238. https://doi.org/10.1002/1098-108X(199411)16:3<227::AID-EAT2260160303>3.0.CO;2-L

Longobardi, C., Prino, L. E., Fabris, M. A., & Settanni, M. (2017). Muscle dysmorphia and psychopathology: Findings from an Italian sample of male bodybuilders. *Psychiatry Research, 256*, 231–236. https://doi.org/10.1016/j.psychres.2017.06.065

Mancuso, S. G., Knoesen, N. P., & Castle, D. J. (2010). The dysmorphic concern questionnaire: A screening measure for body dysmorphic disorder. *Australian & New Zealand Journal of Psychiatry, 44*(6), 535–542. https://doi.org/10.3109/00048671003596055

Marco, J. H., Perpiñá, C., Roncero, M., & Botella, C. (2017). Confirmatory factor analysis and psychometric properties of the Spanish version of the multidimensional body-self relations questionnaire-appearance scales in early adolescents. *Body Image, 21*, 15–18. https://doi.org/10.1016/j.bodyim.2017.01.003

Mayville, S. B., Williamson, D. A., White, M. A., Netemeyer, R. G., & Drab, D. L. (2002). Development of the muscle appearance satisfaction scale: A self-report measure for the assessment of muscle dysmorphia symptoms. *Assessment, 9*(4), 351–360. https://doi.org/10.1177/1073191102238156

McCreary, D. R., & Sasse, D. K. (2000). An exploration of the drive for muscularity in adolescent boys and girls. *Journal of American College Health, 48*(6), 297–304. https://doi.org/10.1080/07448480009596271

McCreary, D. R., Sasse, D. K., Saucier, D. M., & Dorsch, K. D. (2004). Measuring the drive for muscularity: Factorial validity of the drive for muscularity scale in men and women. *Psychology of Men & Masculinity, 5*(1), 49–58. https://doi.org/10.1037/1524-9220.5.1.49

McPherson, K. E., McCarthy, P., McCreary, D. R., & McMillan, S. (2010). Psychometric evaluation of the drive for muscularity scale in a community-based sample of Scottish men participating in an organized sporting event. *Body Image, 7*(4), 368–371. https://doi.org/10.1016/j.bodyim.2010.06.001

Mendelson, B. K., Mendelson, M. J., & White, D. R. (2001). Body-esteem scale for adolescents and adults. *Journal of Personality Assessment, 76*(1), 90–106. https://doi.org/10.1207/S15327752JPA7601_6

Meyer, C., McPartlan, L., Rawlinson, A., Bunting, J., & Waller, G. (2011). Body-related behaviours and cognitions: Relationship to eating psychopathology in non-clinical women and men. *Behavioural and Cognitive Psychotherapy, 39*(5), 591–600. https://doi.org/10.1017/S1352465811000270

Mölbert, S. C., Thaler, A., Streuber, S., Black, M. J., Karnath, H.-O., Zipfel, S., Mohler, B., & Giel, K. E. (2017). Investigating body image disturbance in anorexia nervosa using novel biometric figure rating scales: A pilot study. *European Eating Disorders Review, 25*(6), 607–612. https://doi.org/10.1002/erv.2559

Möllmann, A., & Buhlmann, U. (2021a). *BDD-5 adolescents. Body dysmorphic disorder – self-report criteria according to DSM-5.* https://doi.org/10.17605/OSF.IO/WAH8D

Möllmann, A., & Buhlmann, U. (2021b). *BDD-5 adults. Body dysmorphic disorder – self-report criteria according to DSM-5.* https://doi.org/10.17605/OSF.IO/WAH8D

Mond, J., Hall, A., Brentley, C., Harrison, C., Gratwick-Sarll, K., & Lewis, V. (2014). Eating-disordered behavior in adolescent boys: Eating disorder examination questionnaire norms. *International Journal of Eating Disorders, 47*(4), 335–341. https://doi.org/10.1002/eat.22237

Mond, J. M., Myers, T. C., Crosby, R. D., Hay, P. J., Rodgers, B., Morgan, J. F., Lacey, J. H., & Mitchell, J. E. (2008). Screening for eating disorders in primary care: EDE-Q versus SCOFF. *Behaviour Research and Therapy, 46*(5), 612–622. https://doi.org/10.1016/j.brat.2008.02.003

Mountford, V., Haase, A., & Waller, G. (2006). Body checking in the eating disorders: Associations between cognitions and behaviors. *International Journal of Eating Disorders, 39*(8), 708–715. https://doi.org/10.1002/eat.20279

O'Brien, K. S., Caputi, P., Minto, R., Peoples, G., Hooper, C., Kell, S., & Sawley, E. (2009). Upward and downward physical appearance comparisons: Development of scales and examination of predictive qualities. *Body Image, 6*(3), 201–206. https://doi.org/10.1016/j.bodyim.2009.03.003

Oosthuizen, P., Lambert, T., & Castle, D. J. (1998). Dysmorphic concern: Prevalence and associations with clinical variables. *Australian & New Zealand Journal of Psychiatry, 32*(1), 129–132. https://doi.org/10.3109/00048679809062719

Phillips, K. A., Hollander, E., Rasmussen, S. A., Aronowitz, B. R., DeCaria, C., & Goodman, W. K. (1997). A severity rating scale for body dysmorphic disorder: Development, reliability, and validity of a modified version of the Yale-Brown obsessive compulsive scale. *Psychopharmacological Bulletin, 33*(1), 17–22.

Ralph-Nearman, C., & Filik, R. (2018). New body scales reveal body dissatisfaction, thin-ideal, and muscularity-ideal in males. *American Journal of Men's Health, 12*(4), 740–750. https://doi.org/10.1177/1557988318763516

Ralph-Nearman, C., & Filik, R. (2020). Development and validation of new figural scales for female body dissatisfaction assessment on two dimensions: Thin-ideal and muscularity-ideal. *BMC Public Health, 20*, Article 1114. https://doi.org/10.1186/s12889-020-09094-6

Rand-Giovannetti, D., Cicero, D.C., Mond, J.M., & Latner, J.D. (2020). Psychometric properties of the Eating Disorder Examination–Questionnaire (EDE-Q): A confirmatory factor analysis and assessment of measurement invariance by sex. *Assessment, 27*(1), 164–177. https://doi.org/10.1177/1073191117738046

Reas, D.L., Whisenhunt, B.L., Netemeyer, R., & Williamson, D.A. (2002). Development of the body checking questionnaire: A self-report measure of body checking behaviors. *International Journal of Eating Disorders, 31*(3), 324–333. https://doi.org/10.1002/eat.10012

Rhea, D.J., Lantz, C.D., & Cornelius, A.E. (2004). Development of the muscle dysmorphia inventory (MDI). *Journal of Sports Medicine and Physical Fitness, 44*(4), 428–435.

Rosen, J.C., Srebnik, D., Saltzberg, E., & Wendt, S. (1991). Development of a body image avoidance questionnaire. *Psychological Assessment, 3*(1), 32–37. https://doi.org/10.1037/1040-3590.3.1.32

Ryan, T.A., & Morrison, T.G. (2013). Psychometric evaluation of the drive for leanness scale in a sample of Irish men. *Eating Behaviors, 14*(1), 21–25. https://doi.org/10.1016/j.eatbeh.2012.10.002

Ryan, T.A., Morrison, T.G., Roddy, S., & McCutcheon, J. (2011). Psychometric properties of the revised male body attitudes scale among Irish men. *Body Image, 8*(1), 64–69. https://doi.org/10.1016/j.bodyim.2010.10.004

Salbach-Andrae, H., Schneider, N., Bürger, A., Pfeiffer, E., Lehmkuhl, U., & Holzhausen, M. (2010). Psychometrische Gütekriterien des Eating Disorder Inventory (EDI-2) bei Jugendlichen [Psychometric properties of the eating disorder inventory (EDI-2) in adolescents]. *Zeitschrift für Kinder- und Jugendpsychiatrie und Psychotherapie, 38*(3), 219–228. https://doi.org/10.1024/1422-4917/a000035

Schieber, K., Kollei, I., de Zwaan, M., & Martin, A. (2018). The dysmorphic concern questionnaire in the German general population: Psychometric properties and normative data. *Aesthetic Plastic Surgery, 42*, 1412–1420. https://doi.org/10.1007/s00266-018-1183-1

Sepúlveda, A.R., Anastasiadou, D., Pellegrin, Y. de, Parks, M., Blanco, M., Garcia, P., & Bustos, C. (2017). Confirmatory factor analysis of the male body attitudes scale (MBAS) among Spanish adolescent males. *Men and Masculinities, 20*(3), 345–363. https://doi.org/10.1177/1097184X16634798

Smith, K.E., Mason, T.B., Murray, S.B., Griffiths, S., Leonard, R.C., Wetterneck, C.T., Smith, B.E.R., Farrell, N.R., Riemann, B.C., & Lavender, J.M. (2017). Male clinical norms and sex differences on the Eating Disorder Inventory (EDI) and Eating Disorder Examination Questionnaire (EDE-Q). *International Journal of Eating Disorders, 50*(7), 769–775. https://doi.org/10.1002/eat.22716

Smolak, L., & Murnen, S.K. (2008). Drive for leanness: Assessment and relationship to gender, gender role and objectification. *Body Image, 5*(3), 251–260. https://doi.org/10.1016/j.bodyim.2008.03.004

Stangier, U., Janich, C., Adam-Schwebe, S., Berger, P., & Wolter, M. (2003). Screening for body dysmorphic disorder in dermatological outpatients. *Dermatology and Psychosomatics, 4*(2), 66–71. https://doi.org/10.1159/000072194

Stapleton, P., McIntyre, T., & Bannatyne, A. (2016). Body image avoidance, body dissatisfaction, and eating pathology: Is there a difference between male gym users and non-gym users? *American Journal of Men's Health, 10*(2), 100–109. https://doi.org/10.1177/1557988314556673

Steinfeld, B., Bauer, A., Waldorf, M., Engel, N., Braks, K., Huber, T.J., & Vocks, S. (2017). Validierung einer deutschsprachigen Fassung des Body Checking Questionnaire (BCQ) an Jugendlichen mit Anorexia und Bulimia Nervosa [Validation of a German-language version of the Body Checking Questionnaire (BCQ) in adolescents with anorexia and bulimia nervosa]. *Psychotherapie, Psychosomatik, Medizinische Psychologie, 67*(1), 38–46. https://doi.org/10.1055/s-0042-110851

Steinfeld, B., Hartmann, A.S., Waldorf, M., & Vocks, S. (2020). Development and initial psychometric evaluation of the body image matrix of thinness and muscularity – female bodies. *Journal of Eating Disorders, 8*, Article 75. https://doi.org/10.1186/s40337-020-00345-w

Stice, E. (2001). A prospective test of the dual-pathway model of bulimic pathology: Mediating effects of dieting and negative affect. *Journal of Abnormal Psychology, 110*(1), 124–135. https://doi.org/10.1037/0021-843X.110.1.124

Talbot, D., Smith, E., Cass, J., & Griffiths, S. (2019). Development and validation of the new somatomorphic matrix-male: A figural rating scale for measuring male actual-ideal body discrepancy. *Psychology of Men & Masculinities, 20*(3), 356–367. https://doi.org/10.1037/men0000165

Tantleff-Dunn, S., Thompson, J.K., & Dunn, M.E. (1995). The Feedback on Physical Appearance Scale (FOPAS): Questionnaire development and psychometric evaluation. *Eating Disorders, 3*(4), 332–341. https://doi.org/10.1080/10640269508250063

Thiel, A., & Paul, T. (2006). Test-retest reliability of the eating disorder inventory-2. *Journal of Psychosomatic Research, 61*(4), 567–569. https://doi.org/10.1016/j.jpsychores.2006.02.015

Thompson, J.K., Cattarin, J., Fowler, B., & Fisher, E. (1995). The perception of teasing scale (POTS): A revision and extension of the physical appearance related teasing scale (PARTS). *Journal of Personality Assessment, 65*(1), 146–157. https://doi.org/10.1207/s15327752jpa6501_11

Thompson, J.K., Heinberg, L.J., Altabe, M., & Tantleff-Dunn, S. (1999). *Exacting beauty: Theory, assessment, and treatment of body image disturbance*. American Psychological Association. https://doi.org/10.1037/10312-000

Tod, D., Hall, G., & Edwards, C. (2012). Gender invariance and correlates of the drive for leanness scale. *Body Image, 9*(4), 555–558. https://doi.org/10.1016/j.bodyim.2012.06.004

Tylka, T.L. (2011). Refinement of the tripartite influence model for men: Dual body image pathways to body change behaviors. *Body Image, 8*(3), 199–207. https://doi.org/10.1016/j.bodyim.2011.04.008

Tylka, T.L., Bergeron, D., & Schwartz, J.P. (2005). Development and psychometric evaluation of the Male Body Attitudes Scale (MBAS). *Body Image, 2*(2), 161–175. https://doi.org/10.1016/j.bodyim.2005.03.001

Tylka, T.L., & Wood-Barcalow, N.L. (2015). The Body Appreciation Scale-2: Item refinement and psychometric evaluation. *Body Image, 12*, 53–67. https://doi.org/10.1016/j.bodyim.2014.09.006

Vocks, S., Legenbauer, T., Wächter, A., Wucherer, M., & Kosfelder, J. (2007). What happens in the course of body exposure? Emotional, cognitive, and physiological reactions to mirror confrontation in eating disorders. *Journal of Psychosomatic Research, 6*(2), 231–239. https://doi.org/10.1016/j.jpsychores.2006.08.007

Vossbeck-Elsebusch, A.N., Waldorf, M., Legenbauer, T., Bauer, A., Cordes, M., & Vocks, S. (2014). German version of the Multidimensional Body-Self Relations Questionnaire-Appearance Scales (MBSRQ-AS): Confirmatory factor analysis and validation. *Body Image, 11*(3), 191–200. https://doi.org/10.1016/j.bodyim.2014.02.002

Williamson, D.A., White, M.A., York-Crowe, E., & Stewart, T.M. (2004). Cognitive-behavioral theories of eating disorders. *Behavior Modification, 28*(6), 711–738. https://doi.org/10.1177/0145445503259853

Zeeck, A., Welter, V., Alatas, H., Hildebrandt, T., Lahmann, C., & Hartmann, A. (2018). Muscle Dysmorphic Disorder Inventory (MDDI): Validation of a German version with a focus on gender. *PLoS ONE, 13*(11), Article e0207535. https://doi.org/10.1371/journal.pone.0207535

Chapter 13

Assessment of Physical Activity

Elizabeth W. Lampe[1] and Sasha Gorrell[2]

[1] Center for Weight Eating and Lifestyle Science (WELL Center), Drexel University, PA, USA
[2] Department of Psychiatry and Behavioral Sciences, University of California, San Francisco, CA, USA

Introduction

Exercise is generally encouraged for its physical and mental health benefits (Catalan-Matamoros et al., 2016; Penedo & Dahn, 2005). However, among those with eating disorders (EDs), exercise may be maladaptive in nature (Cook & Hausenblas, 2008; Holland et al., 2014) whereby exercise may be used to control body shape or weight, or compensate for calories consumed (e.g., Monell et al., 2018). Maladaptive exercise is recognized as an important factor in the etiology and maintenance of transdiagnostic EDs (Meyer et al. 2011). An emerging literature also indicates that for some individuals with EDs, exercise may not be driven or compensatory (e.g., Lampe et al., 2021), and entirely adaptive (Kerrigan et al., 2019; Lampe et al., 2021; Wons et al., 2021). Given its complexity, comprehensive understanding of maladaptive and adaptive exercise among ED samples will aid in improving assessment, treatment, and prevention efforts.

Early definitions relied on its "excessive" quality (Bell, 1994), but consensus around a definition of maladaptive exercise remains elusive (Bratland-Sanda, 2011; Dittmer et al., 2018; Voderholzer, 2019; Mond & Gorrell, 2021). Research has coalesced around its compulsive nature (Dittmer et al., 2018; Noetel et al., 2017; Rizk et al., 2015) but models of maladaptive exercise offer disparate mechanisms driving engagement. One model characterizes a behavioral addiction, whereby exercise might initially elicit positive affect, but then lead to tolerance (i.e., increased intensity needed to experience an effect), and withdrawal (e.g., anxiety, guilt; Hausenblas & Downs, 2002b). Another model characterizes a compulsion to exercise to reduce or avoid negative affect or feared consequences (e.g., weight gain; Meyer et al., 2011). Both models describe behavior maintained via negative reinforcement (e.g., reducing negative affect) and positive reinforcement (e.g., increasing positive affect; Coniglio et al., 2021).

Other nuanced factors may interact with exercise pathology such as a focus on leanness or muscularity (Lavender et al., 2017) and athlete status (particularly those in aesthetic or weight-class sports; Gorrell et al., 2021; Plateau et al., 2017). Given that athletic participation may also be protective against disordered eating (Calogero & Pedrotty, 2004), there is an acute need for accurate assessment. To synthesize the current state of exercise assessment in EDs, this chapter reviews measures of general and pathological exercise. We provide guidance around best practices for measuring objective and psychological aspects of exercise, and relative strengths and weaknesses of each approach.

Interview

Eating Disorder Examination

Evaluating exercise often relies on interview assessment, including the Eating Disorder Examination (EDE; Table 13.1). The EDE (Fairburn et al., 1993) and the Children's EDE (Bryant-Waugh et al., 1996) ask, "How many times in the last four weeks (28 days) have you exercised to control your shape or weight?" on a 7-point scale (0 = *no days* to 6 = *every day*). The EDE also assesses exercise over the past 3 months; it measures behavior motivated by weight/shape concern, but does not measure overall or adaptive exercise.

Table 13.1. Interview

Measure	Construct	Time	Psychometrics
Eating Disorder Examination	Exercise frequency to control shape/weight in the last four weeks	Last 3 months	—
Structured Interview for Anorexic & Bulimic Disorders	Five levels of excessive exercise (intended to control shape/weight)	Last 3 months	—
Yale–Brown–Cornell Eating Disorder Scale	Two subscales regarding exercise: (1) Frequency or Intensity of Intrusive Thoughts; (2) Frequency and Type of Rituals	In general	—
Modified Substance Dependence Severity Scale	Seven items, each corresponding to DSM-IV criteria for substance dependence, modified for exercise	In general	—

Structured Interview for Anorexic and Bulimic Disorders

The Structured Interview for Anorexic & Bulimic Disorders (SIAB; Fichter et al., 1998) asks "How much exercise did you engage in?" It refers to the past 3 months and includes five levels: (1) no excessive exercise; (2) rarely exercising to burn calories/reduce weight; (3) occasional excessive exercise (up to twice/week); may report discomfort when prevented; (4) frequent excessive exercise (every day > 1 hour or 3–4 times/week for

≥2 hours); discomfort when prevented; (5) excessive exercise > once/day or for longer periods (> 1.5 hours/day); occurs irrespective of physical pain.

Yale-Brown-Cornell Eating Disorder Scale

The Yale-Brown-Cornell Eating Disorder Scale (YBC-EDS; Mazure et al., 1994) uses eight items to assess ED-related preoccupation or rituals (includes exercise). It has three subscales: (1) Preoccupation (frequency or intensity of intrusive thoughts); (2) Ritual (frequency and type); (3) Motivation to Change Behavior.

Modified Substance Dependence Severity Scale

The Modified Substance Dependence Severity Scale (SDSS; Miele et al., 2000a, 2000b) contains seven items corresponding to DSM-IV criteria for substance dependence (Bell, 1994), modified for exercise: (1) loss of control, more vigorous or longer than intended; (2) persistent desire/unsuccessful attempts to cut down or control; (3) time spent; (4) social, occupational/academic, other activities reduced/given up; (5) tolerance; (6) withdrawal; (7) continued despite physical problem/injury. The scale delineates criterion met fully (2), partially (1), or not at all (0).

Strengths and Weaknesses

Interviews are administered and scored by trained raters, offer standardized ratings, and allow for follow-up questions. However, they are subject to social desirability bias, and ED symptoms are often denied or minimized (Couturier & Lock, 2006). Interviews are also based on recall, with evidence that self-reported exercise frequency is inaccurate (Mâsse & Judith, 2012). The EDE demonstrates adequate content validity in ED samples, but its measure of exercise has not been independently validated. Further, the SDSS has shown good content validity in those with substance abuse, but the exercise-modified version has not been validated.

Self-Report

General Exercise

Seven-Day Physical Activity Recall

Self-report of exercise ranges from six to 51 items (Table 13.2). The Seven-Day Physical Activity Recall (PAR; Blair et al., 1985) queries recall for the previous day, for 7 days. Activity is classified by minute and intensities (i.e., light, moderate, vigorous). The PAR has not been tested for discriminant or content validity in ED samples, but demonstrates good content validity in adults and young adults (Lamb & Brodie, 1990; Washburn et al., 2003).

International Physical Activity Questionnaire

Two versions of the International Physical Activity Questionnaire (IPAQ; Craig et al., 2003) assess exercise over the last 7 days. The nine-item version assesses time spent walking at vigorous or moderate intensity, and sedentary activity. The 31-item version assesses household/yard/occupational/sedentary/leisure-time activity, and self-powered transport. One question asks about walking or cycling pace. The IPAQ has not been preliminarily validated in EDs, but demonstrates adequate internal reliability across samples (Craig et al., 2003; Lee et al., 2011).

Godin Leisure-Time Exercise Questionnaire

The Godin Leisure-Time Exercise Questionnaire (GLTEQ; Amireault & Godin, 2015) assesses the frequency of activity performed for >15 minutes during free time over a 7-day period. Activities are strenuous (e.g., running), moderate (e.g., fast walking), or mild (e.g., yoga) for "long enough to work up a sweat" and responses span *often*, *sometimes*, or *never/ rarely*. The GLTEQ has not been tested for content validity in ED samples, but demonstrates adequate internal reliability in adults and adolescents (Amireault & Godin, 2015; Zelener & Schneider, 2016).

Paffenbarger Physical Activity Questionnaire

The Paffenbarger Physical Activity Questionnaire (PPAQ; Simpson, 2011) assesses city blocks walked and flights of stairs climbed on a typical day, and frequency and type of sports/recreational activity in the past year. Based on responses, energy expenditure is estimated with an exercise index (Paffenbarger et al., 1978). Other questions assess exercise frequency and intensity. The PPAQ has not been tested for content validity in ED samples, but demonstrates adequate internal reliability among adults (Simpson, 2011; Simpson et al., 2015).

Motivation

Reasons for Exercise Inventory

The Reasons for Exercise Inventory (REI; Silberstein et al., 1988) assesses exercise for weight control, fitness, improving health, body tone, physical attractiveness, mood, and enjoyment. Each motive statement refers to a reason to exercise on a 7-point scale (ranging from 1=*not at all important* to 7=*extremely important*). The REI demonstrates adequate content validity in healthy adults (Courneya & McAuley, 1995) and adults with anorexia nervosa (Young et al., 2017).

Table 13.2. Self-Report

Category	Measure	Construct	Time	Psychometrics
General Exercise	Seven-Day Physical Activity Recall	Time spent in "moderate," "hard," or "very hard" activity	Last 7 days	$r = .87$ with 7-day diary
	International Physical Activity Questionnaire	Time spent active, sitting, walking, or engaged in moderate or vigorous activity	"A typical week"	—
	Godin Leisure-Time Exercise Questionnaire	Frequency of bouts of > 15 minutes of mild (e.g., "yoga, easy walking"), moderate (e.g., "fast walking, easy bicycling") or strenuous (e.g., "jogging, vigorous swimming") activity in a typical week	"A typical week"	—
	Paffenbarger Physical Activity Questionnaire	Flights of stairs climbed or city blocks walked in a typical day and duration of weekly sports or recreational activity	"A typical day/ week"	—
General Exercise Motives	Reasons for Exercise Inventory	Exercise for: weight control, fitness, health, improving body tone, physical attractiveness, mood, or enjoyment	In general	$\alpha = .67–.81$ across subscales
	Exercise Motivations Inventory-2	Exercise for: stress management, revitalization, enjoyment, challenge, social recognition, affiliation, competition, health pressures, ill-health avoidance, positive health, weight management, appearance, strength and endurance, nimbleness	In general	$\alpha = .75–.96$ across subscales
	Drive for Muscularity Scale	Desire for muscularity via two subscales: Muscularity Attitudes and Muscularity Behaviors	In general	—
	Muscle Dysmorphia Inventory	Psychological and behavioral aspects of muscle dysmorphia via six subscales: Diet, Supplement, Physique Protection, Exercise Dependence, Size/Symmetry, and Pharmacology	In general	—

Table 13.2. continued

Category	Measure	Construct	Time	Psychometrics
Maladaptive Exercise	Eating Disorder Examination Questionnaire	Frequency of "hard exercise for weight/shape control"	Past 28 days	—
	Diagnostic Survey for Eating Disorders	Frequency and duration of compensatory exercise	In general	—
	Eating Disorders Inventory-Symptom Checklist	Percentage of exercise aimed at controlling weight	In general	α = .90–.97
	Commitment to Exercise Scale	Obligatory aspects (e.g., feeling guilt with a missed exercise session; need to continue in the face of illness or injury)	In general	α = .96
	Compulsive Exercise Test	Avoidance and rule-driven; weight control; mood improvement; lack of enjoyment; rigidity	In general	α = .85–.94 across studies
	[modified] Obligatory Running Questionnaire	*Exercise behaviors:* Frequency and duration, solitary/secret, association between eating and exercise and hyperactivity *Exercise cognitions:* Motives, perceived adequacy and importance of exercise, feelings after or failure to exercise	In general	—
	Obligatory Exercise Questionnaire	Emotional element of exercise; exercise frequency and intensity; exercise preoccupation	In general	*r* = .01–.26 with EDI subscales
	Exercise Addiction Inventory	Exercise salience, mood modification, conflict around exercise, tolerance, withdrawal, relapse	In general	α = .84
	Exercise Beliefs Questionnaire	Beliefs about not being able to exercise regularly	In general	—

Exercise Motivations Inventory-2

The Exercise Motivations Inventory-2 (EMI-2; Markland & Ingledew, 1997) assesses exercise for enjoyment, health improvement, weight management, appearance, and physical fitness. It also queries exercise for stress management, revitalization, challenge, social recognition, affiliation, competition, health pressures, ill-health avoidance, and nimbleness. Responses are made on a 6-point scale (ranging from 1=*not at all true for me* to 6=*very true for me*). The EMI-2 demonstrates adequate content validity in healthy adults (Markland & Ingledew, 1997), but has not been tested for preliminary validity in ED samples.

Drive for Muscularity Scale

The Drive for Muscularity Scale (DMS; McCreary & Sasse, 2000; McCreary et al., 2004) assesses a desire for muscularity with two subscales: Muscularity Attitudes and Muscularity Behaviors. The DMS demonstrates good internal reliability and content validity in adolescents and adults, but has not been tested for content or discriminant validity in ED samples.

Muscle Dysmorphia Inventory

The Muscle Dysmorphia Inventory (MDI; Rhea et al., 2004) assesses muscle dysmorphia with six subscales: Diet, Supplement, Physique Protection, Exercise Dependence, Size/Symmetry, and Pharmacology. The MDI has shown good internal reliability and content validity among weight lifters/bodybuilders but has not been tested for discriminant validity in ED samples.

Maladaptive Exercise

Eating Disorders Inventory-Symptom Checklist

The Eating Disorders Inventory-Symptom Checklist (EDI-SC; Garner & Olmsted, 1986) assesses the proportion of exercise aimed at controlling weight/shape; it has not been independently tested for content validity.

Diagnostic Survey for Eating Disorders

The Diagnostic Survey for Eating Disorders (DSED; Johnson, 1987) assesses exercise for the purpose of "working off" daily calories and includes frequency and duration; it has not been independently tested for content validity.

Exercise Addiction Inventory

The Exercise Addiction Inventory (EAI; Griffiths et al., 2005) assesses exercise for mood modification, conflict around exercise, salience, tolerance, withdrawal, and relapse. It demonstrates adequate internal reliability in adults (Griffiths et al., 2005), but has not been tested for content validity in ED samples.

Compulsive Exercise Test

The Compulsive Exercise Test (CET; Taranis et al., 2011) measures exercise obligation or rigidity on a 6-point scale (0 = *never true* to 5 = *always true*). It demonstrates good content and discriminant validity in adults with anorexia nervosa, but has not been validated in other adult ED samples (Young et al., 2017). The CET was tested for content validity in community youth (Goodwin et al., 2011), and in adolescents with transdiagnostic EDs (Noetel et al., 2017; Swenne, 2016). Two CET subscales, Avoidance and Rule-Driven Exercise and Weight-Control Exercise, show strong correlations with Eating Disorder Examination-Questionnaire (EDE-Q) scores in young females (Taranis & Meyer, 2011) and in college students (Zhan et al., 2022). Two studies used an athlete-adapted CET (Scott et al., 2020; Scott et al., 2021).

Modified Obligatory Running Questionnaire

A modified Modified Obligatory Running Questionnaire (ORQ) has been used to assess obligatory exercise in ED samples (Blumenthal et al., 1984). It assesses exercise behavior (e.g., frequency) and cognitions (e.g., motives); preliminary validity for the modified version is not available.

Obligatory Exercise Questionnaire

The Obligatory Exercise Questionnaire (OEQ) assesses frequency and intensity, emotions, and preoccupation with exercise (Steffen & Brehm, 1999). It shows good content validity in healthy adults (Duncan et al., 2012), and small–moderate correlations between the OEQ and EDI (Steffen & Brehm, 1999). Based on factor loading (Steffen & Brehm, 1999), Homan (2010) and Holland et al. (2017) combined four items that address guilt or depression (e.g., "When I miss a scheduled exercise session, I may feel tense, irritable, or depressed") as a continuous variable.

Exercise Beliefs Questionnaire

The 21-item Exercise Beliefs Questionnaire (EBQ; Loumidis & Wells, 1998) measures exercise beliefs and compulsive attitudes (Hay et al., 2018). It demonstrates adequate reliability and validity in samples with depression or anxiety (Loumidis & Wells, 1998), but has not been tested for discriminant or content validity in ED samples.

Commitment to Exercise Scale

The Commitment to Exercise Scale (CES; Davis et al., 1993) measures exercise obligation/rigidity on a visual analog scale (*never* to *always*) and demonstrates good content validity in ED samples (Davis et al., 1995; Young et al., 2017). It has been used to evaluate exercise interventions in youth (Mang et al., 2021) and adults (Dittmer et al., 2020; Hay et al., 2018).

EDE-Q – Single-Item Measure

The EDE-Q (Fairburn & Beglin, 1994) includes a single item: "Over the past 4 weeks (28 days), how many times have you exercised in a 'driven' or 'compulsive' way as a means of controlling your weight, shape or amount of fat, or to burn off calories?" This item shows good internal reliability in adults with anorexia nervosa, but has not been validated in other ED samples (Young et al., 2017). Due to skewness in nontreatment seeking samples, the item is frequently dichotomized (0 v. ≥1 times; Ganson et al., 2021; Lavender et al., 2010; Lipson & Sonneville, 2017; Nagata et al., 2020; Schaumberg et al., 2014).

Several studies have used EDE-Q items in youth. One study retained wording similar to the original (Schleien & Bardone-Cone, 2016) but in some work, response options have been simplified i.e., "hard exercise specifically for weight control" (Allen et al., 2013) and recall shortened to 2weeks (Davis et al., 2018).

Other Single Items

In community youth, an Eating Disorders Diagnostic Scale item was tested in relation to depression and body dissatisfaction (McCabe & Ricciardelli, 2006) or overweight status (McCabe & Ricciardelli, 2009). College men reported how many times they "engaged in more intense exercise specifically to counteract the effects of overeating" (Dakanalis et al., 2016). In this study, behavior was coded "present" if participants reported it ≥ once in the past 3 months. In a study using the Youth Risk Behavior Surveillance System Questionnaire item, excessive exercise was defined as endorsing yes to exercising frequently for weight loss even when sick, or feeling guilty when not exercising, over the past 12 months (Solmi et al., 2019).

One study used a single DSED item to determine a group of patients with compulsive exercise based on a cut-off score (Brewerton et al., 1995); those reporting ≥60 minutes/day were considered "compulsive exercisers." Another study used a single item from the Bulimia Test Revised to determine the degree to which participants "exercise to burn calories" (Petrie et al., 2008); response allowed for: >2 hours/day, 2 hours/day, 1–2 hours/day, <1 hour/day, or Don't exercise to burn calories. This study used a frequency count (i.e., number endorsing each level of exercise).

Strengths and Weaknesses

Self-report measures of exercise capture its compensatory or driven nature. However, they rely on recall, and many evaluate behavior "on average" rather than on a specific timescale, which makes reporting inaccuracies likely. Only the 7-day PAR, and EDE-Q assess recent objective exercise (ranging from last 7 to 28 days). Many measures used in ED samples have also not been specifically tested for various forms of validity.

The weakness most germane to the evidence base of self-report exercise is the common use of single items. While they are useful, and certainly appropriate in certain contexts, the frequency with which the ED field has used a tremendously varied selection of single items - often modifying their language - precludes our ability to draw conclusions across the literature. Further, the way that single items have been used to bifurcate samples (e.g., groups of those who exercise maladaptively versus those who do not) has been highly variable across studies particularly in the way in which these categorizations have been made based on a yes/no response to a given question, or instead, based on a count. Together, frequent reliance on different single items maintains ambiguity about how we are defining maladaptive exercise as an ED field and contributes to the disparate prevalence rates of this behavior that we find across samples.

Ecological Momentary Assessment

General Exercise and Motivations

Ecological Momentary Assessment (EMA) captures the type and duration of exercise in real-time (Table 13.3), with a yes/no format (Davis et al., 1995; Lampe et al., 2021; Lavender et al., 2013; Lavender et al., 2016; Ma & Kelly, 2020; Pirke et al., 1991). EMA measure of frequency has demonstrated adequate content validity in binge-spectrum EDs (Lampe et al., 2021), but has not been tested for preliminary validity in other ED samples. This study also assessed motivation using items based on the REI and EMI-2, demonstrating high internal reliability (Lampe et al., 2021).

Maladaptive Exercise

EMA has evaluated exercise for "working off" daily calories (Fitzsimmons-Craft, 2017; Lampe et al., 2021; Stein & Corte, 2003), and frequency of thoughts about engaging in compensatory exercise (Fitzsimmons-Craft, 2017). EMA has also assessed the frequency (Fitzsimmons-Craft, 2017; Stein & Corte, 2003) and extent (Lampe et al., 2021) to which each bout was designed to compensate for eating, on a 5-point scale (1=*not at all* to 5=*extremely*). Some work-derived items from the EDE (Stein & Corte, 2003) or the Questionnaire on Eating and Weight Patterns-Revised (Yanovski et al., 2015). EMA demonstrates adequate internal reliability in binge-spectrum EDs (Lampe et al., 2021), but has not been validated in other samples. Only one study assessed driven exercise (i.e., feeling compelled) among those with binge-spectrum EDs on a 5-point scale (1=*not at all* to 5=*extremely*), demonstrating adequate internal reliability (Lampe et al., 2021).

Table 13.3. Ecological Momentary Assessment

Category	Construct	Wording	Psychometrics
General Exercise	Engagement (Yes/No)	*"Have you exercised since the last survey?"*	—
	Activity type (e.g., running)	—	—
	Duration	—	—
General Exercise Motives	Exercise for: health improvement, emotion regulation, routine, enjoyment, shape/weight control, obligation, or guilt	*"Did you exercise for any of the following reasons?"* • *"because it was part of my routine"* • *"because I would feel guilty if I didn't"* • *"to cope with a difficult emotion"* • *"so that I could eat more later"* • *"to improve my health"* • *"because I enjoy the activity"* • *"to control my shape or weight"* • *"other (specify)"*	α = .91
Maladaptive Exercise	Frequency of thoughts about exercise to control weight and/or shape or burn calories	*"Have you thought about exercising as a means of controlling your weight, altering your shape or amount of fat, or burning off calories?"*	—
	Frequency of exercise to control weight/shape or burn calories	*"Did you actually exercise to influence your shape or weight since the last time you were signaled?"*	—
	Extent of exercising to control weight/shape or burn calories (5-point scale from *not at all* to *extremely*)	*"To what extent did you exercise to compensate for eating?"*	α = .79
	Frequency of urges to "over-exercise"	—	—
	Frequency of "excessive exercise" (1 = *not at all* to 6 = *extremely* or *a lot*)	—	—
	Intensity of feeling driven/compelled to exercise measured from 1 = *not at all* to 5 = *extremely*)	*"To what extent did you feel driven or compelled to exercise?"*	α = .79

Three studies measured "excessive" exercise in ED samples (Levinson et al., 2018; Sala et al., 2019; Vanzhula et al., 2020). These included frequency of urges to "over-exercise" (Levinson et al., 2018) or frequency of "excessive exercise" (Sala et al., 2019; Vanzhula et al., 2020). No studies provided a definition of "excessive" or reported internal reliability statistics.

Strengths and Weaknesses

EMA maximizes ecological validity and can reveal precipitants and consequences of exercise. However, EMA is subject to bias and many studies do not include a definition of exercise. Some report only that "ED behaviors were assessed, including exercise" (Lavender et al., 2013; Lavender et al., 2016); one study measured "exercise episodes" in patients with anorexia nervosa but did not describe their methods (Ma & Kelly, 2020); and several studies failed to define "excessive exercise" for readers or participants (Levinson et al., 2018; Sala et al., 2019; Vanzhula et al., 2020). Few studies report training subjects on how to recognize maladaptive exercise (Fitzsimmons-Craft et al., 2016; Lampe et al., 2021) or derive items from established self-report measures (Lampe et al., 2021; Stein & Corte, 2003).

Objective Exercise

Accelerometry, Pedometry, and Heart Rate Sensors

The most frequently used sensors in EDs are accelerometers (Bratland-Sanda et al., 2011; Chen et al., 2012; Warren et al., 2010), pedometers (McNamara et al., 2010; Palavras et al., 2015), and heart rate sensors (Silfee et al., 2018). Accelerometers (e.g., arm band, wrist- or hip-worn devices) measure vibrations, which are translated with an algorithm differentiating locomotive from non-locomotive movement (Choi et al., 2011; Kozey et al., 2010; Nagayoshi et al., 2019). Activity is translated into metabolic equivalents (METs), quantifying minutes of light, moderate, or vigorous activity (Kozey et al., 2010; Wons et al., 2021); accelerometry also detects intensity, duration, frequency, and type (Choi et al., 2011). Pedometers measure step count (McNamara et al., 2010; Palavras et al., 2015), but do not differentiate between activity types.

Heart rate data can be converted into categories of light, moderate, and vigorous activity using METs (Faust et al., 2019). The Physical Activity Trend eXtraction framework is commonly used; it extracts minutes of moderate-vigorous exercise relative to age and heart rate zones, which are calculated and based off of the Center for Disease Control and American College of Sports Medicine recommendations (Faust et al., 2019). Many commercially available wearable fitness trackers combine sensors (e.g., Apple, Garmin, Fitbit; Kaewkannate & Kim, 2016; Liang et al., 2018) with features like step count, activity timer, distance recording, and sleep tracking (Liang et al., 2018); some wearable fitness trackers also include heart rate monitoring (Liang et al., 2018; Paradiso et al., 2020).

Conclusions

When considering recommendations for assessing exercise across clinical and research settings, many suggestions apply for both. Although maladaptive exercise was historically assessed for frequency, duration, and intensity (Davis & Fox, 1993), general consensus now supports the necessity of evaluating the motivation or function of exercise as well (Dittmer et al., 2018; Noetel et al., 2017). Particularly in the context of EDs, exercise for weight and shape reasons or considerable guilt that arises when one is unable to exercise are two domains that are most frequently associated with elevated eating pathology (Hausenblas & Downs, 2002a; Taranis & Meyer, 2011). Of note, weight loss may not be as motivating as a desire for leanness or muscularity (Lavender et al., 2017); therefore, queries about motivation or function of exercise are potentially best open-ended. It may also be important to consider how *avoidance* of exercise (for any reason) may be problematic. In clinical assessment, issues may arise when asking athletes about exercise using a nonathlete specific measure, given that the amount or rigidity around exercise reported may seem excessive when not considered in context.

The traditional approach to exercise within ED treatment generally recommends cessation in the face of medical acuity, particularly among those at low weight (Golden, 2003). However, a weight-centric approach precludes assisting those who might not be dangerously underweight from achieving a more adaptive relationship with exercise in the context of standard treatment. In addition, growing calls in the last decade support further development of guidelines for reintegrating healthy exercise into treatment (Calogero & Pedrotty-Stump, 2010; Cook et al., 2016), across outpatient (Hay et al., 2018) and inpatient settings (Mang et al., 2021). Recent commentary also suggests a potential benefit to neural plasticity that could arise from incorporating exercise into ED treatment (Mathisen et al., 2021).

In research, in-laboratory, acute measurement of response to exercise is critical (Kolar & Gorrell, 2021; Schaumberg et al., 2021) both to elucidate affect-regulatory mechanisms that maintain exercise (Kolar & Gorrell, 2021) and to inform clinical research design (Coniglio et al., 2021). Further, a majority of work has focused either on restrictive EDs (Dalle Grave et al., 2008) *or* on how exercise promotes weight management (Bardone-Cone et al., 2016). This siloed approach prevents understanding of biobehavioral mechanisms that maintain exercise across transdiagnostic EDs, and the weight spectrum (Mond & Gorrell, 2021). Finally, it is important to work towards consensus around definition and measurement of maladaptive exercise. Recent work has been moving the field towards agreement (Noetel et al., 2017), and all efforts should continue to be made to assess exercise in the context of EDs in ways that allow for greater generalizability and harmonization across the field. This includes assessment across the disease state and diagnoses, with appropriate consideration for how intersectionality of sociodemographic and cultural differences may be represented via the tools we design and use.

Acknowledgment

This work was supported by the National Institutes of Mental Health (K23MH126201). The authors have no conflicts of interest to declare.

References

Allen, K.L., Crosby, R.D., Oddy, W.H., & Byrne, S.M. (2013). Eating disorder symptom trajectories in adolescence: Effects of time, participant sex, and early adolescent depressive symptoms. *Journal of Eating Disorders, 1*(1), 32. https://doi.org/10.1186/2050-2974-1-32

Amireault, S., & Godin, G. (2015). The Godin-Shephard leisure-time physical activity questionnaire: Validity evidence supporting its use for classifying healthy adults into active and insufficiently active categories. *Perceptual and Motor Skills, 120*(2), 604–622. https://doi.org/10.2466/03.27.PMS.120v19x7

Bardone-Cone, A.M., Higgins, M., St. George, S.M., Rosenzweig, I., Schaefer, L.M., Fitzsimmons-Craft, E.E., Henning, T.M., & Preston, B.F. (2016). Behavioral and psychological aspects of exercise across stages of eating disorder recovery. *Eating Disorders, 24*(5), 424–439. https://doi.org/10.1080/10640266.2016.1207452

Bell, C.C. (1994). DSM-IV: Diagnostic and statistical manual of mental disorders. *Journal of the American Medical Association, 272*(10), 828–829. https://doi.org/10.1001/jama.1994.03520100096046

Blair, S., Haskell, W., Ho, P., Paffenbarger, R., Vranizan, K., Farquhar, J., & Wood, P. (1985). Assessment of habitual physical activity by a seven-day recall in a community survey and controlled experiments. *American Journal of Epidemiology, 122*(5), 794–804. https://doi.org/10.1093/oxfordjournals.aje.a114163

Blumenthal, J.A., O'Toole, L.C., & Chang, J.L. (1984). Is running an analogue of anorexia nervosa? An empirical study of obligatory running and anorexia nervosa. *Journal of the American Medical Association, 252*(4), 520–523. https://doi.org/10.1001/jama.1984.03350040050022

Bratland-Sanda, S. (2011). Physical activity and exercise in bulimia nervosa: The two-edged sword. In P. Hay (Ed.), *New Insights into the Prevention and Treatment of Bulimia Nervosa* (pp. 167–178). InTech Open. https://doi.org/10.5772/20649

Bratland-Sanda, S., Martinsen, E.W., Rosenvinge, J.H., Rø, Ø., Hoffart, A., & Sundgot-Borgen, J. (2011). Exercise dependence score in patients with longstanding eating disorders and controls: The importance of affect regulation and physical activity intensity. *European Eating Disorders Review, 19*(3), 249–255. https://doi.org/10.1002/erv.971

Brewerton, T.D., Stellefson, E.J., Hibbs, N., Hodges, E.L., & Cochrane, C.E. (1995). Comparison of eating disorder patients with and without compulsive exercising. *International Journal of Eating Disorders, 17*(4), 413–416.

Bryant-Waugh, R.J., Cooper, P.J., Taylor, C.L., & Lask, B.D. (1996). The use of the eating disorder examination with children: A pilot study. *International Journal of Eating Disorders, 19*(4), 391–397.

Calogero, R.M., & Pedrotty, K.N. (2004). The practice and process of healthy exercise: An investigation of the treatment of exercise abuse in women with eating disorders. *Eating Disorders, 12*(4), 273–291. https://doi.org/10.1080/10640260490521352

Calogero, R.M., & Pedrotty-Stump, K.N. (2010). Incorporating exercise into eating disorder treatment and recovery: Cultivating a mindful approach. In M. Maine, D. Bunnell, & B.H. McGiley (Eds.), *Treatment of eating disorders* (pp. 425–441). Elsevier. https://doi.org/10.1016/B978-0-12-375668-8.10025-7

Catalan-Matamoros, D., Gomez-Conesa, A., Stubbs, B., & Vancampfort, D. (2016). Exercise improves depressive symptoms in older adults: An umbrella review of systematic reviews and meta-analyses. *Psychiatry Research, 244*, 202–209. https://doi.org/10.1016/j.psychres.2016.07.028

Chen, K.Y., Janz, K.F., Zhu, W., & Brychta, R.J. (2012). Redefining the roles of sensors in objective physical activity monitoring. *Medicine and Science in Sports and Exercise, 44*(Suppl. 1), S13–S23. https://doi.org/10.1249/MSS.0b013e3182399bc8

Choi, L., Liu, Z., Matthews, C.E., & Buchowski, M.S. (2011). Validation of accelerometer wear and nonwear time classification algorithm. *Medicine and Science in Sports and Exercise, 43*(2), 357–364. https://doi.org/10.1249/MSS.0b013e3181ed61a3

Coniglio, K.A., Cooper, M., & Selby, E.A. (2021). Behavioral reinforcement of pathological exercise in anorexia nervosa. *International Journal of Eating Disorders, 55*(2), 184–192. https://doi.org/10.1002/eat.23626

Cook, B.J., & Hausenblas, H.A. (2008). The role of exercise dependence for the relationship between exercise behavior and eating pathology: Mediator or moderator? *Journal of Health Psychology, 13*(4), 495–502. https://doi.org/10.1177/1359105308088520

Cook, B.J., Wonderlich, S.A., Mitchell, J.E., Thompson, R., Sherman, R., & McCallum, K. (2016). Exercise in eating disorders treatment: Systematic review and proposal of guidelines. *Medicine and Science in Sports and Exercise, 48*(7), 1408. https://doi.org/10.1249/MSS.0000000000000912

Courneya, K.S., & McAuley, E. (1995). Cognitive mediators of the social influence-exercise adherence relationship: A test of the theory of planned behavior. *Journal of Behavioral Medicine, 18*(5), 499–515. https://doi.org/10.1007/BF01904776

Couturier, J.L., & Lock, J. (2006). Denial and minimization in adolescents with anorexia nervosa. *International Journal of Eating Disorders, 39*(3), 212–216. https://doi.org/10.1002/eat.20241

Craig, C.L., Marshall, A.L., Sjöström, M., Bauman, A.E., Booth, M.L., Ainsworth, B.E., Pratt, M., Ekelund, U., Yngve, A., Sallis, J.F., & Oja, P. (2003). International physical activity questionnaire: 12-country reliability and validity. *Medicine & Science in Sports & Exercise, 35*(8), 1381–1395. https://doi.org/10.1249/01.MSS.0000078924.61453.FB

Dakanalis, A., Clerici, M., Caslini, M., Gaudio, S., Serino, S., Riva, G., & Carra, G. (2016). Predictors of initiation and persistence of recurrent binge eating and inappropriate weight compensatory behaviors in college men. *International Journal of Eating Disorders, 49*(6), 581–590.

Dalle Grave, R., Calugi, S., & Marchesini, G. (2008). Compulsive exercise to control shape or weight in eating disorders: Prevalence, associated features, and treatment outcome. *Comprehensive Psychiatry, 49*(4), 346–352. https://doi.org/10.1016/j.comppsych.2007.12.007

Davis, C., Brewer, H., & Ratusny, D. (1993). Behavioral frequency and psychological commitment: Necessary concepts in the study of excessive exercising. *Journal of Behavioral Medicine, 16*(6), 611–628. https://doi.org/10.1007/BF00844722

Davis, C., & Fox, J. (1993). Excessive exercise and weight preoccupation in women. *Addictive Behaviors, 18*(2), 201–211. https://doi.org/10.1016/0306-4603(93)90050-J

Davis, C., Kennedy, S.H., Ralevski, E., Dionne, M., Brewer, H., Neitzert, C., & Ratusny, D. (1995). Obsessive compulsiveness and physical activity in anorexia nervosa and high-level exercising. *Journal of Psychosomatic Research, 39*(8), 967–976. https://doi.org/10.1016/0022-3999(95)00064-X

Davis, H.A., Ortiz, A.M.L., & Smith, G.T. (2018). The occurrence and covariation of binge eating and compensatory behaviors across early to mid-adolescence. *Journal of Pediatric Psychology, 43*(4), 402–412. https://doi.org/10.1093/jpepsy/jsx113

Dittmer, N., Jacobi, C., & Voderholzer, U. (2018). Compulsive exercise in eating disorders: Proposal for a definition and a clinical assessment. *Journal of Eating Disorders, 6*(1), 1–9. https://doi.org/10.1186/s40337-018-0219-x

Dittmer, N., Voderholzer, U., Mönch, C., Cuntz, U., Jacobi, C., & Schlegl, S. (2020). Efficacy of a specialized group intervention for compulsive exercise in inpatients with anorexia nervosa: A randomized controlled trial. *Psychotherapy and Psychosomatics, 89*(3), 161–173. https://doi.org/10.1159/000504583

Duncan, L.R., Hall, C.R., Fraser, S.N., Rodgers, W.M., Wilson, P.M., & Loitz, C.C. (2012). Re-examining the dimensions of obligatory exercise. *Measurement in Physical Education and Exercise Science, 16*(1), 1–22. https://doi.org/10.1080/1091367X.2012.641442

Fairburn, C.G., & Beglin, S.J. (1994). Assessment of eating disorders: Interview or self-report questionnaire? *International Journal of Eating Disorders, 16*(4), 363–370. https://doi.org/10.1002/1098-108X(199412)16:4<363::AID-EAT2260160405>3.0.CO;2-#

Fairburn, C.G., Cooper, Z., & O'Connor, M. (1993). The eating disorder examination. *International Journal of Eating Disorders, 6*, 1–8.

Faust, L., Wang, C., Hachen, D., Lizardo, O., & Chawla, N.V. (2019). Physical activity trend eXtraction: A framework for extracting moderate-vigorous physical activity trends from wearable fitness tracker data. *JMIR Mhealth Uhealth, 7*(3), e11075. https://doi.org/10.2196/11075

Fichter, M.M., Herpertz, S., Quadflieg, N., & Herpertz-Dahlmann, B. (1998). Structured interview for anorexic and bulimic disorders for DSM-IV and ICD-10: Updated (third) revision. *International Jour-*

nal of Eating Disorders, 24(3), 227–249. https://doi.org/10.1002/(SICI)1098-108X(199811)24:3<227::AID-EAT1>3.0.CO;2-O

Fitzsimmons-Craft, E.E. (2017). Eating disorder-related social comparison in college women's everyday lives. *International Journal of Eating Disorders, 50*(8), 893–905. https://doi.org/10.1002/eat.22725

Fitzsimmons-Craft, E.E., Ciao, A.C., & Accurso, E.C. (2016). A naturalistic examination of social comparisons and disordered eating thoughts, urges, and behaviors in college women. *International Journal of Eating Disorders, 49*(2), 141–150. https://doi.org/10.1002/eat.22486

Ganson, K.T., Mitchison, D., Rodgers, R.F., Cunningham, M.L., Murray, S.B., & Nagata, J.M. (2021). Compulsive exercise among college students: 5-year time trends in prevalence and demographic, substance use, and mental health correlates. *Eating and Weight Disorders-Studies on Anorexia, Bulimia and Obesity, 27*, 717–728. https://doi.org/10.1007/s40519-021-01210-8

Garner, D.M., & Olmsted, M.P. (1986). Scoring the eating disorder inventory. *American Journal of Psychiatry, 143*(5), 680-a. https://doi.org/10.1176/ajp.143.5.680-a

Golden, N.H. (2003). Osteopenia and osteoporosis in anorexia nervosa. *Adolescent Medicine Clinics, 14*(1), 97.

Goodwin, H., Haycraft, E., Taranis, L., & Meyer, C. (2011). Psychometric evaluation of the compulsive exercise test (CET) in an adolescent population: Links with eating psychopathology. *European Eating Disorders Review, 19*(3), 269–279. https://doi.org/10.1002/erv.1109

Gorrell, S., Schaumberg, K., Boswell, J.F., Hormes, J.M., & Anderson, D.A. (2021). Female athlete body project intervention with professional dancers: A pilot trial. *Eating Disorders, 29*(1), 56–73.

Griffiths, M., Szabo, A., & Terry, A. (2005). The exercise addiction inventory: A quick and easy screening tool for health practitioners. *British Journal of Sports Medicine, 39*(6), e30. https://doi.org/10.1136/bjsm.2004.017020

Hausenblas, H.A., & Downs, D.S. (2002a). Exercise dependence: A systematic review. *Psychology of Sport and Exercise, 3*(2), 89–123. https://doi.org/10.1016/S1469-0292(00)00015-7

Hausenblas, H.A., & Downs, D.S. (2002b). How much is too much? The development and validation of the exercise dependence scale. *Psychology and Health, 17*(4), 387–404. https://doi.org/10.1080/0887044022000004894

Hay, P., Touyz, S., Arcelus, J., Pike, K., Attia, E., Crosby, R.D., Madden, S., Wales, J., La Puma, M., Heriseanu, A.I., Young, S., & Meyer, C. (2018). A randomized controlled trial of the compuLsive exercise activity TheraPy (LEAP): A new approach to compulsive exercise in anorexia nervosa. *International Journal of Eating Disorders, 51*(8), 999–1004. https://doi.org/10.1002/eat.22920

Holland, L.A., Brown, T.A., & Keel, P.K. (2014). Defining features of unhealthy exercise associated with disordered eating and eating disorder diagnoses. *Psychology of Sport and Exercise, 15*(1), 116–123. https://doi.org/10.1016/j.psychsport.2013.10.005

Holland, G., & Tiggemann, M. (2017). "Strong beats skinny every time": Disordered eating and compulsive exercise in women who post fitspiration on Instagram. *International Journal of Eating Disorders, 50*(1), 76–79. https://doi.org/10.1002/eat.22559

Homan, K. (2010). Athletic-ideal and thin-ideal internalization as prospective predictors of body dissatisfaction, dieting, and compulsive exercise. *Body Image, 7*(3), 240–245. https://doi.org/10.1016/j.bodyim.2010.02.004

Johnson, C. (1987). Diagnostic survey for eating disorders (DSED). In C. Johnson & M. Connors (Eds.), *The etiology and treatment of bulimia nervosa: A biopsychosocial perspective* (pp. 174–194). Basic Books.

Kaewkannate, K., & Kim, S. (2016). A comparison of wearable fitness devices. *BMC Public Health, 16*(1), 433. https://doi.org/10.1186/s12889-016-3059-0

Kerrigan, S.G., Lydecker, J.A., & Grilo, C.M. (2019). Associations between physical activity and eating-disorder psychopathology among individuals categorised with binge-eating disorder and bulimia nervosa. *The International Journal of Clinical Practice, 73*(11), e13401. https://doi.org/10.1111/ijcp.13401

Kolar, D.R., & Gorrell, S. (2021). A call to experimentally study acute affect-regulation mechanisms specific to driven exercise in eating disorders. *International Journal of Eating Disorders, 54*(3), 280–286. https://doi.org/10.1002/eat.23427

Kozey, S.L., Lyden, K., Howe, C.A., Staudenmayer, J.W., & Freedson, P.S. (2010). Accelerometer output and MET values of common physical activities. *Medicine and Science in Sports and Exercise, 42*(9), 1776–1784. https://doi.org/10.1249/MSS.0b013e3181d479f2

Lamb, K., & Brodie, D. (1990). The assessment of physical activity by leisure-time physical activity questionnaires. *Sports Medicine, 10*(3), 159–180. https://doi.org/10.2165/00007256-199010030-00003

Lampe, E.W., Trainor, C., Presseller, E.K., Michael, M.L., Payne-Reichert, A., Juarascio, A.S., & Manasse, S.M. (2021). Characterizing reasons for exercise in binge-spectrum eating disorders. *Eating Behaviors, 43*, 101558. https://doi.org/10.1016/j.eatbeh.2021.101558

Lavender, J.M., Brown, T.A., & Murray, S.B. (2017). Men, muscles, and eating disorders: An overview of traditional and muscularity-oriented disordered eating. *Current Psychiatry Reports, 19*(6), 1–7. https://doi.org/10.1007/s11920-017-0787-5

Lavender, J.M., De Young, K.P., & Anderson, D.A. (2010). Eating Disorder Examination Questionnaire (EDE-Q): Norms for undergraduate men. *Eating Behaviors, 11*(2), 119–121. https://doi.org/10.1016/j.eatbeh.2009.09.005

Lavender, J.M., De Young, K.P., Wonderlich, S.A., Crosby, R.D., Engel, S.G., Mitchell, J.E., Crox, S.J., Peterson, C.B., & Le Grange, D. (2013). Daily patterns of anxiety in anorexia nervosa: Associations with eating disorder behaviors in the natural environment. *Journal of Abnormal Psychology, 122*(3), 672. https://doi.org/10.1037/a0031823

Lavender, J.M., Utzinger, L.M., Crosby, R.D., Goldschmidt, A.B., Ellison, J., Wonderlich, S.A., Engel, S.G., Mitchell, J.E., Crow, S.J., Peterson, C.B., & Le Grange, D. (2016). A naturalistic examination of the temporal patterns of affect and eating disorder behaviors in anorexia nervosa. *International Journal of Eating Disorders, 49*(1), 77–83.

Lee, P.H., Macfarlane, D.J., Lam, T.H., & Stewart, S.M. (2011). Validity of the international physical activity questionnaire short form (IPAQ-SF): A systematic review. *International Journal of Behavioral Nutrition and Physical Activity, 8*(1), 1–11. https://doi.org/10.1186/1479-5868-8-115

Levinson, C.A., Sala, M., Fewell, L., Brosof, L.C., Fournier, L., & Lenze, E.J. (2018). Meal and snack-time eating disorder cognitions predict eating disorder behaviors and vice versa in a treatment seeking sample: A mobile technology based ecological momentary assessment study. *Behaviour Research and Therapy, 105*, 36–42. https://doi.org/10.1016/j.brat.2018.03.008

Liang, J., Xian, D., Liu, X., Fu, J., Zhang, X., Tang, B., & Lei, J. (2018). Usability study of mainstream wearable fitness devices: Feature analysis and system usability scale evaluation. *JMIR mHealth and uHealth, 6*(11), e11066. https://doi.org/10.2196/11066

Lipson, S., & Sonneville, K. (2017). Eating disorder symptoms among undergraduate and graduate students at 12 US colleges and universities. *Eating Behaviors, 24*, 81–88. https://doi.org/10.1016/j.eatbeh.2016.12.003

Loumidis, K.S., & Wells, A. (1998). Assessment of beliefs in exercise dependence: The development and preliminary validation of the exercise beliefs questionnaire. *Personality and Individual Differences, 25*(3), 553–567. https://doi.org/10.1016/S0191-8869(98)00103-2

Ma, R., & Kelly, A.C. (2020). The fragility of perceived social rank following exercise in anorexia nervosa: An ecological momentary assessment study of shame and pride. *Eating and Weight Disorders-Studies on Anorexia, Bulimia and Obesity, 25*(6), 1601–1607. https://doi.org/10.1007/s40519-019-00797-3

Mang, L., Garghan, A., Grant, J., Lacey, H., & Matthews, R. (2021). An evaluation of efficacy and acceptability of a novel manualised JuniorLEAP group programme for compulsive exercise, for children and adolescents with anorexia nervosa, within an inpatient setting. *Eating and Weight Disorders – Studies on Anorexia, Bulimia and Obesity, 26*(2), 591–597. https://doi.org/10.1007/s40519-020-00884-w

Markland, D., & Ingledew, D.K. (1997). The measurement of exercise motives: Factorial validity and invariance across gender of a revised Exercise Motivations Inventory. *British Journal of Health Psychology, 2*(4), 361–376. https://doi.org/10.1111/j.2044-8287.1997.tb00549.x

Mâsse, L.C., & Judith, E. (2012). Sources of validity evidence needed with self-report measures of physical activity. *Journal of Physical Activity and Health, 9*(s1), S44–S55. https://doi.org/10.1123/jpah.9.s1.s44

Mathisen, T.F., Sundgot-Borgen, J., Bulik, C.M., & Bratland-Sanda, S. (2021). The neurostructural and neurocognitive effects of physical activity: A potential benefit to promote eating disorder recovery. *International Journal of Eating Disorders, 54*(10), 1766–1770. https://doi.org/10.1002/eat.23582

Mazure, C.M., Halmi, K.A., Sunday, S.R., Romano, S.J., & Einhorn, A.M. (1994). The Yale-Brown-Cornell eating disorder scale: Development, use, reliability and validity. *Journal of Psychiatric Research, 28*(5), 425–445. https://doi.org/10.1016/0022-3956(94)90002-7

McCabe, M.P., & Ricciardelli, L.A. (2006). A prospective study of extreme weight change behaviors among adolescent boys and girls. *Journal of Youth and Adolescence, 35*(3), 402–411. https://doi.org/10.1007/s10964-006-9062-5

McCabe, M.P., & Ricciardelli, L.A. (2009). Extreme weight change behaviours: Are overweight and normal weight adolescents different, and does this vary over time? *European Eating Disorders Review, 17*(4), 301–314. https://doi.org/10.1002/erv.929

McCreary, D.R., & Sasse, D.K. (2000). An exploration of the drive for muscularity in adolescent boys and girls. *Journal of American College Health, 48*(6), 297–304. https://doi.org/10.1080/07448480009596271

McCreary, D.R., Sasse, D.K., Saucier, D.M., & Dorsch, K.D. (2004). Measuring the drive for muscularity: Factorial validity of the drive for muscularity scale in men and women. *Psychology of Men & Masculinity, 5*(1), 49. https://doi.org/10.1037/1524-9220.5.1.49

McNamara, E., Hudson, Z., & Taylor, S.J.C. (2010). Measuring activity levels of young people: The validity of pedometers. *British Medical Bulletin, 95*(1), 121–137. https://doi.org/10.1093/bmb/ldq016

Meyer, C., Taranis, L., Goodwin, H., & Haycraft, E. (2011). Compulsive exercise and eating disorders. *European Eating Disorders Review, 19*(3), 174–189. https://doi.org/10.1002/erv.1122

Miele, G.M., Carpenter, K.M., Cockerham, M.S., Trautman, K.D., Blaine, J., & Hasin, D.S. (2000a). Concurrent and predictive validity of the Substance Dependence Severity Scale (SDSS). *Drug and Alcohol Dependence, 59*(1), 77–88. https://doi.org/10.1016/S0376-8716(99)00110-6

Miele, G.M., Carpenter, K.M., Cockerham, M.S., Trautman, K.D., Blaine, J., & Hasin, D.S. (2000b). Substance Dependence Severity Scale (SDSS): Reliability and validity of a clinician-administered interview for DSM-IV substance use disorders. *Drug and Alcohol Dependence, 59*(1), 63–75. https://doi.org/10.1037/t04139-000

Mond, J., & Gorrell, S. (2021). "Excessive exercise" in eating disorders research: Problems of definition and perspective. *Eating and Weight Disorders-Studies on Anorexia, Bulimia and Obesity, 26*(4), 1017–1020. https://doi.org/10.1007/s40519-020-01075-3

Monell, E., Levallius, J., Mantilla, E.F., & Birgegård, A. (2018). Running on empty – a nationwide large-scale examination of compulsive exercise in eating disorders. *Journal of Eating Disorders, 6*(1), 11. https://doi.org/10.1186/s40337-018-0197-z

Nagata, J.M., Compte, E.J., Cattle, C.J., Flentje, A., Capriotti, M.R., Lubensky, M.E., Murray, S.B., Obedin-Maliver, J., & Lunn, M.R. (2020). Community norms for the Eating Disorder Examination Questionnaire (EDE-Q) among gender-expansive populations. *Journal of Eating Disorders, 8*(1), 1–11. https://doi.org/10.1186/s40337-020-00352-x

Nagayoshi, S., Oshima, Y., Ando, T., Aoyama, T., Nakae, S., Usui, C., Kumagai, S., & Tanaka, S. (2019). Validity of estimating physical activity intensity using a triaxial accelerometer in healthy adults and older adults. *BMJ Open Sport & Exercise Medicine, 5*(1), e000592–e000592. https://doi.org/10.1136/bmjsem-2019-000592

Noetel, M., Dawson, L., Hay, P., & Touyz, S. (2017). The assessment and treatment of unhealthy exercise in adolescents with anorexia nervosa: A Delphi study to synthesize clinical knowledge. *International Journal of Eating Disorders, 50*(4), 378–388. https://doi.org/10.1002/eat.22657

Paffenbarger Jr., R.S., Wing, A.L., & Hyde, R.T. (1978). Physical activity as an index of heart attack risk in college alumni. *American Journal of Epidemiology, 108*(3), 161–175. https://doi.org/10.1093/oxfordjournals.aje.a112608

Palavras, M.A., Hay, P., Touyz, S., Sainsbury, A., da Luz, F., Swinbourne, J., Estella, N.M., & Claudino, A. (2015). Comparing cognitive behavioural therapy for eating disorders integrated with behavioural weight loss therapy to cognitive behavioural therapy-enhanced alone in overweight or obese people with bulimia nervosa or binge eating disorder: Study protocol for a randomised controlled trial. *Trials, 16*(1), 578. https://doi.org/10.1186/s13063-015-1079-1

Paradiso, C., Colino, F., & Liu, S. (2020). The validity and reliability of the Mi band wearable device for measuring steps and heart rate. *International Journal of Exercise Science, 13*(4), 689–701. https://pubmed.ncbi.nlm.nih.gov/32509127

Penedo, F. J., & Dahn, J. R. (2005). Exercise and well-being: A review of mental and physical health benefits associated with physical activity. *Current Opinion in Psychiatry, 18*(2), 189–193. https://doi.org/10.1097/00001504-200503000-00013

Petrie, T. A., Greenleaf, C., Reel, J., & Carter, J. (2008). Prevalence of eating disorders and disordered eating behaviors among male collegiate athletes. *Psychology of Men & Masculinity, 9*(4), 267–277. https://psycnet.apa.org/doi/10.1037/a0013178

Pirke, K. M., Trimborn, P., Platte, P., & Fichter, M. (1991). Average total energy expenditure in anorexia nervosa, bulimia nervosa, and healthy young women. *Biological Psychiatry, 30*(7), 711–718. https://doi.org/10.1016/0006-3223(91)90016-F

Plateau, C. R., Arcelus, J., & Meyer, C. (2017). Detecting eating psychopathology in female athletes by asking about exercise: Use of the compulsive exercise test. *European Eating Disorders Review, 25*(6), 618–624. https://doi.org/10.1002/erv.2561

Rhea, D., Lantz, C. D., & Cornelius, A. (2004). Development of the muscle dysmorphia inventory (MDI). *Journal of Sports Medicine and Physical Fitness, 44*(4), 428–435.

Rizk, M., Lalanne, C., Berthoz, S., Kern, L., Group, E., & Godart, N. (2015). Problematic exercise in anorexia nervosa: Testing potential risk factors against different definitions. *PloS One, 10*(11), e0143352. https://doi.org/10.1371/journal.pone.0143352

Sala, M., Brosof, L. C., & Levinson, C. A. (2019). Repetitive negative thinking predicts eating disorder behaviors: A pilot ecological momentary assessment study in a treatment seeking eating disorder sample. *Behaviour Research and Therapy, 112*, 12–17. https://doi.org/10.1016/j.brat.2018.11.005

Schaumberg, K., Anderson, L. M., Reilly, E., & Anderson, D. A. (2014). Patterns of compensatory behaviors and disordered eating in college students. *Journal of American College Health, 62*(8), 526–533. https://doi.org/10.1080/07448481.2014.930468

Schaumberg, K., Peters, D., Ahrenholtz, R., Crombie, K. M., Zhang, R., & Gorrell, S. (2021). Registered report: A pilot investigation of acute exercise response among girls and young women with and without eating disorders. *International Journal of Eating Disorders, 54*(11), 2057–2065. https://doi.org/10.1002/eat.23587

Schleien, J. L., & Bardone-Cone, A. M. (2016). Competitiveness as a moderator of the relation between appearance-related factors and disordered eating behaviors. *Body Image, 17*, 30–37.

Scott, C. L., Haycraft, E., & Plateau, C. R. (2021). The influence of social networks within sports teams on athletes' eating and exercise psychopathology: A longitudinal study. *Psychology of Sport and Exercise, 52*, 101786. https://doi.org/10.1016/j.psychsport.2020.101786

Scott, C. L., Plateau, C. R., & Haycraft, E. (2020). Teammate influences, psychological well-being, and athletes' eating and exercise psychopathology: A moderated mediation analysis. *International Journal of Eating Disorders, 53*(4), 564–573. https://doi.org/10.1002/eat.23222

Silberstein, L. R., Striegel-Moore, R. H., Timko, C., & Rodin, J. (1988). Behavioral and psychological implications of body dissatisfaction: Do men and women differ? *Sex Roles, 19*(3), 219–232. https://doi.org/10.1007/BF00290156

Silfee, V. J., Haughton, C. F., Jake-Schoffman, D. E., Lopez-Cepero, A., May, C. N., Sreedhara, M., Rosal, M. C., & Lemon, S. C. (2018). Objective measurement of physical activity outcomes in lifestyle interventions among adults: A systematic review. *Preventive Medicine Reports, 11*, 74–80. https://doi.org/10.1016/j.pmedr.2018.05.003

Simpson, K. (2011). *Validity and reliability of the Paffenbarger Physical Activity Questionnaire among healthy adults*. Master's Thesis, University of Connecticut.

Simpson, K., Parker, B., Capizzi, J., Thompson, P., Clarkson, P., Freedson, P., & Pescatello, L. S. (2015). Validity and reliability of question 8 of the Paffenbarger Physical Activity Questionnaire among healthy adults. *Journal of Physical Activity and Health, 12*(1), 116–123. https://doi.org/10.1123/jpah.2013-0013

Solmi, F., Mascarell, M.C., Zammit, S., Kirkbride, J.B., & Lewis, G. (2019). Polygenic risk for schizophrenia, disordered eating behaviours and body mass index in adolescents. *The British Journal of Psychiatry, 215*(1), 428–433.

Steffen, J.J., & Brehm, B.J. (1999). The dimensions of obligatory exercise. *Eating Disorders, 7*(3), 219–226. https://doi.org/10.1080/10640269908249287

Stein, K.F., & Corte, C.M. (2003). Ecologic momentary assessment of eating-disordered behaviors. *International Journal of Eating Disorders, 34*(3), 349–360. https://doi.org/10.1002/eat.10194

Swenne, I. (2016). Evaluation of the compulsive exercise test (CET) in adolescents with eating disorders: Factor structure and relation to eating disordered psychopathology. *European Eating Disorders Review, 24*(4), 334–340. https://doi.org/10.1002/erv.2439

Taranis, L., & Meyer, C. (2011). Associations between specific components of compulsive exercise and eating-disordered cognitions and behaviors among young women. *International Journal of Eating Disorders, 44*(5), 452–458. https://doi.org/10.1002/eat.20838

Taranis, L., Touyz, S., & Meyer, C. (2011). Disordered eating and exercise: Development and preliminary validation of the compulsive exercise test (CET). *European Eating Disorders Review, 19*(3), 256–268. https://doi.org/10.1002/erv.1108

Vanzhula, I.A., Sala, M., Christian, C., Hunt, R.A., Keshishian, A.C., Wong, V.Z., Wong, V.Z., Ernst, S., Spoor, S.P., & Levinson, C.A. (2020). Avoidance coping during mealtimes predicts higher eating disorder symptoms. *International Journal of Eating Disorders, 53*(4), 625–630. https://doi.org/10.1002/eat.23254

Voderholzer, U., Hessler, J.B., Naab, S., Fichter, M., Graetz, A., Greetfeld, M., ... & Schlegl, S. (2019). Are there differences between men and women in outcome of intensive inpatient treatment for anorexia nervosa? An analysis of routine data. *European Eating Disorders Review, 27*(1), 59–66.

Warren, J.M., Ekelund, U., Besson, H., Mezzani, A., Geladas, N., & Vanhees, L. (2010). Assessment of physical activity – a review of methodologies with reference to epidemiological research: A report of the exercise physiology section of the European Association of Cardiovascular Prevention and Rehabilitation. *European Journal of Cardiovascular Prevention and Rehabilitation, 17*(2), 127–139. https://doi.org/10.1097/HJR.0b013e32832ed875

Washburn, R.A., Jacobsen, D.J., Sonko, B.J., Hill, J.O., & Donnelly, J.E. (2003). The validity of the Stanford Seven-Day Physical Activity Recall in young adults. *Medicine and Science in Sports and Exercise, 35*(8), 1374–1380. https://doi.org/10.1249/01.MSS.0000079081.08476.EA

Wons, O.B., Michael, M.L., Lin, M., & Juarascio, A.S. (2021). Characterizing rates of physical activity in individuals with binge eating disorder using wearable sensor technologies and clinical interviews. *European Eating Disorders Review, 29*(2), 292–299. https://doi.org/10.1002/erv.2811

Yanovski, S.Z., Marcus, M.D., Wadden, T.A., & Walsh, B.T. (2015). The questionnaire on eating and weight patterns-5 (QEWP-5): An updated screening instrument for binge eating disorder. *The International Journal of Eating Disorders, 48*(3), 259. https://doi.org/10.1002/eat.22372

Young, S., Touyz, S., Meyer, C., Arcelus, J., Rhodes, P., Madden, S., Pike, K., Attia, E., Crosby, R.D., Wales, J., & Hay, P. (2017). Validity of exercise measures in adults with anorexia nervosa: The EDE, Compulsive Exercise Test and other self-report scales. *International Journal of Eating Disorders, 50*(5), 533–541. https://doi.org/10.1002/eat.22633

Zelener, J., & Schneider, M. (2016). Adolescents and self-reported physical activity: An evaluation of the modified Godin Leisure-Time Exercise Questionnaire. *International Journal of Exercise Science, 9*(5), 587.

Zhan, C., Heatherington, L., & Klingenberg, B. (2022). Disordered eating-and exercise-related behaviors and cognitions during the first year college transition. *Journal of American College Health, 70*(3), 852–863.

Chapter 14

Assessment of Body Composition and Energy Expenditure

Nuno Casanova,[1] Ruairi O'Driscoll,[2] Graham Finlayson,[2] R. James Stubbs,[2] and Mark Hopkins[3]

[1] KinesioLab, Research Unit in Human Movement Analysis, Instituto Piaget, Almada, Portugal
[2] Appetite Control and Energy Balance Research Group, School of Psychology, Faculty of Medicine and Health, University of Leeds, UK
[3] School of Food Science and Nutrition, Faculty of Environment, University of Leeds, UK

Introduction

The focus of eating behavior studies is commonly directed toward the assessment of food intake and its physiological, psychological, and environmental determinants. However, the importance of measuring these in a quantitative energy balance framework, which includes measures of energy expenditure (EE) and body composition, is often overlooked. Measuring eating behavior in the context of objective measures of energy balance may not only provide important new insight into the determinants of food intake, but also helps address longstanding issues in the measurement of food intake. For example, the importance of fat-free mass (FFM) and EE in the homoeostatic control of appetite is now being recognized (Blundell et al., 2020). Furthermore, mathematical models based upon changes in energy stores (body weight or composition) and total daily EE (TDEE) allow free-living energy intake (EI) to be objectively estimated (Hall & Chow, 2011; Shook et al., 2018; Thomas et al., 2010), providing a much needed alternative to self-report methods of EI assessment (Ravelli & Schoeller, 2020). In the present chapter, we will highlight research examining the influence of body composition and EE on appetite during different states of energy balance. Furthermore, we will discuss how measures of body composition and EE can be used to track changes in EI under free-living conditions, the assumptions of the mathematical models used to calculate EI, and potential areas for future research to improve our ability to track in real time EI and EE in humans.

Appetite Control: General Overview

Appetite is a complex biopsychological phenomenon that can be influenced by metabolic, behavioral, psychological, and environmental factors (Casanova, Finlayson et al., 2019). Energy intake is not controlled exclusively as a result of energy homeostasis (Halford & Blundell, 2000), with food hedonics, prior learned experiences, and environmental contexts (nonhomeostatic factors) also influencing eating behaviors (Finlayson, 2017). While nonhomeostatic factors play an important role in the control of appetite, the focus of the present chapter will be on describing homeostatic appetite control, and in particular, how body composition and EE may influence appetite and EI under different states of energy balance. Early theories of appetite control emphasized the importance of specific features of nutrient balance and the oxidation or storage of carbohydrates, fat, or protein as negative feedback signals, for example, the glucostatic (Mayer, 1953), glycogenostatic (Flatt, 1987), and aminostatic (Mellinkoff et al., 1956) theories. However, limited evidence exists in humans to indicate that the oxidation or storage of individual macronutrients exert strong feedback on EI, and current models of homeostatic appetite control now focus upon the central integration of numerous peripheral neuroendocrine signals of acute energy and nutrient availability (primarily from the gastro-intestinal tract) with longer-term signals of energy storage (primarily from adipose tissue).

Human homeostatic appetite control is thought to comprise of excitatory and inhibitory feedback signals which exert acute (episodic) and long-term (tonic) effects over appetite and EI. Episodic signals such as gastrointestinal peptides (e.g., cholecystokinin, glucagon-like peptide-1, and ghrelin) and gastric distension/emptying provide feedback to the brain regarding acute energy and nutrient availability and signal satiation and satiety in response to the presence or absence of nutrients in the gastrointestinal tract (Hintze et al., 2017; Perry & Wang, 2012). While there is a large variability between individuals (Gibbons et al., 2019), these peptides act as physiological cues that influence subjective appetite sensations (e.g., hunger, satiation, and satiety) and food intake (Gibbons et al., 2013; Hopkins et al., 2017). Tonic feedback mechanisms also exist that exert longer-term influence over appetite, and link daily metabolic energy requirements and stored energy with day-to-day EI. With the discovery of the adipokine leptin (Zhang et al., 1994), the homeostatic control of appetite has centered around the action of fat mass (FM) and leptin on food intake, for example, the "lipostatic" or "adipocentric" theory of appetite (Mayer, 1955). However, it is now being recognized that FFM and EE also play important roles in the control of appetite and may underpin a biological drive to eat (Blundell et al., 2020).

The Influence of Body Composition and Energy Expenditure on Appetite and Energy Intake Under Conditions of Energy Balance

A conceptual model of appetite that incorporates the energetic demands of metabolically active lean tissues has been recently proposed, which suggests a tonic drive to eat arising from components of EE (e.g., resting metabolic rate; RMR) and its main determinants (e.g., FFM). This model is based on a series of studies demonstrating that FFM, but not FM, is associated with hunger and EI under conditions of approximate energy balance (Blundell et al., 2012; Cugini et al., 1998; Lissner et al., 1989; Weise et al., 2014). For example, Blundell et al. reported positive associations between FFM, but not FM, with self-selected meal size and daily EI (Blundell et al., 2012). This finding has been replicated by several independent research groups in different age groups from infants (Wells et al., 2021), adolescents (Cameron et al., 2016; Vainik et al., 2016), young adults (Grannell, Al-Najim, et al., 2019; Hopkins et al., 2018; McNeil et al., 2015; Piaggi et al., 2015; Weise et al., 2014), and older adults (Hopkins et al., 2021; Johnson et al., 2021), and in disease states (Bétry et al., 2019).

Based on work showing associations between FFM and appetite, Blundell et al. have suggested that "any orexigenic drive arising from FFM could be mediated via EE reflected by the RMR" (Blundell et al., 2012). Studies have shown that RMR is associated with subjective hunger (Caudwell et al., 2013) and EI (Bi et al., 2019; Casanova et al., 2021), and the associations between FFM and EI have been shown to be mediated statistically by RMR and TDEE (Hopkins et al., 2019; Hopkins et al., 2018; Piaggi et al., 2015). These findings have been interpreted to suggest that EE per se may exert influence over EI to ensure that daily energy needs are met. However, it is important to refer that these studies showing an association between EE and EI were short-term. Whether this coupling occurs and is maintained in the long-term remains to be examined. Lastly, it is important to acknowledge that components of FFM such as skeletal muscle and the liver are endocrine organs and, thus, the hypothesis that these tissues may exert influence on appetite separate from their influence on EE should not be discarded.

Studies examining the associations between FM and appetite have shown contradictory findings. Some studies have failed to report associations between FM, hunger and EI (Blundell et al., 2012; Grannell, Al-Najim, et al., 2019; Lissner et al., 1989), while others reported negative associations (Blundell et al., 2015; Cugini et al., 1998). Interestingly, the studies that showed a negative association between FM and EI, which is in line with the proposed inhibitory effect of FM and leptin on appetite, were conducted on leaner individuals (Blundell et al., 2015; Cugini et al., 1998). It has been suggested that the inhibitory influence of FM on appetite could be influenced by the levels of body fatness. For example, Casanova et al. observed a statistical moderation of body fat on these relationships, in which the strength of the association between FM and EI (and between FFM, RMR, and EI) weakened with increases in body fatness (as expressed as body mass index, FM index, or body fat percentage; Casanova et al., 2021). These findings corroborated with others that found a negative association between FM and hunger in lean individuals but not in those with obesity (Cugini et al., 1999; Cugini et al., 1998), and weaker associations between FFM and EI at higher levels of body fatness (Grannell, Al-Najim, et al., 2019). The development of leptin and insulin resistance at higher levels of body fatness could contribute to the change in the strength and direction of these associations. However, appetite is not solely determined by biological factors, and factors such as food hedonics, food choices, psychological, and environmental factors may also influence these associations (Hopkins et al., 2018). Furthermore, it is important to note that the aforementioned associations between body composition, EE, and EI have been observed under conditions of approximate energy balance in weight stable individuals. These associations may change under conditions of energy imbalance and weight change.

The Influence of Body Composition and Energy Expenditure on Appetite and Energy Intake Under Conditions of Weight Change

The majority of individuals that lose weight regain most or all of the weight lost over time (Wing & Phelan, 2005). While this likely reflects unfavorable changes in both EE and EI, data suggest that weight regain occurs mostly due to increases in EI (Polidori et al., 2016). Increases in hunger and concentrations of orexigenic hormones have been reported following weight loss (Hintze et al., 2017; Sumithran et al., 2011), but studies have also reported that hunger did not change, or even reduce, after weight loss (Andriessen et al., 2018; Beaulieu et al., 2019; Nymo et al., 2017). The reasons for such discrepancies are unclear, but could be related to the type and extent of energy restriction and the composition of weight loss. It has been suggested that ketogenic diets may attenuate weight loss-induced increases in the orexigenic hormone ghrelin and subjective hunger (Roekenes & Martins, 2021). The composition of the weight lost, which is a function of initial body fat, the rate and extent of weight loss, diet composition, and exercise (Forbes, 1987; Hall, 2007) may also influence compensation, with some suggesting that greater FFM loss is associated with increased hunger (Turicchi et al., 2020) and weight regain (Turicchi et al., 2019) following weight loss. Hunger has been shown to decrease following periods of overfeeding in some individuals (Halliday et al., 2020), but compensatory responses in appetite appear weaker in response to overfeeding than underfeeding (Blundell & Gillett, 2001; Blundell & King, 1996). However, long-term overfeeding studies in which hunger and EI are tracked are sparse. Understanding the relationships between body structure (mass and composition), function, and behavior in the context of energy balance offers a coherent framework to better understand how weight change influences the control of appetite during differing states of energy balance.

During weight loss, losses of both FM and FFM occur and RMR and TDEE usually decrease as a result of these losses in metabolically active tissues (Casanova, Beaulieu et al., 2019; Melby et al., 2017). While evidence on this topic is limited, research suggests that the composition of the weight lost may influence weight loss-induced changes in appetite and weight regain. This was first observed by Dulloo et al. based on a re-analysis of the Minnesota Semi-starvation experiment, which consisted of ≈ 25 % weight loss over 24 weeks, 12 weeks of controlled refeeding, and 8 weeks of *ad libitum* refeeding (12 out of 32 total initial participants followed through the 3 phases). In this study of extreme weight loss, the *ad libitum* refeeding phase was characterized by a hyperphagic response that only ceased once FFM levels were restored to baseline levels, and led to a 70 % overshoot in FM as compared to baseline levels (Dulloo et al., 1997). A similar finding was observed in a group of lean rangers in which after 8 weeks of severe energy deficit, a hyperphagic response was seen in the following 5 weeks of *ad libitum* feeding (Nindl et al., 1997). More recently, Turicchi et al. observed that greater losses of FFM after a 12% weight loss following a low-calorie diet was associated with increases in hunger in men, but not in women (Turicchi et al., 2020). This sex difference could be due to the fact that men lost a greater amount of FFM (men −35.3 % or 4.6kg; women −27.5 % or 2.7kg).

During weight gain, the available evidence is more limited to observational and epidemiological studies. As previously stated, overfeeding will increase energy requirements for a given level of activity and hunger may decrease as a response in some individuals (Halliday et al., 2020). A higher FFM (resulting from weight gain) could result in a higher "passive drive to eat" through an increase in RMR and TDEE. Johnson et al. observed an association between increases in FFM and increases in EI following 12 weeks of resistance training and protein supplementation in older adults (Johnson et al., 2021). When the findings from conditions of energy balance and imbalance are compared, the effect of FFM on appetite appears to be dependent on energy balance status. It has been suggested that FFM may exert a "passive" and an "active" influence on appetite (Dulloo et al., 2017). Under weight-stable conditions, FFM may exert a tonic passive influence on EI to ensure that the energy requirements of metabolic processes are met. During weight loss, the loss of FFM and its constituent tissue-organs may trigger an orexigenic effect over EI, independent of its energy requirements, to preserve or restore them to baseline levels (Stubbs et al., 2018; Dulloo et al., 2018).

In summary, body composition and EE should be considered as sources of feedback in the control of appetite in humans. Including longitudinal measures of motivation to eat and eating behaviors in structured studies where energy balance status is systematically manipulated over periods of a number of weeks, to the extent that body composition is significantly altered, may provide new understanding of the mechanisms influencing human eating behavior. Future studies should examine prospective cause-and-effect relationships between changes in body composition, EE and EI change under conditions of controlled weight change.

Assessing Energy Intake Under Free-Living Conditions: Problems and Potential Solutions

Accurate measures of EI are essential to understand eating behavior, diet–health relationships, and to design effective weight management strategies. Unfortunately, measuring food intake under free-living conditions has been challenging, historically relying on self-report methods. The development of isotopic measures of TDEE using doubly labelled water (DLW) revealed that reporting of EI in study groups usually falls short of actual TDEE, implying that subjects were in a negative energy balance, or they were misreporting their EI. Based on the fundamental principles of energy balance, it is now generally accepted that so called underreporting or misreporting is widespread (Hill & Davies, 2001; Livingstone & Black, 2003; Trabulsi & Schoeller, 2001) and may distort the relationships between diet and health that inform policy. While new strategies for objective EI measurements are in their infancy, there have been recent developments in using mathematical models of energy balance to calculate objective estimates of EI, e.g., the intake–balance method. The intake–balance method can provide an estimate of mean EI over time in free-living conditions based on changes in body energy stores (i.e., changes in body weight or body composition) and measurements of TDEE (Hall & Chow, 2011; Ravelli & Schoeller, 2021; Shook et al., 2018). This approach is reliant on accurate measurements of body composition and TDEE. Detailed descriptions of the methods used to assess body composition (Ackland et al., 2012; Lemos & Gallagher, 2017; Müller et al., 2016) and EE (Hills et al., 2014; Ndahimana & Kim, 2017) have been published elsewhere. The following section provides a brief overview of the techniques commonly used to estimate EI via the intake–balance method, before discussing how this approach can be used to track changes in EI over time under free-living conditions.

Measuring Body Composition

The most precise method to assess whole-body composition is the four-compartment model, which includes measurements of body mass, total body water (typically via deuterium dilution), body volume (typically via air-displacement plethysmography or hydrostatic weighing), and bone mineral content (dual x-ray absorptiometry; DEXA; Ackland et al., 2012; Müller et al., 2016). However, it is often not practical to use four-compartment models in research or clinical settings due to the need to combine multiple (costly) measurement approaches. Therefore, two or three compartmental models of body composition (e.g., FM and FFM, and FM, lean tissue, and bone mineral, respectively) measured using single techniques such via DEXA, air-displacement plethysmography, or bioelectrical impedance are more common. It is important to acknowledge that the more accurate the method is (i.e., lower margin of error), the greater the ability to accurately detect small changes in body composition. This is an important consideration when estimating EI using the intake-balance method over shorter periods of time, as errors in the measurement of body composition will lead to erroneous estimates of EI.

The most common method to measure body composition, as a proxy for changes in energy stores, when using the intake-balance method is DEXA. Dual x-ray absorptiometry passes a low radiation dose (filtered x-ray beams) at two different photon energies through the individual, which are attenuated differentially depending on the tissue in their path (i.e., FM or FFM). Other methods to assess body composition such as air-displacement plethysmography (which estimates body density by measuring body mass and body volume by using air displacement, and estimates FM and FFM assuming a constant energy density for each) and bioelectrical impedance (which measures the impedance that the tissues offer to an electric current, with FFM offering lower resistance than FM due to its higher water content) are common in eating behavior and nutritional research to estimate body composition. However, these approaches have lower accuracy and precision than DEXA (Ackland et al., 2012), and therefore, using these approaches to estimate EI via the intake-balance method should be approached with caution as this could lead to error propagation when calculating EI. Another important limitation to consider when using two compartmental techniques is the assumption of a constant hydration factor for FFM (total body water/FFM is commonly assumed to be 0.732). This assumption may be challenged during a number of situations, particularly the initial phase of weight loss where compartment models do not necessarily hold because initial weight loss is heavily affected by changes in FFM composition (i.e., reductions in body water and glycogen stores; Heymsfield et al., 2011). Greater FFM loss due to reductions in glycogen/protein and associated water in the early phase of weight loss would lead to an underestimation of the loss of metabolically tissue active components of FFM and an underestimation of EI using mathematical models (Hall, 2008).

Measuring Total Daily Energy Expenditure

The calculation of EI using the intake-balance method is also dependent on the accurate measurement of TDEE, which has typically been achieved using DLW. Whole-room direct or indirect calorimetry, which estimates TDEE via measuring the rate of heat loss or O_2 consumption and CO_2 production, respectively, within a metabolic chamber, provide precise values of TDEE (Kenny et al., 2017; Levine, 2005). However, participants are restricted in a small room, which may artificially constrain physical activity levels (Ainslie et al., 2003). As such, it has been more common to estimate TDEE in intake-balance studies using DLW. This technique, in which water rich in stable oxygen and hydrogen isotopes is consumed and the difference in isotopes turnover rates calculated as a measure of carbon dioxide production, is considered the most precise method of measuring free-living TDEE over 10- to 20-day periods (Speakman, 1998). Parenthetically, it also allows a two-compartment model of body composition to be determined. However, while DLW allows for accurate measurements of TDEE, it is an expensive technique which may limit not only sample size but also the number of time-points in which data can be collected.

As an alternative, physical activity monitors (e.g., accelerometers and commercial physical activity devices) have been widely used to estimate TDEE in physical activity and nutritional research settings. These can be worn in different locations (e.g., wrist, upper arm, thigh, or hip) and for long periods of time (if adequately charged) and provide a cheaper alternative to DLW. The accuracy of research-grade and commercial devices for TDEE estimation has been questioned (O'Driscoll, Turicchi, Beaulieu et al., 2020). Recent research has aimed to improve the (often proprietary) algorithms used to estimate TDEE using mathematical techniques such as machine learning. For instance, in a series of studies O'Driscoll et al. demonstrated that machine learning can be applied to consumer and research-grade wearable sensor data to increase the accuracy of physical activity and EE estimates (±5% of simultaneous indirect calorimetry), close to the accepted margins of error for DLW (O'Driscoll, Turicchi, Hopkins, et al., 2020). In two laboratory studies, machine learning algorithms (random forests, gradient boosting, and neural networks) were applied to the sensor data from a Fitbit Charge 2, Sensewear Armband Mini, and Actigraph GT3-x to estimate EE, with EE estimated validated against minute-by-minute indirect calorimetry using a leave-one-subject-out-cross-validation approach across a range of sedentary, ambulatory, exercise, and household activities (O'Driscoll et al., 2021). These data indicated the machine learning algorithms provided high predictive accuracy in EE estimation (root-mean-square error ≈0.91 metabolic equivalent of task) that exceeded accuracy of the SenseWear armband's inbuilt algorithms (regarded as the most accurate research-grade device; O'Driscoll et al., 2021; O'Driscoll, Turicchi, Beaulieu et al., 2020). While more research is needed, improving the accuracy of wearable devices' algorithms may lead to better estimates of TDEE, and in turn, provide a more accessible means of estimating EI using the intake-balance approach.

The Intake–Balance Method

It is possible, through the application of thermodynamic principles, to "solve" the energy balance equation if two of its three components are known. Theoretically, which of the three components are measured should not matter (Heymsfield et al., 2017). However, because of the difficulties inherent in estimating true EI, estimating changes in energy stores and EE, and using them to calculate EI, is the most common approach. This procedure, which has become known as the "intake-balance method," requires two body composition measures, at the start and end of the period of observation, which are used to calculate the composition and energy content of the change in weight. The EE of the subject is then used to calculate EI. Mathematically, the intake balance method can be represented as:

$$EI = 1020 \frac{\Delta FFM}{\Delta t} + 9500 \frac{\Delta FM}{\Delta t} + EE$$

Where and represent changes in FFM (kg) and FM (kg). The coefficients of 1020 (kcal/kg) and 9500 (kcal/kg) are the assumed energy densities of FFM and FM, respectively and is the change in time, expressed in days. These coefficients vary slightly based on assumptions about the composition and therefore energy content of FFM and FM. Estimating EE and body composition with DLW and DEXA can be considered the most precise method (Racette et al., 2012). However, there is approximately 5% error associated with DLW (Black & Cole, 2000; Trabulsi et al., 2003), 1% for DEXA (Sanghvi et al., 2015), and additional error based on different assumptions made about the composition of (mainly) FFM. Furthermore, the method is expensive, requires procedural and analytical expertise, and sample analysis is time-consuming.

Mathematical Modelling of Energy Balance

At present, accurate and precise estimates of EI remain elusive when longitudinal measures are required in large groups of subjects. For this reason, mathematical models which rely on thermodynamic principles relating to EE and energy stores have been developed and these are generally solvable for EI over periods of days or weeks (Thomas et al., 2019). Such approaches are advantageous as they can easily and cheaply be applied to large cohorts. One notable EI model (Thomas et al., 2010) incorporates subject demographics (i.e., age, gender, height, and body weight) into a mathematical approach, from which EI can be derived. The EI estimates from this model have been compared to both food provision (where EI is known) and "intake-balance" with mean bias within ±100 kcal/day, all of which were nonsignificant (Thomas et al., 2010). A comparable model has been developed by a team from the National Institute of Diabetes and Digestive and Kidney Disease (NIDDK; Chow & Hall, 2008). Baseline subject demographic information, height, and weight are required for a differential equation which includes assumed terms for the energy density of FM and FFM, energetic cost of synthesis of FM and FFM, caloric expenditure rate of FM and FFM, and parameters to capture diet-induced thermogenesis and adaptive changes to the rate of EE associated with a change in body weight (Polidori et al., 2016). Physical activity EE is generally approximated as 10 kcal/kg/day ($\approx 1.6 \times$ basal metabolic rate) at baseline and if objective or subjective estimates of activity are unavailable, it is assumed physical activity is constant (Guo et al., 2019). Using this information, over a period of time relative to the baseline maintenance estimate can be derived (Sanghvi et al., 2015). The dataset from the Comprehensive Assessment of Long-term Effects of Reducing Intake of Energy study, which includes repeated body composition and DLW measures, has been used to validate estimates from the NIDDK model. In 140 subjects, the estimates were validated against the most precise intake-balance method repeatedly (Sanghvi et al., 2015). The majority of the estimates were within 132 kcal/day of the most precise method, and the limits of agreement covered an interval 800–1000 kcal/day, which may indicate that the model cannot be applied at the individual-level for (Sanghvi et al., 2015).

The NIDDK model offers ease of use and accurate estimates of at the group level and has consequently been used in several research studies. One study used the NIDDK model to investigate EI in subjects taking canagliflozin, which accelerates urinary excretion of glucose, and therefore imposes an energy deficit. This study showed an increase in EI but a decrease in body weight because of the urinary glucose excretion, and this continued until a stable body weight was reached (Polidori et al., 2016). The NIDDK model has also been applied to estimate patterns of dietary misreporting in the Diet Intervention Examining the Factors Interacting with Treatment Success study (Guo et al., 2019). This study showed that subjects initially reduced model-estimated EI significantly, which then progressively returned to baseline by the last interval in the observation period. Self-reported EI was relatively constant, suggesting that the magnitude of misreporting increased as time progressed. Lastly, the model was applied to investigate EI in a range of randomized-controlled trials evaluating obesity drugs. In placebo and drug-treated patients, EI was estimated as being greatly reduced at the beginning of treatment and progressively returned towards baseline (Göbel et al., 2014).

Despite their application in a range of studies, mathematical models rarely incorporate objective physical activity information. This is problematic because physical activity EE is likely to be highly variable between and within subjects. This is where improvement of EE estimation using wearable devices may further refine such mathematical models of energy balance. There are therefore exciting developments in the use of wearable devices and mathematical modelling to track EI, EE and energy balance in real time. This is a new and developing field and there is a great deal of work yet to be done in improving, refining, and expanding these new approaches. Furthermore, each of these approaches needs to be validated against the most precise measures of EI (e.g., laboratory-weighed food intake), EE (indirect calorimetry via respiratory exchange or DLW), and energy storage (compartmental models of body composition).

Future Directions: Wearable Devices for Real-Time Energy Intake and Expenditure Assessment

Physical activity monitors, which are cheap, cloud-connected, and accessible may assist researchers in overcoming some of the limitations associated with the use of DLW in intake-balance models. Shook et al. replaced the expensive DLW with EE estimated from a research-grade activity monitoring device (SenseWear armband; Shook et al., 2018). This study showed that estimated EI differed by negligible amounts on average when comparing estimates using DLW or the SenseWear armband. However, SenseWear products are no longer in production and alternative devices must be investigated. Commercial devices, which are cloud-connected and more widely available than their research-grade counterparts, have also been investigated. Recently, Shook et al. used the Fitbit Alta device to estimate EE and the Fitbit Aria electronic body composition scales to estimate changes in body composition. In 24 adult subjects, EI calculated by both Fitbit devices demonstrated a lower correlation with the DLW/DEXA method than self-reported dietary intakes (Shook et al., 2021).

In recent years, new approaches have been developed to objectively track food intake such as using wearable cameras and machine learning models of food images (Chen et al., 2021; Qiu et al., 2021), and new developments in biomarkers of nutrient exposure (Posma et al., 2020). These areas are nascent but developing rapidly. For instance, it has been recognized for some time that perhaps one of the most effective ways to monitor actual food intake would be through the use of wearable cameras combined with three-dimensional modelling of food images. This approach creates two key problems. Firstly, there is the issue of privacy which is not trivial. Secondly, there is the issue of modelling images of ingested foods to convert those images into estimates of energy and nutrient intake. These technological and computation approaches involved in identifying and estimating portions sizes of foods are elegant and sophisticated, producing food weight estimates accurate between 50 % and 75 % under experimental conditions, when compared to weighed food intakes (Chen et al., 2021; Qiu et al., 2021). However, there appears to be some way to go in refining and validating such approaches. Privacy issues aside, it is likely that a combination of such approaches with energy balance tracking in the future may lead to interesting real-world applications.

Conclusions

As can be seen throughout this chapter, including measurements of body composition and EE in eating behavior studies offers exciting opportunities to better understand the mechanisms underlying the control of appetite in different states of energy balance. Body composition and EE seem to play a key role in the control of appetite, with FFM, RMR, and TDEE being positively associated with EI and hunger ratings under conditions of weight stability. Furthermore, during periods of negative energy balance, losses of FFM seem to be associated with a hyperphagic response to re-establish FFM to baseline levels. Notably, while one of the hardest parts of conducting eating behavior research is the inability to accurately measure EI under free-living conditions, mathematical models based on the concept of energy balance, which include measurements of body composition and TDEE, allow researchers to significantly improve EI estimates. While still in its infancy, the improvement of research and commercial devices' algorithms to measure TDEE may open doors in the not-so-distant future in which EI can be accurately tracked for extended periods in free-living conditions and in a more ecological and practical manner. Using these approaches to quantify how energy balance behaviors change during periods of energy imbalance will facilitate the design of more effective nutritional and physical activity recommendations and health policies.

References

Ackland, T.R., Lohman, T.G., Sundgot-Borgen, J., Maughan, R.J., Meyer, N.L., Stewart, A.D., & Müller, W. (2012). Current status of body composition assessment in sport: Review and position statement on behalf of the ad hoc research working group on body composition health and performance, under the auspices of the I.O.C. Medical Commission. *Sports Medicine, 42*(3), 227–249. https://doi.org/10.2165/11597140-000000000-00000

Ainslie, P., Reilly, T., & Westerterp, K. (2003). Estimating human energy expenditure: A review of techniques with particular reference to doubly labelled water. *Sports Medicine, 33*(9), 683–698. https://doi.org/10.2165/00007256-200333090-00004

Andriessen, C., Christensen, P., Vestergaard Nielsen, L., Ritz, C., Astrup, A., Meinert Larsen, T., Martinez, J.A., Saris, W.H.M., van Baak, M.A., Papadaki, A., Kunesova, M., Jebb, S., Blundell, J., Lawton, C., & Raben, A. (2018). Weight loss decreases self-reported appetite and alters food preferences in overweight and obese adults: Observational data from the DiOGenes study. *Appetite, 125*, 314–322. https://doi.org/10.1016/j.appet.2018.02.016

Beaulieu, K., Casanova, N., Oustric, P., Turicchi, J., Gibbons, C., Hopkins, M., Varady, K., Blundell, J., & Finlayson, G. (2019). Matched weight loss through intermittent or continuous energy restriction does not lead to compensatory increases in appetite and eating behavior in a randomized controlled trial in women with overweight and obesity. *Journal of Nutrition, 150*(3), 623–633. https://doi.org/10.1093/jn/nxz296

Bétry, C., Lauverjat, M., Mouillot, T., Bergoin, C., Barnoud, D., Ait, S., & Chambrier, C. (2019). Hyperphagia in short bowel patients: Fat-free mass is a strong predictor. *Nutrition, 62*, 146–151. https://doi.org/10.1016/j.nut.2018.12.013

Bi, X., Forde, C.G., Goh, A.T., & Henry, C.J. (2019). Basal metabolic rate and body composition predict habitual food and macronutrient intakes: Gender differences. *Nutrients, 11*(11). https://doi.org/10.3390/nu11112653

Black, A.E., & Cole, T.J. (2000). Within- and between-subject variation in energy expenditure measured by the doubly-labelled water technique: Implications for validating reported dietary energy intake. *European Journal of Clinical Nutrition, 54*(5), 386–394. https://doi.org/10.1038/sj.ejcn.1600970

Blundell, J., Caudwell, P., Gibbons, C., Hopkins, M., Naslund, E., King, N., & Finlayson, G. (2012). Body composition and appetite: Fat-free mass (but not fat-mass or BMI) is positively associated with self-determined meal size and daily energy intake in humans. *British Journal of Nutrition, 107*, 445–459. https://doi.org/10.1017/S0007114511003138

Blundell, J., Finlayson, G., Gibbons, C., Caudwell, P., & Hopkins, M. (2015). The biology of appetite control: Do resting metabolic rate and fat-free mass drive energy intake? *Physiology & Behavior, 152*(Pt B), 473–478. https://doi.org/10.1016/j.physbeh.2015.05.031

Blundell, J.E., Gibbons, C., Beaulieu, K., Casanova, N., Duarte, C., Finlayson, G., Stubbs, R.J., & Hopkins, M. (2020). The drive to eat in homo sapiens: Energy expenditure drives energy intake. *Physiology & Behavior, 219*, 112846. https://doi.org/https://doi.org/10.1016/j.physbeh.2020.112846

Blundell, J.E., & Gillett, A. (2001). Control of food intake in the obese. *Obesity Research, 9* (Suppl. 4), 263s–270s. https://doi.org/10.1038/oby.2001.129

Blundell, J.E., & King, N.A. (1996). Overconsumption as a cause of weight gain: Behavioural-physiological interactions in the control of food intake (appetite). *Ciba Foundation Symposium, 201*, 138–154; discussion 154–138, 188–193. https://doi.org/10.1002/9780470514962.ch9

Cameron, J.D., Sigal, R.J., Kenny, G.P., Alberga, A.S., Prud'Homme, D., Phillips, P., Doucette, S., & Goldfield, G. (2016). Body composition and energy intake – skeletal muscle mass is the strongest predictor of food intake in obese adolescents: The HEARTY trial. *Applied Physiology, Nutrition, and Metabolism, 41*(6), 611–617. https://doi.org/10.1139/apnm-2015-0479

Casanova, N., Beaulieu, K., Finlayson, G., & Hopkins, M. (2019). Metabolic adaptations during negative energy balance and their potential impact on appetite and food intake. *Proceedings of the Nutrition Society, 78*(3), 279–289. https://doi.org/10.1017/s0029665118002811

Casanova, N., Beaulieu, K., Oustric, P., O'Connor, D., Gibbons, C., Duarte, C., Blundell, J., Stubbs, R.J., Finlayson, G., & Hopkins, M. (2021). Body fatness influences associations of body composition and energy expenditure with energy intake in healthy women. *Obesity, 29*(1), 125–132. https://doi.org/10.1002/oby.23034

Casanova, N., Finlayson, G., Blundell, J.E., & Hopkins, M. (2019). Biopsychology of human appetite – understanding the excitatory and inhibitory mechanisms of homeostatic control. *Current Opinion in Physiology, 12*, 33–38. https://doi.org/10.1016/j.cophys.2019.06.007

Caudwell, P., Finlayson, G., Gibbons, C., Hopkins, M., King, N., Naslund, E., & Blundell, J. (2013). Resting metabolic rate is associated with hunger, self-determined meal size, and daily energy intake and may represent a marker for appetite. *American Journal of Clinical Nutrition, 97*(1), 7–14. https://doi.org/doi:10.3945/ajcn.111.029975

Chen, G., Jia, W., Zhao, Y., Mao, Z.-H., Lo, B., Anderson, A.K., Frost, G., Jobarteh, M.L., McCrory, M.A., Sazonov, E., Steiner-Asiedu, M., Ansong, R.S., Baranowski, T., Burke, L., & Sun, M. (2021). Food/non-food classification of real-life egocentric images in low- and middle-income countries based on image tagging features [Original Research]. *Frontiers in Artificial Intelligence*, *4*, Article 644712. https://doi.org/10.3389/frai.2021.644712

Chow, C.C., & Hall, K.D. (2008). The dynamics of human body weight change. *PLoS Computational Biology, 4*(3), e1000045–e1000045. https://doi.org/10.1371/journal.pcbi.1000045
Cugini, P., Salandri, A., Cilli, M., Ceccotti, P., Di Marzo, A., Rodio, A., Fontana, S., Pellegrino, A.M., De Francesco, G.P., Coda, S., De Vito, F., Colosi, L., Petrangeli, C.M., & Giovannini, C. (1999). Daily hunger sensation and body compartments: II. Their relationships in obese patients. *Eating and Weight Disorders, 4*(2), 81–88.
Cugini, P., Salandri, A., Cilli, M., Ceccotti, P., Di Marzo, A., Rodio, A., Marcianò, F., Fontana, S., Pellegrino, A.M., Vacca, K., Di Siena, G., Di Francesco, G.P., Coda, S., Petrangeli, C.M., & Giovannini, C. (1998). Daily hunger sensation and body composition: I. Their relationships in clinically healthy subjects. *Eating and Weight Disorders, 3*(4), 168–172.
Dulloo, A.G., Jacquet, J., & Girardier, L. (1997). Poststarvation hyperphagia and body fat overshooting in humans: A role for feedback signals from lean and fat tissues. *The American Journal of Clinical Nutrition, 65*(3), 717–723. https://doi.org/10.1093/ajcn/65.3.717
Dulloo, A.G., Jacquet, J., Miles-Chan, J.L., & Schutz, Y. (2017). Passive and active roles of fat-free mass in the control of energy intake and body composition regulation. *European Journal of Clinical Nutrition, 71*(3), 353–357. https://doi.org/10.1038/ejcn.2016.256
Dulloo, A.G., Miles-Chan, J.L., & Schutz, Y. (2018). Collateral fattening in body composition autoregulation: Its determinants and significance for obesity predisposition. *European Journal of Clinical Nutrition, 72*(5), 657–664. https://doi.org/10.1038/s41430-018-0138-6
Finlayson, G. (2017). Food addiction and obesity: Unnecessary medicalization of hedonic overeating. *Nature Reviews Endocrinology, 13*(8), 493–498. https://doi.org/10.1038/nrendo.2017.61
Flatt, J. (1987). The difference in the storage capacities for carbohydrate and for fat, and its implications in the regulation of body weight. *Annals of the New York Academy of Sciences, 499*, 104–123.
Forbes, G.B. (1987). Lean body mass-body fat interrelationships in humans. *Nutrition Reviews, 45*(10), 225–231. https://doi.org/doi:10.1111/j.1753-4887.1987.tb02684.x
Gibbons, C., Caudwell, P., Finlayson, G., Webb, D.-L., Hellström, P.M., Näslund, E., & Blundell, J.E. (2013). Comparison of postprandial profiles of ghrelin, active GLP-1, and total PYY to meals varying in fat and carbohydrate and their association with hunger and the phases of satiety. *The Journal of Clinical Endocrinology & Metabolism, 98*(5), E847–E855. https://doi.org/10.1210/jc.2012-3835
Gibbons, C., Hopkins, M., Beaulieu, K., Oustric, P., & Blundell, J.E. (2019). Issues in measuring and interpreting human appetite (satiety/satiation) and its contribution to obesity. *Current Obesity Reports, 8*(2), 77–87. https://doi.org/10.1007/s13679-019-00340-6
Göbel, B., Sanghvi, A., & Hall, K.D. (2014). Quantifying energy intake changes during obesity pharmacotherapy. *Obesity, 22*(10), 2105–2108. https://doi.org/10.1002/oby.20813
Grannell, A., Al-Najim, W., Mangan, A., Kapoor, N., Martin, W.P., Murphy, J.C., Docherty, N.G., le Roux, C.W., & Davenport, C. (2019). Fat free mass is positively associated with hunger and energy intake at extremes of obesity. *Appetite, 143*, Article 104444. https://doi.org/https://doi.org/10.1016/j.appet.2019.104444
Guo, J., Robinson, J.L., Gardner, C.D., & Hall, K.D. (2019). Objective versus self-reported energy intake changes during low-carbohydrate and low-fat diets. *Obesity, 27*(3), 420–426. https://doi.org/10.1002/oby.22389
Halford, J.C.G., & Blundell, J.E. (2000). Separate systems for serotonin and leptin in appetite control. *Annals of Medicine, 32*(3), 222–232. https://doi.org/10.3109/07853890008998829
Hall, K.D. (2007). Body fat and fat-free mass inter-relationships: Forbes's theory revisited. *British Journal of Nutrition, 97*(6), 1059–1063. https://doi.org/10.1017/s0007114507691946
Hall, K.D. (2008). What is the required energy deficit per unit weight loss? *International Journal of Obesity, 32*(3), 573–576. https://doi.org/10.1038/sj.ijo.0803720
Hall, K.D., & Chow, C.C. (2011). Estimating changes in free-living energy intake and its confidence interval. *The American Journal of Clinical Nutrition, 94*(1), 66–74. https://doi.org/10.3945/ajcn.111.014399
Halliday, T.M., Rynders, C.A., Thomas, E., Bergouignan, A., Pan, Z., Kealey, E.H., Cornier, M.A., & Bessesen, D.H. (2020). Appetite-related responses to overfeeding and longitudinal weight change

in obesity-prone and obesity-resistant adults. *Obesity, 28*(2), 259–267. https://doi.org/10.1002/oby.22687

Heymsfield, S.B., Peterson, C.M., Thomas, D.M., Hirezi, M., Zhang, B., Smith, S., Bray, G., & Redman, L. (2017). Establishing energy requirements for body weight maintenance: Validation of an intake-balance method. *BMC Research Notes, 10*(1), 220. https://doi.org/10.1186/s13104-017-2546-4

Heymsfield, S.B., Thomas, D., Nguyen, A.M., Peng, J.Z., Martin, C., Shen, W., Strauss, B., Bosy-Westphal, A., & Muller, M.J. (2011). Voluntary weight loss: Systematic review of early phase body composition changes. *Obesity Review, 12*(5), e348–361. https://doi.org/10.1111/j.1467-789X.2010.00767.x

Hill, R.J., & Davies, P.S. (2001). The validity of self-reported energy intake as determined using the doubly labelled water technique. *British Journal of Nutrition, 85*(4), 415–430. https://doi.org/10.1079/bjn2000281

Hills, A.P., Mokhtar, N., & Byrne, N.M. (2014). Assessment of physical activity and energy expenditure: An overview of objective measures. *Frontiers in Nutrition, 1*, Article 5. https://doi.org/10.3389/fnut.2014.00005

Hintze, L.J., Mahmoodianfard, S., Auguste, C.B., & Doucet, É. (2017). Weight loss and appetite control in women. *Current Obesity Reports, 6*(3), 334–351. https://doi.org/10.1007/s13679-017-0273-8

Hopkins, M., Beaulieu, K., Myers, A., Gibbons, C., & Blundell, J.E. (2017). Mechanisms responsible for homeostatic appetite control: Theoretical advances and practical implications. *Expert Review of Endocrinology & Metabolism, 12*(6), 401–415. https://doi.org/10.1080/17446651.2017.1395693

Hopkins, M., Casanova, N., Finlayson, G., Stubbs, R.J., & Blundell, J.E. (2021). Fat-free mass and total daily energy expenditure estimated using doubly labelled water predict energy intake in a large sample of community-dwelling older adults. *Journal of Nutrition, 152*(4), 971–980. https://doi.org/10.1093/jn/nxab434

Hopkins, M., Duarte, C., Beaulieu, K., Finlayson, G., Gibbons, C., Johnstone, A.M., Whybrow, S., Horgan, G.W., Blundell, J.E., & Stubbs, R.J. (2019). Activity energy expenditure is an independent predictor of energy intake in humans. *International Journal of Obesity, 43*, 1466–1474. https://doi.org/10.1038/s41366-018-0308-6

Hopkins, M., Finlayson, G., Duarte, C., Gibbons, C., Johnstone, A., Whybrow, S., Horgan, G.W., Blundell, J.E., & Stubbs, J. (2018). Biological and psychological mediators of the relationships between fat mass, fat-free mass and energy intake. *International Journal of Obesity, 43*, 233–242. https://doi.org/10.1038/s41366-018-0059-4

Johnson, K.O., Holliday, A., Mistry, N., Cunniffe, A., Howard, K., Stanger, N., O'Mahoney, L.L., Matu, J., & Ispoglou, T. (2021). An increase in fat-free mass is associated with higher appetite and energy intake in older adults: A randomised control trial. *Nutrients, 13*(1), 141. https://doi.org/10.3390/nu13010141

Kenny, G.P., Notley, S.R., & Gagnon, D. (2017). Direct calorimetry: A brief historical review of its use in the study of human metabolism and thermoregulation. *European Journal of Applied Physiology, 117*(9), 1765–1785. https://doi.org/10.1007/s00421-017-3670-5

Lemos, T., & Gallagher, D. (2017). Current body composition measurement techniques. *Current Opinion in Endocrinology, Diabetes, and Obesity, 24*(5), 310–314. https://doi.org/10.1097/MED.0000000000000360

Levine, J.A. (2005). Measurement of energy expenditure. *Public Health Nutrition, 8*(7a), 1123–1132. https://doi.org/10.1079/phn2005800

Lissner, L., Habicht, J.-P., Strupp, B.J., Levitsky, D., Haas, J.D., & Roe, D. (1989). Body composition and energy intake: Do overweight women overeat and underreport? *The American Journal of Clinical Nutrition, 49*(2), 320–325. https://doi.org/10.1093/ajcn/49.2.320

Livingstone, M.B., & Black, A.E. (2003). Markers of the validity of reported energy intake. *Journal of Nutrition, 133* (Suppl 3), 895s–920s. https://doi.org/10.1093/jn/133.3.895S

Mayer, J. (1953). Glucostatic mechanism of regulation of food intake. *The New England Journal of Medicine, 249*(1), 13. https://doi.org/10.1056/NEJM195307022490104

Mayer, J. (1955). Regulation of energy intake and the body weight: The glucostatic theory and the lipostatic hypothesis. *Annals of New York Academy of Sciences, 63*(1), 15–43. https://doi.org/10.1111/j.1749-6632.1955.tb36543.x

McNeil, J., Lamothe, G., Cameron, J.D., Riou, M.-È., Cadieux, S., Lafrenière, J., Goldfield, G., Willbond, S., Prud'homme, D., & Doucet, É. (2015). Investigating predictors of eating: Is resting metabolic rate really the strongest proxy of energy intake? *Canadian Journal of Diabetes, 39*, S59. https://doi.org/10.1016/j.jcjd.2015.01.221

Melby, C.L., Paris, H.L., Foright, R.M., & Peth, J. (2017). Attenuating the biologic drive for weight regain following weight loss: Must what goes down always go back up? *Nutrients, 9*(5), 468. https://doi.org/10.3390/nu9050468

Mellinkoff, S.M., Frankland, M., Boyle, D., & Greipel, M. (1956). Relationship between serum amino acid concentration and fluctuations in appetite. *Journal of Applied Physiology, 8*(5), 535. https://doi.org/10.1152/jappl.1956.8.5.535

Müller, M.J., Braun, W., Pourhassan, M., Geisler, C., & Bosy-Westphal, A. (2016). Application of standards and models in body composition analysis. *Proceedings of the Nutrition Society, 75*(2), 181–187. https://doi.org/10.1017/s0029665115004206

Ndahimana, D., & Kim, E.-K. (2017). Measurement methods for physical activity and energy expenditure: A review. *Clinical Nutrition Research, 6*(2), 68–80. https://doi.org/10.7762/cnr.2017.6.2.68

Nindl, B.C., Friedl, K.E., Frykman, P.N., Marchitelli, L.J., Shippee, R.L., & Patton, J.F. (1997). Physical performance and metabolic recovery among lean, healthy men following a prolonged energy deficit. *International Journal of Sports Medicine, 18*(5), 317–324. https://doi.org/10.1055/s-2007-972640

Nymo, S., Coutinho, S.R., Jorgensen, J., Rehfeld, J.F., Truby, H., Kulseng, B., & Martins, C. (2017). Timeline of changes in appetite during weight loss with a ketogenic diet. *International Journal of Obesity, 41*(8), 1224–1231. https://doi.org/10.1038/ijo.2017.96

O'Driscoll, R., Turicchi, J., Beaulieu, K., Scott, S., Matu, J., Deighton, K., Finlayson, G., & Stubbs, J. (2020). How well do activity monitors estimate energy expenditure? A systematic review and meta-analysis of the validity of current technologies. *British Journal of Sports Medicine, 54*(6), 332–340. https://doi.org/10.1136/bjsports-2018-099643

O'Driscoll, R., Turicchi, J., Hopkins, M., Duarte, C., Horgan, G.W., Finlayson, G., & Stubbs, R.J. (2021). Comparison of the validity and generalizability of machine learning algorithms for the prediction of energy expenditure: Validation study. *JMIR mHealth & uHealth, 9*(8), e23938. https://doi.org/10.2196/preprints.23938

O'Driscoll, R., Turicchi, J., Hopkins, M., Horgan, G.W., Finlayson, G., & Stubbs, J.R. (2020). Improving energy expenditure estimates from wearable devices: A machine learning approach. *Journal of Sport Sciences, 38*(13), 1496–1505. https://doi.org/10.1080/02640414.2020.1746088

Perry, B., & Wang, Y. (2012). Appetite regulation and weight control: The role of gut hormones. *Nutrition and Diabetes, 2*, e26. https://doi.org/10.1038/nutd.2011.21

Piaggi, P., Thearle, M.S., Krakoff, J., & Votruba, S.B. (2015). Higher daily energy expenditure and respiratory quotient, rather than fat free mass, independently determine greater ad libitum overeating. *The Journal of Clinical Endocrinology & Metabolism, 100*(8), 3011–3020. https://doi.org/10.1210/jc.2015-2164

Polidori, D., Sanghvi, A., Seeley, R.J., & Hall, K.D. (2016). How strongly does appetite counter weight loss? Quantification of the feedback control of human energy intake. *Obesity, 24*(11), 2289–2295. https://doi.org/10.1002/oby.21653

Posma, J.M., Garcia-Perez, I., Frost, G., Aljuraiban, G.S., Chan, Q., Van Horn, L., Daviglus, M., Stamler, J., Holmes, E., Elliott, P., & Nicholson, J.K. (2020). Nutriome-metabolome relationships provide insights into dietary intake and metabolism. *Nature Food, 1*(7), 426–436. https://doi.org/10.1038/s43016-020-0093-y

Qiu, J., Lo, F.P.W., Jiang, S., Tsai, Y.Y., Sun, Y., & Lo, B. (2021). Counting bites and recognizing consumed food from videos for passive dietary monitoring. *IEEE Journal of Biomedical and Health Informatics, 25*(5), 1471–1482. https://doi.org/10.1109/JBHI.2020.3022815

Racette, S.B., Das, S.K., Bhapkar, M., Hadley, E.C., Roberts, S.B., Ravussin, E., Pieper, C., DeLany, J.P., Kraus, W.E., Rochon, J., Redman, L.M., & CALERIE Study Group (2012). Approaches for quantifying energy intake and %calorie restriction during calorie restriction interventions in humans: The multicenter CALERIE study. *American Journal of Physiology, Endocrinology and Metabolism, 302*(4), E441–E448. https://doi.org/10.1152/ajpendo.00290.2011

Ravelli, M.N., & Schoeller, D.A. (2020). Traditional self-reported dietary instruments are prone to inaccuracies and new approaches are needed. *Frontiers in Nutrition, 7*, Article 90. https://doi.org/10.3389/fnut.2020.00090

Ravelli, M.N., & Schoeller, D.A. (2021). An objective measure of energy intake using the principle of energy balance. *International Journal of Obesity, 45*(4), 725–732. https://doi.org/10.1038/s41366-021-00738-0

Roekenes, J., & Martins, C. (2021). Ketogenic diets and appetite regulation. *Current Opinion in Clinical Nutrition and Metabolic Care, 24*(4), 359–363. https://doi.org/10.1097/mco.0000000000000760

Sanghvi, A., Redman, L.M., Martin, C.K., Ravussin, E., & Hall, K.D. (2015). Validation of an inexpensive and accurate mathematical method to measure long-term changes in free-living energy intake. *The American Journal of Clinical Nutrition, 102*(2), 353–358. https://doi.org/10.3945/ajcn.115.111070

Shook, R.P., Hand, G.A., O'Connor, D.P., Thomas, D.M., Hurley, T.G., Hébert, J.R., Drenowatz, C., Welk, G.J., Carriquiry, A.L., & Blair, S.N. (2018). Energy intake derived from an energy balance equation, validated activity monitors, and dual X-ray absorptiometry can provide acceptable caloric intake data among young adults. *The Journal of Nutrition, 148*(3), 490–496. https://doi.org/10.1093/jn/nxx029

Shook, R.P., Yeh, H.W., Welk, G.J., Davis, A.M., & Ries, D. (2021). Commercial devices provide estimates of energy balance with varying degrees of validity in free-living adults. *Journal of Nutrition, 152*(2), 630–638. https://doi.org/10.1093/jn/nxab317

Speakman, J.R. (1998). The history and theory of the doubly labeled water technique. *The American Journal of Clinical Nutrition, 68*(4), 932s–938s. https://doi.org/10.1093/ajcn/68.4.932S

Stubbs, R.J., Hopkins, M., Finlayson, G., Duarte, C., Gibbons, C., & Blundell, J. (2018). Potential effects of fat mass and fat-free mass on energy intake in different states of energy balance. *European Journal of Clinical Nutrition, 72*(5), 698. https://doi.org/10.1038/s41430-018-0146-6

Sumithran, P., Prendergast, L.A., Delbridge, E., Purcell, K., Shulkes, A., Kriketos, A., & Proietto, J. (2011). Long-term persistence of hormonal adaptations to weight loss. *New England Journal of Medicine, 365*(17), 1597–1604. https://doi.org/10.1056/NEJMoa1105816

Thomas, D.M., Schoeller, D.A., Redman, L.A., Martin, C.K., Levine, J.A., & Heymsfield, S.B. (2010). A computational model to determine energy intake during weight loss. *The American Journal of Clinical Nutrition, 92*(6), 1326–1331. https://doi.org/10.3945/ajcn.2010.29687

Thomas, D.M., Scioletti, M., & Heymsfield, S.B. (2019). Predictive mathematical models of weight loss. *Current Diabetes Reports, 19*(10), 93. https://doi.org/10.1007/s11892-019-1207-5

Trabulsi, J., & Schoeller, D.A. (2001). Evaluation of dietary assessment instruments against doubly labeled water, a biomarker of habitual energy intake. *American Journal of Physiology, Endocrinology and Metabolism, 281*(5), E891–899. https://doi.org/10.1152/ajpendo.2001.281.5.E891

Trabulsi, J., Troiano, R.P., Subar, A.F., Sharbaugh, C., Kipnis, V., Schatzkin, A., & Schoeller, D.A. (2003). Precision of the doubly labeled water method in a large-scale application: Evaluation of a streamlined-dosing protocol in the Observing Protein and Energy Nutrition (OPEN) study. *European Journal of Clinical Nutrition, 57*(11), 1370–1377. https://doi.org/10.1038/sj.ejcn.1601698

Turicchi, J., O'Driscoll, R., Finlayson, G., Beaulieu, K., Deighton, K., & Stubbs, R.J. (2019). Associations between the rate, amount, and composition of weight loss as predictors of spontaneous weight regain in adults achieving clinically significant weight loss: A systematic review and meta-regression. *Obesity Review, 20*(7), 935–946. https://doi.org/10.1111/obr.12849

Turicchi, J., O'Driscoll, R., Finlayson, G., Duarte, C., Hopkins, M., Martins, N., Michalowska, J., Larsen, T.M., van Baak, M.A., Astrup, A., & Stubbs, R.J. (2020). Associations between the proportion of fat-free mass loss during weight loss, changes in appetite, and subsequent weight change: Results from a randomized 2-stage dietary intervention trial. *The American Journal of Clinical Nutrition, 111*(3), 536–544. https://doi.org/10.1093/ajcn/nqz331

Vainik, U., Konstabel, K., Latt, E., Maestu, J., Purge, P., & Jurimae, J. (2016). Diet misreporting can be corrected: Confirmation of the association between energy intake and fat-free mass in adolescents. *British Journal of Nutrition, 116*(8), 1425–1436. https://doi.org/10.1017/s0007114516003317

Weise, C.M., Hohenadel, M.G., Krakoff, J., & Votruba, S.B. (2014). Body composition and energy expenditure predict ad-libitum food and macronutrient intake in humans. *International Journal of Obesity, 38*(2), 243–251. https://doi.org/10.1038/ijo.2013.85

Wells, J.C., Davies, P.S., Hopkins, M., & Blundell, J.E. (2021). The "drive to eat" hypothesis: Energy expenditure and fat-free mass but not adiposity are associated with milk intake and energy intake in 12 week infants. *The American Journal of Clinical Nutrition, 114*(2), 505–514. https://doi.org/10.1093/ajcn/nqab067

Wing, R.R., & Phelan, S. (2005). Long-term weight loss maintenance. *The American Journal of Clinical Nutrition, 82*(1), 222S–225S. https://doi.org/10.1093/ajcn/82.1.222S

Zhang, Y., Proenca, R., Maffei, M., Barone, M., Leopold, L., & Friedman, J. (1994). Positional cloning of the mouse obese gene and its human homologue. *Nature, 372*(6505), 425–432.

Chapter 15

Assessment of Food Neophobia and Disgust Sensitivity

Christina Hartmann[1] and Klazine van der Horst[2]

[1] ETH Zurich, Department Health Science and Technology (D-HEST), Consumer Behavior, Switzerland
[2] Bern University of Applied Sciences, School of Health Professions, Nutrition & Dietetics, Switzerland

Introduction

The following chapter is separated into two major parts. In the first part, the concept food neophobia is explained and how it can be measured. In that vein, not only the established Food Neophobia Scale published in 1992 is addressed, but also the more recently developed Motivation to Eat New Foods Scale is introduced. Potential limitations and newer developments in the field are discussed. In the second part of the chapter, the focus is on disgust sensitivity and how it can be assessed with questionnaires, facial, physiological, and behavioral measures. A distinction is made between state disgust (instant sensation) and trait disgust (personality-like trait). Critical aspects in the field of disgust research regarding linguistic challenges and differentiation from neighboring emotions such as fear are briefly addressed as well.

Assessment of Food Neophobia

Introduction

Food neophobia is the fear or reluctance to eat unfamiliar or new foods (Dovey et al., 2008). Food neophobia is considered to be an important factor influencing food choice and eating behaviors in both children and adults. The influence of food neophobia on food choice, eating behaviors, and diversity in the diet varies between individuals. Food neophobia has been hypothesized to occur because of the omnivore dilemma: In the search for food, humans also need to approach novel and unknown foods, but to protect themselves from potentially poisonous foods, the diet is restricted by a tendency to only consume what is familiar and safe (Armelagos, 2014).

Several studies have explored the associations between food neophobia and dietary intake. In these studies, higher scores of neophobia have been mainly associated with less dietary variety and lower food intake in children (Dovey et al., 2008; Elkins & Zickgraf, 2018). The evidence for the association between neophobia and food intake in adults is much less substantial. Few studies have explored this, finding lower food intake in neophobic adults (Capiola & Raudenbush, 2012) and an association between higher food neophobia and adherence to the Mediterranean Diet Index adapted for the Italian diet (Predieri et al., 2020). In a Portuguese study, food neophobia was not significantly associated with adherence to a healthy dietary pattern but was found to be negatively associated with reduced preferences for specific foods (Costa et al., 2020). However, it is also important to notice that in this study, neophobia did not affect the macronutrients and energy intake, as well as sodium, added sugars, and fiber intake. In adults, food neophobia might have implications for food choice and food intake, but an association with a less healthy diet cannot be confirmed (Rabadán & Bernabéu, 2021). When examining individual foods, more evidence is available (e.g., on consumer acceptance) mainly because this is critical for new food products entering the market, such as meat alternatives (Idowu-Adebayo et al., 2021; Tuorila & Hartmann, 2020).

The Food Neophobia Scale

The most widely used measure of neophobia is the Food Neophobia Scale (FNS), which was developed by Pliner and Hobden in 1992. This scale has been translated into many languages and used in numerous research projects (Alley, 2018). Variations of the scale have been used, such as shortened versions with eight items in a study with children (Laureati et al., 2015) or a six-item scale in studies with adolescents (Flight et al., 2003) and adults (Alemu et al., 2017; Ritchey et al., 2003; Verbeke, 2015). However, based on confirmatory factor analyses, different researchers excluded different items, and different response scales were used, such as a 5-point scale versus a 7-point scale. It is important to keep in mind that such changes affect the outcome. For example, on the 5-point scale, adults scored relatively lower on average for neophobia than they did on a 7-point scale (Meiselman et al., 2010). Unless there is a clear improvement of the shorter scale over the original one, researchers should be hesitant to make changes to the original FNS scale because it has been shown to decrease the comparability of the scores between studies. Moreover there is no consensus on which item(s) should be excluded (Alley, 2018). Summarizing studies that have used the FNS (including studies targeting children), food neophobia is at least partially determined genetically (Rabadán & Bernabéu, 2021). Several studies have shown associations between food neophobia and demographic factors such as a decrease with increased age, and lower scores in those with higher education, income, and urbanization (Elkins & Zickgraf, 2018; Rabadán & Bernabéu, 2021; Heuvel et al., 2019).

Limitations of the FNS Scale

The development of the FNS scale through confirmatory factor analysis dates back to 2003 (Ritchey et al., 2003). A systematic review on available food neophobia measures confirmed that so far, the FNS is the only neophobia measure that has been compared to a behavior test (Damsbo-Svendsen et al., 2017). After 30 years, it is questionable if the FNS is still relevant and reflecting the current food environment; several studies argued that the change and adaptation of the scale is a necessity to ensure its validity for specific uses, to ensure the relevance of its items, and to ensure a critical assessment on the one-dimensionality of its structure (Damsbo-Svendsen et al., 2017). Items on the liking and acceptance of foods from other cultures or ethnic foods such as "I like foods from different cultures" and "Ethnic food looks too weird to eat," might have declined in importance, while the acceptance of novel foods like plant-based meat and dairy alternatives and, for example, products with or based on insects would better define neophobia nowadays (Tuorila & Hartmann, 2020). Items regarding eating ethic foods from different cultures may also not be relevant because these may be familiar foods simply imported from foreign countries (Damsbo-Svendsen et al., 2017). This aspect highlights that even though the FNS was translated into various languages for various countries, it might need additional changes to better reflect the neophobia trait in the country of study and in the current diverse food environments. More recently, a Revised Food Neophobia Scale (FNS-R) was validated for the Italian context (Guidetti et al., 2018). As presented in Table 15.1, four items of the questionnaire were omitted based on diagnostics and psychometric tests performed on its factorial structure. However, a study evaluating the wording of the items and if ethnic foods are considered familiar or unfamiliar is still lacking.

One of the main criticisms of the FNS is summarized by Nezlek et al. (2021) who argued that the scale has shown two factors instead of representing only one dimension. The first dimension is represented by so-called "approach" items, such as "I am constantly sampling new and different foods," which are then reverse coded (Items 1, 4, 6, 9, and 10) to measure the avoidance of new foods. Nezlek et al. (2021) argued that the lack of an approach motive is not the same as the presence of a corresponding avoidance motive and that these motives need to be clearly distinguished. Therefore, a new scale, the Motivation to Eat New Food Scale, was developed specifically for adults to address the aspects mentioned above (Table 15.1). Another element in the development of this scale was the removal of wording like "ethnic" or foods from culinary traditions that are different from one's own, which was done to avoid ambiguity around these words. In using the scale, the avoidance and approach motivations can be used as related but independent constructs (Nezlek et al., 2021). Future research is needed to further examine and develop this instrument by linking the scale to actual consumption of new foods and applying the measure in various populations, as was done with the FNS of Pliner and Hobden (Pliner & Hobden, 1992).

Other Measures of Neophobia

More food neophobia scales exist, but many of them focus on food neophobia in children, such as the Children's Eating Behavior Questionnaire (Wardle et al., 2001) and the Fruit and Vegetable Food Neophobia Scale (Hollar et al., 2013). A detailed overview of

Table 15.1. The 10-item Food Neophobia Scale from Pliner and Hobden (1992), the six-item FNS-Revised Scale from Guidetti et al. (2018), and the Motivation to Eat New Food Scale from Nezlek et al. (2021)

Food Neophobia Scale (FNS) and FNS-Revised Scale (FNS-R)	Motivation to Eat New Food Scale
1. I am constantly sampling new and different foods. (R) **2. I don't trust new foods.** 3. If I don't know what a food is, I won't try it. 4. I like foods from different cultures. (R) **5. Ethnic food looks too weird to eat.** **6. At dinner parties, I will try new foods. (R)** **7. I am afraid to eat things I have never had before.** 8. I am very particular about the foods I eat. 9. I will eat almost anything. (R) **10. I like to try new ethnic restaurants. (R)**	**Motivation to approach new foods** 1. I enjoy trying foods that I have never eaten before. 2. I enjoy learning about new foods. 3. I am interested in trying familiar foods that have been prepared with new ingredients. 4. I am curious about the flavors of new foods and ingredients. 5. I get sort of excited when I know I am going to eat some new types of food. **Motivation to avoid new foods** 1. I don't trust new foods. 2. I am afraid to eat things I have never had before. 3. I think that if I eat something I have not eaten before that it will taste strange. 4. I think that if I eat something I have not eaten before that I will not like it. 5. Foods I have never eaten before seem sort of disgusting.
Each item is rated on a 7-point scale labeled as: −3 = *disagree strongly*, −2 = *disagree moderately*, −1 = *disagree slightly*, 0 = *neither disagree nor agree*, 1 = *agree slightly*, 2 = *agree moderately*, 3 = *agree strongly*. Items indicated with (R) are reverse scored. Items in bold are the FNS-R items.	The items are rated on a 5-point scale labeled as: 1 = *not at all like me*, 2 = *a little like me*, 3 = *somewhat like me*, 4 = *like me*, 5 = *very much like me*.

Note. Items have been reprinted from: *Food Quality and Preference, 88*, John B. Nezlek, Catherine A. Forestell, Marzena Cypryanska, "Approach and avoidance motivation and interest in new foods: Introducing a measure of the motivation to eat new foods," p. 104111, © 2021, with permission from Elsevier; *Appetite, 19*(2), Patricia Pliner, Karen Hobden, "Development of a scale to measure the trait of food neophobia in humans", Table 1, © 1992, with permission from Elsevier; *Appetite, 128*, Margherita Guidetti, Luciana Carraro, Nicoletta Cavazza, Michele Roccato, "Validation of the revised Food Neophobia Scale (FNS-R) in the Italian context", Table 3, © 2018, with permission from Elsevier.

the available measures has been given in the systematic review of Damsbo-Svendsen et al. (2017). An instrument that was developed in the same year as the FNS is the VAR-SEEK Questionnaire, which aims to measure consumers' variety seeking tendency in relation to foods (Trijp et al., 1992). The items in the questionnaire focus on trying out new recipes, unusual items, exotic foods, and unfamiliar foods. The Food Attitude Scale (FAS; Frank & Klaauw, 1994) consists of food preference ratings for 455 foods and beverages, including some unusual and fictitious foods. A FAS score can reflect a general attitude toward novel foods, which may reflect neophobia. However, preference may not fully reflect the concept of neophobia and willingness to try unfamiliar foods (Damsbo-Svendsen et al., 2017).

Conclusion

Food consumption and food choice is influenced by many interrelated factors. Food neophobia is one of these and should, for instance, be taken into account in the development of new food products and in consumer behavior studies. In general, food neophobia does not have a clear influence on the healthiness of adults' dietary patterns, and a low willingness to include novel foods in the diet might not be of significant importance. However, food neophobia could play an important role when it comes to recent developments trying to create new, sustainable, vegan, or healthier products.

Assessment of Disgust and Disgust Sensitivity

Introduction

Disgust is considered to serve as a disease-avoidance function that aims to limit contact with and, thus, the likelihood of infection from bacteria, parasites, and viruses. It aims to avoid potential health threats by cognitively triggering disease preventive behavior (Terrizzi et al., 2013). A feeling of disgust is typically accompanied by feeling unpleasant or even having nausea. Apart from distaste, disgust can be triggered by cues that symbolize hazardous items and the presence of pathogens such as certain odors (e.g., smell of decayed food), visual (e.g., mold, runny nose), and tactile (e.g., slime) cues, as well as auditory input (e.g., clear one's throat; Curtis & Biran, 2001). Likewise, objects that have had contact with a disease vector can be perceived as contaminated and a trigger of disgust.

The ability to experience disgust is innate, and researchers have stated that genetics also determine an individual's disgust sensitivity (Sherlock et al., 2016). However, disgust evolves within cultural boundaries and is primarily shaped through social learning (Rottman, 2014). Parental influences during early childhood play a substantial role when it comes to learning new disgust elicitors (Stevenson et al., 2010). People vary in the intensity of experienced disgust (Tybur et al., 2018). In fact, although some people simply feel uncomfortable in the presence of disgust triggers, others feel a very intense aversion up to the point of nausea. The underlying reasons for these differences are not fully understood, but it is assumed that physiological state, perceived vulnerability to diseases, or experiences such as food borne illnesses are responsible for the variations (Duncan et al., 2009; Egolf et al., 2018).

Assessment of Individual Differences in Disgust Responding Using Questionnaires

Variability in people's proneness to experiencing disgust and disgust propensity can be measured using questionnaires. Various questionnaires have been proposed; they vary in their conceptualization of disgust, the disgust elicitors and contexts that are used, and how disgust elicitors are grouped together. Factor analysis of disgust elicitors has consistently produced multidimensional factor solutions (e.g., Kleinknecht et al., 1997; Olatunji, Williams, et al., 2007). Thus, most scales consist of two to eight subscales that measure disgust in different (functional) domains or groups of elicitors.

The oldest scale is the 32-item Disgust Scale (DS) developed by Haidt et al. (1994). It measures disgust sensitivity in eight domains. Example items read "It bothers me to hear someone clear a throat full of mucous" and "You are walking barefoot on concrete, and you step on an earthworm." However, the scale has been criticized for low alpha reliabilities in the domain subscales. Olatunji, Williams et al. (2007) proposed a revised version of the DS (DS-R) with a reorganized item structure and reduced number of subscales (core disgust, contamination-based disgust, and animal reminder disgust).

Tybur et al. (2009) proposed the 21-item Three Domains DS. An example item reads "Stepping on dog poop," "Accidentally touching a person's bloody cut," or "Stealing from a neighbor." The scale includes three distinct functional domains of disgust: pathogen disgust, sexual disgust, and moral disgust. The pathogen domain functions to stimulate avoidance with infectious microorganisms. Sexual disgust motivates avoidance with costly sexual behaviors, and moral disgust motivates avoidance of antisocial norm violations (Tybur et al., 2009). However, the moral subscale (e.g., "Shoplifting a candy bar from a convenience store") might not be understood as a source of disgust in any language equally well.

In 2006, Overveld et al. (2006) published the Disgust Propensity and Sensitivity Scale, which measures how easily people are disgusted (propensity) and how unpleasant they consider the disgust experience (sensitivity). It does not measure disgust for specific elicitors. Accordingly, example items read "I avoid disgusting things" (propensity) and "It embarrasses me when I feel disgusted" (sensitivity). A revised version was proposed by Olatunji et al. (2007) and Fergus and Valentiner (2009) with a reduced number of items but with the same two-factor structure.

In 2018, a new scale was published – the Food Disgust Sensitivity scale (FDS) – that focuses on the domain of food and food-related disgust stimuli (Hartmann & Siegrist, 2018). It measures disgust experience when confronted with food-related cues such as indicated pathogen presence via a moldy surface, animal origin of the food, and unhygienic food preparation. A 32-item long version and an eight-item short version were published, as well as a picture-based version (Ammann et al., 2018a). The questionnaire consists of eight pictures showing different potentially disgusting situations, and people must indicate how disgusting they perceive the displayed situation/food product to be. In contrast to the word-based FDS, participants' perception of the disgust cues is not subject to imagination: they are directly confronted with a picture of the elicitor. The picture-based tool was developed to facilitate cross-cultural research by being independent of text understanding.

Assessment of State Disgust Using Questionnaires

The questionnaire and scales presented so far are measures of trait-like disgust, which is correlated with state disgust. To measure an instant sensation of disgust and the subjective feeling, researchers have often used a single item such as "To what extent are you feeling disgust right now?" or "How disgusting do you perceive the following situation?" (e.g., Egolf et al., 2019). To increase reliability of the state measure, a multi-item state

DS was developed and tested (Ihme & Mitte, 2009). The 15 items were developed in a German context, and the sample items (translated) are "I feel miserable," "I feel sick," and "I have an urge to choke." The 4-point response scale ranges from *not at all* to *very*. An advantage of the scale is that it measures both subjective feeling and motor expression of disgust. An English language version has been evaluated and published, too (Bates & Chadwick, 2015). So far, the scale has not been comprehensively applied in different samples and contexts and still needs to be tested. It is also not clear to what extent the scale outperforms a single item measure of a disgust sensation.

Assessment of Disgust Response in the Face

Facial expressions are considered as having different communicative values. Next to happiness, anger, fear, and surprise, disgust is one of the emotions reliably recognized by people from a variety of Western and non-Western societies (Ekman & Friesen, 1971; Haidt & Keltner, 1999). In emotion research, facial expressions can be measured via direct (anatomical analysis of facial actions) and indirect (observer judgments) methods. For instance, researchers can observe the different variations of a disgusted face in behavioral experiments and link the intensity of disgust responses to various elicitors. In the past couple of years, automated expression recognition systems have been applied, too, but it is questionable how mature the technology is by now when it comes to measuring emotions (Buck & Miller, 2016; Hwang & Matsumoto, 2016). Researchers are referred to more recent publications in the area (e.g., Adjabi et al., 2020; Briot et al., 2021; Dzedzickis et al., 2020). Facial measurements are rather difficult, and many potential biases and difficulties can occur, such as emotional reactions toward the research process, different facial structures between ethnicities, and individual and cultural differences in emotion expression (Hwang & Matsumoto, 2016).

Physiological Measures and Behavioral Assessment

Other measures of a disgust sensation have been used, including measures of anatomic nervous system measures (skin conductance) or eye tracking (measuring oculomotor avoidance). However, they are not introduced in the present chapter, and interested readers are referred to for instance Armstrong et al. (2021).

Behavioral assessments of disgust have been used to assess disgust reactivity or state disgust. In behavioral avoidance tasks, participants are exposed to potentially disgust-provoking stimuli and nondisgusting control tasks (e.g., Ammann et al., 2018b; Rozin et al., 1999). Correlations with disgust sensitivity scales and behavioral tasks can facilitate a more sophisticated assessment of disgust.

Caveats in the Assessment of Disgust and Disgust Sensitivity

The English emotion term for disgust does not have one straightforward equivalent in other languages. According to the Oxford dictionary of current English, the term "disgust" can be used to indicate a strong feeling of dislike or disapproval of somebody or something that one feels is unacceptable (Turnbull et al., 2010). Yet, it can also be used to indicate anger. In German, for example, disgust [German: *Ekel*] is usually not used to indicate anger. Instead, it is used to indicate that something is unpleasant or vomitous. Following that, some items from the moral domain of the Three Domains DS (e.g., "Shoplifting a candy bar from a convenience store") might not work in the German translation. Some scholars have even called into question whether moral transgressions (without reference to the body and its products) can be linked to the term disgust at all (Armstrong et al., 2021). The present use of the term "disgust" in emotion research has been generally criticized, here stating that a lexical fallacy drives its usage (e.g., Armstrong et al., 2021; Nabi, 2002). Like others in the field, researchers draw attention to the lay usage of the term, which does not correspond with the scientific construct and sometimes mislabels anger or neighboring states (Armstrong et al., 2021). Likewise, the difference between fear and disgust is not always obvious, and both might have common elicitors like in the field of anxiety-related disorders or genetic modification. Whether disgust (from an oral inhibition) or fear (in terms of creeped out) is really driving the emotional response is not always clear and has been debated (Cusimano et al., 2018; Inbar & Scott, 2018; Royzman et al., 2017). Thus, potential variations in emotion vocabulary should be considered when disgust measures are developed or translated to other languages and cultural contexts. For a more thorough discussion about the term disgust and translatability cross-cultural studies, see Nabi (2002), Fiske (2020), and Ogarkova (2016).

Conclusion

Disgust can have functional and dysfunctional effects, and its consequences for behavior are not fully understood yet. A diverse set of possibilities are available to assess disgust either as a trait-like measure or state measure. There are a couple of questionnaires available that can be used to measure disgust in different domains, but cultural and lexical challenges remain.

Conclusions

Although food neophobia exclusively operates when it comes to suspiciousness toward the unknown or unfamiliar in the domain of food intake, disgust sensitivity – as a preventive measure – has more functional domains than just oral rejection like sexual or pathogen-related disgust sensitivity. Studies showed correlational associations between disgust sensitivity and food neophobia (Al-Shawaf et al., 2015; Hartmann & Siegrist, 2018), but the direction of the relationship remains unclear. Although some have argued that disgust is one influential factor among many on food neophobia (Al-Shawaf et al., 2015), others found evidence that food neophobia has an direct and indirect relationships via perceived vulnerability to disease on (food) disgust sensitivity (Santisi et al., 2021).

Both food neophobia and disgust sensitivity have been linked to eating behavior and rejection of novel foods, unfamiliar foods and food technologies in particular (Egolf et al., 2018; Siegrist et al., 2013; Tuorila & Hartmann, 2020). Thus, theoretically and empirically, it could be shown that both constructs are linked to how consumers process novelty in foods. Therefore, it seems advisable to assess both constructs because they are not conceptually the same.

References

Adjabi, I., Ouahabi, A., Benzaoui, A., & Taleb-Ahmed, A. (2020). Past, present, and future of face recognition: A review. *Electronics, 9*(8), 1188. https://doi.org/10.3390/electronics9081188

Alemu, M.H., Olsen, S.B., Vedel, S.E., Pambo, K.O., & Owino, V.O. (2017). Combining product attributes with recommendation and shopping location attributes to assess consumer preferences for insect-based food products. *Food Quality and Preference, 55*, 45–57. https://doi.org/10.1016/j.foodqual.2016.08.009

Alley, T.R. (2018). Conceptualization and measurement of human food neophobia. *Food Neophobia*, 169–192. https://doi.org/10.1016/b978-0-08-101931-3.00009-4

Al-Shawaf, L., Lewis, D.M., Alley, T.R., & Buss, D.M. (2015). Mating strategy, disgust, and food neophobia. *Appetite, 85*, 30–35. https://doi.org/10.1016/j.appet.2014.10.029

Ammann, J., Hartmann, C., & Siegrist, M. (2018a). Development and validation of the food disgust picture scale. *Appetite, 125*, 367–379. https://doi.org/10.1016/j.appet.2018.02.020

Ammann, J., Hartmann, C., & Siegrist, M. (2018b). Does food disgust sensitivity influence eating behaviour? Experimental validation of the Food Disgust Scale. *Food Quality and Preference, 68*, 411–414. https://doi.org/10.1016/j.foodqual.2017.12.013

Armelagos, G.J. (2014). Brain evolution, the determinates of food choice, and the omnivore's dilemma. *Critical Reviews in Food Science and Nutrition, 54*(10), 1330–1341. https://doi.org/10.1080/10408398.2011.635817

Armstrong, T., Wilbanks, D.B.A., Leong, D., & Hsu, K. (2021). Beyond vernacular: Measurement solutions to the lexical fallacy in disgust research. *Journal of Anxiety Disorders, 82*, 102408.

Bates, B.R., & Chadwick, A.E. (2015). Measuring state disgust: Initial evidence for the reliability and validity of an English-language version of the Ekel-State-Fragebogen. *Communication Research Reports, 32*(1), 73–82. https://doi.org/10.1080/08824096.2014.989978

Briot, K., Pizano, A., Bouvard, M., & Amestoy, A. (2021). New technologies as promising tools for assessing facial emotion expressions impairments in ASD: A systematic review. *Frontiers in Psychiatry, 12*, Article 530. https://doi.org/10.3389/fpsyt.2021.634756

Buck, R., & Miller, M. (2016). Measuring the dynamic stream of display: Spontaneous and intentional facial expression and communication. In D. Matsumoto, H. Hwang, & M. Frank (Eds.), *APA handbook of nonverbal communication* (pp. 425–458). American Psychological Association. https://doi.org/10.1037/14669-017

Capiola, A., & Raudenbush, B. (2012). The effects of food neophobia and food neophilia on diet and metabolic processing. *Food and Nutrition Sciences, 3*(10), 1397–1403. https://doi.org/10.4236/fns.2012.310183

Costa, A., Silva, C., & Oliveira, A. (2020). Food neophobia and its association with food preferences and dietary intake of adults. *Nutrition & Dietetics: The Journal of the Dietitians Association of Australia, 77*(5), 542–549. https://doi.org/10.1111/1747-0080.12587

Cusimano, C., Royzman, E.B., Leeman, R.F., & Metas, S. (2018). Methodology is the core disgust problem: Response to Inbar and Scott (2018). *Judgment and Decision Making, 13*(6), 639.

Curtis, V., & Biran, A. (2001). Dirt, disgust, and disease: Is hygiene in our genes? *Perspectives in Biology and Medicine, 44*(1), 17–31.

Damsbo-Svendsen, M., Frøst, M.B., & Olsen, A. (2017). A review of instruments developed to measure food neophobia. *Appetite, 113*, 358–367. https://doi.org/10.1016/j.appet.2017.02.032

Dovey, T.M., Staples, P.A., Gibson, E.L., & Halford, J.C.G. (2008). Food neophobia and "picky/fussy" eating in children: A review. *Appetite, 50*(2–3), 181–193. https://doi.org/10.1016/j.appet.2007.09.009

Duncan, L.A., Schaller, M., & Park, J.H. (2009). Perceived vulnerability to disease: Development and validation of a 15-item self-report instrument. *Personality and Individual Differences, 47*(6), 541–546. https://doi.org/10.1016/j.paid.2009.05.001

Dzedzickis, A., Kaklauskas, A., & Bucinskas, V. (2020). Human emotion recognition: Review of sensors and methods. *Sensors, 20*(3), 592. https://doi.org/10.3390/s20030592

Egolf, A., Siegrist, M., & Hartmann, C. (2018). How people's food disgust sensitivity shapes their eating and food behaviour. *Appetite, 127*, 28–36. https://doi.org/10.1016/j.appet.2018.04.014

Egolf, A., Siegrist, M., & Hartmann, C. (2019). When evolution works against the future: Disgust's contributions to the acceptance of new food technologies. *Risk Analysis, 39*(7), 1546–1559. https://doi.org/10.1111/risa.13279

Ekman, P., & Friesen, W.V. (1971). Constants across cultures in the face and emotion. *Journal of Personality and Social Psychology, 17*(2), 124. https://doi.org/10.1037/h0030377

Elkins, A., & Zickgraf, H.F. (2018). Picky eating and food neophobia: Resemblance and agreement in parent/young adult dyads. *Appetite, 126*, 36–42. https://doi.org/10.1016/j.appet.2018.02.021

Fergus, T.A., & Valentiner, D.P. (2009). The Disgust Propensity and Sensitivity Scale–Revised: An examination of a reduced-item version. *Journal of Anxiety Disorders, 23*(5), 703–710. https://doi.org/10.1016/j.janxdis.2009.02.009

Fiske, A.P. (2020). The lexical fallacy in emotion research: Mistaking vernacular words for psychological entities. *Psychological Review, 127*(1), 95. https://doi.org/10.1037/rev0000174

Flight, I., Leppard, P., & Cox, D.N. (2003). Food neophobia and associations with cultural diversity and socio-economic status amongst rural and urban Australian adolescents. *Appetite, 41*(1), 51–59. https://doi.org/10.1016/S0195-6663(03)00039-4

Frank, R.A., & Klaauw, N.J. van der (1994). The contribution of chemosensory factors to individual differences in reported food preferences. *Appetite, 22*(2), 101–123. https://doi.org/10.1006/appe.1994.1011

Guidetti, M., Carraro, L., Cavazza, N., & Roccato, M. (2018). Validation of the revised Food Neophobia Scale (FNS-R) in the Italian context. *Appetite, 128*, 95–99. https://doi.org/10.1016/j.appet.2018.06.004

Haidt, J., & Keltner, D. (1999). Culture and facial expression: Open-ended methods find more expressions and a gradient of recognition. *Cognition and Emotion, 13*(3), 225–266. https://doi.org/10.1080/026999399379267

Haidt, J., McCauley, C., & Rozin, P. (1994). Individual differences in sensitivity to disgust: A scale sampling seven domains of disgust elicitors. *Personality and Individual Differences, 16*, 701–713. https://doi.org/10.1016/0191-8869(94)90212-7

Hartmann, C., & Siegrist, M. (2018). Development and validation of the Food Disgust Scale. *Food Quality and Preference, 63*, 38–50. https://doi.org/10.1016/j.foodqual.2017.07.013

Heuvel, E. van den, Newbury, A., & Appleton, K.M. (2019). The psychology of nutrition with advancing age: Focus on food neophobia. *Nutrients, 11*(1). https://doi.org/10.3390/nu11010151

Hollar, D., Paxton-Aiken, A., & Fleming, P. (2013). Exploratory validation of the Fruit and Vegetable Neophobia Instrument among third- to fifth-grade students. *Appetite, 60*(1), 226–230. https://doi.org/10.1016/j.appet.2012.09.030

Hwang, H.C., & Matsumoto, D. (2016). Measuring emotions in the face. In H.L. Meiselman (Ed.), *Emotion measurement* (pp. 125–144). Elsevier. https://doi.org/10.1016/B978-0-08-100508-8.00006-0

Idowu-Adebayo, F., Fogliano, V., Oluwamukomi, M.O., Oladimeji, S., & Linnemann, A.R. (2021). Food neophobia among Nigerian consumers: A study on attitudes towards novel turmeric-fortified drinks. *Journal of the Science of Food and Agriculture, 101*(8), 3246–3256. https://doi.org/10.1002/jsfa.10954

Ihme, J.M., & Mitte, K. (2009). Measuring state disgust: Evaluation of a German state disgust scale. *European Journal of Psychological Assessment, 25*(3), 150–156. https://doi.org/10.1027/1015-5759.25.3.150

Inbar, Y., & Scott, S.E. (2018). People respond to GM food with disgust more than fear: Comment on Royzman, Cusimano and Leeman (2017). *Judgment and Decision Making, 13*(6), 636 –638.

Kleinknecht, R.A., Kleinknecht, E.E., & Thorndike, R.M. (1997). The role of disgust and fear in blood and injection-related fainting symptoms: A structural equation model. *Behaviour Research and Therapy, 35*(12), 1075–1087. https://doi.org/10.1016/S0005-7967(97)10010-9

Laureati, M., Bergamaschi, V., & Pagliarini, E. (2015). Assessing childhood food neophobia: Validation of a scale in Italian primary school children. *Food Quality and Preference, 40*, 8–15. https://doi.org/10.1016/j.foodqual.2014.08.003

Meiselman, H.L., King, S.C., & Gillette, M. (2010). The demographics of neophobia in a large commercial US sample. *Food Quality and Preference, 21*(7), 893–897. https://doi.org/10.1016/j.foodqual.2010.05.009

Nabi, R.L. (2002). The theoretical versus the lay meaning of disgust: Implications for emotion research. *Cognition & Emotion, 16*(5), 695–703. https://doi.org/10.1080/02699930143000437

Nezlek, J., Forestell, C., & Cypryańska, M. (2021). Approach and avoidance motivation and interest in new foods: Introducing a measure of the motivation to eat new foods. *Food Quality and Preference, 88*, 104111. https://doi.org/10.1016/j.foodqual.2020.104111

Ogarkova, A. (2016). Translatability of emotions. In H.L. Meiselman (Ed.), *Emotion measurement* (pp. 575–599). Elsevier. https://doi.org/10.1016/B978-0-08-100508-8.00023-0

Olatunji, B.O., Cisler, J.M., Deacon, B.J., Connolly, K., & Lohr, J.M. (2007). The Disgust Propensity and Sensitivity Scale-Revised: Psychometric properties and specificity in relation to anxiety disorder symptoms. *Journal of Anxiety Disorders, 21*, 918–930. https://doi.org/10.1016/j.janxdis.2006.12.005

Olatunji, B.O., Williams, N.L., Tolin, D.F., Abramowitz, J.S., Sawchuk, C.N., Lohr, J.M., & Elwood, L.S. (2007). The Disgust Scale: Item analysis, factor structure, and suggestions for refinement. *Psychological Assessment, 19*(3), 281–297. https://doi.org/10.1037/1040-3590.19.3.281

Overveld, M. van, Jong, P.J. de, Peters, M.L., Cavanagh, K., & Davey, G. (2006). Disgust propensity and disgust sensitivity: Separate constructs that are differentially related to specific fears. *Personality and Individual Differences, 41*(7), 1241–1252. https://doi.org/10.1016/j.paid.2006.04.021

Pliner, P., & Hobden, K. (1992). Development of a scale to measure the trait of food neophobia in humans. *Appetite, 19*(2), 105–120. https://doi.org/10.1016/0195-6663(92)90014-w

Predieri, S., Sinesio, F., Monteleone, E., Spinelli, S., Cianciabella, M., Daniele, G.M., Dinnella, C., Gasperi, F., Endrizzi, I., Torri, L., & Gallina Toschi, T. (2020). Gender, age, geographical area, food neophobia and their relationships with the adherence to the Mediterranean diet: New insights from a large population cross-sectional study. *Nutrients, 12*(6), 1778. https://doi.org/10.3390/nu12061778

Rabadán, A., & Bernabéu, R. (2021). A systematic review of studies using the Food Neophobia Scale: Conclusions from thirty years of studies. *Food Quality and Preference, 93*, 104241. https://doi.org/10.1016/j.foodqual.2021.104241

Ritchey, P.N., Frank, R.A., Hursti, U.-K., & Tuorila, H. (2003). Validation and cross-national comparison of the food neophobia scale (FNS) using confirmatory factor analysis. *Appetite, 40*(2), 163–173. https://doi.org/10.1016/s0195-6663(02)00134-4

Rottman, J. (2014). Evolution, development, and the emergence of disgust. *Evolutionary Psychology, 12*(2), 147470491401200209. https://doi.org/10.1177/147470491401200209

Royzman, E., Cusimano, C., & Leeman, R.F. (2017). What lies beneath? Fear vs. disgust as affective predictors of absolutist opposition to genetically modified food and other new technologies. *Judgment and Decision Making, 12*(5), 466–480.

Rozin, P., Haidt, J., McCauley, C., Dunlop, L., & Ashmore, M. (1999). Individual differences in disgust sensitivity: Comparisons and evaluations of paper-and-pencil versus behavioral measures. *Journal of Research in Personality, 33*(3), 330–351. https://doi.org/10.1006/jrpe.1999.2251

Santisi, G., Magnano, P., & Scuderi, V.E. (2021). Food neophobia and food disgust: The mediating role of perceived vulnerability to disease. *Behavioral Sciences, 11*(5), Article 65. https://doi.org/10.3390/bs11050065

Sherlock, J.M., Zietsch, B.P., Tybur, J.M., & Jern, P. (2016). The quantitative genetics of disgust sensitivity. *Emotion, 16*(1), 43–51. https://doi.org/10.1037/emo0000101

Siegrist, M., Hartmann, C., & Keller, C. (2013). Antecedents of food neophobia and its association with eating behavior and food choices. *Food Quality and Preference, 30*(2), 293–298. https://doi.org/10.1016/j.foodqual.2013.06.013

Stevenson, R.J., Oaten, M.J., Case, T.I., Repacholi, B.M., & Wagland, P. (2010). Children's response to adult disgust elicitors: Development and acquisition. *Developmental Psychology, 46*(1), 165–177. https://doi.org/10.1037/a0016692

Terrizzi, J.A., Shook, N.J., & McDaniel, M.A. (2013). The behavioral immune system and social conservatism: A meta-analysis. *Evolution and Human Behavior, 34*(2), 99–108. https://doi.org/10.1016/j.evolhumbehav.2012.10.003

Trijp, H.C.M. van, Steenkamp, J., & Benedict, E.M. (1992). Consumers' variety seeking tendency with respect to foods: Measurement and managerial implications. *European Review of Agricultural Economics, 19*(2), 181–195. https://doi.org/10.1093/erae/19.2.181

Tuorila, H., & Hartmann, C. (2020). Consumer responses to novel and unfamiliar foods. *Current Opinion in Food Science, 33*, 1–8. https://doi.org/10.1016/j.cofs.2019.09.004

Turnbull, J., Lea, D., Parkinson, D., Phillips, P., Francis, B., Webb, S., & Ashby, M. (2010). *Oxford advanced learner's dictionary. International Student's Edition*. Oxford University Press.

Tybur, J.M., Çınar, Ç., Karinen, A.K., & Perone, P. (2018). Why do people vary in disgust? *Philosophical Transactions of the Royal Society B Biological Sciences, 373*(1751), 20170204. https://doi.org/10.1098/rstb.2017.0204

Tybur, J.M., Lieberman, D., & Griskevicius, V. (2009). Microbes, mating, and morality: Individual differences in three functional domains of disgust. *Journal of Personality and Social Psychology, 97*(1), 103–122. https://doi.org/10.1037/a0015474

Verbeke, W. (2015). Profiling consumers who are ready to adopt insects as a meat substitute in a Western society. *Food Quality and Preference, 39*, 147–155. https://doi.org/10.1016/j.foodqual.2014.07.008

Wardle, J., Guthrie, C.A., Sanderson, S., & Rapoport, L. (2001). Development of the children's eating behaviour questionnaire. *Journal of Child Psychology and Psychiatry, 42*(7), 963–970. https://doi.org/10.1111/1469-7610.00792

Chapter 16

Assessment of Weight-Related Stigmatization

Megan Lindloff[1] and Angela Meadows[2]

[1] Department of Psychology, Western University, Ontario, Canada
[2] Department of Psychology, University of Essex, UK

Introduction

Anecdotal, observational, and empirical evidence has documented the frequency and severity of weight stigma encountered by higher-weight individuals, often driven by negative stereotypes that depict higher-weight people as lazy, ugly, stupid, or lacking self-discipline and self-control (Puhl & Heuer, 2009). Few areas are left untouched by weight stigma, as it occurs across many life domains, including relationships, work, school, healthcare, and the legal system (Meadows et al., 2020; Puhl & King, 2013). In addition to experiencing weight stigma (EWS) from others, some higher-weight individuals also devalue themselves because of their weight, a phenomenon termed internalized weight stigma (IWS; Durso & Latner, 2008). Both EWS and IWS have been linked to a host of detrimental psychological, physical, and behavioral consequences, including depression, anxiety, and suicidal ideation, increased physiological stress, disordered eating, reduced participation in physical activity, and healthcare avoidance (Meadows & Bombak, 2019; Mensinger et al., 2018; Pearl & Puhl, 2018; Wu & Berry, 2018).

There has been increased scholarship around weight stigma particularly in the past 15 years, as well as a proliferation of assessment tools. Though the research around weight stigma over the last decade and a half has raised awareness of the extent of the problem and the critical need to address it, weight stigma research suffers from the use of limited and inconsistent methods for assessing key constructs. In this chapter, we will provide an overview of existing measures of EWS and IWS, their limitations and suggestions for future research and clinical use.

Experienced Weight Stigma

There have been many scales developed for measuring EWS across a variety of samples and contexts. In this section, we will briefly summarize some of these measures, their psychometric properties, and their limitations, focusing on scales that have been more extensively tested, are used more widely, or offer a unique tool for measuring weight stigma in specific contexts.

Stigmatizing Situations Inventory

The most comprehensive of existing measures of EWS is the Stigmatizing Situations Inventory (SSI; Myers & Rosen, 1999), a 50-item questionnaire that measures lifetime stigmatization frequency. The 11 subscales assess weight stigma originating from a variety of sources (e.g., romantic partners, family members, children, doctors) and different situational contexts (e.g., employment, in public, physical barriers). An example item is, "Having strangers suggest diets to you." The scale was developed and tested in both a clinical sample and a higher-weight sample drawn from the fat acceptance movement, and demonstrated excellent internal reliability and good criterion validity.

There have been several adaptions of the SSI. A brief 10-item version (Vartanian, 2015) demonstrated similarly good criterion and convergent validity in several community samples of higher-weight adults (Vartanian, 2015). A 12-item version of the SSI was created for use in university student samples (Douglas et al., 2021). The Stigmatizing Situations Questionnaire-Extended was developed to measure EWS across the lifespan, adding 53 items relating to stigma during adolescence and 25 items for stigma during childhood, resulting in a 126-item measure (Annis et al., 2004). One issue with some of these measures is that higher-weight adults were not necessarily heavy as children, and items asking about their experiences in their youth may not be applicable.

Measures of Childhood Weight Stigma in Adult Samples

Some measures are intended specifically for adults to retroactively measure childhood experiences. The Weight-Related Abuse Questionnaire (Salwen & Hymowitz, 2015) is a 15-item measure that assesses both the frequency and emotional impact of weight-related verbal and physical abuse experienced before the age of 21 years. The 12-item Body Image Victimization Experiences Scale (Duarte & Pinto-Gouveia, 2016) assesses the frequency and impact of victimization pertaining to body image from peers and parents during childhood with eight items referring to weight or body shape. The Perception of Teasing Scale (POTS; Thompson et al., 1995) is a commonly used measure intended to assess the frequency and impact of weight-related teasing between the ages of 5 and 16 years. The POTS has since been adapted to measure teasing specifically from family members and from peers (Berg et al., 2002).

Measures for Children or Adolescents

While originally intended to retrospectively assess childhood experiences, POTS and its modifications are often used in samples of children and adolescents. Additionally, Najjar et al. (2018) developed a 42-item SSI-Adolescents, removing items specific to adults (e.g., "Losing your job because of your size") and altering wording of other items to be clearer for adolescents. Several measures have been developed specifically for use with children or adolescents. The 22-item Adolescent Weight-Based Victimization scale (Puhl et al., 2013) was used in adolescents aged 14–18 years and assesses verbal teasing, relational victimization, cyberbullying, and physical aggression. Puhl and Luedicke (2012) used similar items with additional subscales to assess sources and locations of the bullying, and how students responded. Shorter measures include a five-item scale assessing weight-related teasing and criticism from parents or siblings (Levine et al., 1994); a six-item measure of EWS during sports and physical activity (Faith et al., 2002); a four-item scale adapted from an adolescent racial discrimination scale (Golaszewski et al., 2018); and the five-item Peer Teasing Scale for use in younger children (Young-Hyman et al., 2003).

Cultural-Specific Measures

In contrast to the number of age-specific scales that have been developed, few culturally appropriate measures exist specific to non-White populations. One good example, however, is the 43-item Perceived Weight Stigmatization Scale, written in Urdu, which measures stigma experiences, perceptions of societal rejection, and the impact of weight-related stigma in Pakistani adults (Rafeh & Hanif, 2019). Development of this scale included focus groups with weight- and gender-diverse samples of Pakistani university students and a formal Delphi review to ensure both scientific and cultural validity.

Setting-Specific Measures

Other measures have been developed for use in specific settings, some expanding on items included in the SSI. For example, the 20-item Stigma Situations in Healthcare (Ferrante et al., 2016) includes items such as, "A doctor saying your weight is a health problem even when you are in good health"; the six-item Healthcare Weight-Related Stigma (Raves et al., 2016) asks about feeling stigmatized by various healthcare professionals (e.g., doctors, nurses, nutritionists); and the 10-item Healthcare Questionnaire (Wadden et al., 2000) assesses negative weight-related interactions with patients' physicians, (e.g., "Doctors have said critical or insulting things to me about my weight").

Beyond the healthcare setting, scales are available for weight-related teasing or criticism specifically from romantic partners (4 items; Befort et al., 2001); weight stigma in a school or work environment (5 items, Puhl et al., 2020); in the family, at work, and in public places (14 items; Rand & MacGregor, 1990); and in the military (26 items; Schvey et al., 2017).

Adaptation of Measures of Other Types of Stigma

Many studies have used measures adapted from scales for other types of discrimination. The nine-item Everyday Discrimination Scale (Williams et al., 1997), originally intended for racial discrimination, is commonly modified to assess weight stigma experiences. An example item is "You receive poorer service than other people at restaurants or stores." Additional measures of weight stigma have been adapted from other racial discrimination scales (Carr et al., 2007; Hatzenbuehler et al., 2009), gender discrimination scales (Farrow & Tarrant, 2009), and measures of stigma against those with chronic illness

(Truong et al., 2016) or Human Immunodeficiency Virus (Polk & Hullman, 2011). The Multidimensional Scale of Perceived Discrimination (Magallares et al., 2017) was created to assess discrimination against any stigmatized group, which then can be adapted for any target group.

Limitations of Existing Measures

Issues of Validity

While most authors report the internal reliability of their scales, the majority of measures of EWS are lacking further psychometric assessment. Additionally, many of the existing measures have been developed and tested in predominantly White and female samples, excluding the likely unique experiences of fat non-White and nonfemale-identifying people. Consequently, even when studies use these measures in more diverse samples, findings as to the extent and type of weight stigma experiences should not be considered uncritically.

Relatedly, several weight stigma measures have been adapted from measures of other forms of discrimination, such as racial or gender discrimination. However, because experiences of stigmatized groups are unique and rooted in a history of discrimination towards that group, these measures may not be fully capturing higher-weight people's experiences of weight discrimination. For example, qualitative studies have reported that one of the more commonly reported experiences of weight stigma is a lack of seating that fits (Hunt & Rhodes, 2018; Owen, 2012). This is a unique obstacle that higher-weight people face, and therefore would not be included in a measure that has been adapted from a scale for racial discrimination.

Stigma Awareness

Many higher-weight individuals may not recognize what experts would consider stigmatizing events as being a form of stigma because their high levels of IWS may normalize these occurrences. As such, items that phrase experiences in more general terms (e.g., "Have you experienced discrimination because of your weight?") rather than describing specific scenarios (e.g., "Being glared at or harassed by bus passengers for taking up 'too much' room") risk underestimating the frequency with which higher-weight people experience stigma. Studies using scenario-specific measures such as the SSI consistently report greater rates of experienced stigma (nearly 100 % of participants in community samples have experienced at least one type of stigma at least once in their life) than those using more generic questions, which tend to find only 30 %–50 % of individuals in community samples report having experienced weight stigma (Himmelstein et al., 2017; Puhl et al., 2018). Yet even SSI studies tend to produce a total frequency score equivalent to only "several times in their life." Further, the SSI is now over 20 years old, and may no longer reflect the current lived reality of many higher-weight people. For example, none of the items refer to any form of media, now a major source of stigmatizing messaging.

Recall Bias

All retrospective experience measures are likely to underestimate prevalence due to recall bias. This is likely to be especially true of stigma, where day-to-day microaggressions are much more common than major or overt forms of discrimination, but the latter are more likely to be remembered in the longer term (Swim et al., 2001). This problem will be further compounded in the case of low stigma awareness.

While most studies assess EWS through questionnaire measures, experience sampling techniques are becoming increasingly popular. For example, ecological momentary assessment (EMA) is a technique using mobile devices or other technological equipment to gather data in real time, reducing recall bias and increasing ecological validity (Potter et al., 2021; Smyth & Heron, 2014). Due to the everyday nature of weight stigma and fat microaggressions, EMA may be particularly useful to capture the full extent of these experiences. A small but growing number of studies have used EMA to assess everyday experiences of weight stigma (Carels et al., 2019; Potter et al., 2021; Vartanian et al., 2014, 2018) and have often found more frequent reports of daily stigmatizing experiences than studies using retrospective questionnaires. Lower-tech experience sampling techniques are also available. A study that used daily diary entries to capture the frequency of the 50 events included in the SSI experienced by 50 higher-weight women recruited from weight-related discussion boards and forums found that the women reported an average of 3.1 events per day over a 1-week period (Seacat et al., 2016).

Internalized Weight Stigma

Several measures have now been developed to assess IWS, all of which operationalize the construct slightly differently. A 2018 review of the health correlates of IWS identified 74 studies (Pearl & Puhl, 2018), of which over 70 % used the Weight Bias Internalization Scale (WBIS; Durso & Latner, 2008) or one of its modifications. A further 20 % used the Weight Self-Stigma Questionnaire (WSSQ; Lillis et al., 2010). Other less frequently used measures include the Weight- and Body-Related Shame and Guilt Scale (WEB-SG; Conradt et al., 2007), which assesses feelings of shame about one's size and guilt at failing to lose weight, and the Acceptance and Action Questionnaire-Weight (AAQW; Lillis & Hayes, 2008), a measure of experiential avoidance and psychological inflexibility around weight-related feelings and behaviors.

Weight Bias Internalization Scale

The Weight Bias Internalization Scale (WBIS; Durso & Latner, 2008) is an 11-item unidimensional measure with good internal reliability, convergent and predictive validity reported in multiple studies (Lacroix et al., 2017; Papadopoulos et al., 2021). The scale was originally developed using a higher-weight community sample but is now frequently used in both clinical and nonclinical samples. An example item is, "I don't feel that I deserve to have a really fulfilling social life, as long as I'm overweight." Item 1 on the scale, "As an overweight person, I feel that I am just as competent as anyone," is sometimes found to be unreliable (Durso et al., 2016; Lee & Dedrick, 2016), and many researchers use a 10-item version of the scale; some studies have also used further reduced scales.

Scores on the WBIS tend to be higher in clinical or treatment-seeking populations (Meadows, 2018), although no population norms or clinical cut-offs have been determined (Pearl & Puhl, 2018; for an exception, see Hilbert et al., 2014, who provided gender-specific population norms in a German population). The WBIS has been translated into German (Hilbert et al., 2014; which also led to development and validation of a German version for adolescents; Ciupitu-Plath et al., 2017), Spanish (Sarrías-Gómez & Baile, 2015; two-factor structure), Italian (Innamorati et al., 2017), Chinese (Wong et al., 2019), and Persian (Lin et al., 2020).

However, doubts have been raised about the operationalization of the WBIS and whether it does indeed assess weight-related self-devaluation (Meadows & Higgs, 2020a). Although IWS as measured by the WBIS did mediate the relationship between EWS and disordered eating behaviors in an international sample of higher-weight individuals, the majority of the variance was explained by general aspects of body image and global self-esteem, rather than weight-related self-worth specifically, challenging the construct validity of the scale (Meadows & Higgs, 2020a). A 13-item two-factor version of the scale (WBIS-2F; Meadows & Higgs, 2019) comprises a separate self-devaluation subscale and a weight-related distress subscale, and evidence from a large international study of self-classified higher-weight individuals suggests that distress may be a major component of individuals' scores on the WBIS, rather than self-devaluation per se (Meadows & Higgs, 2022).

A modified version of the WBIS (WBIS-M) replaces wording related to "overweight" to wording such as "because of my weight" (Pearl & Puhl, 2014) to facilitate use of the measure in a weight-diverse sample (i.e., not only those who are objectively or subjectively "overweight"). While the WBIS-M tends to perform well on standard psychometric tests (Lacroix et al., 2017; Papadopoulos et al., 2021), there is some evidence that the scale is not measurement-invariant across the weight spectrum (Meadows, 2018), indicating that weight category membership may introduce an element of measurement bias. It is possible that the WBIS-M is not measuring the same thing in higher-weight and normative-weight samples, and it may be unwise to treat it as such. In particular, IWS appears to be more focused on desire for weight change and low fat identity in normative-weight individuals, compared with a more even representation of items relating to reduced self-worth and fear of stigma in higher-weight individuals (Meadows, 2018). Thus, for slimmer individuals, high WBIS-M scores may be more indicative of body image distortion or eating disorder cognitions than of weight-related self-devaluation or even weight-related distress.

The WBIS-M has been translated into Turkish (Apay et al., 2017), Chinese (Pakpour et al., 2019), Spanish (Macho et al., 2021), and Greek (Argyrides et al., 2021), and a version for children (WBIS-C) was developed in German (Zuba & Warschburger, 2018). The WBIS-C was subsequently validated in a sample of Chinese children and adolescents (Chen & Ye, 2021). Aimé et al. (2020) tested measurement invariance of the WBIS-M across eight countries (Australia, Belgium, Canada, China, Italy, Japan, Spain, United States) and found only partial metric and scalar invariance, meaning that the comparability of findings cannot be assumed across countries, and differences should not be overinterpreted. Interestingly, a recent three-item German version of the WBIS-M (WBIS-3) demonstrated metric and scalar invariance across weight categories, suggesting that group mean scores can be meaningfully compared for "overweight" and "nonoverweight" individuals (Kliem et al., 2020). This improvement compared with the standard WBIS-M may be because the problematic items previously identified in the full scale were not included in the WBIS-3. However, all three included items capture aspects of weight-related distress rather than weight-related self-devaluation.

Weight Self-Stigma Questionnaire

The Weight Self-Stigma Questionnaire (WSSQ) is a 12-item measure comprising two subscales: Self-Devaluation and Fear of Enacted Stigma (Lillis et al., 2010). The Self-Devaluation subscale captures shame and guilt around body weight, but again, is not specifically about a weight-related devalued global self. Three of the 6 items do assess devaluation, but all three pertain to only one of the stereotypes associated with higher-weight individuals, namely lack of willpower (e.g., "I became overweight because I'm a weak person,") rather than a devalued social identity. The Fear of Enacted Stigma subscale primarily assesses beliefs about others' negative judgments. A sample item is, "Others will think I lack self-control because of my weight problems." As such, this subscale overlaps somewhat with the conceptualization of weight-related distress in the WBIS-2F. While the two subscales are generally strongly correlated and have similar predictive characteristics across many cognitive, affective, and behavioral outcomes, some studies have found differential associations for the subscales and some outcomes, including dietary restraint and eating and weight concerns (Almenara et al., 2017), weight loss during an online weight management intervention (Lillis et al., 2020), and worsening of addictive-like eating patterns over time (Meadows & Higgs, 2020b).

The WSSQ was originally developed and validated in two higher-weight community samples: one from the general population and one that recruited active dieters, and demonstrated good convergent and discriminant validity in both (Lillis et al., 2010). Participants from the dieting sample were randomized to either receive a 1-day mindfulness and acceptance-based workshop or to a control group, with the WSSQ being completed both at baseline and at 3-month follow-up. Significant differences between the two groups at follow-up indicated that the WSSQ is sensitive to change and may be used to evaluate treatment success. Based on follow-up data from the control group, test–retest reliability at 3 months was acceptable (Lillis et al., 2010). As with the WBIS, the scale is now routinely used in both clinical and nonclinical samples. The WSSQ has been translated into German (Hain et al., 2015), Portuguese (Palmeira et al., 2016), Chinese (Lin & Lee, 2017), Romanian (Puia et al., 2017), Turkish (Erdogan et al., 2018; Sevincer et al., 2017), French (Maïano et al., 2019), Arabic (BinDhim et al., 2020), and Persian (Lin et al., 2020).

Although the wording of the WSSQ tends to limit its use to higher-weight individuals, some studies have used the measure in weight-diverse samples (e.g., Meadows et al., 2017; Pakpour et al., 2019). In a Hong Kong study of children aged 8 to 12 years old, the Chinese version of the WSSQ was found to be measurement invariant across weight categories (Pakpour et al., 2019). To our knowledge, cross-country measurement invariance of the WSSQ has yet to be assessed.

Weight- and Body-Related Shame and Guilt Scale

The Weight- and Body-Related Shame and Guilt Scale (WEB-SG) assesses feelings of shame at one's size and guilt about not pursuing or achieving weight loss (Conradt et al., 2007). The scale was originally developed in a German community sample of "obese" participants, in which it showed good convergent and test-retest reliability at 6 months. Both the Shame and Guilt subscales explained additional variance in scores on body self-acceptance, depressive symptoms, and self-esteem, beyond that accounted for by shame and guilt related specifically to eating, although only the Guilt subscale explained additional variance in dietary restraint (Conradt et al., 2007). Other studies in nonclinical samples have linked both subscales in the expected directions with a range of eating behaviors, including emotional eating, binge eating, and intuitive eating (Craven & Fekete, 2019; Schulte, 2016). The Guilt subscale perhaps aligns most closely with measures of disordered eating cognitions, and will not be discussed further here.

Shame can be conceptualized as a trait-level perception of self-worth (i.e., being a bad person) whereas guilt captures state negative affect relating to specific non-normative behaviors (i.e., doing a bad thing; Lewis, 1971). Thus, the Shame subscale of the WEB-SG could be expected to capture weight-related self-devaluation aligning with the conceptualization of IWS. Indeed, the Shame, but not the Guilt, subscale mediated the negative relationships between objective weight status and global self-esteem (Pila et al., 2015) and perceived weight and engagement in physical activity (Lucibello et al., 2020) in a weight-diverse sample of Canadian young adults. Both weight-related shame and guilt tend to be higher in women than in men, and significantly increase across body mass index (BMI) categories (Pila et al., 2016). A trait version of the Shame subscale has been used in experimental studies, and was responsive to social-evaluative body-related threat (Cloudt et al., 2014).

However, more recent work on the operationalization of shame suggests that the construct comprises not only aspects of global self-devaluation, but also perceived judgment and devaluation by others (Gausel & Leach, 2011; Gausel et al., 2016), and it is this latter component that is assessed by 5 of the 6 items on the WEB-SG Shame subscale, for example, "When I am in a situation where others can see my body (e.g., pool, changing room), I feel ashamed." Thus, the Shame subscale of the WEB-SG appears to capture weight-related distress rather than weight-related self-devaluation.

Acceptance and Action Questionnaire – Weight

The AAQW is a 22-item measure assessing experiential avoidance and psychological inflexibility with respect to negative weight-related thoughts, feelings, and behaviors (Lillis & Hayes, 2008). Initial development and testing were carried out in a clinical population participating in a study of Acceptance and Commitment Therapy (ACT) for weight-maintenance (Lillis & Hayes, 2008). Within this population, several of the items could be considered to encapsulate weight-related self-devaluation, for example, "I should be ashamed of my body." Other items relate more to weight-related distress, such as, "I need to avoid social situations where people might judge me," or to weight-related eating behaviors, for example, "If I eat something bad, the whole day is a waste." The AAQW is moderately to strongly correlated in the expected directions with weight-related quality of life, psychological wellbeing, objective binge episodes, intuitive eating, and exercise engagement (Lillis & Hayes, 2008) and is responsive to ACT interventions in clinical populations (Levin et al., 2018; Lillis & Hayes, 2008; Weineland et al., 2013). The scale is also strongly correlated with both the Self-Devaluation and the Fear of Enacted Stigma subscales of the WSSQ (Lillis et al., 2010). The scale has been translated into Finnish (Sairanen et al., 2015), Portuguese (Palmeira et al., 2016), and Swedish (Weineland et al., 2013). A study in a Swedish bariatric surgery sample suggested a five-factor structure, including a three-item Body Acceptance factor and a five-item Self-Stigma factor (Weineland et al., 2013). However, the items in the Self-Stigma subscale comprise a mix of weight-related self-devaluation, weight-related distress, and disordered eating cognitions. Validation in a weight-diverse sample of Hispanic US college students suggested a six-item, single-factor solution that included items related to both weight-related self-devaluation and weight-related distress (AAQW-6; Flynn et al., 2019). The AAQW-6 was strongly negatively correlated with scores on the Eating Attitudes Test; however, surprisingly, there was a small to moderate positive correlation with BMI (Flynn et al., 2019), possibly due to cultural differences in this sample.

A revised version of the scale (AAQW-R) includes 10 items across three subscales – Food as Control, Weight as a Barrier to Living, and Weight Stigma – and was developed and validated in two samples of Portuguese women: a weight-diverse community sample and a higher-weight treatment-seeking sample (Palmeira et al., 2016). The latter two subscales comprise items relating predominantly, but not exclusively, to weight-related self-devaluation and weight-related distress, respectively, and align closely with the Body-Acceptance and Self-Stigma factors in the five-factor Swedish AAQW. Both correlate in the expected directions with eating pathology and subjective happiness, and scores on all three subscales are significantly higher in high- versus normative-BMI individuals (Palmeira et al., 2016). The three-factor structure was confirmed in a US sample of treatment-seeking higher-weight adults (Dochat et al., 2020). The AAQW-R is responsive to ACT interventions in clinical samples (Palmeira et al., 2016).

Limitations of Existing Measures

Operationalization of Internalized Weight Stigma

The major limitation of existing measures of IWS is the lack of consistency in operationalization of the construct. Weight stigma in general can be defined as being marked and devalued because of one's weight. As such, most researchers would agree that internalization of weight stigma should reflect accepting that mark and devaluing *oneself* because of one's weight. Yet many measures of IWS fail to clearly distinguish this construct from other, related, phenomena, in particular, conflation with body image, concern about others' perceptions, and general negative affect related to living in a fat body. Thus, great care must be taken in choice of measure used depending on the specific construct being targeted, and is not always self-evident from the name of the scale or subscale. Self-devaluation is best captured by the WBIS-2F Self-Devaluation subscale or the AAQW-R Weight as a Barrier to Living subscale. Weight-related distress may be best captured by the standard WBIS, the WSSQ-Fear of Enacted Stigma subscale, the WEB-SG Shame subscale, or the AAQW-R Weight Stigma subscale. Distress could further be broken down into concern about other-judgment (i.e., what people think about you), and fear of other-discrimination (i.e., how people will treat you). This latter could be classified as anticipation or expectation of stigma. While several of the scales above include items that assess this construct, none are ideally suited to measuring it exclusively. If anticipated stigma is the construct of interest, the Weight-Based Rejection Sensitivity scale (Brenchley & Quinn, 2016) would be the best choice.

Issues of Validity

Beyond the major concern about whether these scales are indeed measuring what they are supposed to, measures of IWS share some of the same issues as measures of EWS. Most scales have been developed and tested in predominantly White, predominantly female samples, by researchers working within a medicalized model of body weight. None have drawn on the lived experiences of higher-weight people, and in particular, higher-weight people not seeking to lose weight, in their development. As such, these measures should not be assumed to represent the lived experience of all, or even most, higher-weight individuals.

In addition, while most of these measures demonstrate excellent internal reliability, and good convergent and predictive validity in reported studies, further psychometric testing is often lacking. Only the WSSQ, AAQW-R (both 3 months) and the WEB-SG (6 months) have data confirming test-retest reliability. And there is little evidence of discriminant validity or of measurement invariance across populations in which many measures are routinely used. Perhaps the most serious of these omissions, given the widespread use of the WBIS-M, is the lack of evidence for measurement invariance across the weight spectrum.

Conclusions

There are a range of options available for measuring both EWS and IWS. In choosing an appropriate scale, researchers should take into consideration the specific aspect of stigma that they are interested in measuring, the sample of interest, as well as the limitations associated with each measure. Some of these limitations, such as lack of psychometric testing, are relatively easily remedied. However, other issues are more fundamental. Inconsistencies in operationalization (and terminology), development of measures without input from diverse populations with lived experience, or those outside treatment-seeking environments, limit the validity of most of the currently available measures. In addition, the widespread acceptability of weight stigma in society and high levels of IWS in higher-weight people compound the difficulties associated with measuring experiences of other forms of stigma.

Future measures of EWS should use situation-specific items that can prompt both awareness and recall, rather than generic questions about having "experienced discrimination" that will likely underestimate the extent of weight stigma experienced by many participants. Experience sampling techniques, which need not be high-tech, can also be used to address the issue of recall bias, although this may not be feasible for many studies.

Weight stigma intersects with various other axes of discrimination, including gender, race and ethnicity, and socioeconomic status, among others. New measures should be grounded in the lived experiences of higher-weight people, preferably capturing experiences from more diverse populations, including those with different gender and racial identities, and individuals who tend to be more stigma-aware, such as those in the fat acceptance community. It is only by doing so that measures will likely reflect the current lived experience of higher-weight people, rather than weight stigma as it is imagined by academics. In particular, many current measures focus on less common forms of weight stigma than on the everyday microaggressions that make up the totality of living in a fat body in our current cultural environment (Munro, 2017). While it is of course critical that overt weight discrimination in employment contexts, refusal of access to medical treatment, or physical attacks on higher-weight people are documented (and addressed by policymakers), it is the cumulative nature of more minor slights that have the larger impact on the health and wellbeing of stigmatized groups, as evidenced both in the wider stigma literature and in qualitative studies with higher-weight individuals. The Fat Microaggression Scale (Lindloff et al., 2023) and the Antifat Microaggression Experiences Questionnaire (J. Webb, personal communication, February 11, 2022) are two measures currently in development looking to include these more "everyday" experiences of weight stigma, or fat microaggressions.

Notwithstanding the limitations of our current measures of EWS and IWS, weight stigma is demonstrably associated with a wide range of negative outcomes. Despite the proliferation of measures in recent years, most do not address the problems inherent in existing measures, and better approaches are needed if the field is to produce robust research that can inform intervention and policy.

References

Aimé, A., Fuller-Tyskiewicz, M., Dion, J., Markey, C.H., Strodl, E., McCabe, M., Mellor, D., Gallegos, A.G., Pietrabissa, G., Alcaraz-Ibánez, M., Bégin, C., Blackburn, M.-E., Caltabiano, M., Castelnuovo, G., Gullo, S., Hayami-Chisuwa, N., He, Q., Lo Coco, G., Manzonie, G.M., ... & Maïano, C. (2020). Assessing positive body image, body satisfaction, weight bias, and appearance comparison in emerging adults: A cross-validation study across eight countries. *Body Image, 35*, 320–332. https://doi.org/10.1016/j.bodyim.2020.09.014

Almenara, C.A., Aimé, A., Maïano, C., Ejova, A., Guèvremont, G., Bournival, C., & Ricard, M.-M. (2017). Weight stigmatization and disordered eating in obese women: The mediating effects of self-esteem and fear of negative appearance evaluation. *European Review of Applied Psychology, 67*, 155–162. https://doi.org/10.1016/j.erap.2017.02.004

Annis, N.M., Cash, T.F., & Hrabosky, J.I. (2004). Body image and psychosocial differences among stable average weight, currently overweight, and formerly overweight women: The role of stigmatizing experiences. *Body Image, 1*(2), 155–167. https://doi.org/10.1016/j.bodyim.2003.12.001

Apay, S.E., Yilmaz, E., Aksoy, M., & Akalin, H. (2017). Validity and reliability study of Modified Weight Bias Internalization Scale in Turkish. *International Journal of Caring Sciences, 10*(3), 1341–1347.

Argyrides, M., Charalambous, Z., Anastasiades, E., & Michael, K. (2021). Translation and validation of the Greek version of the Modified Weight Bias Internalization Scale in an adult population. *Clinical Obesity*, e12503. https://doi.org/10.1111/cob.12503

Befort, C., Nicpon, M.F., Robinson Kurpius, S.E., Huser, L., Hull-Blanks, E., & Sollenberger, S. (2001). Body image, self-esteem, and weight-related criticism from romantic partners. *Journal of College Student Development, 42*(5), 407–419.

Berg, P. van den, Thompson, J.K., Obremski-Brandon, K., & Coovert, M. (2002). The Tripartite Influence model of body image and eating disturbance: A covariance structure modeling investigation testing the mediational role of appearance comparison. *Journal of Psychosomatic Research, 53*(5), 1007–1020. https://doi.org/10.1016/s0022-3999(02)00499-3

BinDhim, N.F., Althumiri, N.A., Basyouni, M.H., Sims, O.T., Alhusseini, N., & Alqahtani, S.A. (2020). Arabic translation of the Weight Self-Stigma Questionnaire: Instrument validation study of factor structure and reliability. *JMIR Formative Research, 4*(11), e24169. https://doi.org/10.2196/24169

Brenchley, K.J.M., & Quinn, D.M. (2016). Weight-based rejection sensitivity: Scale development and implications for well-being. *Body Image, 16*, 79–92. https://doi.org/10.1016/j.bodyim.2015.11.005

Carels, R.A., Rossi, J., Solar, C., & Selensky, J.C. (2019). An ecological momentary assessment of weight stigma among weight loss participants. *Journal of Health Psychology, 24*(9), 1155–1166. https://doi.org/10.1177/1359105317692855

Carr, D., Friedman, M.A., & Jaffe, K. (2007). Understanding the relationship between obesity and positive and negative affect: the role of psychosocial mechanisms. *Body Image, 4*(2), 165–177. https://doi.org/10.1016/j.bodyim.2007.02.004

Chen, H., & Ye, Y.D. (2021). Validation of the Weight Bias Internalization Scale for mainland Chinese children and adolescents. *Frontiers in Psychology, 11*, Article 594949. https://doi.org/10.3389/fpsyg.2020.594949

Ciupitu-Plath, C., Wiegand, S., & Babitsch, B. (2017). The Weight Bias Internalization Scale for youth: Validation of a specific tool for assessing internalized weight bias among treatment-seeking German adolescents with overweight. *Journal of Pediatric Psychology, 43*(1), 40–51. https://doi.org/10.1093/jpepsy/jsx079

Cloudt, M.C., Lamarche, L., & Gammage, K.L. (2014). The impact of the amount of social evaluation on psychobiological responses to a body image threat. *Body Image, 11*(4), 350–356. https://doi.org/10.1016/j.bodyim.2014.06.003

Conradt, M., Dierk, J.M., Schlumberger, P., Rauh, E., Hebebrand, J., & Rief, W. (2007). Development of the Weight- and Body-Related Shame and Guilt scale (WEB-SG) in a nonclinical sample of obese individuals. *Journal of Personality Assessment, 88*(3), 317–327. https://doi.org/10.1080/00223890701331856

Craven, M.P., & Fekete, E.M. (2019). Weight-related shame and guilt, intuitive eating, and binge eating in female college students. *Eating Behaviors, 33*, 44–48. https://doi.org/10.1016/j.eatbeh.2019.03.002

Dochat, C., Afari, N., Wooldridge, J.S., Herbert, M.S., Gasperi, M., & Lillis, J. (2020). Confirmatory factor analysis of the Acceptance and Action Questionnaire for Weight-Related Difficulties-Revised (AAQW-R) in a United States sample of adults with overweight and obesity. *Journal of Contextual Behavioral Science, 15*, 189–196. https://doi.org/10.1016/j.jcbs.2020.01.006

Douglas, V.J., Kwan, M.Y., & Gordon, K. (2021). The roles of weight stigma, emotion dysregulation, and eating pathology in suicide risk. *Body Image, 38*, 162–170. https://doi.org/10.1016/j.bodyim.2021.04.005

Duarte, C., & Pinto-Gouveia, J. (2016). Body image as a target of victimization by peers/parents: Development and validation of the Body Image Victimization Experiences Scale. *Women & Health, 57*(9), 1061–1079. https://doi.org/10.1080/03630242.2016.1243603

Durso, L.E., & Latner, J.D. (2008). Understanding self-directed stigma: Development of the Weight Bias Internalization Scale. *Obesity, 16*, S80–S86. https://doi.org10.1038/oby.2008.448 https://doi.org/10.1038/oby.2008.448

Durso, L.E., Latner, J.D., & Ciao, A.C. (2016). Weight bias internalization in treatment-seeking overweight adults: Psychometric validation and associations with self-esteem, body image, and mood symptoms. *Eating Behavior, 21*, 104–108. https://doi.org/10.1016/j.eatbeh.2016.01.011

Erdogan, Z., Kurcer, M.A., Kurtuncu, M., & Catalcam, S. (2018). Validity and reliability of the Turkish version of the weight self-stigma questionnaire. *Journal of Pakistan Medical Association, 68*(12), 1798–1803.

Faith, M.S., Leone, M.A., Ayers, T.S., Heo, M., & Pietrobelli, A. (2002). Weight criticism during physical activity, coping skills, and reported physical activity in children. *Pediatrics, 110*(2), e23. https://doi.org/10.1542/peds.110.2.e23

Farrow, C.V., & Tarrant, M. (2009). Weight-based discrimination, body dissatisfaction and emotional eating: The role of perceived social consensus. *Psychology & Health, 24*(9), 1021–1034. https://doi.org/10.1080/08870440802311348

Ferrante, J.M., Seaman, K., Bator, A., Ohman-Strickland, P., Gundersen, D., Clemow, L., & Puhl, R. (2016). Impact of perceived weight stigma among underserved women on doctor-patient relationships. *Obesity Science & Practice, 2*(2), 128–135. https://doi.org/10.1002/osp4.40

Flynn, M.K., Kurz, A.S., & Berkout, O.V. (2019). Psychological inflexibility among Hispanic college students: Introducing the 6-item Acceptance and Action Questionnaire for weight-related difficulties. *Journal of Latinx Psychology, 7*(2), 123–136. https://doi.org/10.1037/lat0000110

Gausel, N., & Leach, C.W. (2011). Concern for self-image and social image in the management of moral failure: Rethinking shame. *European Journal of Social Psychology, 41*(4), 468–478. https://doi.org/10.1002/ejsp.803

Gausel, N., Vignoles, V.L., & Leach, C.W. (2016). Resolving the paradox of shame: Differentiating among specific appraisal-feeling combinations explains pro-social and self-defensive motivation. *Motivation and Emotion, 40*, 118–139. https://doi.org/10.1007/s11031-015-9513-y

Golaszewski, N.M., Pasch, K.E., Fernandez, A., Poulos, N.S., Batanova, M., & Loukas, A. (2018). Perceived weight discrimination and school connectedness among youth: Does teacher support play a protective role? *Journal of School Health, 88*(10), 754–761. https://doi.org/10.1111/josh.12682

Hain, B., Langer, L., Hünnemeyer, K., Rudofsky, G., Zech, U., & Wild, B. (2015). Translation and validation of the German version of the Weight Self-Stigma Questionnaire (WSSQ). *Obesity Surgery, 25*(4), 750–753. https://doi.org/10.1007/s11695-015-1598-6

Hatzenbuehler, M.L., Keyes, K.M., & Hasin, D.S. (2009). Associations between perceived weight discrimination and the prevalence of psychiatric disorders in the general population. *Obesity, 17*(11), 2033–2039. https://doi.org/10.1038/oby.2009.131

Hilbert, A., Baldofski, S., Zenger, M., Löwe, B., Kersting, A., & Braehler, E. (2014). Weight Bias Internalization Scale: Psychometric properties and population norms. *PLoS One, 9*(1), e86303. https://doi.org/10.1371/journal.pone.0086303

Himmelstein, M.S., Puhl, R.M., & Quinn, D.M. (2017). Intersectionality: An understudied framework for addressing weight stigma. *American Journal of Preventive Medicine, 53*(4), 421–431. https://doi.org/10.1016/j.amepre.2017.04.003

Hunt, A.N., & Rhodes, T. (2018). Fat pedagogy and microaggressions: Experiences of professionals working in higher education settings. *Fat Studies, 7*(2), 21–32. https://doi.org/10.1080/21604851.2017.1360671

Innamorati, M., Imperatori, C., Lamis, D.A., Contardi, A., Castelnuovo, G., Tamburello, S., Manzoni, G.M., & Fabbricatore, M. (2017). Weight Bias Internalization Scale discriminates obese and overweight patients with different severity levels of depression: The Italian version of the WBIS. *Current Psychology, 36*(2), 242–251. https://doi.org/10.1007/s12144-016-9406-6

Kliem, S., Puls, H.-C., Hinz, A., Kersting, A., Brähler, E., & Hilbert, A. (2020). Validation of a three-item short form of the Modified Weight Bias Internalization Scale (WBIS-3) in the German population. *Obesity Facts, 13*, 560–571. https://doi.org/10.1159/000510923

Lacroix, E., Alberga, A., Russell-Mathew, S., McLaren, L., & von Ranson, K. (2017). Weight bias: A systematic review of characteristics and psychometric properties of self-report questionnaires. *Obesity Facts, 10*(3), 223–237. https://doi.org/10.1159/000475716

Lee, M.S., & Dedrick, R.F. (2016). Weight Bias Internalization Scale: Psychometric properties using alternative weight status classification approaches. *Body Image, 17*, 25–29. https://doi.org/10.1016/j.bodyim.2016.01.008

Levin, M.E., Potts, S., Haeger, J., & Lillis, J. (2018). Delivering acceptance and commitment therapy for weight self-stigma through guided self-help: Results from an open pilot trial. *Cognitive and Behavioral Practice, 25*(1), 87–104. https://doi.org/10.1016/j.cbpra.2017.02.00

Levine, M.P., Smolak, L., & Hayden, H. (1994). The relation of sociocultural factors to eating attitudes and behaviors among middle school girls. *The Journal of Early Adolescence, 14*(4), 471–490. https://doi.org/10.1177/0272431694014004004

Lewis, H.B. (1971). Shame and guilt in neurosis. *Psychoanalytic Review, 58*(3), 419–438.

Lillis, J., & Hayes, S.C. (2008). Measuring avoidance and inflexibility in weight related problems. *International Journal of Behavioral Consultation and Therapy, 4*(4), 348–354. https://doi.org/10.1037/h0100865

Lillis, J., Luoma, J.B., Levin, M.E., & Hayes, S.C. (2010). Measuring weight self-stigma: The Weight Self-Stigma Questionnaire. *Obesity, 18*(5), 971–976. https://doi.org/10.1038/oby.2009.353

Lillis, J., Thomas, J.G., Levin, M.E., & Wing, R.R. (2020). Self-stigma and weight loss: The impact of fear of being stigmatized. *Journal of Health Psychology, 25*(7), 922–930. https://doi.org//10.1177/1359105317739101

Lin, C.-Y., Imani, V., Cheung, P., & Pakpour, A.H. (2020). Psychometric testing on two weight stigma instruments in Iran: Weight Self-Stigma Questionnaire and Weight Bias Internalized Scale. *Eating and Weight Disorders, 25*, 889–901. https://doi.org/10.1007/s40519-019-00699-4

Lin, K.P., & Lee, M.L. (2017). Validating a Chinese version of the Weight Self-stigma Questionnaire for use with obese adults. *International Journal of Nursing Practice, 23*(4), e12537. https://doi.org/10.1111/ijn.12537

Lindloff, M.R., Meadows, A.M., & Calogero, R.M. (2023). *Development and validation of the Fat Microaggressions Scale* [Manuscript in preparation]. Department of Psychology, Western University. Manuscript submitted for publication.

Lucibello, K.M., Sabiston, C.M., O'Loughlin, E.K., & O'Loughlin, J.L. (2020). Mediating role of body-related shame and guilt in the relationship between weight perceptions and lifestyle behaviours. *Obesity Science & Practice, 6*(4), 365–372. https://doi.org/10.1002/osp4.415

Macho, S., Andrés, A., & Saldaña, C. (2021). Validation of the modified weight bias internalization scale in a Spanish adult population. *Clinical Obesity, 11*(4), e12454. https://doi.org/10.1111/cob.12454

Magallares, A., Bolaños-Rios, P., Ruiz-Prieto, I., Benito de Valle, P., Irles, J.A., & Jáuregui-Lobrera, I. (2017). The mediational effect of weight self-stigma in the relationship between blatant and subtle discrimination and depression and anxiety. *The Spanish Journal of Psychology, 20*(e4), 1–7. https://doi.org/10.1017/sjp.2017.1

Maïano, C., Aimé, A., Lepage, G., & Morin, A.J.S. (2019). Psychometric properties of the Weight Self-Stigma Questionnaire (WSSQ) among a sample of overweight/obese French-speaking adolescents. *Eating and Weight Disorders, 4*(3), 575–583. https://doi.org/10.1007/s40519-017-0382-0

Meadows, A. (2018). *Fear and self-loathing: Internalised weight stigma and maladaptive coping in higher-weight individuals* [Doctoral dissertation]. University of Birmingham. https://etheses.bham.ac.uk//id/eprint/8465/

Meadows, A., & Bombak, A.E. (2019). Yes, we can (no, you can't): Weight stigma, exercise self-efficacy, and active fat identity development. *Fat Studies, 8*(2), 135–153. https://doi.org/10.1080/21604851.2019.1550303

Meadows, A., Daníelsdóttir, S., Goldberg, D., & Mercedes, M. (2020). Fighting for a (wide enough) seat at the table: Weight stigma in law and policy. *Fat Studies, 10*(2), 101–124. https://doi.org/10.1080/21604851.2020.1835295

Meadows, A., & Higgs, S. (2019). The multifaceted nature of weight-related self-stigma: Validation of the Two-Factor Weight Bias Internalization Scale (WBIS-2F). *Frontiers in Psychology, 10*, Article 808. https://doi.org/10.3389/fpsyg.2019.00808

Meadows, A., & Higgs, S. (2020a). A bifactor analysis of the Weight Bias Internalization Scale: What are we really measuring? *Body Image, 33*, 137–151. https://doi.org/10.1016/j.bodyim.2020.02.013

Meadows, A., & Higgs, S. (2020b). Internalized weight stigma and the progression of food addiction over time. *Body Image, 34*, 67–71. https://doi.org/10.1016/j.bodyim.2020.05.002

Meadows, A., & Higgs, S. (2022). *Challenging oppression: A social identity model of stigma resistance in high-weight individuals* [Manuscript submitted for publication]. School of Psychology, University of Birmingham.

Meadows, A., Nolan, L.J., & Higgs, S. (2017). Self-perceived food addiction: Prevalence, predictors, and prognosis. *Appetite, 114*, 282–298. https://doi.org/10.1016/j.appet.2017.03.051

Mensinger, J.L., Tylka, T.L., & Calamari, M.E. (2018). Mechanisms underlying weight status and health-care avoidance in women: A study of weight stigma, body-related shame and guilt, and healthcare stress. *Body Image, 25*, 139–147. https://doi.org/10.1016/j.bodyim.2018.03.001

Munro, L. (2017). Everyday indignities: Using the microaggressions framework to understand weight stigma. *The Journal of Law, Medicine & Ethics, 45*(4), 502–509. https://doi.org/10.1177/1073110517750584

Myers, A., & Rosen, J.C. (1999). Obesity stigmatization and coping: Relation to mental health symptoms, body image, and self-esteem. *International Journal of Obesity, 23*, 221–230. https://doi.org/10.1038/sj.ijo.0800765

Najjar, R.H., Jacob, E., & Evangelista, L. (2018). Eating behaviors, weight bias, and psychological functioning in multi-ethnic low-income adolescents. *Journal of Pediatric Nursing, 38*, 81–87. https://doi.org/10.1016/j.pedn.2017.11.008

Owen, L. (2012). Living fat in a thin-centric world: Effects of spatial discrimination on fat bodies and selves. *Feminism & Psychology, 22*(3), 290–306. https://doi.org/10.1177/0959353512445360

Pakpour, A.H., Tsai, M.-C., Lin, Y.-C., Strong, C., Latner, J.D., Fung, X.C.C., Lin, C.-Y., & Tsang, H.W.H. (2019). Psychometric properties and measurement invariance of the Weight Self-Stigma Questionnaire and Weight Bias Internalization Scale in children and adolescents. *International Journal of Clinical and Health Psychology, 19*(2), 150–159. https://doi.org/10.1016/j.ijchp.2019.03.001

Palmeira, L., Cunha, M., Pinto-Gouveia, J., Carvalho, S., & Lillis, J. (2016). New developments in the assessment of weight-related experiential avoidance (AAQW-Revised). *Journal of Contextual Behavioral Science, 5*(3), 193–200. https://doi.org/10.1016/j.jcbs.2016.06.001

Papadopoulos, S., Piedad Garcia, X. de la, & Brennan, L. (2021). Evaluation of the psychometric properties of self-reported weight stigma measures: A systematic literature review. *Obesity Reviews, 22*(8), e13267. https://doi.org/10.1111/obr.13267.

Pearl, R.L., & Puhl, R.M. (2014). Measuring internalized weight attitudes across body weight categories: Validation of the Modified Weight Bias Internalization Scale. *Body Image, 11*(1), 89–92. https://doi.org/10.1016/j.bodyim.2013.09.005

Pearl, R.L., & Puhl, R.M. (2018). Weight bias internalization and health: A systematic review. *Obesity Reviews, 19*(8), 1141–1163. https://doi.org/10.1111/obr.12701

Pila, E., Brunet, J., Crocker, P.R.E., Kowalski, K.C., & Sabiston, C.M. (2016). Intrapersonal characteristics of body-related guilt, shame, pride, and envy in Canadian adults. *Body Image, 16*, 100–106. https://doi.org/10.1016/j.bodyim.2016.01.001

Pila, E., Sabiston, C.M., Brunet, J., Castonguay, A.L., & O'Loughlin, J. (2015). Do body-related shame and guilt mediate the association between weight status and self-esteem? *Journal of Health Psychology, 20*(5), 659–669. https//doi.org/10.1177/1359105315573449

Polk, D.M., & Hullman, G.A. (2011). Weight-related stigma as a predictor of self-disclosure patterns in women. *The Open Communications Journal, 5*, 1–10. https://doi.org/10.2174/1874916X01105010001

Potter, L., Meadows, A., & Smyth, J. (2021). Experiences of weight stigma in everyday life: An ecological momentary assessment study. *Journal of Health Psychology, 26*(14), 2781–2793. https://doi.org/10.1177/1359105320934179

Puhl, R.M., & Heuer, C.A. (2009). The stigma of obesity: A review and update. *Obesity, 17*(5), 941–964. https://doi.org/10.1038/oby.2008.636

Puhl, R.M., Himmelstein, M.S., & Quinn, D.M. (2018). Internalizing weight stigma: Prevalence and sociodemographic considerations in US adults. *Obesity, 26*(1), 167–175. https://doi.org/10.1002/oby.22029

Puhl, R.M., & King, K.M. (2013). Weight discrimination and bullying. *Best Practice & Research Clinical Endocrinology & Metabolism, 27*(2), 117–127. https://doi.org/10.1016/j.beem.2012.12.002

Puhl, R.M., & Luedicke, J. (2012). Weight-based victimization among adolescents in the school setting: Emotional reactions and coping behaviors. *Journal of Youth and Adolescence, 41*(1), 27–40. https://doi.org/10.1007/s10964-011-9713-z

Puhl, R.M., Peterson, J.L., & Luedicke, J. (2013). Weight-based victimization: Bullying experiences of weight loss treatment-seeking youth. *Pediatrics, 131*(1), e1–9. https://doi.org/10.1542/peds.2012-1106

Puhl, R.M., Telke, S., Larson, N., Eisenberg, M.E., & Neumark-Stzainer, D. (2020). Experiences of weight stigma and links with self-compassion among a population-based sample of young adults from diverse ethnic/racial and socio-economic backgrounds. *Journal of Psychosomatic Research, 134*, 1–8. https://doi.org/10.1016/j.jpsychores.2020.110134

Puia, I.C., Stanculete, M.F., Hopulele-Petri, A., Muresan, D., & Puia, A. (2017). Patients' perception of weight-related stigma in a Romanian sample. *Journal of Evidence-Based Psychotherapies, 17*(2), 147–157. https://doi.org/10.24193/jebp.2017.2.9

Rafeh, A., & Hanif, R. (2019). Understanding perception of weight stigma: Development and validation of Perceived Weight Stigmatization Scale. *Pakistan Journal of Psychological Research, 34*(4), 869–897. https://doi.org/10.33824/PJPR.2019.34.4.47

Rand, C.S., & MacGregor, A.M. (1990). Morbidly obese patients' perceptions of social discrimination before and after surgery for obesity. *Southern Medical Journal, 83*(12), 1390–1395. https://doi.org/10.1097/00007611-199012000-00006

Raves, D.M., Brewis, A., Trainer, S., Han, S.-Y., & Wutich, A. (2016). Bariatric surgery patients' perceptions of weight-related stigma in healthcare settings impair post-surgery dietary adherence. *Frontiers in Psychology, 7*, 1–13. https://doi.org/10.3389/fpsyg.2016.01497

Sairanen, E., Tolvanen, A., Karhunen, L., Kolehmainen, M., Järvelä, E., Rantala, S., Peuhkuri, K., Korpela, R., & Lappalainen, R. (2015). Psychological flexibility and mindfulness explain intuitive eating in overweight adults. *Behavior Modification, 39*(4), 557–579. https://doi.org/10.1177/0145445515576402

Salwen, J.K., & Hymowitz, G.F. (2015). The Weight-Related Abuse Questionnaire (WRAQ): Reliability, validity, and clinical utility. *Eating Behaviors, 19*, 150–154. https://doi.org/10.1016/j.eatbeh.2015.09.001

Sarrías-Gómez, S., & Baile, J.I. (2015). Psychometric properties of a Spanish adaptation of the Weight bias Internalization Scale (WBIS). *Nutrición Hospitalaria, 32*(4), 1510–1515. https://doi.org/10.3305/nh.2015.32.4.9343

Schulte, S.J. (2016). Predictors of binge eating in male and female youths in the United Arab Emirates. *Appetite, 105*, 312–319. https://doi.org/10.1016/j.appet.2016.06.00

Schvey, N.A., Barmine, M., Bates, D., Oldham, K., Bakalar, J.L., Spieker, E., Maurer, D., Stice, E., Stephens, M., Tanofsky-Kraff, M., & Sbrocco, T. (2017). Weight stigma among active duty U.S. military personnel with overweight and obesity. *Stigma and Health, 2*(4), 281–291. https://doi.org/10.1037/sah0000057

Seacat, J.D., Dougal, S.C., & Roy, D. (2016). A daily diary assessment of female weight stigmatization. *Journal of Health Psychology, 21*(2), 228–240. https://doi.org/10.1177/1359105314525067

Sevincer, G.M., Kaya, A., Bozkurt, S., Akin, E., & Kose, S. (2017). Reliability, validity, and factorial structure of the Turkish version of the Weight Self-Stigma Questionnaire (Turkish WSSQ). *Psychiatry and Clinical Psychopharmacology, 27*(4), 386–392. https://doi.org/10.1080/24750573.2017.1379717

Smyth, J.M., & Heron, K.E. (2014). Ecological momentary assessment (EMA) in family research. In S.M. McHale, P. Amato, & A. Booth (Eds.), *Emerging methods in family research* (pp. 145–161). Springer International Publishing. https://doi.org/10.1007/978-3-319-01562-0_9

Swim, J.K., Hyers, L.L., Cohen, L.L., & Ferguson, M.J. (2001). Everyday sexism: Evidence for its incidence, nature, and psychological impact from three daily diary studies. *Journal of Social Issues, 57*, 31–53. https://doi.org/10.1111/0022-4537.00200

Thompson, J.K., Cattarin, J., Fowler, B., & Fisher, E. (1995). The Perception of Teasing Scale (POTS): A revision and extension of the Physical Appearance Related Teasing Scale (PARTS). *Journal of Personality Assessment, 65*(1), 146–157. https://doi.org/10.1207/s15327752jpa6501_11

Truong, E.A.K., Olson, K.L., & Emery, C.F. (2016). Repressive coping, stigmatization, psychological distress, and quality of life among behavioral weight management participants. *Eating Behaviors, 22*, 206–210. https://doi.org/10.1016/j.eatbeh.2016.06.007

Vartanian, L.R. (2015). Development and validation of a brief version of the Stigmatizing Situations Inventory. *Obesity Science & Practice, 1*(2), 119–125. https://doi.org/10.1002/osp4.11

Vartanian, L.R., Pinkus, R.T., & Smyth, J.M. (2014). The phenomenology of weight stigma in everyday life. *Journal of Contextual Behavioral Science, 3*(3), 196–202. https://doi.org/10.1016/j.jcbs.2014.01.003

Vartanian, L.R., Pinkus, R.T., & Smyth, J.M. (2018). Experiences of weight stigma in everyday life: Implications for health motivation. *Stigma and Health, 3*(2), 85–92. https://doi.org/10.1037/sah0000077

Wadden, T.A., Anderson, D.A., Foster, G.D., Bennett, A., Steinberg, C., & Sarwer, D.B. (2000). Obese women's perceptions of their physicians' weight management attitudes and practices. *Archives of Family Medicine, 9*(9), 854–860. https://doi.org/10.1001/archfami.9.9.854

Weineland, S., Lillis, J., & Dahl, J. (2013). Measuring experiential avoidance in a bariatric surgery population – psychometric properties of AAQ-W. *Obesity Research & Clinical Practice, 7*(6), e464–e475. https://doi.org/10.1016/j.orcp.2012.06.002

Williams, D. R., Yu, Y., Jackson, J. S., & Anderson, N. B. (1997). Racial differences in physical and mental health: Socio-economic status, stress and discrimination. *Journal of Health Psychology, 2*(3), 335–351. https://doi.org/10.1177/135910539700200305

Wong, P. C., Hsieh, Y.-P., Ng, H. H., Kong, S. F., Chan, K. L., Au, T. Y. A., Lin, C.-Y., & Fung, X. C. C. (2019). Investigating the self-stigma and quality of life for overweight/obese children in Hong Kong: A preliminary study. *Child Indicators Research, 12*, 1065–1082. https://doi.org/10.1007/s12187-018-9573-0

Wu, Y., & Berry, D. C. (2018). Impact of weight stigma on physiological and psychological health outcomes for overweight and obese adults: A systematic review. *Journal of Advanced Nursing, 74*(5), 1030–1042. https://doi.org/10.1111/jan.13511

Young-Hyman, D., Schlundt, D. G., Herman-Wenderoth, L., & Bozylinski, K. (2003). Obesity, appearance, and psychosocial adaptation in young African American children. *Journal of Pediatric Psychology, 28*(7), 463–472.https://doi.org/10.1093/jpepsy/jsg037

Zuba, A., & Warschburger, P. (2018). Weight bias internalization across weight categories among school-aged children: Validation of the Weight Bias Internalization Scale for children. *Body Image, 25*, 56–65. https://doi.org/10.1016/j.bodyim.2018.02.008

Part IV

Assessment Methods and Issues

Chapter 17

Measuring Food Intake in the Laboratory

Suzanne Higgs

School of Psychology, University of Birmingham, UK

Introduction

Laboratory-based measures of food intake have been used extensively by researchers to gain insight into the factors that influence human eating. A commonly used approach is to examine the effect of an experimental manipulation on consumption. For example, it has been found that people eat more when they eat in the laboratory with a friend compared with when they eat alone (social context manipulation; for review Ruddock et al., 2019), and so it has been concluded that one factor that promotes intake is the presence of a familiar dining companion. Laboratory studies are suited to identifying factors that cause people to increase or decrease their food intake and may also provide insight into the underlying mechanisms because the causal and mediating variables can be manipulated and/or measured while controlling for other factors that affect intake. However, controlled laboratory studies do not tell us about the importance of any identified influences on intake in real life eating situations. For this, naturalistic studies are required to assess the relative impact of a specific factor, for example eating with others, on intake under free living conditions (Meiselman, 1992; De Castro, 1991).

At face value, the assessment of food intake in the laboratory appears straightforward: Volunteers are invited to consume foods in a controlled environment and if the amount of food is weighed beforehand, it is possible to determine accurately how much has been consumed by weighing any leftovers and calculating the difference between the two measures. Despite this apparent simplicity, there are many issues that need to be considered in the design and conduct of laboratory-based studies of food intake if meaningful insight is to be gained into the mechanisms underlying the control of eating. This is because there are many factors relating to the way in which the study is set up and conducted that will have a powerful influence on how much is consumed by participants. These influences may override any effects of an experimental manipulation or act as confounding variables, making interpretation of the results difficult. How a study is carried out will also affect the reproducibility of the findings. If the many factors that affect intake are not well controlled using rigorous standardized procedures, the results may vary widely across studies.

The aim of this chapter is to describe standard procedures that are used to measure food intake in the laboratory and to highlight key issues that should be addressed during the design of studies that involve intake measures, so that methodological rigor and reproducibility can be maximized, and interpretation of the results made more straightforward. Other methodological practices related to assessment of appetite sensations and hedonic evaluation of foods are out of scope for this chapter but have been reviewed elsewhere (Blundell et al., 2010; Gibbons et al., 2014). There are additional issues that relate to the reporting of laboratory studies of human eating behavior that have also been covered in detail elsewhere (Hetherington & Rolls, 2018; Robinson et al., 2018) and are not considered here.

Where to Measure and What to Measure

An eating behavior laboratory usually consists of a kitchen area in which food can be prepared/weighed and an associated set of furnished test rooms in which participants consume the food. Responses to food are influenced by context in which the food is presented (Best et al., 2018) and so providing contextual cues that are found in typical consumption situations, such as tableware, wall décor, and ambient lighting may promote more naturalistic behavior in the testing environment. However, the testing environment should be consistent across participants and test days and participants should not access their mobile phone or be exposed to other random distractions during testing (e.g., noise). This is because distractions at the time of consumption have been reported to increase intake (Bellisle et al., 2004; Brunstrom & Mitchell, 2006) and affect later appetite (Higgs & Woodward, 2009). Unless social eating is of interest then participants should be tested alone to avoid effects of the behavior of others on intake. It is common for an eating behavior laboratory to also have a waiting area where participants can be given information about the study and complete additional measures, such as questionnaire-based assessment of eating traits. It is useful to have a separate, private space for the assessment of height and weight so that participants are not exposed to cues about weight while eating.

It is possible to assess intake at different types of eating occasion in the laboratory, for example snack or meal, and the choice of what type of intake to measure will depend on the research questions being asked and the facilities available.

Snack Intake

A paradigm employed commonly to assess food intake in the laboratory is the snack taste test. Participants are asked to sample a few different snacks (e.g., plates of different flavored cookies) and then complete a series of ratings (e.g., how sweet is the cookie?) in a set time (e.g., 10 min). They are informed that once they have completed the ratings, they are free to eat as much of the snack as they please (e.g., Rogers & Hill, 1989; Higgs, 2002). Using snacks has the advantage that complex food preparation is not necessary, but the factors influencing snack intake may be different from those influencing meal intake and so it may not be possible to generalize across eating occasions. However, an analysis of 31 studies suggests that intake in taste tests is influenced by factors known to influence intake generally, such as baseline hunger and food liking (Robinson et al., 2017).

Meal Intake

In studies that assess meal intake, participants are usually provided with a fixed portion of food and are asked to eat until they are comfortably full. Intake of a homogenous food (e.g., pasta and sauce; see Gray et al., 2003) as well as multicomponent meals (e.g., fish and vegetables; see Diktas et al., 2021) have been assessed. In some studies intake over two courses (starter and main or main course and dessert) has been assessed (e.g., Caton et al., 2007; Yeomans & Chambers, 2011). Understanding the factors that influence meal intake is important because meals are the major source of calories for most people. However, providing meals is more costly than providing snacks and preparation of meals on site requires approved kitchen facilities.

Buffet Intake

In a buffet study, a wide variety of different foods is made available from which participants can serve themselves to make up a meal (Shide & Rolls, 1995). The buffet meal may be more suited to answer research questions regarding food choice rather than food intake (Robinson & Higgs, 2013). In the buffet situation overall energy intake can be similar but the choice of foods differs (Oliver et al., 2000). However, the sheer variety of food on offer is likely to stimulate choice (Rolls et al., 1981) meaning that as a method it may not be very sensitive to detecting effects of experimental manipulations.

Portion Size

The amount of food or portion size provided to participants in a study will affect amounts consumed, which may then obscure any effect of a manipulation. If a small meal is provided, then participants may eat all the food on their plate. In this scenario, intake would be the same regardless of the experimental condition due to ceiling effects and it might be concluded erroneously that the manipulation had no effect when it was just that the study was not set up in a way that allowed an effect to be detected. Plate clearing is a commonly observed behavior for meals but for snack intake another problematic issue can arise when small portions are provided. If participants are provided with four cookies on a plate, then they may be inclined to eat less than they would like because they may be concerned about appearing greedy to the experimenter or seeming to be rude for not leaving any snacks on the plate. For these reasons, it is usual in intake studies to provide plenty of food so that participants can eat as much as they would like without feeling self-conscious. However, if a very large personal portion is provided then all participants may eat a lot because intake is known to increase as a function of the portion size provided (Rolls et al., 2002). One way to address these problems is to allow participants to self-serve a portion of food, for example pasta from a large pot or cookies from a large serving plate. In this case, plenty of food is provided but individual portion size cues are reduced (Ruddock et al., 2021). Other studies have provided participants with an initial portion of food, but they are then told that if they finish that portion more will be provided (Yeomans & Gray, 1996).

Presentation of Food

How a food is presented can also affect consumption and so needs to be considered. Intake of familiar foods can be very habitual, such that a particular amount of food, for example two cookies, is consumed as a matter of routine. This habitual amount might be unlikely to be altered by an experimental manipulation. To know whether a habitual amount has been consumed, a participant needs to monitor consumption, which is obviously straightforward if the food is provided in a standard portion (i.e., the participant would easily know if they had consumed their habitual amount of two cookies). However, habitual consumption can be disrupted if food is provided in a more unfamiliar format/portion size. For example, a common tactic used in intake studies is to provide cookies that have been broken into small irregular pieces so that participants are less able to monitor consumption (Higgs, 2015; Thomas et al., 2018). Another approach that has been used to reduce the likelihood of monitoring of familiar portion size consumption is to provide small portion of a homogenous food, for example 200 g of pasta, and then just before that portion is finished (after 150 g has been consumed) ask the participant if they would like another portion. In this way, the participants can continue to consume these unfamiliar portion sizes until they have had enough without plate clearing (Yeomans, 2000; Thomas et al., 2014). This approach is facilitated by using a universal eating monitor (Kissileff et al., 1980), which is a set up that allows constant monitoring of amounts consumed during a meal. The participant's plate is placed upon a concealed weighing balance that is located underneath, but protruding through, the surface of a table. The balance is connected to a computer and the progressive reductions in the weight of the plate as food is eaten are recorded. Although in many studies the participants are not made aware of the presence of the balance, similar results have been obtained when they have been informed of its presence (Thomas et al., 2015). It may be helpful to inform participants of the presence of the balance so that they cannot lean inadvertently on it during testing.

Study Design

Several key questions should be answered before a study commences, including specifying the study design and analysis, deciding who the participants will be, how many participants will be tested, and how they will be recruited. Good experimental design requires that the clear hypotheses are tested and that there is a plan before the study begins as to how the data will be analyzed. Study preregistration is available as an option for researchers. This involves researchers committing to and making their research predictions and methods/analyses publicly available before starting their experiments. Preregistering formal data analysis plans may be helpful in reducing selective reporting and publication bias that hamper scientific progress (Munafò et al., 2017).

Participants

Who to Recruit?

When recruiting participants to a food intake study, decisions must be made as to who to recruit and what the inclusion and exclusion criteria might be. Some exclusionary criteria are advised because of ethical issues. For example not recruiting people with food allergies to reduce possibility that a participant might have an adverse reaction to a food being offered. Other exclusionary criteria may serve the purpose of reducing the influence of extraneous factors on intake. For example, participants may be excluded from participation if they have a health condition that affects appetite or are taking prescribed drugs that might interfere with appetite. Similarly it is common to exclude participants who smoke or are following special diets for the same reason. Of course, if participants do not like or are not willing to consume a test food for whatever reason then this will affect intake and so it should be made clear in recruitment materials that consumption of a particular food is part of the testing protocol and that willingness to consume the food(s) is a prerequisite of participation.

Specifying eligibility criteria and recruiting a homogenous sample will reduce the variability in intake observed and thus increase the likelihood of detecting an effect of a manipulation if it exists. However, the generalizability of the results will be unclear. One way of dealing with this problem is to recruit a sufficiently large sample size to allow stratification of participants according to characteristics expected to influence intake such as sex/gender, age, dieting status, and weight (e.g., see Haynes et al., 2019). If there is equal allocation of subgroups of participants to experimental conditions, then the variability in intake associated with these characteristics can be accounted for in the analysis. At the very least the population being tested should be characterized by gathering demographic information so that the sample is clearly defined, and conclusions can be drawn about the representativeness of the sample.

How Many to Recruit?

The number of participants to be tested should be specified beforehand based on the expected size of the effect. Sample sizes will therefore vary depending on the predicted effect and the design of the study (for further guidance on sample size decisions, see Lakens, 2022; Gruijters & Peters, 2020). However, it should be noted that very small sample sizes are to be avoided because with small samples there is a greater likelihood that a true effect will go undetected but also a lower likelihood that a detected effect is true (Button et al., 2013; Szucs & Ioannidis, 2017).

How to Recruit?

As part of the recruitment process participants should provide written confirmation of their voluntary and informed consent to take part. A participant information sheet should explain to participants what they will be asked to do in the study, and it should be clear to the participants that they may withdraw at any time and that their data will be treated appropriately, for example according to data protection legislation. While providing an incentive to take part, such as offering a small amount of monetary compensation, may be appropriate to motivate participation, there should be no coercion involved such as requiring that a student take part in a study because it is part of their course. Ethical approval by an independent institutional review board is normally a requirement for publication of lab-based studies.

Participant demand characteristics are an important consideration in studies of food intake. These are cues which convey information about the study hypotheses to the participant. If demand characteristics are high and a participant guesses what the study is about then they may behave in a way consistent with their understanding of the study aims to please the experimenter or because these expectations drive their behavior (Orne, 1962). For example, a participant may increase their intake of vegetables on offer if they believe that is how the experimenter expects them to behave. They may also wish to present themselves in a positive light to the experimenter by making what they believe to be "good" food choices (Vartanian, 2015). Merely being aware that intake is being monitored may also lead to reduced consumption in the laboratory (Robinson et al., 2015), possibly because participants believe that eating minimally will convey a positive impression (Vartanian, 2015).

Presenting a cover story as part of the recruitment to a study can be useful to detract from the aims so it is less likely that the participant guesses the study hypotheses, for example presenting a study as an investigation of the effect of personality or mood on taste preferences when the outcome of interest is intake (Robinson & Higgs, 2012). In this case, the participant is aware of the study procedures, but the specific aims and hypotheses are not revealed. Another approach is to present the food as an incidental part of the study rather than the focus, for example, presenting snacks as part of a study on problem solving (Robinson et al., 2011). Alternatively, the experimental manipulation part of the study can be separated from the intake part by recruiting participants to two ostensibly separate studies run by different experimenters (Liu et al., 2019). In this case, the participants may be less likely to link the two parts of the study and guess that the manipulation was intended to alter intake.

Even when a cover story or incidental intake is deployed, participants may still guess the aims of the study or be aware of the hypotheses. After all, participants cannot be blinded to the fact that they have signed up to a session at which food is being offered, even if it is not presented as the main event. To probe participants awareness, participants should be asked what they thought the study was about as part of the debrief. A funnel debrief can be useful for finding out what participants were aware of and when they were aware of it during the study (Vartanian et al., 2016). In a funnel debrief, participants are first asked some abstract and open-ended questions about the study such as what they thought the overall aims were. After this, the questions funnel down to the more specific and closed-ended questions, such as questions about when realized that their intake was being assessed and whether an increase or decrease in intake was predicted.

Researchers should be aware that how a study is advertised could result in a bias towards recruiting participants with particular characteristics. For example, there is some evidence that study adverts containing information about food could attract a population with a high interest in food and low social appearance anxiety (Haynes & Robinson, 2019). This kind of self-selection bias poses a threat to the generalizability of the results. While participants need to be informed about what they will be asked to do as part of a study, self-selection bias could be minimized if the eating part were presented as an incidental or minor part of the study in the advert/cover story.

Control Condition(s)

An appropriate control or comparison condition should be used in which the study set up is the same as in the experimental condition and the only difference relates to the manipulation of interest. For example, if the manipulation of interest involves adding a supplement to a food, then the control condition should include a food formulation that is identical in all respects to the experimental version but minus the supplement of interest. In this case it is also important that the control and experimental formulation are matched for visual and sensory characteristics (Yeomans et al., 2001). Using appropriate control conditions can also help in understanding whether responses to a manipulation are being driven by demand characteristics.

Within- or Between-Subjects Design?

An important design decision is whether one should choose a within- or between-subjects design. In a within-subjects design, a participant experiences all conditions in the study design, which is often preferred in appetite research. This is because there can be large between-subject variability in food intake and so it is more powerful to be able to examine the effect of a manipulation using a participant as their own control. However, the decision about whether to employ a within- or between-subjects design will be influenced by the type of manipulation. Exposing a participant to all conditions in a study may result in them becoming aware of the study aims/hypotheses and behaving accordingly. For example, a researcher interested in examining the effect of communicating a social norm message about the eating behavior of others on food intake might present such a study as an evaluation of educational materials (e.g., see Thomas et al., 2016). This cover story might be credible in a between-subject design, but if participants experienced both the experimental (social norm) condition and a control condition that presented a similar but health-oriented message then the participants might guess that the study was about social influences. Whether a within- or between-subjects design is chosen the order in which the conditions are experienced or allocation of participants to condition should be randomized to avoid order effects and to reduce the possibility that the manipulation is confounded with another variable, for example time of year of testing.

Test Procedures

Pilot Testing

Running through standardized testing procedures before recruiting participants and having a standardized script for researchers will maximize the likelihood that a study will run smoothly and consistently. Researchers should be prepared, organized, professional, and courteous. Showing respect for participants is not only ethical but will increase the likelihood that participants take their role seriously and adhere to the study protocols.

Pilot testing is also helpful for checking that manipulations are having the expected effects, for example checking that a mood manipulation does indeed affect mood (Herman et al., 1987).

Test Day

Taking accurate logs of testing sessions and ensuring data that is backed up regularly is important for data integrity and auditing of data. A data management plan should be in place that specifies how data will be checked, stored, shared, secured, and preserved.

The ordering of tasks within an experiment should be considered. Researchers should try and avoid any carry over effects from performing one task to anther task, for example, performing a stressful cognitive task might affect subsequent food intake (Wallis & Hetherington, 2009). Asking someone about their dieting behavior or weight before an eating episode might differentially affect responses based on concerns about weight. For example, it has been reported that exposure to weight-related cues reduces the tendency to model the high intake of an eating companion (Brunner, 2010). Therefore, it is often best to take eating trait and weight measures at the end of a study protocol rather than before any experimental manipulation intended to affect intake. The number of measures to be taken should be considered carefully, considering the total burden on participants. Too many measures may induce fatigue and unreliable responding.

During testing, extraneous variables predicted to affect appetite should be controlled or measured so that their influence may be minimized or taken into account the analysis, for example by including a measure as covariate in the analysis. The main extraneous variables that are usually considered are: baseline appetite, time of day, and eating traits.

Baseline Appetite

If participants begin an intake study in different states of baseline appetite, then this adds variability to the results: Hungry participants will usually eat more than sated participants. For this reason many researchers attempt to standardize baseline hunger. There are various ways in which this can be achieved including asking the participants not to eat for a few hours before attending the session (Fedoroff et al., 1997) or providing a standardized meal in the laboratory (Yeomans et al., 2001). While these procedures may result in more consistent baseline appetite ratings there are also some downsides. For example, asking a person who never eats breakfast to consume a standard amount of food at 7 am will disrupt their normal habit, which could have consequences for their later consumption (Yeomans, 2018). In addition, asking participants not to eat 3 hours before a study may mean that some participants skip having a (late) breakfast and so end up not having eaten since the previous day (Meule, 2018). Therefore, it is also common to measure rather than attempt to standardize baseline hunger by asking participants to report their current levels of appetite, for example using visual analogue scales or by reporting the time they last ate (Vartanian et al., 2013). Such questions can be mixed in with other questions, for example mood-related questions if the researchers also wish to reduce the focus of the study on appetite (Higgs et al., 2008).

Time of Day

The time of day that the test session takes place should be controlled. Hunger levels will be variable through the day and so testing participants at a similar time of day should reduce baseline variability in appetite, but it should be considered that participants may be unwilling to eat certain foods at some times of day due to cultural conventions and habits. For example offering ice cream for breakfast may mean that consumption is generally low because it is not the kind of food that participants would normally consume at that time. Similarly, asking participants to eat lunch at 4 pm may also result in unrepresentative intake. Hence, the time of testing should fit with the type of meal/foods offered and testing should occur in the same time frame across conditions or else be included as a factor in the analysis.

Eating Traits

There are individual differences in eating traits that are known to influence eating behavior that could influence responses to an experimental manipulation. For example, in the classic study on responses to a preload, restrained eaters exhibited counterregulatory behavior by consuming more ice cream after they had consumed a milkshake preload compared with having consumed no preload, whereas unrestrained eaters exhibited the opposite behavior and reduced their ice cream intake after the preload (Herman & Mack, 1975). Various questionnaires have been developed to assess different types of eating traits, including dietary restraint (Herman & Polivy, 1980), tendency toward disinhibited eating (Stunkard & Messick, 1985), and restrained, external, and emotional eating (Strien et al., 1986). If a researcher hypothesizes that a manipulation will depend upon an eating trait then the measure can be analyzed as a moderator of any effect. It is advised to use a standardized questionnaire(s) to be able to characterize a population in terms of eating traits. The choice of which questionnaire is most appropriate will depend on the specific questions being asked (Polivy et al., 2020).

Conclusions

Studying intake in the laboratory has yielded many important insights into human appetite but it is not an easy endeavor. There is no one correct way to conduct a laboratory-based study of food intake but there are some general practices and issues that have been highlighted here that should be considered when designing and running a study.

References

Bellisle, F., Dalix, A.M., & Slama, G. (2004). Non food-related environmental stimuli induce increased meal intake in healthy women: Comparison of television viewing versus listening to a recorded story in laboratory settings. *Appetite, 43*(2), 175–180. https://doi.org/10.1016/j.appet.2004.04.004

Best, M., Barsalou, L.W., & Papies, E.K. (2018). Studying human eating behaviour in the laboratory: Theoretical considerations and practical suggestions. *Appetite, 130*, 339–343. https://doi.org/10.1016/j.appet.2018.06.001

Blundell, J., De Graaf, C., Hulshof, T., Jebb, S., Livingstone, B., Lluch, A., Mela, D., Salah, S., Schuring, E., Van Der Knaap, H., & Westerterp, M. (2010). Appetite control: methodological aspects of the evaluation of foods. *Obesity Reviews, 11*(3), 251–270.

Brunner, T.A. (2010). How weight-related cues affect food intake in a modeling situation. *Appetite, 55*(3), 507–511. https://doi.org/10.1016/j.appet.2010.08.018

Brunstrom, J.M., & Mitchell, G.L. (2006). Effects of distraction on the development of satiety. *British Journal of Nutrition, 96*, 761–769.

Button, K.S., Ioannidis, J.P., Mokrysz, C., Nosek, B.A., Flint, J., Robinson, E.S., & Munafò, M.R. (2013). Power failure: Why small sample size undermines the reliability of neuroscience. *Nature Reviews Neuroscience, 14*(5), 365–376. https://doi.org/10.1038/nrn3475

Caton, S.J., Bate, L., & Hetherington, M.M. (2007). Acute effects of an alcoholic drink on food intake: Aperitif versus co-ingestion. *Physiology & Behavior, 90*(2–3), 368–375. https://doi.org/10.1016/j.physbeh.2006.09.028

De Castro, J.M. (1991). Social facilitation of the spontaneous meal size of humans occurs on both weekdays and weekends. *Physiology & Behavior, 49*(6), 1289–1291. https://doi.org/10.1016/0031-9384(91)90365-U

Diktas, H.E., Roe, L.S., Keller, K.L., Sanchez, C.E., & Rolls, B.J. (2021). Promoting vegetable intake in preschool children: Independent and combined effects of portion size and flavor enhancement. *Appetite, 164*, 105250. https://doi.org/10.1016/j.appet.2021.105250

Fedoroff, I.D., Polivy, J., & Herman, C.P. (1997). The effect of pre-exposure to food cues on the eating behavior of restrained and unrestrained eaters. *Appetite, 28*(1), 33–47. https://doi.org/10.1006/appe.1996.0057

Gibbons, C., Finlayson, G., Dalton, M., Caudwell, P., & Blundell, J.E. (2014). Metabolic phenotyping guidelines: Studying eating behaviour in humans. *Journal of Endocrinology, 222*(2), G1–G12. https://doi.org/10.1530/JOE-14-0020

Gray, R.W., French, S.J., Robinson, T.M., & Yeomans, M.R. (2003). Increasing preload volume with water reduces rated appetite but not food intake in healthy men even with minimum delay between preload and test meal. *Nutritional Neuroscience, 6*(1), 29–37. https://doi.org/10.1080/1028415021000056032

Gruijters, S.L., & Peters, G.J.Y. (2020). Meaningful change definitions: Sample size planning for experimental intervention research. *Psychology & Health, 37*(1), 1–16. https://doi.org/10.1080/08870446.2020.1841762

Haynes, A., Hardman, C.A., Makin, A.D., Halford, J.C., Jebb, S.A., & Robinson, E. (2019). Visual perceptions of portion size normality and intended food consumption: A norm range model. *Food Quality and Preference, 72*, 77. https://doi.org/10.1016/j.foodqual.2018.10.003

Haynes, A., & Robinson, E. (2019). Who are we testing? Self-selection bias in laboratory-based eating behaviour studies. *Appetite, 141*, 104330. https://doi.org/10.1016/j.appet.2019.104330

Herman, C.P., & Mack, D. (1975). Restrained and unrestrained eating. *Journal of Personality, 43*, 647–660. https://doi.org/10.1111/j.1467-6494.1975.tb00727.x

Herman, C.P., & Polivy, J. (1980). Experimental and clinical aspects of restrained eating. In A. Stunkard (Ed.), *Obesity: Basic mechanisms and treatment* (pp. 208–225). W.B. Saunders.

Herman, C.P., Polivy, J., Lank, C.N., & Heatherton, T.F. (1987). Anxiety, hunger, and eating behavior. *Journal of Abnormal Psychology, 96*(3), 264. https://doi.org/10.1037/0021-843X.96.3.264

Hetherington, M.M., & Rolls, B.J. (2018). Favouring more rigour when investigating human eating behaviour is like supporting motherhood and apple pie: A response to Robinson, Bevelander, Field, and Jones (2018). *Appetite, 130*, 330–333. https://doi.org/10.1016/j.appet.2018.05.013

Higgs, S. (2002). Memory for recent eating and its influence on subsequent food intake. *Appetite, 39*(2), 159–166. https://doi.org/10.1006/appe.2002.0500

Higgs, S. (2015). Manipulations of attention during eating and their effects on later snack intake. *Appetite, 92*, 287–294. https://doi.org/10.1016/j.appet.2015.05.033

Higgs, S., Williamson, A.C., & Attwood, A.S. (2008). Recall of recent lunch and its effect on subsequent snack intake. *Physiology & Behavior, 94*(3), 454–462. https://doi.org/10.1016/j.physbeh.2008.02.011

Higgs, S., & Woodward, M. (2009). Television watching during lunch increases afternoon snack intake of young women. *Appetite, 52*(1), 39–43. https://doi.org/10.1016/j.appet.2008.07.007

Kissileff, H.R., Kilngsberg, G., & Italie, T.B. van (1980). Universal eating monitor for continuous recording of solid or liquid consumption in man. *American Journal of Physiology, 238*, R14–R22. https://doi.org/10.1152/ajpregu.1980.238.1.R14

Lakens, D. (2022). Sample size justification. *Collabra: Psychology, 8*(1), 33267. https://doi.org/10.31234/osf.io/9d3yf

Liu, J., Thomas, J., & Higgs, S. (2019). The relationship between social identity, descriptive social norms and eating intentions and behaviors. *Journal of Experimental Social Psychology, 82*, 217–230. https://doi.org/10.1016/j.jesp.2019.02.002

Meiselman, H.L. (1992). Methodology and theory in human eating research. *Appetite, 19*(1), 49–55. https://doi.org/10.1016/0195-6663(92)90235-X

Meule, A. (2018). Standardizing versus measuring food deprivation and hunger. *Appetite, 130*, 328–329. https://doi.org/10.1016/j.appet.2018.05.014

Munafò, M.R., Nosek, B.A., Bishop, D.V., Button, K.S., Chambers, C.D., Percie du Sert, N., Simonsohn, U., Wagenmakers, E.J., Ware, J.J., & Ioannidis, J. (2017). A manifesto for reproducible science. *Nature Human Behaviour, 1*(1), Article 0021. https://doi.org/10.1038/s41562-016-0021

Oliver, G., Wardle, J., & Gibson, E.L. (2000). Stress and food choice: A laboratory study. *Psychosomatic Medicine, 62*(6), 853–865. https://doi.org/10.1097/00006842-200011000-00016

Orne, M.T. (1962). On the social psychology of the psychological experiment: With particular reference to demand characteristics and their implications. *American Psychologist, 17*(11), 776–783. https://doi.org/10.1037/h0043424

Polivy, J., Herman, C.P., & Mills, J.S. (2020). What is restrained eating and how do we identify it? *Appetite*, 104820. https://doi.org/10.1016/j.appet.2020.104820

Robinson, E., Bevelander, K.E., Field, M., & Jones, A. (2018). Methodological and reporting quality in laboratory studies of human eating behavior. *Appetite, 125*, 486–491. https://doi.org/10.1016/j.appet.2018.02.008

Robinson, E., Hardman, C.A., Halford, J.C., & Jones, A. (2015). Eating under observation: A systematic review and meta-analysis of the effect that heightened awareness of observation has on laboratory measured energy intake. *The American Journal of Clinical Nutrition, 102*(2), 324–337. https://doi.org/10.3945/ajcn.115.111195

Robinson, E., Haynes, A., Hardman, C.A., Kemps, E., Higgs, S., & Jones, A. (2017). The bogus taste test: Validity as a measure of laboratory food intake. *Appetite, 116*, 223–231. https://doi.org/10.1016/j.appet.2017.05.002

Robinson, E., & Higgs, S. (2012). Liking food less: The impact of social influence on food liking evaluations in female students. *PloS One, 7*(11), e48858. https://doi.org/10.1371/journal.pone.0048858

Robinson, E., & Higgs, S. (2013). Food choices in the presence of "healthy" and "unhealthy" eating partners. *British Journal of Nutrition, 109*(4), 765–771. https://doi.org/10.1017/S0007114512002000

Robinson, E., Tobias, T., Shaw, L., Freeman, E., & Higgs, S. (2011). Social matching of food intake and the need for social acceptance. *Appetite, 56*(3), 747–752. https://doi.org/10.1016/j.appet.2011.03.001

Rogers, P.J., & Hill, A.J. (1989). Breakdown of dietary restraint following mere exposure to food stimuli: Interrelationships between restraint, hunger, salivation, and food intake. *Addictive Behaviors, 14*(4), 387–397. https://doi.org/10.1016/0306-4603(89)90026-9

Rolls, B.J., Morris, E.L., & Roe, L.S. (2002). Portion size of food affects energy intake in normal-weight and overweight men and women. *American Journal of Clinical Nutrition, 76*, 1207–1213. https://doi.org/10.1093/ajcn/76.6.1207

Rolls, B.J., Rowe, E.A., Rolls, E.T., Kingston, B., Megson, A., & Gunary, R. (1981). Variety in a meal enhances food intake in man. *Physiology & Behavior, 26*(2), 215–221. https://doi.org/10.1016/0031-9384(81)90014-7

Ruddock, H.K., Brunstrom, J.M., Vartanian, L.R., & Higgs, S. (2019). A systematic review and meta-analysis of the social facilitation of eating. *The American Journal of Clinical Nutrition, 110*(4), 842–861. https://doi.org/10.1093/ajcn/nqz155

Ruddock, H.K., Long, E.V., Brunstrom, J.M., Vartanian, L.R., & Higgs, S. (2021). People serve themselves larger portions before a social meal. *Scientific Reports, 11*(1), 1–8. https://doi.org/10.1038/s41598-021-90559-y

Shide, D.J., & Rolls, B.J. (1995). Information about the fat content of preloads influences energy intake in healthy women. *Journal of the American Dietetic Association, 95*(9), 993–998. https://doi.org/10.1016/S0002-8223(95)00273-1

Strien, T. van, Frijters, J.E., Bergers, G., & Defares, P.B. (1986). The Dutch Eating Behavior Questionnaire (DEBQ) for assessment of restrained, emotional, and external eating behavior. *International Journal of Eating Disorders, 5*(2), 295–315. https://doi.org/10.1002/1098-108X(198602)5:2<295::AID-EAT2260050209>3.0.CO;2-T

Stunkard, A.J., & Messick, S. (1985). The three-factor eating questionnaire to measure dietary restraint, disinhibition and hunger. *Journal of Psychosomatic Research, 29*(1), 71–83. https://doi.org/10.1016/0022-3999(85)90010-8

Szucs, D., & Ioannidis, J.P. (2017). Empirical assessment of published effect sizes and power in the recent cognitive neuroscience and psychology literature. *PLoS Biology, 15*(3), e2000797. https://doi.org/10.1371/journal.pbio.2000797

Thomas, J.M., Dourish, C.T., & Higgs, S. (2015). Effects of awareness that food intake is being measured by a universal eating monitor on the consumption of a pasta lunch and a cookie snack in healthy female volunteers. *Appetite, 92*, 247–251. https://doi.org/10.1016/j.appet.2015.05.034

Thomas, J.M., Dourish, C.T., Tomlinson, J., Hassan-Smith, Z., Hansen, P.C., & Higgs, S. (2018). The 5-HT 2C receptor agonist meta-chlorophenylpiperazine (mCPP) reduces palatable food consumption and BOLD fMRI responses to food images in healthy female volunteers. *Psychopharmacology, 235*(1), 257–267. https://doi.org/10.1007/s00213-017-4764-9

Thomas, J.M., Dourish, C.T., Tomlinson, J.W., Hassan-Smith, Z., & Higgs, S. (2014). Effects of the 5-HT 2C receptor agonist meta-chlorophenylpiperazine on appetite, food intake and emotional processing in healthy volunteers. *Psychopharmacology, 231*(12), 2449–2459. https://doi.org/10.1007/s00213-013-3409-x

Thomas, J.M., Liu, J., Robinson, E.L., Aveyard, P., Herman, C.P., & Higgs, S. (2016). The effects of liking norms and descriptive norms on vegetable consumption: A randomized experiment. *Frontiers in Psychology, 7*, Article 442. https://doi.org/10.3389/fpsyg.2016.00442

Vartanian, L.R. (2015). Impression management and food intake. Current directions in research. *Appetite, 86*, 74–80. https://doi.org/10.1016/j.appet.2014.08.021

Vartanian, L.R., Chen, W.H., Reily, N.M., & Castel, A.D. (2016). The parallel impact of episodic memory and episodic future thinking on food intake. *Appetite, 101*, 31–36. https://doi.org/10.1016/j.appet.2016.02.149

Vartanian, L.R., Sokol, N., Herman, C.P., & Polivy, J. (2013). Social models provide a norm of appropriate food intake for young women. *PLoS One, 8*(11), e79268. https://doi.org/10.1371/journal.pone.0079268

Wallis, D.J., & Hetherington, M.M. (2009). Emotions and eating. Self-reported and experimentally induced changes in food intake under stress. *Appetite, 52*(2), 355–362.

Yeomans, M.R. (2000). Rating changes over the course of meals: What do they tell us about motivation to eat? *Neuroscience and Biobehavioral Reviews, 24*, 249–259. https://doi.org/10.1016/S0149-7634(99)00078-0

Yeomans, M.R. (2018). Measuring appetite and food intake. In G. Areas & P. Varela (Eds.), *Methods in consumer research, volume 2* (pp. 119–149). Woodhead Publishing. https://doi.org/10.1016/B978-0-08-101743-2.00006-6

Yeomans, M.R., & Chambers, L. (2011). Satiety-relevant sensory qualities enhance the satiating effects of mixed carbohydrate-protein preloads. *The American Journal of Clinical Nutrition, 94*(6), 1410–1417. https://doi.org/10.3945/ajcn.111.011650

Yeomans, M.R., & Gray, R.W. (1996). Selective effects of naltrexone on food pleasantness and intake. *Physiology & Behavior, 60*(2), 439–446. https://doi.org/10.1016/S0031-9384(96)80017-5

Yeomans, M.R., Lee, M.D., Gray, R.W., & French, S.J. (2001). Effects of test-meal palatability on compensatory eating following disguised fat and carbohydrate preloads. *International Journal of Obesity, 25*(8), 1215–1224. https://doi.org/10.1038/sj.ijo.0801653

Chapter 18

Ecological Momentary Assessment of Eating Behavior

Diana Zhang,[1] Tyler Mason,[1] and Kathryn Smith[2]

[1] Department of Population and Public Health Sciences, University of Southern California, CA, USA
[2] Department of Psychiatry and Behavioral Sciences, University of Southern California, CA, USA

Introduction

Historically, most research on normative and maladaptive eating behaviors has relied on retrospective self-reports and laboratory-based assessment. However, retrospective recall and laboratory measures are inherently limited by their ability to capture the complex dynamics of everyday life, including those related to eating behavior. As a result, these methods pose serious challenges in understanding and generalizing findings to behaviors in real-world settings, which may further affect the ability to effectively inform behavior change interventions. As a response to these concerns, behavioral research has increasingly integrated methods to study every day, real-world behavior (Shiffman et al., 2008). This chapter will review an alternative to retrospective self-report and laboratory measures known as ecological momentary assessment (EMA; Shiffman et al., 2008). The next sections will first provide a summary of EMA methodology, followed by a synthesis of EMA research across various domains (i.e., restrained eating and dieting, hedonic eating, dysregulated and disordered eating, and self-reported dietary intake). Last, limitations and future directions for this field will be discussed.

Overview of EMA Methodology

EMA is a real-time data capture methodology that involves repeated sampling of an individual's current behavior and experiences in real-time, naturalistic environments (Shiffman et al., 2008). This method consists of prompted or participant-initiated self-reports on a wide range of factors related to behavioral, physical, psychological, and contextual aspects of daily life. EMA allows participants to repeatedly report on concurrent experiences in real time in their natural environments over a specified period of time. This research generally utilizes mobile electronic devices to capture real-time data, including smartphone applications, SMS messaging, and web-based programs (Shiffman et al., 2008). EMA protocols can employ different data collection methods, either alone or in combination (Shiffman et al., 2008). In event-contingent sampling, participants record events (e.g., eating episodes) as they occur. Participants can also be prompted (e.g., receive a signal on their electronic device) at random or semirandom times throughout the day to complete a similar assessment (signal-contingent sampling). Lastly, interval-contingent sampling protocols prompt participants to make recordings at fixed time intervals (e.g., beginning of each day; Shiffman et al., 2008). Importantly, evidence suggests EMA research on eating and dietary intake behavior has shown to provide the most flexibility when using a combination of signal-, event-, and interval-contingent prompts (Mason et al., 2020). In addition to assessing eating behaviors, EMA research in this area often assesses other variables at these assessments, such as mood, social context, and activities that happen shortly before, during, and/or after eating behaviors. These data can help capture contextual variables that may be concurrently associated with eating behaviors, as well as elucidate temporal relationships between eating behaviors and such factors, for example, mood, social context, and environment (Mason et al., 2020).

Advantages of EMA

As previously noted, EMA can address several limitations of more traditional methods of collecting dietary intake data, such as 24-hour dietary recall (a method that requires relatively high level of motivation and is likely burdensome for respondents). The use of EMA can increase ecological validity, reduce retrospective recall bias, provide a more nuanced and temporal understanding of data, and disaggregate within- versus between-subjects effects (Shiffman et al., 2008).

Increased ecological validity is one key advantage of EMA. Gathering participants' reports on current behavior in their usual environments while performing regular daily activities increases the validity and generalizability of findings to real-life settings. Retrospective recall bias is also reduced when participants are asked to respond to questions in real time rather than to provide a summary over long periods of time (Shiffman et al., 2008). This may be related to increased saliency, as details and information are more likely to be accurately reported if asked in real time compared to reports on past events (Shiffman et al., 2008).

EMA has also shown utility in assessing how behavior changes over time and across various contexts. Further, momentary antecedents and consequences can be more accurately assessed in real-world settings compared to laboratory settings. Another unique advantage of EMA is the capacity to disaggregate data into between- and within-subjects measures (Shiffman et al., 2008). As an example, EMA can measure changes in binge eating relative to an individual's usual level of binge eating (within-subjects effect); how an individual's average level of binge eating over the course of an EMA protocol compares to other individuals' average level of binge eating (between-subjects effect); and how individual differences (e.g., trait impulsivity) may moderate momentary associations between negative affect and binge eating (state-trait or cross-level effects). This can be particularly important for understanding microtemporal functional relationships that serve as maintaining mechanisms of eating behaviors, as well as who may be most susceptible to these mechanisms.

Populations Assessed With EMA

EMA has been used to measure eating behaviors across a diverse range of populations. Among adults, EMA has shown to be a useful tool for assessing a wide range of behaviors across diverse clinical and nonclinical populations, such as individuals with disordered eating, obesity, and diabetes across various age groups (Goldschmidt et al., 2018; Miller et al., 2016).

Populations With Disordered Eating

Several decades of EMA research has accumulated focusing on eating psychopathology and maladaptive eating behaviors, including among individuals with eating disorders such as anorexia nervosa, bulimia nervosa, and binge eating disorder (e.g., Engel et al., 2016). EMA studies have helped advance eating disorder research and clinical practice by increasing understanding of proximal antecedents of symptoms (Mason et al., 2021). More specifically, EMA has elucidated functional associations between eating disorder symptoms and other constructs, such as affect, rumination, body image, hunger, feelings of guilt, disgust, and depressed mood (Goldschmidt et al., 2018). Additionally, theoretical models, especially affect regulation models, have been tested using EMA (Schaefer et al., 2020; Smyth et al., 2007). Study findings have subsequently helped to inform targets of interventions. For example, evidence supports the importance of developing momentary interventions to 'de-couple' or decrease the association between negative affect and binge eating more effectively (Smith et al., 2022).

Populations With Obesity

EMA has also been a valuable tool in research examining everyday and normative eating behavior of individuals with overweight/obesity. Employing EMA with these populations has furthered the understanding of momentary correlates and predictors of obesogenic eating behavior, including emotional, physiological, and environment factors, such as affect and mood, stress, hunger, craving, distracting stimuli (e.g., eating while watching television), and social cues (e.g., eating because others are eating; Goldschmidt et al., 2018). These findings highlight an ongoing need to understand the interplay of the diverse and temporally dynamic factors that contribute to the rising obesity epidemic.

Populations With Diabetes

Research has also used EMA among individuals with diabetes to monitor eating behavior and its relation to the adoption of a lower glycemic index diet. A pilot study examined the dietary intake of six patients with Type II diabetes for 6 weeks, in which signal-contingent EMA was used to assess intake of low glycemic index foods, with results suggesting that EMA has potential to be an effective monitoring instrument in the context of nutrition therapy (Miller et al., 2016). Other studies have tested the feasibility of event-contingent EMA to measure factors such as insulin administration and dietary intake (Nam et al., 2021). This study and other literature suggest that EMA has potential utility in clinical settings as it relates to diabetes self-management assessment, as well as for development of individualized diabetes interventions (Nam et al., 2021). Further and large randomized controlled trials should be conducted to better assess the feasibility, efficacy, and generalizability.

Youth Populations

While the majority of EMA research has focused on eating behavior in adults, there is a growing body of a recent systematic review indicated EMA can be an effective tool for capturing relevant factors that influence eating behavior among youths (for a review see Mason et al., 2021). The EMA literature among youths has assessed the following contextual factors: affect, stress, cognition, social and environmental factors, behavior, and caregiver-related factors; notably, cognitive and social factors appear to be the most consistently related to eating behaviors. In particular, findings extend existing literature on the temporal relationship between momentary situational triggers (e.g., interpersonal problems and negative social evaluation) and eating disorder symptoms, and the utility of EMA for developing novel ecological momentary interventions, in which participants receive intervention material in real time when it may be most impactful (Mason et al., 2021).

Review of EMA Across Relevant Domains

The following section will review the use of EMA across various domains related to eating behavior and dietary intake: restrained eating and dieting, craving and hunger, dysregulated eating and disordered eating (e.g., binge eating, emotional eating, purging, and restriction), and self-reported dietary intake.

Restrained Eating and Dieting

Dietary restraint has been implicated in the development and maintenance of eating pathology as well as adaptive eating regulation. As such, this construct remains a subject of debate due in part to variability in conceptual definitions and assessment methods (Johnson et al., 2012). Researchers have distinguished between restraint intentions versus behaviors, with dietary restraint being regarded as intentions to decrease or limit one's dietary intake (Rodgers et al., 2018). A study that examined chronic dieting and self-regulation of food desires by measuring dietary restraint and inhibitory control found significant differences between restrained eaters and unrestrained eaters; behavioral inhibition, for example, was a key factor that distinguished successful from unsuccessful dieters (Hofmann et al., 2014). Previous EMA research has assessed momentary dietary restraint in a variety of ways, including adapted items from the Concern for Dieting questionnaire, a six-item subscale of the Revised Restraint Scale (Hofman et al., 2014), the Dutch Eating Behavior Questionnaire (Mason et al., 2019), and the Three Factor Eating Questionnaire (Thomas et al., 2011). Overall, studies have shown promise for the use of EMA to measure dietary restraint. However, findings remain mixed; further research is needed to examine the ecological validity of the various adapted items, and may benefit from developing standardized measures. Other research has found that trait-level restraint behavior is predictive of daily presence and frequency of dietary restraint behaviors measured via EMA (Rodgers et al., 2018).

Craving and Hunger

Physiological and homeostatic processes (e.g., hunger and satiety), as well as hedonic eating (e.g., food- and cue-elicited craving), also play a role in food intake and eating behavior (Reichenberger, Kuppens, et al., 2018). Difficulties with distinguishing between physiological and subjective hunger and craving may be a significant factor contributing to unhealthy eating, such as eating in the absence of hunger (Reichenberger, Richard, et al., 2018), and can lead to uncontrolled overeating, especially among individuals with obesity (Goldschmidt et al., 2018). EMA measures of craving and hunger have consisted of adapted items from standardized instruments, such as the Food Cravings Questionnaire-State (FCQ-S; Cepeda-Benito et al., 2000), such as "How hungry are you right now?" to measure hunger on a scale of 0 to 100 (*not at all* to *very much*), and "What do you feel like eating right now?" followed by listings of food categories with response options to level of desire for each category ranging from 0 to 100 (i.e., *nothing* to *very much*) to measure craving (Reichenberger, Richard, et al., 2018). Food categories included high-fat and high-sugar foods (e.g., fatty foods such as fries and pizza, and sweets such as chocolate and cookies), as well as health food categories (e.g., vegetables, salads, and fruits) adapted from the Yale Food Addiction Scale 2.0 (Reichenberger, Richard, et al., 2018; Gearhardt et al., 2016). Of note, EMA studies have found that hunger is significantly associated with anxiety and depression, and food craving is significantly associated with stress, anxiety, and depression (Kikuchi et al., 2015).

Dysregulated and Disordered Eating

Binge Eating and Emotional Eating

Various forms of dysregulated and disordered eating, including binge eating, emotional eating, purging, and restriction have been examined using EMA. Binge eating behavior is a multifaceted construct and presents in several types of eating disorders. Binge eating has been assessed categorically (e.g., presence versus absence of behavior) and dimensionally (e.g., frequency of specific symptoms of binge eating) with EMA. Previous EMA research has assessed binge eating with adapted items from instruments such as the Eating Disorder Examination interview and questionnaire (Fairburn & Beglin, 2008; Fairburn et al., 1993) to measure the extent to which binge episodes were characterized by overeating and loss of control over eating (Schaefer et al., 2020). Overeating has been assessed with questions such as, "To what extent do you feel that you overate?" and "To what extent do you feel that you ate an excessive amount of food?" Items that have assessed loss of control over eating included, "While you were eating, to what extent did you feel that you could not stop eating once you had started?" and "While you were eating, to what extent did you feel driven or compelled to eat?" (Schaefer et al., 2020). EMA responses to such questions are typically assessed on ordinal scales (e.g., 1 to 5 ranging from *not at all* to *extremely*) and can be analyzed as a dimensional variable or coded dichotomously to indicate the occurrence of binge episodes (e.g., when individuals have scores of three or more on both overeating and loss of control items). Binge eating has also been linked with emotional eating, which is defined as eating in response to negative or positive emotions (though much of existing literature is focused on negative emotional eating; Reichenberger, Kuppens, et al., 2018). EMA studies have measured emotional eating using adapted items from the Emotional Overeating Questionnaire (Masheb & Grilo, 2006; Juarascio et al., 2020). While extant literature indicates EMA methodology can be a useful tool for research on emotional eating, further studies are needed to increase understanding of momentary predictors, correlates, and consequences of emotional eating (e.g., affect, appetite regulation, physical activity; Smith et al., 2021). For example, research on stress-related eating and positive emotional eating have suggested that engaging in physical activity prior to psychological stress may lower stress-related eating and positive emotional eating (Smith et al., 2021).

Purging

Purging behavior has been assessed using EMA questions about the recent occurrence of self-induced vomiting, laxative abuse, and diuretic use behavior, including how long ago purging occurred compared to time of completing assessment (Haedt-Matt & Keel, 2015). Negative affect has often been studied in relation to purging behavior using EMA, and has shown to mediate relationships between stress-related constructs (e.g., interpersonal and environmental stressors, daily hassles and activities, stress appraisal) and purging (Goldschmidt et al., 2014). Other EMA research has highlighted complex relationships between antecedents and consequences of purging among individuals with purging disorder (i.e., characterized by purging after consuming normal amounts of food). For example, positive affect can trigger purging, while negative affect may play a role in maintaining purging behavior, suggesting an affect regulation function of purging among individuals with this disorder (Haedt-Matt & Keel, 2015).

Dietary Restriction

EMA has also been used for research on restrictive eating, which differs from dietary restraint in that restraint refers to an attempt to restrict what one eats (Johnson et al., 2012), while restrictive eating refers to undereating associated with physical, physiological, and/or psychosocial symptoms (e.g., extreme weight loss and malnutrition; Rastogi & Rome, 2020). EMA research on dietary restriction has usually been conducted among individuals with eating disorders. This has consisted of questions about the type of eating episode (e.g., snack or meal) in addition to items specifically related to restricting food intake, such as "I limited calories" and "I ate as little as possible," in which endorsements of either of these items are classified as restrictive eating episodes (Haynos et al., 2015). Further, restriction has also been assessed via end of day ratings in which participants are asked to report if they "went 8 or more hours without eating" or "limited food intake to less than 1200 calories"; endorsement of either item has been operationalized as restrictive eating (Haynos et al., 2015). Based on responses to the aforementioned 4 items, each day of EMA can be categorized as either a high or low restriction day (Haynos et al., 2015). Findings from EMA studies on relationships between restrictive eating and other constructs have been mixed (Haynos et al., 2015). Some EMA research has found that dietary restriction is predictive of subsequent binge eating, while other studies did not find significant associations between restrictive eating and binge eating (Haynos et al., 2015; Zunker et al., 2011). Therefore, additional research utilizing EMA is warranted to explore temporal relationships between restrictive eating and binge eating, including relationships with potential correlates such as affect (De Young et al., 2014).

Self-Reported Dietary Intake

EMA of dietary intake consists of repeated sampling in the form of event- or signal-contingent assessments, which can also be combined with an end-of-day survey (Schembre et al., 2018). Self-reported dietary assessments using EMA allow participants to report their food intake in real time (event-contingent), while also capturing factors that may otherwise not be recorded through the use of signal-contingent prompts. Studies using EMA methodology can generate a wide range of data in addition to dietary intake, such as physical, behavioral, psychological, social, and contextual information, allowing for examination of concurrent events and exposures (Schembre et al., 2018). EMA of dietary intake has shown utility in capturing full days of food consumption and estimating energy and nutrient intake (Schembre et al., 2018).

Limitations and Future Directions

Although EMA addresses important limitations of more traditional methods of data collection, there are some challenges to consider. EMA is generally administered via electronic devices, which can be more expensive than other forms of data collection such as paper-and-pencil surveys. However, studies may offer the option of loaning devices to participants. While this can be beneficial for ensuring consistency in data collection methodology and may help increase participant response rates (for example, if participants do not have regular, reliable access to data usage via their personal phones or electronic devices), funding may limit the overall sample size of the study. Nevertheless, alternative options are available to mitigate costs, such as establishing inclusion criteria that require ownership of personal smartphone. Using open-source software also reduces costs associated with EMA platform licenses.

Another challenge is related to EMA prompt schedules and the timing of participants' responses, as these factors can contribute to mixed findings. For example, concurrent relationships between factors are examined in some studies, while others explored time-lagged relationships. Studies that examine time-lagged associations should consider the time between EMA prompts because the intervals can vary widely depending on the structure of the EMA schedule. This is particularly important, as contextual factors and eating behavior may have highly dynamic relationships, and findings may be less meaningful unless appropriate time frames are used for EMA prompts. Additionally, contextual factors may serve as antecedents and/or consequences of eating, and these differences could be missed due to issues with timing of EMA signals and participant reporting.

The utility of EMA may also be limited by the wide variety of instruments that have been used to measure eating and dietary intake behavior across the literature. Future studies should consider standardizing EMA methods of dietary intake to maximize quality of dietary data and ecological validity, keeping in mind issues related to participant burden (Schembre et al., 2018). Other strategies may include the use of relatively novel measures, such as food photos and monitors (e.g., wearable devices), which could provide informative data that aforementioned traditional methods cannot.

Relatedly, the association between momentary factors and eating behavior can be influenced by a wide range of factors, such as individual differences (e.g., personality, affect, stress, cognition), contextual, social, and environmental components. More studies are needed that include items related to appetite, food cravings, and food-related thoughts, as existing studies indicate these factors are salient momentary correlates of eating behavior. Failing to account for such factors may lead to inconsistent and potentially inaccurate findings. Moving forward, more EMA research is also needed to explore the effects of individual differences, particularly as potential moderators or mediators, on observed associations.

Finally, issues related to participant burden represent an important limitation. Given that it can be time consuming to complete surveys multiple times per day, this may lead to low compliance. There are potential technical issues that may arise with EMA platforms, and some populations may be less receptive to electronic methods of data collection, such as individuals who are older and/or have less experience or feel less comfortable with using electronic devices. Despite the potential challenges with EMA methodology, strategies are available to help mitigate these issues. For example, tailoring protocols to the target study population to increase interest in participation; incentivizing participants based on compliance to address potential low response rates; and limiting the number of items or survey prompts to reduce participant burden. In addition, future EMA research in youth is needed to evaluate how participant burden and compliance relates to EMA signal schedules, choice of measures, individual differences, and contextual factors (Mason et al., 2021).

Conclusions

Taken together, EMA is an effective method for assessing eating behaviors and examining relationships between eating behaviors and other relevant factors. Although EMA studies have revealed associations between a wide variety of factors and eating behavior, some findings remain mixed (e.g., particularly restrained eating and dietary restriction; De Young et al., 2014; Hofman et al., 2014; Thomas et al., 2011), which underscores the need for further research to clarify these relationships. The current literature also highlights several areas of focus that may help to improve EMA methodology in this field, including further consideration of: the timing and scheduling of EMA prompts and reporting, choice of instruments and measures of dietary intake, as well as the influence of individual differences and contextual factors on eating behaviors (Mason et al., 2020).

References

Cepeda-Benito, A., Gleaves, D.H., Williams, T.L., & Erath, S.A. (2000). The development and validation of the state and trait food-cravings questionnaires. *Behavior Therapy, 31*(1), 151–173. https://doi.org/10.1016/S0005-7894(00)80009-X

De Young, K.P., Lavender, J.M., Crosby, R.D., Wonderlich, S.A., Engel, S.G., Mitchell, J.E., Crow, S.J., Peterson, C.B., & Le Grange, D. (2014). Bidirectional associations between binge eating and restriction in anorexia nervosa. An ecological momentary assessment study. *Appetite, 83*, 69–74.

Engel, S.G., Crosby, R.D., Thomas, G., Bond, D., Lavender, J.M., Mason, T., Steffen, K.J., Green, D.D., & Wonderlich, S.A. (2016). Ecological momentary assessment in eating disorder and obesity research: a review of the recent literature. *Current Psychiatry Reports, 18*(4), 37. https://doi.org/10.1007/s11920-016-0672-7

Fairburn, C.G., & Beglin, S.J. (2008). Eating disorder examination questionnaire. In C.G. Fairburn (Ed.), *Cognitive behavior therapy and eating disorders* (pp. 309–313). Guilford Press.

Fairburn, C.G., Cooper, Z., & O'Connor, M. (1993). The eating disorder examination. *International Journal of Eating Disorders, 6*, 1–8.

Gearhardt, A.N., Corbin, W.R., & Brownell, K.D. (2016). Development of the Yale Food Addiction Scale version 2.0. *Psychology of Addictive Behaviors, 30*(1), 113–121. https://doi.org/10.1037/adb0000136

Goldschmidt, A.B., Smith, K.E., Crosby, R.D., Boyd, H.K., Dougherty, E., Engel, S.G., & Haedt-Matt, A. (2018). Ecological momentary assessment of maladaptive eating in children and adolescents with overweight or obesity. *International Journal of Eating Disorders, 51*(6), 549–557. https://doi.org/10.1002/eat.22864

Goldschmidt, A.B., Wonderlich, S.A., Crosby, R.D., Engel, S.G., Lavender, J.M., Peterson, C.B., Crow, S.J., Cao, L., & Mitchell, J.E. (2014). Ecological momentary assessment of stressful events and negative affect in bulimia nervosa. *Journal of Consulting and Clinical Psychology, 82*(1), 30–39.

Haedt-Matt, A.A., & Keel, P.K. (2015). Affect regulation and purging: An ecological momentary assessment study in purging disorder. *Journal of Abnormal Psychology, 124*(2), 399–411. https://doi.org/10.1037/a0038815

Haynos, A.F., Crosby, R.D., Engel, S.G., Lavender, J.M., Wonderlich, S.A., Mitchell, J.E., Peterson, C.B., Crow, S.J., & Le Grange, D. (2015). Initial test of an emotional avoidance model of restriction in anorexia nervosa using ecological momentary assessment. *Journal of Psychiatric Research, 68*, 134–139.

Hofmann, W., Adriaanse, M., Vohs, K.D., & Baumeister, R.F. (2014). Dieting and the self-control of eating in everyday environments: An experience sampling study. *British Journal of Health Psychology, 19*(3), 523–539. https://doi.org/10.1111/bjhp.12053

Johnson, F., Pratt, M., & Wardle, J. (2012). Dietary restraint and self-regulation in eating behavior. *International Journal of Obesity, 36*(5), 665–674. https://doi.org/10.1038/ijo.2011.156

Juarascio, A.S., Crochiere, R.J., Tapera, T.M., Palermo, M., & Zhang, F. (2020). Momentary changes in heart rate variability can detect risk for emotional eating episodes. *Appetite, 152*, 104698. https://doi.org/10.1016/j.appet.2020.104698

Kikuchi, H., Yoshiuchi, K., Inada, S., Ando, T., & Yamamoto, Y. (2015). Development of an ecological momentary assessment scale for appetite. *BioPsychoSocial Medicine, 9*(1), 1–8. https://doi.org/10.1186/s13030-014-0029-6

Masheb, R.M., & Grilo, C.M. (2006). Emotional overeating and its associations with eating disorder psychopathology among overweight patients with binge eating disorder. *International Journal of Eating Disorders, 39*(2), 141–146. https://doi.org/10.1002/eat.20221

Mason, T.B., Do, B., Wang, S., & Dunton, G.F. (2020). Ecological momentary assessment of eating and dietary intake behaviors in children and adolescents: A systematic review of the literature. *Appetite, 144*, 104465. https://doi.org/10.1016/j.appet.2019.104465

Mason, T.B., Pacanowski, C.R., Lavender, J.M., Crosby, R.D., Wonderlich, S.A., Engel, S.G., Mitchell, J.E., Crow, S.J., & Peterson, C.B. (2019). Evaluating the ecological validity of the Dutch eating behavior questionnaire among obese adults using ecological momentary assessment. *Assessment, 26*(5), 907–914.

Mason, T.B., Smith, K.E., Crosby, R.D., Engel, S.G., & Wonderlich, S.A. (2021). Examination of momentary maintenance factors and eating disorder behaviors and cognitions using ecological momentary assessment. *Eating Disorders, 29*(1), 42–55. https://doi.org/10.1080/10640266.2019.1613847

Miller, C.K., Weinhold, K.R., & Mitchell, D.C. (2016). Using ecological momentary assessment to track goal progress toward the adoption of a low glycemic index diet among adults with type 2 diabetes: A pilot study. *Topics in Clinical Nutrition, 31*(4), 323–334. https://doi.org/10.1097/TIN.0000000000000083

Nam, S., Griggs, S., Ash, G.I., Dunton, G.F., Huang, S., Batten, J., Parekh, N., & Whittemore, R. (2021). Ecological momentary assessment for health behaviors and contextual factors in persons with diabetes: A systematic review. *Diabetes Research and Clinical Practice, 174*, 108745. https://doi.org/10.1016/j.diabres.2021.108745

Rastogi, R., & Rome, E.S. (2020). Restrictive eating disorders in previously overweight adolescents and young adults. *Cleveland Clinic Journal of Medicine, 87*(3), 165–171. https://doi.org/10.3949/ccjm.87a.19034

Reichenberger, J., Kuppens, P., Liedlgruber, M., Wilhelm, F.H., Tiefengrabner, M., Ginzinger, S., & Blechert, J. (2018). No haste, more taste: An EMA study of the effects of stress, negative and positive emotions on eating behavior. *Biological Psychology, 131*, 54–62. https://doi.org/10.1016/j.biopsycho.2016.09.002

Reichenberger, J., Richard, A., Smyth, J.M., Fischer, D., Pollatos, O., & Blechert, J. (2018). It's craving time: Time of day effects on momentary hunger and food craving in daily life. *Nutrition, 55*, 15–20. https://doi.org/10.1016/j.nut.2018.03.048

Rodgers, R.F., Fuller-Tyszkiewicz, M., Holmes, M., Skouteris, H., & Broadbent, J. (2018). When does behavior follow intent? Relationships between trait level dietary restraint and daily eating behaviors. *Appetite, 120*, 449–455. https://doi.org/10.1016/j.appet.2017.09.030

Schaefer, L.M., Smith, K.E., Anderson, L.M., Cao, L., Crosby, R.D., Engel, S.G., Crow, S.J., Peterson, C.B., & Wonderlich, S.A. (2020). The role of affect in the maintenance of binge-eating disorder: Evidence from an ecological momentary assessment study. *Journal of Abnormal Psychology, 129*(4), 387–396. https://doi.org/10.1037/abn0000517

Schembre, S.M., Liao, Y., O'Connor, S.G., Hingle, M.D., Shen, S.E., Hamoy, K.G., Huh, J., Dunton, G.F., Weiss, R., Thomson, C.A., & Boushey, C.J. (2018). Mobile ecological momentary diet assessment methods for behavioral research: systematic review. *JMIR mHealth and uHealth, 6*(11), e11170.

Shiffman, S., Stone, A.A., & Hufford, M.R. (2008). Ecological momentary assessment. *Annual Review of Clinical Psychology, 4*, 1–32. https://doi.org/10.1146/annurev.clinpsy.3.022806.091415

Smith, K.E., Mason, T.B., Schaefer, L.M., Anderson, L.M., Hazzard, V.M., Crosby, R.D., Engel, S.G., Crow, S.J., Wonderlich, S.A., & Peterson, C.B. (2022). Micro-level de-coupling of negative affect and binge eating in relationship to macro-level outcomes in binge eating disorder treatment. *Psychological Medicine, 52*(1), 140–148.

Smith, K.E., O'Connor, S.M., Mason, T.B., Wang, S., Dzubur, E., Crosby, R.D., Wonderlich, S.A., Salvy, S.J., Feda, D.M., & Roemmich, J.N. (2021). Associations between objective physical activity and emotional eating among adiposity-discordant siblings using ecological momentary assessment and accelerometers. *Pediatric Obesity, 16*(3), e12720.

Smyth, J.M., Wonderlich, S.A., Heron, K.E., Sliwinski, M.J., Crosby, R.D., Mitchell, J.E., & Engel, S.G. (2007). Daily and momentary mood and stress are associated with binge eating and vomiting in bulimia nervosa patients in the natural environment. *Journal of Consulting and Clinical Psychology, 75*(4), 629–638. https://doi.org/10.1037/0022-006X.75.4.629

Thomas, J.G., Doshi, S., Crosby, R.D., & Lowe, M.R. (2011). Ecological momentary assessment of obesogenic eating behavior: Combining person-specific and environmental predictors. *Obesity, 19*(8), 1574–1579. https://doi.org/10.1038/oby.2010.335

Zunker, C., Peterson, C.B., Crosby, R.D., Cao, L., Engel, S.G., Mitchell, J.E., & Wonderlich, S.A. (2011). Ecological momentary assessment of bulimia nervosa: Does dietary restriction predict binge eating? *Behaviour Research and Therapy, 49*(10), 714–717. https://doi.org/10.1016/j.brat.2011.06.006

Chapter 19

Behavioral Tasks for Measuring and Changing Reactions to Food

Sarah Masterton and Andrew Jones

Department of Psychology, University of Liverpool, UK

Introduction

While the development of overweight and obesity is linked to the excess consumption of energy-dense, highly palatable food items, there is considerable variability in body weight status across the population. It is clear that the obesogenic environment can influence food choice and consumption behaviors. However, not all individuals respond in the same way to their environment and the food cues within. Subsequently, not all individuals will develop overweight and obesity. Examination of individual variations in responsivity to food cues is critical and has led to the development of behavioral tasks that attempt to both measure and modify individual responses to food cues, known as cognitive biases and cognitive bias modification. This chapter aims to outline three commonly used behavioral tasks utilized within appetitive contexts (focusing on biases related to approach, attention, and inhibition behaviors) and evaluate their use as tools of change and measurement. First, however, we briefly discuss the theoretical underpinnings of cognitive biases.

Cognitive Biases and Dual Process Theory

Cognitive Bias and Cognitive Bias Modification (CBM) paradigms are broadly based on theories of dual-processing which state that (un)healthy food consumption and related behaviors are regulated by two distinct but related processing systems: automatic and reflective processes (Hofmann et al., 2008; Strack & Deutsch, 2004). Automatic processes are somewhat fast and nonconscious, activated by memory formations that are consolidated and driven by the rewarding and pleasurable aspects of food consumption (e.g., "in the past I have received pleasure from eating chocolate cake, therefore I should act to get a slice now"). In isolation, these processes require little cognitive effort, which can free up resources for other demanding tasks, but can lead to "eating without thinking". Reflective processes on the other hand are slow, deliberate, and effortful. They are driven by our longer-term health goals (e.g., "I should not get a slice of cake now as I am trying to reduce my weight"). These dual-process systems are prevalent throughout psychology, often under different names (e.g., System 1 and System 2; automatic and volitional, etc.,), in an attempt to explain several behavioral outcomes (e.g., addiction: Weirs et al., 2007).

Both intra- and inter-individual differences in eating behaviors are postulated to be a result of conflict between these two processes, with automatic and reflective processes competing to regulate behavioral outcomes, and the stronger of the two processes determining food consumption behaviors at any given point in time (Hofmann et al., 2009). While understanding dual-process models may help to predict behavioral responses to stimuli (e.g., an individual having a weaker reflective system unable to resist the immediate pleasure of the chocolate cake), they have also informed dietary interventions which attempt to either target reflective (e.g., attempting to increase the capacity of executive functions involved in reflective processes) or automatic (e.g., attempting to change or weaken the associations that drive automatic processes) processes to support reducing unhealthy food consumption (Jones et al., 2018).

In order to be able to both measure these processes and create novel interventions which target these processes, behavioral tasks need to be developed that operationalize these cognitive biases. Below, we focus on three of the most researched cognitive biases and discuss their measurement, and modification in the eating behavior literature: approach bias, attentional bias, and inhibition bias.

Approach Bias

Approach biases refer to the process of food cues triggering an automatic approach behavior towards the cue (which is relatively faster than an avoidance behavior towards the same cue: Wiers et al., 2013). Typically, approach biases are measured using tasks that involve the presentation of food (and control) images, and participants are required to approach or avoid these images using a motor response (often termed approach-avoidance tasks, AATs). Generally, participants observe an equal number of food and nonfood images and for 50 % of trials make an "approach" response, and 50 % of trials make an "avoid" response to each.

There are several variations of this design. The Stimulus-Response Compatibility task requires participants to move an on-screen manikin towards or away from food-related and nonfood-related images, by pressing a key on a keyboard (Brignell et al, 2009).

A second variation of the task (the approach and avoid task) uses a joystick as the input mechanism to increase face validity. To approach the images, participants are required to pull the joystick towards their body, whereas to avoid the images participants are required to push the joystick away from their body. Animation of the images on the screen reflects the action initiated by participants, with approached images zooming in and getting larger (simulating movement *towards* the participant), and avoided images zooming out and getting smaller (simulating movement *away* from the participant). These animations are thought to further increase face validity by emphasizing the action taken (Stacy & Wiers, 2010; Wiers et al., 2013; Figure 19.1).

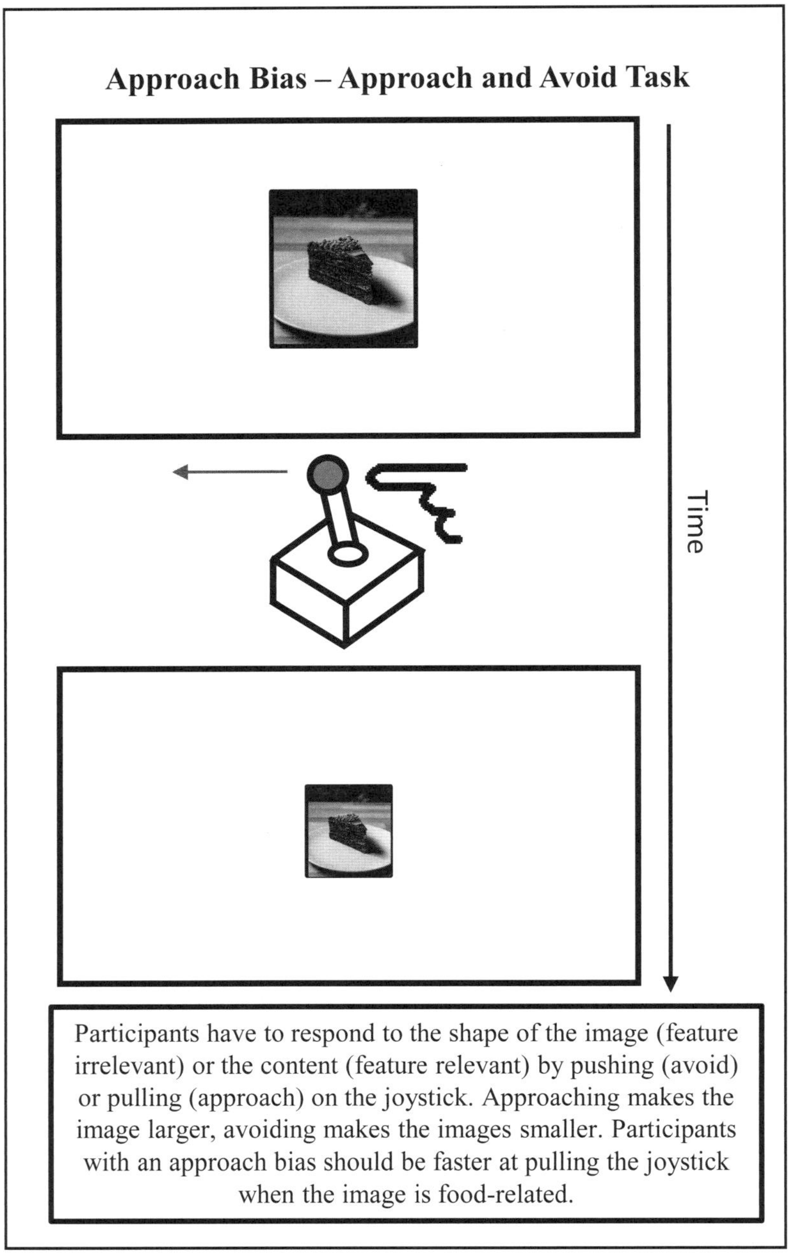

Figure 19.1. Schematic of a typical trial in the approach and avoidance task

When using these tasks to assess approach biases for unhealthy foods, a bias towards unhealthy foods is identified when "approach" responses for one image type are faster than "avoid" responses (i.e., participants pull the joystick more quickly than push it away when food images are presented: Wiers et al., 2013).

Previous work has discovered that participants with obesity demonstrated approach biases for food using a joystick AAT (Mehl et al, 2019), and also in individuals of normal weight in a novel touch screen AAT (Kahveci et al. 2020). Research has also demonstrated positive associations between approach biases for food and food craving using an alternative approach bias measure (Kemps et al., 2013). However, Meule et al. (2020) demonstrated that that approach biases were not influenced by hunger or food deprivation. Finally, Paslakis et al., (2017) discovered that participants with obesity and binge eating disorder showed an avoidance bias for low-calorie food cues compared to high-calorie foods. These findings suggest that the examination of approach biases may allow researchers and clinicians to predict (or target) undesirable responses to food cues. However, Meule et al. (2020) suggest that overall, findings are inconsistent.

While the interpretation of approach responses in these tasks and across studies is relatively consistent, there are differences in relation to the task designs which can influence exactly what is being measured. While some studies present images of food and ask participants to respond to the content of the images (feature relevant tasks: i.e., push the joystick away for foods, pull the joystick towards you for objects), others ask participants to respond to stimulus irrelevant features when determining the required response (feature irrelevant tasks: i.e., the orientation of the image, e.g., portrait or landscape). While it is argued that a feature irrelevant (more indirect) task minimizes demand characteristics and reflects more automatic responses to food cues (Rinck & Becker, 2007), more recent work has suggested that robust approach biases are contingent on image valence, with stronger approach biases detected in the feature relevant version of the task (Lender et al., 2018). Previous research investigating AAT within alcohol contexts discovered that the feature relevant feature AAT was a reliable predictor of alcohol consumption and hazardous drinking behaviors, unlike the feature irrelevant version of the task (Kersbergen et al., 2015), however, it has been argued that the lack of naturalistic movements in approach bias tasks (i.e., participants do not have to "reach" or "grasp" for items) may threaten the translation of these measures to real-world food consumption behaviors (Meule et al., 2020). The predictive validity of approach bias tasks (in relation to food behavior) is currently understudied and should be a focus of future research.

Modifying Approach Biases to Change Food Behaviors

AATs have also been adapted for interventions that aim to reduce approach biases for unhealthy food items (known as approach-avoidance training). While approach bias tasks employ a 50 % approach, 50 % avoid contingency for each type of stimuli presented in order to *measure* biases accurately, these percentages can be manipulated to *train* participants to "avoid" target stimuli (i.e., 90 % of unhealthy food images would be accompanied by an "avoid" joystick movement, see Wiers et al., 2010) and reduce approach bias for these specific items. Over time and through associative learning, participants are thought to ascertain that food-related cues are more likely to signal an avoidance response.

There is laboratory evidence to support the use of approach-avoidance training to reduce approach bias for foods, with work by Schumacher et al., (2016) demonstrating that training participants to avoid chocolate stimuli (by "pushing" chocolate images away during a training phase) resulted in a reduced bias towards chocolate, but also reduced consumption of chocolate items in a subsequent taste test, compared to a group of individuals who were trained to approach chocolate. While promising, these results are not necessarily consistent across studies, with work by Dickson et al. (2016) finding that while training reduced approach biases for chocolate stimuli, there were no significant differences in consumption of chocolate between "approach" and "avoid" training groups.

Systematic reviews have concluded that overall approach–avoidance training positively influenced approach biases across various appetitive stimuli and was an effective behavior change technique (Kakoschke et al., 2017), however, there was substantial variation across studies in terms of effect size – ranging between $d=0.37$ (Schumacher et al., 2016) and $d=1.11$ (Brockmeyer et al., 2015) for studies measuring eating behaviors. Researchers have questioned the validity of this conclusion within the eating domain, calling for suitably powered studies with appropriately designed control groups (Becker et al., 2018). While not a problem unique to approach–avoidance training, the use of reverse contingency control groups across the literature (where participants are trained to approach unhealthy foods rather than avoid unhealthy foods) may inflate between-group differences, resulting in overestimations in relation to training efficacy (Jones et al., 2018). Finally, whilst training appears to consistently reduce approach bias for unhealthy foods, this does not necessarily translate to food-related behavioral change: meta-analytic work by Aulbach et al. (2019) revealed that although implicit process interventions resulted in a small and significant cumulative effect (Hedges' $g=-0.17$) on dietary outcomes, this effect was not significant after correcting for publication bias and only a minority of studies reported dietary changes post-training.

Attentional Bias

Attentional bias refers to the tendency for food-related cues to capture and hold visual attention (Field et al., 2016). Several tasks have been developed to measure attentional bias. The emotional Stroop task presents food-related words (e.g., "chocolate," "crisps," "burger") and control-words (e.g., "wardrobe," "chair," "ceiling") in various colors. Participants are asked to identify the color of the word whilst ignoring the content. If participants are relatively faster at identifying the control-word colors versus the food-related-word colors, this is inferred as the content of the food-words grabbing the attention and slowing the color naming process (Field et al., 2016). Alternatively, the visual probe task involves presenting participants with a food-related image and a non-food (control) image concurrently on screen. After a fixed duration (e.g., 500 ms), both images disappear, and one is replaced by a probe (e.g., a small dot or arrow). Participants are instructed to respond to the location or the content of the probe on the screen using a keyboard (Figure 19.2). Attentional bias is identified by faster response latencies for trials where the probe is presented in the spatial location previously occupied by the target stimuli (i.e., food image) in comparison to trials where the probe appears behind the control/comparison stimulus. That is, if a bias is present participants' attention would already be directed to the location of the target stimuli, which would result in a faster response time (Werthmann et al., 2015). However, it is also possible to directly measure attention in which gaze durations to each stimulus during their onscreen presentation are calculated, using eye-tracking technology (Hardman et al., 2013).

Attentional biases for food cues have been linked to various appetitive measures, with meta-analytic work by Hardman et al. (2021), demonstrating small (yet robust) associations between food attentional bias and craving ($r=.13$), hunger ($r=.05$), and food intake

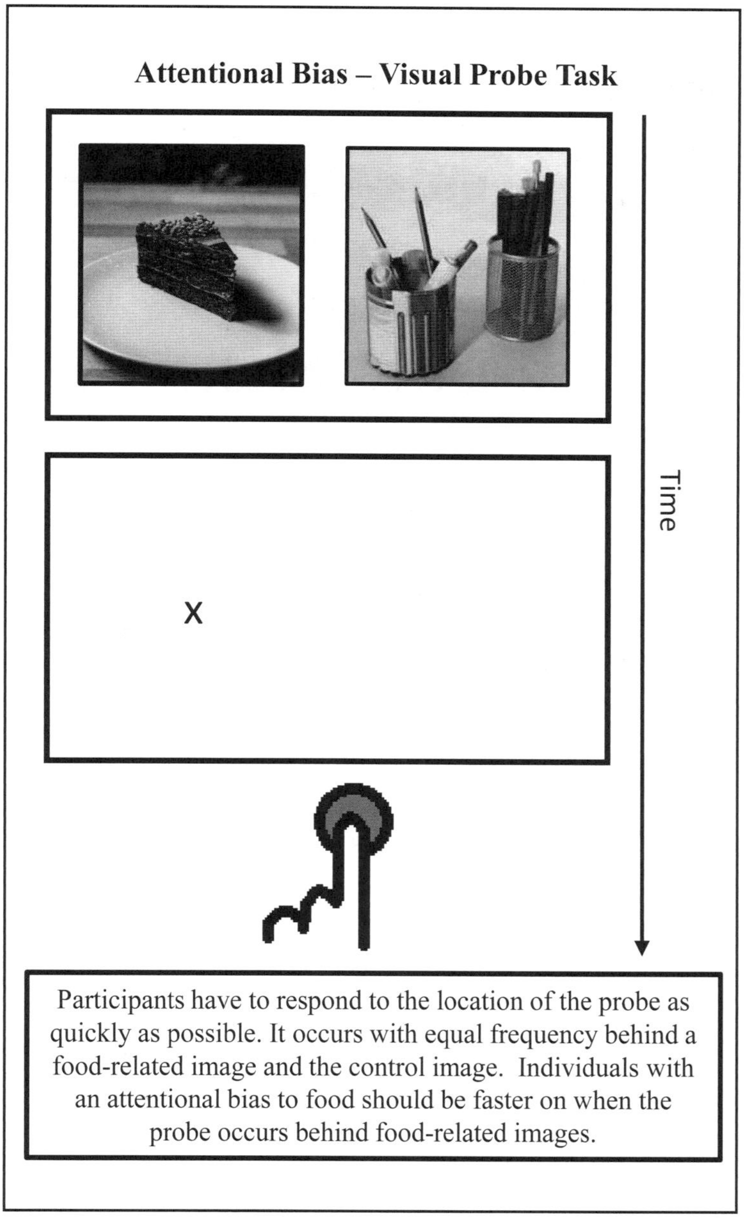

Figure 19.2. Schematic of a typical trial in the visual probe task

(r=.09). Despite this, there is evidence to suggest that these biases may not be related to body mass index (BMI) or bodyweight, with a review by Hagan et al. (2020) finding no evidence to support differences between individuals with overweight/obesity and healthy weight in terms of attentional bias for food stimuli (as measured by both visual probe and Stroop tasks).

There are wider concerns in relation to the nature of attentional bias measures and their reliability. Work by Field et al. (2016) argues that attentional bias is not a trait variable, but a dynamic construct. It is hypothesized that attentional biases are influenced by incentive value and motivational conflict at the time of assessment (in addition to contextual factors; Field et al., 2016), which may account for some of the poor reliability observed within attentional bias tasks (Rodebaugh et al., 2016). It is suggested that using more dynamic data analysis and assessment methods (such as trial-level bias scores or ecological momentary assessment designs; Shiffman et al., 2008) would allow researchers to capture rapid changes in attentional bias, increasing measurement reliability and predictive utility (Hardman et al., 2021). However, few studies to date have applied these measures to food-related attentional bias contexts.

Modifying Attentional Biases to Change Food Behavior

Similar to AATs, the visual probe task has been modified in an attempt to reduce attentional biases for target stimuli (i.e., unhealthy food cues), known as attentional bias modification (ABM). For the intervention variation of the task, the probe appears in the same spatial location as the control (or neutral) cue on a large majority of trials, which is thought to train participants to "avoid" attending to the food cues (as the probe rarely appears in that location; Wiers et al., 2013). Work by Kemps et al. (2016) discovered that participants with overweight and obesity trained to "avoid" food cues had decreased attentional bias for food items, and more recent meta-analytic work has reported that ABM training appears to positively influence eating behavior (g=.19 [95% CI: .06–.32]), with relatively low heterogeneity between studies (indicating between study effects are relatively consistent; Yang et al., 2019).

Although these findings are promising, the mechanisms through which ABM influences eating behavior are relatively unclear, as reductions to food attentional biases posttraining are not consistently observed across studies, despite positive behavioral outcomes (Boutelle et al., 2016). It has also been suggested that perceived improvements to bias (i.e., reaction time increases) may be the result of task practice, with work by Franja et al., (2021) discovering that response times significantly decreased for both food and animal stimuli (indicating decreased bias) after 14 days (with no intervention). Additionally, the indirect nature of reaction time tasks mean that participants may not actually be directing attention towards or away from cues as instructed, instead focusing on the presentation of the probe, which may further explain some variability in attentional biases and inconsistent training outcomes (Liu et al., 2021). Another consideration relates to the longevity of training effects: while Kemps et al. (2016) discovered weekly ABM training reduced attentional biases for food in "avoid" training groups both 24 hours and 1 week post-training for individuals with overweight and obesity, the subsequent impact on direct measures of food behavior was not measured, and the lack of association between BMI/weight change and attentional biases (Hardman et al., 2021) raises questions in relation to the use of training within intervention contexts. These findings (combined with the dynamic and context-dependent nature of attentional biases; Field et al., 2016) suggest that more research is needed to fully understand the potential for ABM in long term behavior change strategies.

Inhibitory Biases

Inhibitory biases refer to the (in)ability to inhibit behavior in response to food-related cues (Jones et al., 2018). These inhibitory biases have been linked to the existence of approach biases, as individuals cannot approach and inhibit responses towards appetitive cues simultaneously. However, the difference in their operationalization lies in that whilst approach biases measure fast automatic approach responses, inhibitory biases measure the failure to inhibit these fast motor responses. Inhibitory biases are measured using inhibitory control tasks such as the stop signal and go/no-go tasks, with food- and nonfood related cues embedded (Verbruggen & Logan, 2008). In the stop signal task participants are required to make a speeded categorization motor response (e.g., press left if you see a food image, press right if you see a nonfood image). On a majority of trials, usually 75 % or greater, this response is uninterrupted. However, on a minority of trials a stop signal occurs after the stimulus presentation. Participants are required to inhibit or override their speeded response when this occurs. In the go/no-go tasks participants observe a stimulus appear on the screen and are instructed to respond if it is a "go stimulus" or not to respond if it is a "no-go" stimulus. Like the AAT, the go and no-go stimuli may be feature relevant (respond if you see a nonfood image, do not respond if you see a food image) or feature irrelevant (respond if you see a portrait image, do not respond if you see a landscape image; Figure 19.3).

In general, both these tasks conceptualize inhibitory biases as the failure to inhibit a response in the presence of food-related images, or in the case of the stop signal task the "stop signal reaction time" is computed as an unobserved latency of inhibition (Verbruggen & Logan, 2008). Across these various outcome measures, research supports the role of inhibitory control in food choice and consumption: work by Houben et al. (2014) discovered an association between poor food-related inhibitory control abilities and BMI, and Meule et al. (2014) found that lower inhibitory performance predicted craving (particularly for items related to desire for food and lack of control over consumption).

While the use of various tasks (and outcome measures) allows for some researcher flexibility in relation to study design, the generalization of results across both task paradigms and outcome measures is potentially problematic. Work by Verbruggen and Logan (2008) highlighted that different tasks may place more emphasis on different elements of response inhibition (i.e., either top-down - conscious decisions to withhold - or bottom-up - automatic withholding of responses), which would influence both task performance and interpretation of results. These concerns have been echoed by other researchers, with increasing calls for the standardization of task paradigms across studies in addition to the careful interpretation of task performance based on the outcome measure used (Meule, 2017).

Modifying Inhibitory Biases to Change Food Behavior

Cue-inhibitory control training (cue-ICT: sometimes referred to as motor response training) is an established intervention paradigm that attempts to train participants to automatically engage inhibitory control in response to food cues by forming associations between food cues and the engagement of inhibitory control (Jones et al., 2018). This involves the completion of inhibitory control tasks, designed to ensure that target stim-

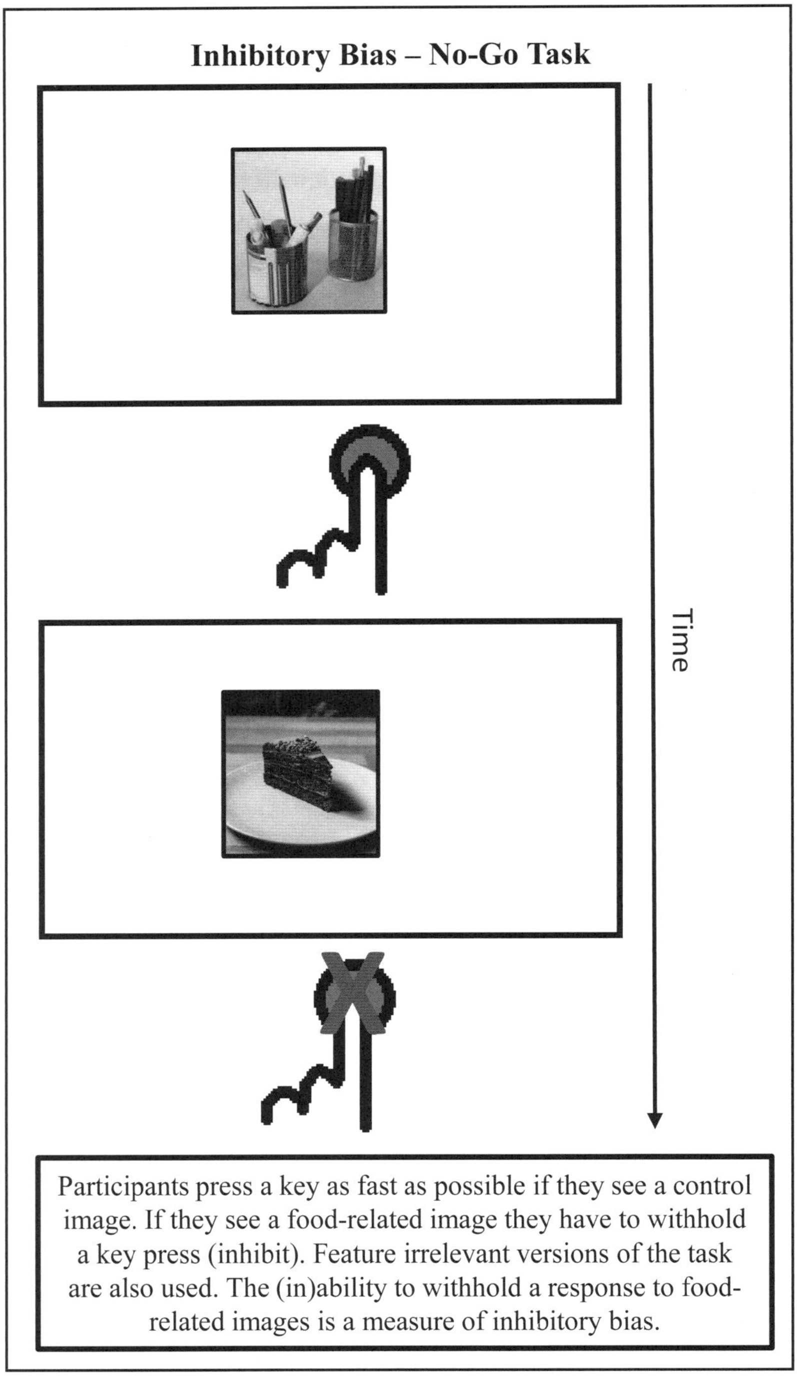

Figure 19.3. Schematic of typical trials in the go/no-go task

uli (e.g., unhealthy food cues) are disproportionately paired with a no-go cue or stop signal. Meta-analytic work has supported the use of cue-ICT within appetitive contexts, with Jones et al. (2016) revealing that a single session leads to a small yet robust reduction in food consumption in the laboratory, supporting earlier meta-analytic work (Allom et al., 2016) which discovered a small ($d = 0.38$) but homogenous effect of training on behavior across various health behavior contexts. Outside of the laboratory, there has been some evidence to suggest repeated cue-ICT can lead to reductions in weight loss (Allom & Mullan, 2015; Lawrence et al, 2015; Veling et al, 2014). However, not all studies report significant training effects, with work by Bongers et al. (2018) discovering no between-group differences in ad-libitum chocolate consumption post-cue-ICT, and Carbine et al. (2021) finding that cue-ICT had no influence on caloric intake or weight loss over a 12-week period.

To investigate these inconsistent training outcomes, Carbine et al. (2019) performed a *p*-curve analysis for cue-ICT research. When performing a *p*-curve analysis, researchers plot the distribution of published (and significant) *p*-values within a particular research area and compare these to expected distributions (no effect, true effect, selective reporting; Simonsohn et al., 2014) to assess evidential value (i.e., the presence of a true underlying effect). The analysis revealed that while there was some evidence to support the existence of a true underlying effect there was also evidence to support selective reporting (i.e., where only statistically significant results are reported). While an updated analysis provided increased support for evidential value (Veling et al., 2020), the high proportion of published *p*-values close to .05 still raises questions related to the true effectiveness of cue-ICT in food contexts, highlighting the need for higher-powered studies in the area (Carbine et al., 2019). A lack of standardized training paradigms further complicates evaluations of training efficacy (Jones et al., 2018), and there is also evidence to suggest that the *type* of training selected can influence reported outcomes, with larger effect sizes observed for go/no-go in comparison to stop signal training paradigms (Allom et al., 2016; Jones et al., 2016), despite these tasks being used to target the same cognitive bias.

Limitations and Wider Considerations of the Evidence Base

Control Groups and Standardization of Paradigms

A significant limitation of many of these modification paradigms relates to the utilization of inappropriate control groups in intervention studies. While control groups in CBM research should implement active control conditions (where participants respond and withhold responses to stimuli equally to not influence biases: Jones et al., 2018), this is often not the case, with many researchers implementing reversed contingency groups (i.e., for cue-ICT, instead of responding to 0 % of unhealthy food items, participants respond to of 100 % unhealthy food items) as control groups. This may have the unintended consequence of training participants to respond to unhealthy food items, increasing cognitive biases towards these items and inflating between-group differences (Jones et al., 2016). Recent work investigating AAT design has demonstrated that participants in an "avoid" training group (90 % probes followed by control image) displayed decreased attentional bias in comparison to an "attend" (90 % probes followed by chocolate image) training group who displayed an increased attentional bias for chocolate stimuli (Kemps & Tiggemann, 2021) supporting the idea of between-group inflations when using reverse contingency control groups. Whilst this is interesting from a theoretical perspective, it raises ethical concerns to have control groups who are being trained towards unhealthy foods should these interventions become clinically implemented. Future work should ensure appropriate control groups which do not directly influence cognitive biases are implemented. Results and conclusions should be interpreted with caution where no such group exists.

A further complication relates to the lack of standardization of both measurement and intervention tasks, and stimuli used within. While some researchers use images of unrelated stimuli in control trials (e.g., Kakoschke et al., 2015), others use healthy food images as control stimuli (e.g., Lawrence et al., 2015), which may have implications for task performance and outcome measures involving food choice. There are also issues in relation to the accessibility and transparency of task stimuli within CBM research: not all studies specify the type of stimuli used in control tasks (e.g., stating "neutral" images were used), which can make building on previous work difficult, and direct replication of studies impossible (Pennington et al., 2021).

In relation to CBM as a training paradigm, although most studies ensure that a high percentage of food cues are avoided/inhibited to, there is some variability between studies. For cue-ICT, the cue-inhibition contingency can vary between 87.5 % (e.g., Adams et al., 2017) and 100 % (e.g., Carbine et al., 2021), which has implications for task performance and outcomes (Jones et al., 2016). These task variations complicate attempts to evaluate training (and measure) efficacy, and further work is needed to develop standardized paradigms (and task stimuli) to be used in future research.

Individual Variability, Personalization, and Reliability

Although dual-process models have informed CBM training paradigms, a key prediction of these models is that not all individuals experience cognitive biases to food stimuli, hence the variation in food behaviors across the population (Jones et al., 2018). While the use of CBM tasks as measurement tools can help to differentiate participants with specific biases, questions have been raised in relation to the reliability of these measures (e.g., Becker et al., 2018; Pennington et al., 2021) and the measures are not often used to identify individuals who would benefit most from a specific type of intervention (e.g., participants who display high approach biases for food are not necessarily targeted and recruited for AAT interventions). It is argued that targeting these individuals specifically may improve intervention outcomes (as they possess the specific cognitive bias being targeted; Jones et al., 2018). It has also been suggested that participant-level factors external to training (such as motivation to change behavior; Jones et al., 2016) may influence CBM intervention outcomes, however, research investigating these factors in isolation is limited.

A second important consideration relates to the type of stimuli used within training. While the majority of training paradigms adopt a one size fits all approach (i.e., training participants to not respond to unhealthy food items; e.g., Lawrence et al., 2015), some researchers focus on specific categories of food (e.g., chocolate; Schumacher et al., 2016) to measure and manipulate cognitive biases. Previous work investigating alcohol-related biases discovered that using personalized stimuli (i.e., asking participants to select their favorite alcoholic drink and using images of this drink during tasks) resulted in increased internal reliability for the visual probe task (Christiansen et al., 2015) and in the eating domain, work by Kahveci et al. (2020) found that desire to eat *specific* food items predicted participants approach biases for these items, independently of general desire to eat. Future work should further investigate the impact of personalization within CBM paradigms to develop effective interventions to support behavioral change.

A final issue in relation to the use of CBM paradigms is the (un)reliability of these tasks within eating behavior contexts. Work by Ens et al. (2019) discovered that there is considerable variability in reliability between measures of attentional bias for food items, with measures of bias ranging between poor (e.g., gaze direction) and acceptable (e.g., reaction times) in terms of internal and test–retest reliability. Franja et al. (2021) discovered that correlations were poor between different versions of the visual probe task, and the wide variety of measures (and scoring strategies) utilized across the research area further complicate attempts to assess reliability, with work by Vervoort et al. (2021) suggesting that some reliability indices may be reflective of consistent response speeds to stimuli rather than attentional biases. Finally, Kahveci et al. (2020) demonstrated low-to-acceptable reliability in their novel AAT. Overall, the lack of robust reliability of these tasks is problematic (particularly where CBM tasks are used within behavior change contexts) as if observed results are not reliable (and standardized measures cannot be agreed upon), the potential effectiveness and feasibility of long term CBM intervention programs is difficult to ascertain.

Conclusions

Behavioral tasks present an alternative to traditional laboratory assessments of behavior, while also offering a noninvasive intervention strategy to reduce unhealthy eating behaviors. Despite their promise, there are issues across the literature in relation to the standardization of tasks, the reliability of measures and the poor utilization of control groups, which makes it difficult to draw overall conclusions in relation to task and intervention efficacy. Additional research is needed to address these issues and support the development of optimum paradigms to reliably measure and manipulate cognitive biases within food behavior contexts.

References

Adams, R.C., Lawrence, N.S., Verbruggen, F., & Chambers, C.D. (2017). Training response inhibition to reduce food consumption: Mechanisms, stimulus specificity and appropriate training protocols. *Appetite, 109*, 11–23. https://doi.org/10.1016/j.appet.2016.11.014

Allom, V., & Mullan, B. (2015). Two inhibitory control training interventions designed to improve eating behaviour and determine mechanisms of change. *Appetite, 89*, 282–290. https://doi.org/10.1016/j.appet.2015.02.022

Allom, V., Mullan, B., & Hagger, M. (2016). Does inhibitory control training improve health behaviour? A meta-analysis. *Health Psychology Review, 10*(2), 168–186. https://doi.org/10.1080/17437199.2015.1051078

Aulbach, M.B., Knittle, K., & Haukkala, A. (2019). Implicit process interventions in eating behaviour: A meta-analysis examining mediators and moderators. *Health Psychology Review, 13*(2), 179–208. https://doi.org/10.1080/17437199.2019.1571933

Becker, D., Jostmann, N. B., & Holland, R. W. (2018). Does approach bias modification really work in the eating domain? A commentary on Kakoschke et al. (2017). *Addictive Behaviors, 77*, 293–294. https://doi.org/10.1016/j.addbeh.2017.02.025

Bongers, P., Houben, K., & Jansen, A. (2018). Double up! Examining the effects of adding inhibition training to food cue exposure in chocolate-loving female students. *Appetite, 121*, 154–162. https://doi.org/10.1016/j.appet.2017.11.096

Boutelle, K. N., Monreal, T., Strong, D. R., & Amir, N. (2016). An open trial evaluating an attention bias modification program for overweight adults who binge eat. *Journal of Behavior Therapy and Experimental Psychiatry, 52*, 138–146. https://doi.org/10.1016/j.jbtep.2016.04.005

Brignell, C., Griffiths, T., Bradley, B. P., & Mogg, K. (2009). Attentional and approach biases for pictorial food cues. Influence of external eating. *Appetite, 52*(2), 299–306. https://doi.org/10.1016/j.appet.2008.10.007

Brockmeyer, T., Hahn, C., Reetz, C., Schmidt, U., & Friederich, H. C. (2015). Approach bias and cue reactivity towards food in people with high versus low levels of food craving. *Appetite, 95*, 197–202. https://doi.org/10.1016/j.appet.2015.07.013

Carbine, K. A., & Larson, M. J. (2019). Quantifying the presence of evidential value and selective reporting in food-related inhibitory control training: A p-curve analysis. *Health Psychology Review, 13*, 318–353. https://doi.org/10.1080/17437199.2019.1622144

Carbine, K. A., Muir, A. M., Allen, W. D., LeCheminant, J. D., Baldwin, S. A., Jensen, C. D., Kirwan, C. B., & Larson, M. J. (2021). Does inhibitory control training reduce weight and caloric intake in adults with overweight and obesity? A pre-registered, randomized controlled event-related potential (ERP) study. *Behaviour Research and Therapy, 136*, 103784. https://doi.org/10.1016/j.brat.2020.103784

Christiansen, P., Mansfield, R., Duckworth, J., Field, M., & Jones, A. (2015). Internal reliability of the alcohol-related visual probe task is increased by utilising personalised stimuli and eye-tracking. *Drug and Alcohol Dependence, 155*, 170–174. https://doi.org/10.1016/j.drugalcdep.2015.07.672

Dickson, H., Kavanagh, D. J., & MacLeod, C. (2016). The pulling power of chocolate: Effects of approach-avoidance training on approach bias and consumption. *Appetite, 99*, 46–51. https://doi.org/10.1016/j.appet.2015.12.026

Ens, W. van, Schmidt, U., Campbell, I. C., Roefs, A., & Werthmann, J. (2019). Test-retest reliability of attention bias for food: Robust eye-tracking and reaction time indices. *Appetite, 136*, 86–92. https://doi.org/10.1016/j.appet.2019.01.020

Field, M., Werthmann, J., Franken, I., Hofmann, W., Hogarth, L., & Roefs, A. (2016). The role of attentional bias in obesity and addiction. *Health Psychology, 35*(8), 767–780. https://doi.org/10.1037/hea0000405

Franja, S., McCrae, A. E., Jahnel, T., Gearhardt, A. N., & Ferguson, S. G. (2021). Measuring food-related attentional bias. *Frontiers in Psychology, 12*, Article 629115. https://doi.org/10.3389/fpsyg.2021.629115

Hagan, K. E., Alasmar, A., Exum, A., Chinn, B., & Forbush, K. T. (2020). A systematic review and meta-analysis of attentional bias toward food in individuals with overweight and obesity. *Appetite, 151*, 104710. https://doi.org/10.1016/j.appet.2020.104710

Hardman, C. A., Jones, A., Burton, S., Duckworth, J. J., McGale, L. S., Mead, B. R., Roberts, C. A., Field, M., & Werthmann, J. (2021). Food-related attentional bias and its associations with appetitive motivation and body weight: A systematic review and meta-analysis. *Appetite, 157*, 104986. https://doi.org/10.1016/j.appet.2020.104986

Hardman, C. A., Rogers, P. J., Etchells, K. A., Houstoun, K. V., & Munafò, M. R. (2013). The effects of food-related attentional bias training on appetite and food intake. *Appetite, 71*, 295–300. https://doi.org/10.1016/j.appet.2013.08.021

Hofmann, W., Friese, M., & Strack, F. (2009). Impulse and self-control from a dual-systems perspective. *Perspectives on Psychological Science, 4*(2), 162–176. https://doi.org/10.1111/j.1745-6924.2009.01116.x

Hofmann, W., Friese, M., & Wiers, R. W. (2008). Impulsive versus reflective influences on health behavior: A theoretical framework and empirical review. *Health Psychology Review, 2*(2), 111–137, https://doi.org/10.1080/17437190802617668

Houben, K., Nederkoorn, C., & Jansen, A. (2014). Eating on impulse: The relation between overweight and food-specific inhibitory control. *Obesity, 22*(5), E6–E8. https://doi.org/10.1002/oby.20670

Jones, A., Di Lemma, L.C., Robinson, E., Christiansen, P., Nolan, S., Tudur-Smith, C., & Field, M. (2016). Inhibitory control training for appetitive behaviour change: A meta-analytic investigation of mechanisms of action and moderators of effectiveness. *Appetite, 97*, 16–28. https://doi.org/10.1016/j.appet.2015.11.013

Jones, A., Hardman, C.A., Lawrence, N., & Field, M. (2018). Cognitive training as a potential treatment for overweight and obesity: A critical review of the evidence. *Appetite, 124*, 50–67. https://doi.org/10.1016/j.appet.2017.05.032

Kahveci, S., Meule, A., Lender, A., & Blechert, J. (2020). Food approach bias is moderated by the desire to eat specific foods. *Appetite, 154*, 104758. https://doi.org/10.1016/j.appet.2020.104758

Kakoschke, N., Kemps, E., & Tiggemann, M. (2015). Combined effects of cognitive bias for food cues and poor inhibitory control on unhealthy food intake. *Appetite, 87*, 358–364. https://doi.org/10.1016/j.appet.2015.01.004

Kakoschke, N., Kemps, E., & Tiggemann, M. (2017). Approach bias modification training and consumption: A review of the literature. *Addictive Behaviors, 64*, 21–28. https://doi.org/10.1016/j.addbeh.2016.08.007

Kemps, E., & Tiggemann, M. (2021). Attentional bias modification for chocolate: Sham-n training as a new control group. *PloS One, 16*(11), e0260294. https://doi.org/10.1371/journal.pone.0260294

Kemps, E., Tiggemann, M., & Hollitt, S. (2016). Longevity of attentional bias modification effects for food cues in overweight and obese individuals. *Psychology & Health, 31*(1), 115–129. https://doi.org/10.1080/08870446.2015.1077251

Kemps, E., Tiggemann, M., Martin, R., & Elliott, M. (2013). Implicit approach-avoidance associations for craved food cues. *Journal of Experimental Psychology: Applied, 19*(1), 30–38. https://doi.org/10.1037/a0031626

Kersbergen, I., Woud, M.L., & Field, M. (2015). The validity of different measures of automatic alcohol action tendencies. *Psychology of Addictive Behaviors, 29*(1), 225–230. https://doi.org/10.1037/adb0000009

Lawrence, N.S., O'Sullivan, J., Parslow, D., Javaid, M., Adams, R.C., Chambers, C.D., Kos, K., & Verbruggen, F. (2015). Training response inhibition to food is associated with weight loss and reduced energy intake. *Appetite, 95*, 17–28. https://doi.org/10.1016/j.appet.2015.06.009

Lender, A., Meule, A., Rinck, M., Brockmeyer, T., & Blechert, J. (2018). Measurement of food-related approach-avoidance biases: Larger biases when food stimuli are task relevant. *Appetite, 125*, 42–47. https://doi.org/10.1016/j.appet.2018.01.032

Liu, Y., Roefs, A., & Nederkoorn, C. (2021). Fluctuations in attentional bias for food and the role of executive control. *Appetite, 168*, 105761. https://doi.org/10.1016/j.appet.2021.105761

Mehl, N., Morys, F., Villringer, A., & Horstmann, A. (2019). Unhealthy yet avoidable – how cognitive bias modification alters behavioural and brain responses to food cues in individuals with obesity. *Nutrients, 11*, 874. https://doi.org/10.3390/nu11040874

Meule, A. (2017). Reporting and interpreting task performance in go/no-go affective shifting tasks. *Frontiers in Psychology, 8,* Article 701. https://doi.org/10.3389/fpsyg.2017.00701

Meule, A., Lutz, A.P., Vögele, C., & Kübler, A. (2014). Impulsive reactions to food-cues predict subsequent food craving. *Eating Behaviors, 15*(1), 99–105. https://doi.org/10.1016/j.eatbeh.2013.10.023

Meule, A., Richard, A., Lender, A., Dinic, R., Brockmeyer, T., Rinck, M., & Blechert, J. (2020). Measuring approach-avoidance tendencies towards food with touchscreen-based arm movements. *Psychological Research, 84*(7), 1789–1800. https://doi.org/10.1007/s00426-019-01195-1

Paslakis, G., Kühn, S., Grunert, S., & Erim, Y. (2017). Explicit and implicit approach vs. avoidance tendencies towards high vs. low calorie food cues in patients with obesity and active binge eating disorder. *Nutrients, 9*(10), 1068. https://doi.org/10.3390/nu9101068

Pennington, C.R., Jones, A., Bartlett, J.E., Copeland, A., & Shaw, D.J. (2021). Raising the bar: Improving methodological rigour in cognitive alcohol research. *Addiction, 116*(11), 3243–3251. https://doi.org/10.1111/add.15563

Rinck, M., & Becker, E.S. (2007). Approach and avoidance in fear of spiders. *Journal of Behavior Therapy and Experimental Psychiatry, 38*(2), 105–120. https://doi.org/10.1016/j.jbtep.2006.10.001

Rodebaugh, T.L., Scullin, R.B., Langer, J.K., Dixon, D.J., Huppert, J.D., Bernstein, A., Zvielli, A., & Lenze, E.J. (2016). Unreliability as a threat to understanding psychopathology: The cautionary tale of attentional bias. *Journal of Abnormal Psychology, 125*(6), 840–851. https://doi.org/10.1037/abn0000184

Schumacher, S.E., Kemps, E., & Tiggemann, M. (2016). Bias modification training can alter approach bias and chocolate consumption. *Appetite, 96*, 219–224. https://doi.org/10.1016/j.appet.2015.09.014

Shiffman, S., Stone, A.A., & Hufford, M.R. (2008). Ecological momentary assessment. *Annual Review of Clinical Psychology, 4*, 1–32. https://doi.org/10.1146/annurev.clinpsy.3.022806.091415

Simonsohn, U., Nelson, L.D., & Simmons, J.P. (2014). P-curve: A key to the file-drawer. *Journal of Experimental Psychology: General, 143*, 534–547. https://doi.org/10.1037/a0033242

Stacy, A.W., & Wiers, R.W. (2010). Implicit cognition and addiction: A tool for explaining paradoxical behavior. *Annual Review of Clinical Psychology, 6*, 551–575. https://doi.org/10.1146/annurev.clinpsy.121208.131444

Strack, F., & Deutsch, R. (2004). Reflective and impulsive determinants of social behavior. *Personality and Social Psychology Review, 8*(3), 220–247. https://doi.org/10.1207/s15327957pspr0803_1

Veling, H., Chen, Z., Liu, H., Quandt, J., & Holland, R.W. (2020). Updating the p-curve analysis of Carbine and Larson with results from preregistered experiments. *Health Psychology Review, 14*(2), 215–219. https://doi.org/10.1080/17437199.2019.1669482

Veling, H., Koningsburggen, H. van, Aarts, H., & Stroebe, W. (2014). Targeting impulsive processes of eating behaviour via the internet. Effects on body weight. *Appetite, 78,* 102–109.

Verbruggen, F., & Logan, G.D. (2008). Automatic and controlled response inhibition: Associative learning in the go/no-go and stop-signal paradigms. *Journal of Experimental Psychology: General, 137*(4), 649–672. https://doi.org/10.1037/a0013170

Vervoort, L., Braun, M., De Schryver, M., Naets, T., Koster, E., & Braet, C. (2021). A pictorial dot probe task to assess food-related attentional bias in youth with and without obesity: Overview of indices and evaluation of their reliability. *Frontiers in Psychology, 12*, Article 644512. https://doi.org/10.3389/fpsyg.2021.644512

Werthmann, J., Jansen, A., & Roefs, A. (2015). Worry or craving? A selective review of evidence for food-related attention biases in obese individuals, eating-disorder patients, restrained eaters and healthy samples. *The Proceedings of the Nutrition Society, 74*(2), 99–114. https://doi.org/10.1017/S0029665114001451

Wiers, R.W., Bartholow, B.D., van den Wildenberg, E., Thush, C., Engels, R.C., Sher, K.J., Grenard, J., Ames, S.L., & Stacy, A.W. (2007). Automatic and controlled processes and the development of addictive behaviors in adolescents: A review and a model. *Pharmacology, Biochemistry, and Behavior, 86*(2), 263–283. https://doi.org/10.1016/j.pbb.2006.09.021

Wiers, R.W., Gladwin, T.E., Hofmann, W., Salemink, E., & Ridderinkhof, K.R. (2013). Cognitive bias modification and cognitive control training in addiction and related psychopathology: Mechanisms, clinical perspectives, and ways forward. *Clinical Psychological Science, 1*(2), 192–212. https://doi.org/10.1177/2167702612466547

Wiers, R.W., Rinck, M., Kordts, R., Houben, K., & Strack, F. (2010). Retraining automatic action-tendencies to approach alcohol in hazardous drinkers. *Addiction, 105*(2), 279–287. https://doi.org/10.1111/j.1360-0443.2009.02775.x

Yang, Y., Shields, G.S., Wu, Q., Liu, Y., Chen, H., & Guo, C. (2019). Cognitive training on eating behaviour and weight loss: A meta-analysis and systematic review. *Obesity Reviews, 20*(11), 1628–1641. https://doi.org/10.1111/obr.12916

Chapter 20

Psychophysiological Measures in Eating Behavior Research

Annika P.C. Lutz, Zoé van Dyck, and Claus Vögele

Department of Behavioural and Cognitive Sciences,
University of Luxembourg, Luxembourg

Introduction

Over the last decades, psychophysiological assessment has become a core method for evaluating autonomic and central nervous system function while an individual interacts with their (internal and external) environment. Psychological processes investigated with psychophysiological measures range from cognitive ability (e.g., attention, memory) to affective processing (e.g., stress, reward) and decision-making (e.g., problem solving). Physiological responses evaluated during experimental manipulations of those psychological processes can be recorded noninvasively from several organs, for example, the brain, the skin, the heart, the eyes, and muscles. The most widely used psychophysiological methods include electroencephalography (EEG), electromyography (EMG), electrooculography, pupillometry, electrodermal activity (EDA), electrocardiography (ECG), and blood pressure (BP). Laboratory-based studies recording psychophysiological measures in the context of psychological manipulations have resulted in important insights into the contributions of autonomic and central nervous system functions to cognitive, affective, and behavioral functioning in the general population (Andreassi, 2013) and the etiology and maintenance of mental disorders (e.g., mood and anxiety disorders; Lang, 1985).

There are several advantages to laboratory testing (Steptoe & Vögele, 1991) in that psychophysiological monitoring in a standardized environment offers precise control over the stimuli under investigation, together with the possibility to use sophisticated physiological measurements. In addition, experimental manipulations of the psychological processes under investigation allow for the closest approximation to come to conclusions on cause-and-effect relations that psychological research designs can offer. Nevertheless, and despite of all these advantages, laboratory testing has been increasingly criticized due to its artificial environment, rendering ecological validity and, therefore, generalizability of results to responses under everyday-life conditions doubtful. A complementary approach concerns ecological momentary assessment (EMA), which entails the sampling of experiences (e.g., activities, mood, cognitions, etc.) as they occur in everyday life (Shiffman et al., 2008), also including the monitoring of psychophysiological parameters (Raugh et al., 2019). These developments have good potential to overcome some of the limitations of laboratory-based assessments, but they come with their own challenges and complex problems. As in other studies, for example, power and sample-size calculations are required (although rarely reported; Trull & Ebner-Priemer, 2020), but these are made more complex in EMA research because of the multilevel nature of the data (Bolger et al., 2012). In addition, EMA methods put considerable burden on the respondents as they are required to wear psychophysiological equipment and are prompted several times per day to respond to questions, thus increasing risk of attrition and affecting the very phenomenon under investigation by the method of investigation (*sensu lato* Heisenberg's uncertainty principle; Stamm, 1985), which can be experienced as intrusive.

As psychophysiological EMA research in eating disorders (EDs) is still in its infancy, as of now the vast majority of studies involving the psychophysiological assessment of individuals with EDs are laboratory-based. In this chapter we will, therefore, provide an overview of laboratory-based investigations of etiological processes considered of particular importance for the development or maintenance of EDs, that is, physiological responses to food stimuli, body stimuli, and interoceptive cues. In terms of psychophysiological parameters, we will focus on event-related potentials (ERPs), EMG, EDA, and cardiovascular reactions, although other techniques have also been used in EDs, albeit more rarely. In doing so, we concentrate on those psychophysiological parameters that are based on electrophysiological signals, as they share the feature of high temporal resolution over time, as opposed to neuroimaging techniques, which provide a snapshot of central nervous system activity with the advantage of exact localization of where the process occurs in the brain.

Overview of Measures and Paradigms

Event-Related Potentials

Event-related potentials are calculated from scalp EEG by averaging the responses to repeatedly presented stimuli. In the resulting ERP, positive and negative peaks at different time delays are traditionally interpreted as reflecting various sensory and cognitive processes. Although peaks occur at specific scalp locations, they do not allow any conclusions on which brain areas are implicated. The major advantage of the EEG/ERP method is its high temporal resolution, which reflects neural activity directly as it happens (Luck, 2014). When interpreting ERP findings, we need to keep in mind, however, that peaks are the result of a summation of underlying components, that is, the actual neural processes the researcher is interested in (Luck, 2014). In addition, decades of research have associated specific ERPs with various cognitive processes, but findings are diverse and depend on the experimental setup (Luck, 2014). For example, a P300 extracted from a passive viewing paradigm probably does not reflect the same neural processes as a P300 extracted from an oddball paradigm. These issues need to be considered when using the EEG/ERP method to help understand the etiology of EDs. One of the major issues in

ERP ED research today is the heterogeneity of paradigms and components used, which makes the aggregation of results across studies difficult. Passive viewing of disorder-relevant stimuli and analysis of a broad range of peaks is a rather coarse method, which is only suitable for exploratory studies. Careful experimental design is required, if ERP research is to contribute to a better understanding of neural and cognitive processes underlying the etiology of EDs. Physiological consequences of EDs, such as reduced cortical excitability in anorexia nervosa (AN; Khedr et al., 2014) also need to be considered.

Startle Eye-Blink Modulation

The startle reflex is the response to a sudden threatening stimulus, resulting, among others, in protective eyelid closure. It is a brainstem reflex, but modulated by the affective motivational state of the individual. A congruent, negative affective state potentiates the startle response, while an incongruent, positive affective state attenuates it (Lang et al., 1990). Thus, when a startling stimulus, for example, a loud burst of white noise, is presented concurrently with a visual stimulus, for example, the photograph of a pleasant or threatening scene, the resulting startle response provides an indication of the implicit evaluation of the photograph. The startling stimulus mainly used in ED research consists of a short burst of white noise, with the startle response quantified with the EMG of the orbicularis oculi (eyelid closure) muscle. Reactions to food and body pictures are usually compared with reactions to positive, neutral, and negative normative pictures, often taken from the International Affective Picture System (Lang et al., 2008), as startle attenuation and potentiation are relative indicators. The interpretability of results is limited in studies lacking adequate comparison stimuli.

One study showed an attenuated baseline (blank screen) startle eyeblink response in AN (Bellodi et al., 2013). Regarding affective startle modulation, women with AN showed no attenuation or even potentiated (negative) startle responses regarding positive normative pictures in two studies (Friederich et al., 2006; Lutz et al., 2017), though not in a third (Reichel et al., 2014). It is possible that at least some patients, for example, with longer illness duration, experience a failure to activate their appetitive motivational system. No such effects were reported for patients with bulimia nervosa (BN; Friederich et al., 2006; Mauler et al., 2006).

Facial Electromyogram

Most extant studies recorded surface EMG from the corrugator supercilii muscle, the "frowning" muscle, which is located above the eyebrows, or the zygomaticus major muscle, the "smiling" muscle, which draws back the corners of the mouth. The activity of both muscles is sensitive to affective state, in particular the valence of a stimulus (Cacioppo et al., 1986). Facial EMG is sensitive to small changes in muscle activity, even if they are not registered by a human observer.

Electrodermal and Cardiovascular Activity

Electrodermal activity is a summary term for methods quantifying the activity of the sweat glands, usually recorded from the palm of the hand or the fingers. As these are exclusively innervated by the sympathetic nervous system, EDA provides an index of sympathetic arousal (Critchley, 2002). Most studies on EDs investigated tonic skin conductance level or the number of nonspecific phasic skin conductance responses. Some studies report lower skin conductance level at baseline in AN (Knejzlíková et al., 2021) and baseline skin conductance responses correlated positively with body mass index (BMI; Bellodi et al., 2013). This suggests that weight status needs to be considered when interpreting EDA in EDs.

A small number of studies reported changes in heart rate in response to disorder-relevant stimuli, while other cardiovascular measures are more frequently applied as baseline measures and thus not the focus of our review. Cardiovascular complications are frequent in AN, BN (Casiero & Frishman, 2006), and binge eating disorder (BED; Mitchell, 2016), and should be considered in all studies assessing cardiovascular responses. Heart rate is modulated through a complex interplay between the sympathetic and parasympathetic nervous systems. This autonomic balance is often investigated with heart rate variability (HRV), a summary term for indices reflecting parasympathetic or sympathetic modulation of heart rate to different degrees (Task Force of The European Society of Cardiology and The North American Society of Pacing and Electrophysiology, 1996). Reviews and meta-analyses of HRV in AN (Mazurak et al., 2011) and BN (Peschel et al., 2016a, 2016b) report parasympathetic dominance during the resting state and an impaired activation of the sympathetic system during stress in most studies, while at the same time acknowledging the heterogeneity of results. Especially in AN, where a larger number of studies has been conducted, sympathetic dominance or no alterations have also been reported (Mazurak et al., 2011). One study found an association between autonomic balance and disorder duration, leading to the suggestion that over the course of the AN the balance shifts from parasympathetic to sympathetic dominance (Nakai et al., 2015; Sachs et al., 2016).

Reactions to Food Stimuli

When interpreting results from psychophysiological studies investigating responses to pictorial food stimuli in patients with EDs, it needs to be considered that not all studies included appropriate comparison conditions (e.g., normative neutral, positive, and negative pictures). Only a subset of studies investigated differential responding to high- and low-calorie foods, or chose disorder-relevant foods, for example, binge foods. Accordingly, the extant literature does not allow for firm conclusions to be drawn regarding responses to particular food types.

Event-Related Potentials

Food stimuli are motivationally relevant stimuli. This is reflected, among others, in a larger P300 (motivated attention allocation) and a larger late positive potential (LPP; sustained attention), as compared to neutral stimuli (Carbine et al., 2018; Nijs et al.,

2008; Nijs, Franken, et al., 2010; Nijs, Muris, et al., 2010; Sarlo et al., 2013). Differences between low- and high-calorie foods are reported in some, but not all studies. The P300 and LPP have been associated with cue reactivity in the context of substance use disorders (Littel et al., 2012) and are thus the focus of this chapter.

The LPP seems to be increased for pictures of binge foods in BN (Delgado-Rodríguez et al., 2019), for high- but not low-calorie foods in BED (Svaldi et al., 2010), and for low-calorie foods in AN (Novosel et al., 2014), reflecting the expected motivational tendencies in the different disorder groups. Other studies found contradicting results, with no LPP differences between women with versus without BN (Lutz et al., 2021), and no difference between high- and low-calorie foods in BED (Schienle et al., 2017).

Several studies have demonstrated how food ERPs can be influenced by certain cognitive states, for example attempts to regulate food cravings (Meule et al., 2013; Sarlo et al., 2013; Svaldi et al., 2015), or emotional states (Blechert et al., 2014; Lutz et al., 2021; Schnepper et al., 2020). A study with women with BN (Lutz et al., 2021) showed that inducing a negative versus a neutral emotional state led to globally reduced P300 amplitudes for foods and objects, but a specific increase in LPP for high-calorie foods only, as compared to low-calorie foods and objects. Decreased P300 amplitudes have been associated with reduced inhibitory processing in obesity (Babiloni et al., 2009; Hill et al., 2013), while increased LPP for high-calorie foods could be a sign of motivational salience (Hajcak et al., 2010), motivational conflict (Field et al., 2016), or craving regulation (see above). Disentangling these effects requires careful experimental designs in future studies.

Startle Eyeblink Modulation

The extant literature does not show any affective startle eyeblink modulation regarding food pictures in acute, chronic, or recovered AN; both individuals with and without AN show reactions, which are similar to those for neutral normative pictures (Erdur et al., 2017; Friederich et al., 2006). For BN, one study found attenuated startle responses during the presentation of food pictures (Friederich et al., 2006), while another showed startle potentiation (Mauler et al., 2006). The latter study, however, reported changes in food-related startle magnitude dependent on whether patients with BN had fasted before the experiment or had consumed smaller or larger meals. Especially, fasting and eating small amounts of food reduced food-related startle potentiation, possibly due to a sense of control and thus reduced threat of overeating (Mauler et al., 2006). Accordingly, when assessing food-related startle responses in BN, the current fasting/overeating state of the individual needs to be considered.

Facial Electromyogram

Activity of the corrugator muscle during the viewing of food pictures appears to be increased in BN (Mauler et al., 2006), and for high- but not low-calorie foods in AN (Schnepper et al., 2021), suggesting a negative evaluation of food pictures. One study found negative facial reactions (increased corrugator activity) for food cues in all participants irrespective of BED diagnosis, but the largest discrepancy between positive ratings and negative facial reaction in the group diagnosed with BED (Leehr et al., 2016). Negative mood induction led to decreased corrugator activity, that is, more pleasant evaluation, for high- but not low-calorie foods in individuals with BN, but not those with AN (Schnepper et al., 2021). Recording from the zygomatic muscle, one study reported rapidly decreasing activity for food and pleasurable cues in individuals with AN, suggesting generally reduced hedonic processing (Soussignan et al., 2011).

Electrodermal and Cardiovascular Activity

Contrary to the studies reported above, which mostly used pictorial food stimuli, the majority of the following studies investigated reactions to exposure with real food items over the course of 20 minutes or more. In some studies, psychophysiological responses to food exposure are conceptualized as cephalic phase responses, that is, responses to sensory signals that prepare the gastrointestinal tract for the processing of food. Cephalic phase responses can be operationalized as salivation, often measured noninvasively in terms of amount of saliva secreted monitored using cotton swabs, in addition to psychophysiological parameters. Two studies found increases in EDA during exposure to food-related words or actual food items in AN, indicating increased sympathetic arousal, but no significant effects in BN (Léonard et al., 1998; Perpiña et al., 1998). One study found smaller increases in EDA, but stronger salivation responses during food exposure, in participants with BN than in a healthy comparison group (Legenbauer et al., 2004). Individuals with recent binge eating episodes showed different patterns in BP and EDA during 20 minutes of food exposure than a healthy comparison group (Vögele & Florin, 1997). Interestingly, heart rate during the exposure correlated with the number of calories consumed afterwards. The only recent study found no significant differences between groups with AN, BN, BED, or no ED in vagally mediated HRV and EDA during food exposure (Christensen et al., 2020).

Reactions to Body Stimuli

The studies reviewed in this section differ markedly in the types of body stimuli included, for example, photographs of models versus the participants themselves, or different BMI categories. As with food stimuli, this limits the conclusions, which can be drawn regarding specific types of body stimuli.

Event-Related Potentials

Most studies looked at two different types of body-related ERPs. On the one hand, there are earlier ERPs, such as the P1/P100 and N1/N170, which reflect featural and configural processing, respectively, and are particularly sensitive to human faces and bodies (de Gelder et al., 2010). On the other hand, there are later ERPs, such as the P3/P300 and LPP, which are associated with emotional and motivational processing.

Some studies found general alterations in early processing (P1, N1), which were not specific to body or face stimuli, but extended to objects, as well. One study with partially recovered patients with AN and BN found shortened P1 and N1 latencies for bodies and houses (Groves et al., 2017), while another found lower P1 and N1 amplitudes for faces and houses in AN (Li et al., 2015). Regarding body images, no significant N1 effects were found in individuals with BN (Mai et al., 2015). Another study reported larger N1 amplitudes for female than male bodies in individuals with EDs, but not in the healthy comparison group (Groves et al., 2017).

Later components show complex differences in the processing of bodies of different weight categories between individuals with and without BN (Mai et al., 2015). Findings regarding the LPP suggest increased cue reactivity, especially for underweight bodies, in AN (Horndasch et al., 2018). Given the small number of studies with heterogenous methodology, general conclusions about the brain-electric processing of body images in EDs cannot be drawn at this point.

Startle Eyeblink Modulation

One study found no differences between individuals with AN, BN, and no ED regarding eye-blink startle responses during the presentation of photographs of slim fashion models, thus indicating a similar affective evaluation in the groups (Friederich et al., 2006). This effect was confirmed in individuals with different stages of AN (i.e., acute, chronic, and recovered). None of these groups or the healthy comparison sample showed affective startle modulation by body images (Erdur et al., 2017). Another study reported startle attenuation, that is, a positive evaluation and approach motivation, for photographs of emaciated bodies in women with AN (Reichel et al., 2014). Only one study used photographs of the participants themselves and found no differential modulation of the startle response for different identities (self versus other) or different degrees of distortion of the body image (thinner versus actual body versus fatter) in women with and without AN (Lutz et al., 2017). Summarizing these results, it seems possible that only emaciated bodies with clearly visible signs of cachexia, for example, protruding bones, as in the study by Reichel et al., produce a strong approach motivation in individuals with AN, reflecting their drive for extreme thinness.

Electrodermal and Cardiovascular Activity

Two studies found no significant differences between women with EDs (AN, BN) and those without in their reaction to mirror exposure regarding heart rate and EDA, despite higher levels of negative emotions and cognitions in the group with EDs (Knejzlíková et al., 2021; Vocks et al., 2007). While negative emotions and cognitions decreased during exposure, physiological reactions did not, indicating poor habituation of physiological arousal (Vocks et al., 2007). A third study reported that EDA increased from before to after a body-related film clip in women with BED, but decreased in an overweight comparison group. None of the groups showed significant changes in cardiovascular parameters (Svaldi et al., 2009).

Interoception

Interoception refers to the perception of signals from within the body. A recent model (Suksasilp & Garfinkel, 2022) differentiates between several dimensions of interoception, which may potentially be assessed. Of particular relevance for this chapter on psychophysiological assessment are the dimensions: neural representation, strength of afferent signals, and interoceptive accuracy. These dimensions may be assessed with regards to different organ systems, with the current chapter focusing on the cardiovascular and the gastrointestinal system, due to their potential relevance for EDs. Interoception research in EDs necessarily needs to consider the physiological changes caused by disordered eating behavior, which impact the strength of the afferent signal. This has not always been the case in the literature, making it difficult to disentangle alterations with respect to different interoceptive dimensions.

Cardiovascular System

A large number of studies have assessed self-reported interoception with the interoceptive deficits subscale of the Eating Disorder Inventory-2 (Garner, 1991), for which a recent review reports consistent deficits in patients with EDs, even after recovery (Jenkinson et al., 2018). Regarding studies using psychophysiological assessment, however, the literature is much more heterogeneous. Several studies assessed interoceptive accuracy, that is, the correspondence between perceived and actual heartbeats, using heartbeat perception tasks. Some studies found reduced heartbeat perception in patients with AN (Pollatos et al., 2008, 2016) and women recovered from BN (Klabunde et al., 2013). Other studies, however, found no significant differences between healthy persons and individuals with AN (Kinnaird et al., 2020; Lutz, Schulz, et al., 2019; Richard et al., 2019), BN (Lutz, van Dyck, et al., 2019; Pollatos & Georgiou, 2016), or mixed ED samples (Eshkevari et al., 2014). To our knowledge, only two studies assessed the cortical processing of cardio-afferent signals in EDs to date. This is assessed with heartbeat-evoked potentials, that is, brain-electric activity related to the R peak of the ECG. One study found increased cortical representation in women with AN (Lutz, Schulz, et al., 2019), the other found no differences between women with BN and healthy women (Lutz, van Dyck, et al., 2019).

Taken together, these findings suggest that dimensions of interoception assessed with self-report and psychophysiological measures may vary within and between ED diagnoses. More research with multidimensional assessment is needed to produce a clearer picture of interoceptive alterations in EDs. Alterations in interoception regarding cardiac activity may be particularly relevant for emotion processing (Herbert et al., 2007; Pollatos et al., 2005), which is known to be altered in EDs (for a review, see Lavender et al., 2015). Psychophysiological research on interoception may shed light on the mechanisms underlying such deficits and thus provide potential intervention targets in the future.

Gastrointestinal System

The gastrointestinal system plays an important role for EDs. Gastrointestinal disturbances such as postprandial fullness, constipation, abdominal distension, nausea, early satiety, and abdominal discomfort are common (Hadley & Walsh, 2003; Hetterich et al., 2019).

Furthermore, individuals with EDs present alterations in different gastric functions that are closely interrelated. Studies report diminished release of cholecystokinin (Devlin et al., 1997; Geracioti & Liddle, 1988), delays in gastric emptying (Geliebter et al., 2004), diminished gastric relaxation reflex (Walsh et al., 2003), and abnormal gastric motor activity (Ogawa et al., 2004) across ED diagnoses.

Gastric motor activity can be noninvasively measured using electrogastrography (EGG), which captures the myoelectric activity of gastric smooth muscles through cutaneous electrodes placed on the abdomen. The frequency of the EGG signal is identical with the frequency of peristaltic contractions in the postprandial period and corresponds to the frequency of the signal recorded from the serosal surface (Levine, 2005). The main functions of the stomach consist of mixing and grinding food after ingestion, and emptying the chyme to the duodenum (Stern et al., 2007). Stomach motility, however, not only regulates the rates at which nutrients are being processed, but also contributes to the development of satiation.

The frequency and propagation of gastric contractions is determined by electrical slow waves, an omnipresent myoelectrical activity originating in the stomach proximal body, and transmitted annularly toward the pylorus (Koch & Stern, 2004). In healthy humans, the gastric rhythm has a normal frequency of 0.05 Hz or three cycles per minute, which is referred to as normal gastric myoelectrical activity (GMA; normogastria). Gastric dysrhythmias, that is, abnormally slow (bradygastria) or abnormally fast (tachygastria) rhythms, have been repeatedly associated with upper gastrointestinal symptoms, such as nausea, epigastric distress, and bloating (Koch et al., 1990; Koch & Stern, 2004).

The EGG has so far mostly been used for clinical purposes in gastroenterology (Koch & Stern, 2004), but it also represents an appealing method to study brain-viscera interactions in psychophysiological studies (Wolpert et al., 2020). The potential relevance of visceral signals for understanding cognition and behavior has long been emphasized for emotions (Cannon, 1927; Damasio, 1996), and more recently also for physical and mental health (Khalsa et al., 2018; Quadt et al., 2018), including EDs (Herbert, 2020).

Studies using EGG in individuals with EDs remain sparse, and usually measure the neuromuscular activity of the stomach in response to a provocative stimulus, such as the water load test (WLT). During the WLT, study participants ingest a noncaloric physical volume of water over a predefined time period, which evokes pure stomach neuromuscular activity without the complex hormonal response of a caloric meal and without the influence of visual, gustatory, or olfactory cues (Koch et al., 2000). In healthy individuals, water ingestion during the WLT has been shown to increase normal GMA (Koch & Stern, 2004). In addition, loading the stomach with water induces gastric distention, which in turn plays an important role in the development of satiation (Powley & Phillips, 2004). The WLT has been adapted for the ED field (WLT-II; van Dyck et al., 2016). The WLT-II is a standardized 2-step drink test that both measures the perception of gastric signals and evokes gastric motility responses, making it an interesting tool to study brain-stomach interactions.

Recording the EGG in combination with a WLT, Ogawa et al. (2004) found a significantly smaller percentage of normogastria and increased bradygastria in patients with EDs compared to healthy controls. When comparing different ED diagnoses (AN versus BN versus eating disorder not otherwise specified), they found no differences in terms of EGG spectrum distribution. In another study only patients with BN, but not AN, differed from healthy controls regarding EGG variables (Diamanti et al., 2003). Using the WLT-II, a more recent study also found less normogastric and more bradygastric activity after water ingestion in BN and BED compared to a healthy control group (van Dyck et al., 2021). This study further reports a negative relationship between the percentage of normal GMA and the number of objective binge eating episodes per week, together with a delayed response to satiation, in individuals with BED or BN. A preponderance of bradygastria in BN was also reported by Koch et al. (1998).

Overall, these results suggest a potential role for gastric motility alterations in the development and/or maintenance of EDs, but additional research is warranted to examine the unique associations of dietary restriction, binge eating, and purging with gastric electrical activity. The empirical evidence on AN is still inconclusive and only one study included participants with BED. The investigation of participants with BED is particularly challenging as they are frequently overweight or obese, and a thicker abdominal wall results in a lower amplitude of the EGG signal (Farajidavar, 2018). Furthermore, individuals with a high BMI show more activity outside the normogastric range (Tolj et al., 2007). Other ED related factors that might affect the recordings of GMA are fasting or postprandial status, meal contents, and physical and psychological stressors (Koch et al., 2000; Wolpert et al., 2020). Also, the phase of the menstrual cycle might impact EGG frequency (Tolj et al., 2007) and should be considered especially in AN, where amenorrhea is a frequent condition.

Conclusions

The current overview of laboratory-based investigations of physiological responses to food stimuli, body stimuli, and interoceptive cues shows very mixed results. Some studies found converging evidence considering self-reports and physiological responses, while other studies found divergent results for these observation levels. This heterogeneity in findings may not be surprising when considering the psychophysiological literature on other mental disorders, such as anxiety and depression. In the early days of psychophysiology, the divergence of physiological responses and self-reports was observed so often that the concept of response fractionation was introduced to describe the lack of covariation, nonsignificant common variance or dyssynchrony of overt behavioral, self-report, and physiological measures (Haynes & Wilson, 1979). In this sense, psychophysiological assessment offers additional information at an observational level that may avoid effects of social desirability, or even uncover underlying conflicts and ambivalence that may be important for etiological models or interventions for EDs. It is important to note, however, that in contrast to many publications in this field, results derived from physiological measures are not in any way more "objective" than self-reports, which are sometimes denoted "subjective." As the term "subjective" is not supposed to imply that these measures are less true than "objective" measures, it stands to reason that this distinction is somewhat misleading.

Notwithstanding these potential advantages of psychophysiological assessment (and some caveats), based on the current evidence we conclude that the general methodological standard of psychophysiological assessment in many studies leaves considerable room for improvement. Among the many areas that should be considered for future advancement are for target samples to not only include women, and also less well-researched conditions (e.g., BED), to ensure proper statistical power, and to consider potentially important moderating variables such as illness duration, age-of-onset of the disorder and treatment status. In addition, some "state" variables at the time of investigation are important to control for, for example, fasting status and emotional well-being. Finally, in some studies the lack of observed differences in body dissatisfaction, restrained eating, or emotional eating between women with and without EDs reflects the fact that these problem behaviors are not unique to EDs but are very common in the general (female) population.

References

Andreassi, J.L. (2013). *Psychophysiology*. Psychology Press. https://doi.org/10.4324/9780203880340

Babiloni, C., del Percio, C., Valenzano, A., Marzano, N., de Rosas, M., Petito, A., Bellomo, A., Rossi, G., Lecce, B., Mundi, C., Lizio, R., Eusebi, F., & Cibelli, G. (2009). Frontal attentional responses to food size are abnormal in obese subjects: An electroencephalographic study. *Clinical Neurophysiology, 120*(8), 1441–1448. https://doi.org/10.1016/j.clinph.2009.06.012

Bellodi, L., Martoni, R.M., Galimberti, E., & Cavallini, M.C. (2013). Low baseline startle in anorexia nervosa patients. *Progress in Neuro-Psychopharmacology & Biological Psychiatry, 40*, 26–29. https://doi.org/10.1016/j.pnpbp.2012.08.007

Blechert, J., Goltsche, J.E., Herbert, B.M., & Wilhelm, F.H. (2014). Eat your troubles away: Electrocortical and experiential correlates of food image processing are related to emotional eating style and emotional state. *Biological Psychology, 96*, 94–101. https://doi.org/10.1016/j.biopsycho.2013.12.007

Bolger, N., Stadler, G., & Laurenceau, J.-P. (2012). Power analysis for intensive longitudinal studies. In M.R. Mehl & T.S. Conner (Eds.), *Handbook of research methods for studying daily life* (pp. 285–301). Guilford Press.

Cacioppo, J.T., Petty, R.E., Losch, M.E., & Kim, H.S. (1986). Electromyographic activity over facial muscle regions can differentiate the valence and intensity of affective reactions. *Journal of Personality and Social Psychology, 50*(2), 260–268. https://doi.org/10.1037/0022-3514.50.2.260

Cannon, W.B. (1927). *Bodily changes in pain, hunger, fear and rage: An account of recent researches into the function of emotional excitement*. D. Appleton.

Carbine, K.A., Duraccio, K.M., Kirwan, C.B., Muncy, N.M., LeCheminant, J.D., & Larson, M.J. (2018). A direct comparison between ERP and fMRI measurements of food-related inhibitory control: Implications for BMI status and dietary intake. *NeuroImage, 166*, 335–348. https://doi.org/10.1016/j.neuroimage.2017.11.008

Casiero, D., & Frishman, W.H. (2006). Cardiovascular complications of eating disorders. *Cardiology in Review, 14*(5), 227–231. https://doi.org/10.1097/01.crd.0000216745.96062.7c

Christensen, K.A., French, M.N., & Chen, E.Y. (2020). Multi-method assessment of palatable food exposure in women with and without eating disorders. *European Eating Disorders Review, 28*(5), 594–602. https://doi.org/10.1002/erv.2746

Critchley, H.D. (2002). Review: Electrodermal responses: What happens in the brain. *The Neuroscientist, 8*(2), 132–142. https://doi.org/10.1177/107385840200800209

Damasio, A.R. (1996). The somatic marker hypothesis and the possible functions of the prefrontal cortex. *Philosophical Transactions: Biological Sciences, 351*, 1413–1420.

de Gelder, B., van den Stock, J., Meeren, H.K.M., Sinke, C.B.A., Kret, M.E., & Tamietto, M. (2010). Standing up for the body. Recent progress in uncovering the networks involved in the perception of bodies and bodily expressions. *Neuroscience and Biobehavioral Reviews, 34*(4), 513–527. https://doi.org/10.1016/j.neubiorev.2009.10.008

Delgado-Rodríguez, R., Hernández-Rivero, I., Fernández-Santaella, M.C., Vila, J., Guerra, P., & Miccoli, L. (2019). Neural processing of food and erotic cues in bulimia nervosa. *Psychosomatic Medicine, 81*(6), 527–535. https://doi.org/10.1097/PSY.0000000000000704

Devlin, M.J., Walsh, B.T., Guss, J.L., Kissileff, H.R., Liddle, R.A., & Petkova, E. (1997). Postprandial cholecystokinin release and gastric emptying in patients with bulimia nervosa. *American Journal of Clinical Nutrition, 65*(1), 114–120. https://doi.org/10.1093/ajcn/65.1.114

Diamanti, A., Bracci, F., Gambarara, M., Ciofetta, G.C., Sabbi, T., Ponticelli, A., Montecchi, F., Marinucci, S., Bianco, G., & Castro, M. (2003). Gastric electric activity assessed by electrogastrography and gastric emptying scintigraphy in adolescents with eating disorders. *Journal of Pediatric Gastroenterology and Nutrition, 37*(1), 35–41. https://doi.org/10.1097/00005176-200307000-00006

Erdur, L., Weber, C., Zimmermann-Viehoff, F., Rose, M., & Deter, H.-C. (2017). Affective responses in different stages of anorexia nervosa: Results from a startle-reflex paradigm. *European Eating Disorders Review, 25*(2), 114–122. https://doi.org/10.1002/erv.2502

Eshkevari, E., Rieger, E., Musiat, P., & Treasure, J. (2014). An investigation of interoceptive sensitivity in eating disorders using a heartbeat detection task and a self-report measure. *European Eating Disorders Review, 22*(5), 383–388. https://doi.org/10.1002/erv.2305

Farajidavar, A. (2018). Bioelectronics for mapping gut activity. *Brain Research, 1693*, 169–173. https://doi.org/10.1016/j.brainres.2018.03.004

Field, M., Werthmann, J., Franken, I., Hofmann, W., Hogarth, L., & Roefs, A. (2016). The role of attentional bias in obesity and addiction. *Health Psychology, 35*(8), 767–780. https://doi.org/10.1037/hea0000405

Friederich, H.-C., Kumari, V., Uher, R., Riga, M., Schmidt, U., Campbell, I.C., Herzog, W., & Treasure, J. (2006). Differential motivational responses to food and pleasurable cues in anorexia and bulimia nervosa: A startle reflex paradigm. *Psychological Medicine, 36*(9), 1327–1335. https://doi.org/10.1017/S0033291706008129

Garner, D.M. (1991). *Eating Disorder Inventory-2. Professional manual.* Psychological Assessment Resources.

Geliebter, A., Yahav, E.K., Gluck, M.E., & Hashim, S.A. (2004). Gastric capacity, test meal intake, and appetitive hormones in binge eating disorder. *Physiology and Behavior, 81*(5), 735–740. https://doi.org/10.1016/j.physbeh.2004.04.014

Geracioti, T.D., & Liddle, R.A. (1988). Impaired cholecystokinin secretion in bulimia nervosa. *New England Journal of Medicine, 319*(11), 683–688. https://doi.org/10.1056/NEJM198809153191105

Groves, K., Kennett, S., & Gillmeister, H. (2017). Evidence for ERP biomarkers of eating disorder symptoms in women. *Biological Psychology, 123*, 205–219. https://doi.org/10.1016/j.biopsycho.2016.12.016

Hadley, S., & Walsh, B. (2003). Gastrointestinal disturbances in anorexia nervosa and bulimia nervosa. *Current Drug Target - CNS & Neurological Disorders, 2*(1), 1–9. https://doi.org/10.2174/1568007033338715

Hajcak, G., Macnamara, A., & Olvet, D.M. (2010). Event-related potentials, emotion, and emotion regulation: An integrative review. *Developmental Neuropsychology, 35*(2), 129–155. https://doi.org/10.1080/87565640903526504

Haynes, S.N., & Wilson, C.L. (1979). *Behavioral assessment: Recent advances in methods, concepts and applications.* Jossey-Bass.

Herbert, B.M. (2020). Interoception and its role for eating, obesity, and eating disorders. *European Journal of Health Psychology, 27*(4), 188–205. https://doi.org/10.1027/2512-8442/a000062

Herbert, B.M., Pollatos, O., & Schandry, R. (2007). Interoceptive sensitivity and emotion processing: An EEG study. *International Journal of Psychophysiology, 65*(3), 214–227. https://doi.org/10.1016/j.ijpsycho.2007.04.007

Hetterich, L., Mack, I., Giel, K.E., Zipfel, S., & Stengel, A. (2019). An update on gastrointestinal disturbances in eating disorders. *Molecular and Cellular Endocrinology, 497*, 110318. https://doi.org/10.1016/j.mce.2018.10.016

Hill, C., Wu, J., Crowley, M.J., & Fearon, P. (2013). Restrictive feeding practices and adiposity are differentially related to P3b cortical responses to food stimuli in children. *Appetite, 63*, 7–17. https://doi.org/10.1016/j.appet.2012.11.025

Horndasch, S., Kratz, O., van Doren, J., Graap, H., Kramer, R., Moll, G.H., & Heinrich, H. (2018). Cue reactivity towards bodies in anorexia nervosa – common and differential effects in adolescents and adults. *Psychological Medicine, 48*(3), 508–518. https://doi.org/10.1017/S0033291717001994

Jenkinson, P.M., Taylor, L., & Laws, K.R. (2018). Self-reported interoceptive deficits in eating disorders: A meta-analysis of studies using the eating disorder inventory. *Journal of Psychosomatic Research, 110*, 38–45. https://doi.org/10.1016/j.jpsychores.2018.04.005

Khalsa, S.S., Adolphs, R., Cameron, O.G., Critchley, H.D., Davenport, P.W., Feinstein, J.S., Feusner, J.D., Garfinkel, S.N., Lane, R.D., Mehling, W.E., Meuret, A.E., Nemeroff, C.B., Oppenheimer, S., Petzschner, F.H., Pollatos, O., Rhudy, J.L., Schramm, L.P., Simmons, W.K., Stein, M.B., ... Zucker, N. (2018). Interoception and mental health: A roadmap. *Biological Psychiatry: Cognitive Neuroscience and Neuroimaging, 3*(6), 501–513. https://doi.org/10.1016/j.bpsc.2017.12.004

Khedr, E.M., Fetoh, N.A. el, Bieh, E. el, Ali, A.M., & Karim, A.A. (2014). Altered cortical excitability in anorexia nervosa. *Clinical Neurophysiology, 44*, 291–299. https://doi.org/10.1016/j.neucli.2014.08.002

Kinnaird, E., Stewart, C., & Tchanturia, K. (2020). Interoception in anorexia nervosa: Exploring associations with alexithymia and autistic traits. *Frontiers in Psychiatry, 11*, Article 64. https://doi.org/10.3389/fpsyt.2020.00064

Klabunde, M., Acheson, D.T., Boutelle, K.N., Matthews, S.C., & Kaye, W.H. (2013). Interoceptive sensitivity deficits in women recovered from bulimia nervosa. *Eating Behaviors, 14*(4), 488–492. https://doi.org/10.1016/j.eatbeh.2013.08.002

Knejzlíková, T., Světlák, M., Malatincová, T., Roman, R., Chládek, J., Najmanová, J., Theiner, P., Linhartová, P., & Kašpárek, T. (2021). Electrodermal response to mirror exposure in relation to subjective emotional responses, emotional competences and affectivity in adolescent girls with restrictive anorexia and healthy controls. *Frontiers in Psychology, 12*, Article 673597. https://doi.org/10.3389/fpsyg.2021.673597

Koch, K.L., Bingaman, S., Tan, L., & Stern, R.M. (1998). Visceral perceptions and gastric myoelectrical activity in healthy women and in patients with bulimia nervosa. *Neurogastroenterol Motil, 10*(1), 3–10. https://doi.org/10.1046/j.1365-2982.1998.00080.x

Koch, K.L., Hong, S.P., & Xu, L. (2000). Reproducibility of gastric myoelectrical activity and the Water Load Test in patients with dysmotility-like dyspepsia symptoms and in control subjects. *Journal of Clinical Gastroenterology, 31*(2), 125–129. https://doi.org/10.1097/00004836-200009000-00007

Koch, K.L., & Stern, R.M. (2004). *Handbook of electrogastrography*. Oxford University Press.

Koch, K.L., Stern, R.M., Vasey, M., Botti, J.J., Creasy, G.W., & Dwyer, A. (1990). Gastric dysrhythmias and nausea of pregnancy. *Digestive Diseases and Sciences, 35*(8), 961–968. https://doi.org/10.1007/BF01537244

Lang, P.J. (1985). The cognitive psychophysiology of emotion: Fear and anxiety. In A.H. Tuma & J.D. Maser (Eds.), *Anxiety and the anxiety disorders* (pp. 131–170). Lawrence Erlbaum Associates, Inc.

Lang, P.J., Bradley, M.M., & Cuthbert, B.N. (1990). Emotion, attention, and the startle reflex. *Psychological Review, 97*(3), 377–395. https://doi.org/10.1037/0033-295X.97.3.377

Lang, P.J., Bradley, M.M., & Cuthbert, B.N. (2008). *International Affective Picture System (IAPS): Affective ratings of pictures and instruction manual. Technical Report A-8*. University of Florida, Gainesville, FL.

Lavender, J.M., Wonderlich, S.A., Engel, S.G., Gordon, K.H., Kaye, W.H., & Mitchell, J.E. (2015). Dimensions of emotion dysregulation in anorexia nervosa and bulimia nervosa: A conceptual review of the empirical literature. *Clinical Psychology Review, 40*(3), 111–122. https://doi.org/10.1016/j.cpr.2015.05.010

Leehr, E.J., Schag, K., Brinkmann, A., Ehlis, A.C., Fallgatter, A.J., Zipfel, S., Giel, K.E., & Dresler, T. (2016). Alleged approach-avoidance conflict for food stimuli in binge eating disorder. *PLoS One, 11*(4). https://doi.org/10.1371/journal.pone.0152271

Legenbauer, T., Vögele, C., & Rüddel, H. (2004). Anticipatory effects of food exposure in women diagnosed with bulimia nervosa. *Appetite, 42*(1), 33–40. https://doi.org/10.1016/S0195-6663(03)00114-4

Léonard, T., Pepinà, C., Bond, A., & Treasure, J. (1998). Assessment of test-meal induced autonomic arousal in anorexic, bulimic and control females. *European Eating Disorders Review, 6*(3), 188–200. https://doi.org/10.1002/(SICI)1099-0968(199809)6:3<188::AID-ERV227>3.0.CO;2-G

Levine, M.E. (2005). Sickness and satiety: Physiological mechanisms underlying perceptions of nausea and stomach fullness. *Current Gastroenterology Reports, 7*(4), 280–288. https://doi.org/10.1007/s11894-005-0020-2

Li, W., Lai, T.M., Loo, S.K., Strober, M., Mohammad-Rezazadeh, I., Khalsa, S., & Feusner, J. (2015). Aberrant early visual neural activity and brain-behavior relationships in anorexia nervosa and body dysmorphic disorder. *Frontiers in Human Neuroscience, 9*, Article 301. https://doi.org/10.3389/fnhum.2015.00301

Littel, M., Euser, A.S., Munafò, M.R., & Franken, I.H.A. (2012). Electrophysiological indices of biased cognitive processing of substance-related cues: A meta-analysis. *Neuroscience and Biobehavioral Reviews, 36*(8), 1803–1816. https://doi.org/10.1016/j.neubiorev.2012.05.001

Luck, S.J. (2014). *An introduction to the event-related potential technique*. MIT Press.

Lutz, A.P.C., Dierolf, A., van Dyck, Z., Georgii, C., Schnepper, R., Blechert, J., & Vögele, C. (2021). Mood-induced changes in the cortical processing of food images in bulimia nervosa. *Addictive Behaviors, 113*, 106712. https://doi.org/10.1016/j.addbeh.2020.106712

Lutz, A.P.C., Herbert, C., Schulz, A., Voderholzer, U., Koch, S., & Vögele, C. (2017). Affective evaluation of body images in anorexia nervosa. *Psychophysiology, 54*(S1). https://doi.org/10.1111/psyp.13033

Lutz, A.P.C., Schulz, A., Voderholzer, U., Koch, S., van Dyck, Z., & Vögele, C. (2019). Enhanced cortical processing of cardio-afferent signals in anorexia nervosa. *Clinical Neurophysiology, 130*(9), 1620–1627. https://doi.org/10.1016/j.clinph.2019.06.009

Lutz, A.P.C., van Dyck, Z., Schulz, A., & Vögele, C. (2019). Interoception in bulimia nervosa: Evidence at cortical and self-report levels. *Psychophysiology, 56*(S1), S117. https://doi.org/10.1111/psyp.13502

Mai, S., Gramann, K., Herbert, B.M., Friederich, H.C., Warschburger, P., & Pollatos, O. (2015). Electrophysiological evidence for an attentional bias in processing body stimuli in bulimia nervosa. *Biological Psychology, 108*, 105–114. https://doi.org/10.1016/j.biopsycho.2015.03.013

Mauler, B.I., Hamm, A.O., Weike, A.I., & Tuschen-Caffier, B. (2006). Affect regulation and food intake in bulimia nervosa: Emotional responding to food cues after deprivation and subsequent eating. *Journal of Abnormal Psychology, 115*(3), 567–579. https://doi.org/10.1037/0021-843X.115.3.567

Mazurak, N., Enck, P., Muth, E., Teufel, M., & Zipfel, S. (2011). Heart rate variability as a measure of cardiac autonomic function in anorexia nervosa: A review of the literature. *European Eating Disorders Review, 19*, 87–99. https://doi.org/10.1002/erv.1081

Meule, A., Kübler, A., & Blechert, J. (2013). Time course of electrocortical food-cue responses during cognitive regulation of craving. *Frontiers in Psychology, 4*, Article 669. https://doi.org/10.3389/fpsyg.2013.00669

Mitchell, J.E. (2016). Medical comorbidity and medical complications associated with binge-eating disorder. *International Journal of Eating Disorders, 49*(3), 319–323. https://doi.org/10.1002/eat.22452

Nakai, Y., Fujita, M., Nin, K., Noma, S., & Teramukai, S. (2015). Relationship between duration of illness and cardiac autonomic nervous activity in anorexia nervosa. *BioPsychoSocial Medicine, 9*(1), 10–13. https://doi.org/10.1186/s13030-015-0032-6

Nijs, I.M.T., Franken, I.H.A., & Muris, P. (2008). Food cue-elicited brain potentials in obese and healthy-weight individuals. *Eating Behaviors, 9*(4), 462–470. https://doi.org/10.1016/j.eatbeh.2008.07.009

Nijs, I.M.T., Franken, I.H.A., & Muris, P. (2010). Food-related Stroop interference in obese and normal-weight individuals: Behavioral and electrophysiological indices. *Eating Behaviors, 11*(4), 258–265. https://doi.org/10.1016/j.eatbeh.2010.07.002

Nijs, I.M.T., Muris, P., Euser, A.S., & Franken, I.H.A. (2010). Differences in attention to food and food intake between overweight/obese and normal-weight females under conditions of hunger and satiety. *Appetite, 54*(2), 243–254. https://doi.org/10.1016/j.appet.2009.11.004

Novosel, A., Lackner, N., Unterrainer, H.F., Dunitz-Scheer, M., Scheer, P.J.Z., Wallner-Liebmann, S.J., & Neuper, C. (2014). Motivational processing of food cues in anorexia nervosa: A pilot study. *Eating and Weight Disorders, 19*(2), 169–175. https://doi.org/10.1007/s40519-014-0114-7

Ogawa, A., Mizuta, I., Fukunaga, T., Takeuchi, N., Honaga, E., Sugita, Y., Mikami, A., Inoue, Y., & Takeda, M. (2004). Electrogastrography abnormality in eating disorders. *Psychiatry and Clinical Neurosciences, 58*(3), 300–310. https://doi.org/10.1111/j.1440-1819.2004.01236.x

Perpiña, C., Leonard, T., Treasure, J., Bond, A., & Baños, R. (1998). Selective processing of food – and body – related information and autonomic arousal in patients with eating disorders. *Spanish Journal of Psychology, 1*(1), 3–10. https://doi.org/10.1017/S1138741600005357

Peschel, S.K.V., Feeling, N.R., Vögele, C., Kaess, M., Thayer, J.F., & Koenig, J. (2016a). A systematic review on heart rate variability in bulimia nervosa. *Neuroscience and Biobehavioral Reviews, 63*, 78–97. https://doi.org/10.1016/j.neubiorev.2016.01.012

Peschel, S.K.V., Feeling, N.R., Vögele, C., Kaess, M., Thayer, J.F., & Koenig, J. (2016b). A meta-analysis on resting state high-frequency heart rate variability in bulimia nervosa. *European Eating Disorders Review, 24*(5), 355–365. https://doi.org/10.1002/erv.2454

Pollatos, O., & Georgiou, E. (2016). Normal interoceptive accuracy in women with bulimia nervosa. *Psychiatry Research, 240*, 328–332. https://doi.org/10.1016/j.psychres.2016.04.072

Pollatos, O., Herbert, B.M., Berberich, G., Zaudig, M., Krauseneck, T., & Tsakiris, M. (2016). Atypical self-focus effect on interoceptive accuracy in anorexia nervosa. *Frontiers in Human Neuroscience, 10*, Article 484. https://doi.org/10.3389/fnhum.2016.00484

Pollatos, O., Kirsch, W., & Schandry, R. (2005). On the relationship between interoceptive awareness, emotional experience, and brain processes. *Cognitive Brain Research, 25*(3), 948–962. https://doi.org/10.1016/j.cogbrainres.2005.09.019

Pollatos, O., Kurz, A.-L., Albrecht, J., Schreder, T., Kleemann, A.M., Schöpf, V., Kopietz, R., Wiesmann, M., & Schandry, R. (2008). Reduced perception of bodily signals in anorexia nervosa. *Eating Behaviors, 9*(4), 381–388. https://doi.org/10.1016/j.eatbeh.2008.02.001

Powley, T.L., & Phillips, R.J. (2004). Gastric satiation is volumetric, intestinal satiation is nutritive. *Physiology and Behavior, 82*(1), 69–74. https://doi.org/10.1016/j.physbeh.2004.04.037

Quadt, L., Critchley, H.D., & Garfinkel, S.N. (2018). The neurobiology of interoception in health and disease. *Annals of the New York Academy of Sciences, 1428*(1), 112–128. https://doi.org/10.1111/nyas.13915

Raugh, I.M., Chapman, H.C., Bartolomeo, L.A., Gonzalez, C., & Strauss, G.P. (2019). A comprehensive review of psychophysiological applications for ecological momentary assessment in psychiatric populations. *Psychological Assessment, 31*(3), 304–317. https://doi.org/10.1037/pas0000651

Reichel, V.A., Schneider, N., Grünewald, B., Kienast, T., Pfeiffer, E., Lehmkuhl, U., & Korte, A. (2014). "Glass fairies" and "bone children": Adolescents and young adults with anorexia nervosa show positive reactions towards extremely emaciated body pictures measured by the startle reflex paradigm. *Psychophysiology, 51*(2), 168–177. https://doi.org/10.1111/psyp.12160

Richard, A., Meule, A., Georgii, C., Voderholzer, U., Cuntz, U., Wilhelm, F.H., & Blechert, J. (2019). Associations between interoceptive sensitivity, intuitive eating, and body mass index in patients with anorexia nervosa and normal-weight controls. *European Eating Disorders Review, 27*(5), 571–577. https://doi.org/10.1002/erv.2676

Sachs, K.V., Harnke, B., Mehler, P.S., & Krantz, M.J. (2016). Cardiovascular complications of anorexia nervosa: A systematic review. *International Journal of Eating Disorders, 49*(3), 238–248. https://doi.org/10.1002/eat.22481

Sarlo, M., Ubel, S., Leutgeb, V., & Schienle, A. (2013). Cognitive reappraisal fails when attempting to reduce the appetitive value of food: An ERP study. *Biological Psychology, 94*(3), 507–512. https://doi.org/10.1016/j.biopsycho.2013.09.006

Schienle, A., Scharmüller, W., & Schwab, D. (2017). Processing of visual food cues during bitter taste perception in female patients with binge-eating symptoms: A cross-modal ERP study. *Clinical Neurophysiology, 128*(11), 2184–2190. https://doi.org/10.1016/j.clinph.2017.08.017

Schnepper, R., Georgii, C., Eichin, K., Arend, A.-K., Wilhelm, F.H., Vögele, C., Lutz, A.P.C., van Dyck, Z., & Blechert, J. (2020). Fight, flight – or grab a bite! Trait emotional and restrained eating style predicts food cue responding under negative emotions. *Frontiers in Behavioral Neuroscience, 14*, Article 91. https://doi.org/10.3389/fnbeh.2020.00091

Schnepper, R., Richard, A., Georgii, C., Arend, A.K., Naab, S., Voderholzer, U., Wilhelm, F.H., & Blechert, J. (2021). Bad mood food? Increased versus decreased food cue reactivity in anorexia nervosa and bulimia nervosa during negative emotions. *European Eating Disorders Review, 29*(5), 756–769. https://doi.org/10.1002/erv.2849

Shiffman, S., Stone, A.A., & Hufford, M.R. (2008). Ecological momentary assessment. *Annual Review of Clinical Psychology, 4*, 1–32. https://doi.org/10.1146/annurev.clinpsy.3.022806.091415

Soussignan, R., Schaal, B., Rigaud, D., Royet, J.P., & Jiang, T. (2011). Hedonic reactivity to visual and olfactory cues: Rapid facial electromyographic reactions are altered in anorexia nervosa. *Biological Psychology, 86*(3), 265–272. https://doi.org/10.1016/j.biopsycho.2010.12.007

Stamm, J.S. (1985). The uncertainty principle in psychology. *Behavioral and Brain Sciences, 8*(4), 553–554. https://doi.org/10.1017/S0140525X0004509X

Steptoe, A., & Vögele, C. (1991). Methodology of mental stress testing in cardiovascular research. *Circulation, 83*(Suppl. 4), II14–24. http://www.ncbi.nlm.nih.gov/pubmed/2009622

Stern, R.M., Koch, K.L., Levine, M.E., & Muth, E.R. (2007). Gastrointestinal response. In J.T. Cacioppo, L.G. Tassinary, & G.G. Berntson (Eds.), *Handbook of psychophysiology* (3rd ed., pp. 211–230). Cambridge University Press. https://doi.org/10.1017/CBO9780511546396.009

Suksasilp, C., & Garfinkel, S.N. (2022). Towards a comprehensive assessment of interoception in a multidimensional framework. *Biological Psychology, 168*, 108262. https://doi.org/10.1016/j.biopsycho.2022.108262

Svaldi, J., Caffier, D., Blechert, J., & Tuschen-Caffier, B. (2009). Body-related film clip triggers desire to binge in women with binge eating disorder. *Behaviour Research and Therapy, 47*(9), 790–796. https://doi.org/10.1016/j.brat.2009.06.005

Svaldi, J., Tuschen-Caffier, B., Biehl, S.C., Gschwendtner, K., Wolz, I., & Naumann, E. (2015). Effects of two cognitive regulation strategies on the processing of food cues in high restrained eaters. An event-related potential study. *Appetite, 92*, 269–277. https://doi.org/10.1016/j.appet.2015.05.026

Svaldi, J., Tuschen-Caffier, B., Peyk, P., & Blechert, J. (2010). Information processing of food pictures in binge eating disorder. *Appetite, 55*(3), 685–694. https://doi.org/10.1016/j.appet.2010.10.002

Task Force of The European Society of Cardiology and The North American Society of Pacing and Electrophysiology. (1996). Guidelines. Heart rate variability. Standards of measurement, physiological interpretation, and clinical use. *European Heart Journal, 17*, 354–381. https://doi.org/10.1111/j.1542-474X.1996.tb00275.x

Tolj, N., Luetić, K., Schwarz, D., Bilić, A., Jurcić, D., & Gabrić, M. (2007). The impact of age, sex, body mass index and menstrual cycle phase on gastric myoelectrical activity characteristics in a healthy Croatian population. *Collegium Antropologicum, 31*(4), 955–962.

Trull, T.J., & Ebner-Priemer, U.W. (2020). Ambulatory assessment in psychopathology research: A review of recommended reporting guidelines and current practices. *Journal of Abnormal Psychology, 129*(1), 56–63. https://doi.org/10.1037/abn0000473

van Dyck, Z., Schulz, A., Blechert, J., Herbert, B.M., Lutz, A.P.C., & Vögele, C. (2021). Gastric interoception and gastric myoelectrical activity in bulimia nervosa and binge-eating disorder. *International Journal of Eating Disorders, 54*(7), 1106–1115. https://doi.org/10.1002/eat.23291

van Dyck, Z., Vögele, C., Blechert, J., Lutz, A.P.C., Schulz, A., & Herbert, B.M. (2016). The Water Load Test as a measure of gastric interoception: Development of a two-stage protocol and application to a healthy female population. *PLOS One, 11*(9), e0163574. https://doi.org/10.1371/journal.pone.0163574

Vocks, S., Legenbauer, T., Wächter, A., Wucherer, M., & Kosfelder, J. (2007). What happens in the course of body exposure? Emotional, cognitive, and physiological reactions to mirror confrontation in eating disorders. *Journal of Psychosomatic Research, 62*, 231–239. https://doi.org/10.1016/j.jpsychores.2006.08.007

Vögele, C., & Florin, I. (1997). Psychophysiological responses to food exposure: An experimental study in binge eaters. *International Journal of Eating Disorders, 21*(2), 147–157. https://doi.org/10.1002/(SICI)1098-108X(199703)21:2<147::AID-EAT5>3.0.CO;2-L

Walsh, B.T., Zimmerli, E., Devlin, M.J., Guss, J., & Kissileff, H.R. (2003). A disturbance of gastric function in bulimia nervosa. *Biological Psychiatry, 54*(9), 929–933. https://doi.org/10.1016/S0006-3223(03)00176-8

Wolpert, N., Rebollo, I., & Tallon-Baudry, C. (2020). Electrogastrography for psychophysiological research: Practical considerations, analysis pipeline, and normative data in a large sample. *Psychophysiology, 57*(9), 1–26. https://doi.org/10.1111/psyp.13599

Contributors

Sophie R. Abber
Department of Psychology
Florida State University
1107 W Call St, A203
Tallahassee, FL 32304
USA
abber@psy.fsu.edu

Sarrah I. Ali
Department of Psychology
Florida State University
1107 W Call St, A203
Tallahassee, FL 32304
USA
ali@psy.fsu.edu

Kelly C. Allison
Department of Psychiatry
Perelman School of Medicine
University of Pennsylvania
Philadelphia, PA 19104
USA
kca@pennmedicine.upenn.edu

Rike Arkenau-Kathmann
Department of Clinical Psychology and Psychotherapy
Osnabrück University
Lise-Meitner-Str. 3
49076 Osnabrück
Germany
rike.arkenau@uni-osnabrueck.de

Caroline Braet
Department of Developmental, Personality and Social Psychology
Ghent University
Henri Dunantlaan 2
9000 Ghent
Belgium
caroline.braet@ugent.be

Nuno Casanova
KinesioLab
Research Unit in Human Movement Analysis
Instituto Piaget
Av. Jorge Peixinho 30 Quinta da Arreinela
2805-059 Almada
Portugal
nuno.martins@ipiaget.pt

Eva M. Conceição
Campus Gualtar
School of Psychology
University of Minho
4710-057 Braga
Portugal
econceicao@psi.uminho.pt

Heather A. Davis
Department of Psychology
Virginia Tech
319 Williams Hall
890 Drillfield Dr.
Blacksburg, VA 24061-1052
USA
heatherdavis@vt.edu

Caroline Donovan
School of Applied Psychology
Griffith University
M24 Room 2.21
Mt Gravatt QLD 4122
Australia
c.donovan@griffith.edu.au

Zoé van Dyck
Department of Behavioural and Cognitive Sciences
University of Luxembourg
11, Porte des Sciences
4366 Esch-sur-Alzette
Luxembourg
zoe.vandyck@ext.uni.lu

Amy H. Egbert
Department of Psychological Sciences
University of Connecticut
406 Babbidge Road
U-1020
Storrs, CT 06269-1020
USA
aheard2@luc.edu

Catharine Evers
Department of Social, Health, and Organizational Psychology
Utrecht University
PO Box 80140
3508 TC Utrecht
The Netherlands
c.evers@uu.nl

Graham Finlayson
Appetite Control and Energy Balance Research Group
School of Psychology
Faculty of Medicine and Health
University of Leeds
Leeds LS2 9JT
UK
G.S.Finlayson@leeds.ac.uk

Ashley N. Gearhardt
Department of Psychology
University of Michigan
530 Church Street
Ann Arbor, MI 48109
USA
agearhar@umich.edu

Andrea B. Goldschmidt
Department of Psychiatry
University of Pittsburgh School of Medicine
3811 O'Hara St.
Pittsburgh, PA 15213
USA
goldscha@pitt.edu

Sasha Gorrell
Department of Psychiatry and Behavioral Sciences
Weill Institute for Neurosciences
University of California, San Francisco
675 18th St.
San Francisco, CA 94143
USA
Sasha.Gorrell@ucsf.edu

Christina Hartmann
ETH Zurich
Department Health Science and Technology (D-HEST)
Consumer Behavior
Universitaetstrasse 22, CHN H75.3
8092 Zurich
Switzerland
christina.hartmann@hest.ethz.ch

C. Peter Herman
Department of Psychology
University of Toronto
100 St. George St.
Toronto, Ontario M5S 3G3
Canada
herman@psych.utoronto.ca

Suzanne Higgs
School of Psychology
University of Birmingham
Edgbaston
Birmingham, B15 2TT
UK
s.higgs.1@bham.ac.uk

Lindzey V. Hoover
Department of Psychology
University of Michigan
530 Church Street
Ann Arbor, MI 48109
USA
lindzeyh@umich.edu

Mark Hopkins
School of Food Science and Nutrition
Faculty of Environment
University of Leeds
Leeds LS2 9JT
UK
m.hopkins@leeds.ac.uk

Klazine van der Horst
School of Health Professions,
Nutrition & Dietetics
Bern University of Applied Sciences
Murtenstr. 10
3009 Bern
Switzerland
klazine.vanderhorst@bfh.ch

Andrew Jones
Department of Psychology
University of Liverpool
Bedford St South
L69 7ZA
UK
a.j.jones@ljmu.ac.uk

Pamela K. Keel
Department of Psychology
Florida State University
1107 W Call St, A203
Tallahassee, FL 32304
USA
keel@psy.fsu.edu

Meredith Kells
University of Rochester
School of Nursing
601 Elmwood Avenue
Rochester, NY 14642
USA
meredith_kells@urmc.rochester.edu

Jessica Kerin
School of Applied Psychology
Griffith University
Parklands Dr. G40
Southport QLD 4222
Australia
jessica.kerin2@griffithuni.edu.au

Elizabeth W. Lampe
Drexel University
Psychology, Arts & Sciences
Stratton Hall Rm. 281
3201 Chestnut St.
Philadelphia, PA 19104
USA
ewl34@drexel.edu

Megan Lindloff
Department of Psychology
Western University
361 Windermere Rd
London, ON N6G 2K3
Canada
mlindlof@uwo.ca

Marta de Lourdes
Campus Gualtar
School of Psychology
University of Minho
4710-057 Braga
Portugal
martamagalhaeslourdes@outlook.com

Annika P. C. Lutz
Department of Behavioural and
Cognitive Sciences
University of Luxembourg
11, Porte des Sciences
4366 Esch-sur-Alzette
Luxembourg
annika.lutz@uni.lu

Tyler Mason
Department of Population and Public
Health Sciences
Keck School of Medicine
University of Southern California
1845 N Soto St
Los Angeles, CA 90032
USA
tylermas@usc.edu

Sarah Masterton
Department of Psychology
University of Liverpool
Bedford St South
L69 7ZA
UK
s.masterton@liverpool.ac.uk

Angela Meadows
Department of Psychology
University of Essex
Wivenhoe Park
Colchester CO4 3SQ
UK
a.meadows@essex.ac.uk

Adrian Meule
Schön Klinik Roseneck
Am Roseneck 6
83209 Prien am Chiemsee
Germany
ameule@med.lmu.de

Nathalie Michels
Department of Developmental
Personality and Social Psychology
Ghent University
Henri Dunantlaan 2
9000 Ghent
Belgium
nathalie.michels@ugent.be

Jennifer S. Mills
Department of Psychology
York University
4700 Keele St.
Toronto ON M3J 1P3
Canada
jsmills@yorku.ca

Carmen Beatriz Neufeld
Department of Psychology
Faculty of Philosophy, Sciences and
Languages
Ribeirão Preto University of São Paulo
Av. Bandeirantes, 3900
CEP 14040-901
Bairro Monte Alegre
Ribeirão Preto – SP
Brazil
cbneufeld@usp.br

Natalie A. Noebel
Department of Psychiatry
University of Texas
Southwestern Medical Center
6363 Forest Park Road
Dallas, TX 75235
USA
nan53@txstate.edu

Crystal D. Oberle
Department of Psychology
Texas State University
601 University Dr.
San Marcos, TX 78666
USA
oberle@txstate.edu

Ruairi O'Driscoll
Appetite Control and Energy Balance
Research Group
School of Psychology
Faculty of Medicine and Health
University of Leeds
Leeds LS2 9JT
UK
r.odriscoll@leeds.ac.uk

Janet Polivy
Department of Psychology
University of Toronto
100 St George St.
Toronto, ON M5S 3G3
Canada
polivy@psych.utoronto.ca

Hannah L. Quittkat
Department of Clinical Psychology and
Psychotherapy
Osnabrück University
Lise-Meitner-Str. 3
49076 Osnabrück
Germany
hannah.quittkat@uni-osnabrueck.de

Kathryn Smith
Department of Psychiatry and Behavioral Sciences
University of Southern California
2250 Alcazar Street
Los Angeles, CA 90033
USA
ksmith41@usc.edu

Harley J. Stansfield
School of Applied Psychology
Griffith University
Mt Gravatt QLD 4122
Australia
harley.stansfield@griffithuni.edu.au

R. James Stubbs
Appetite Control and Energy Balance Research Group
School of Psychology
Faculty of Medicine and Health
University of Leeds
Leeds LS2 9JT
UK
r.j.stubbs@leeds.ac.uk

Sandra Verbeken
Department of Developmental, Personality and Social Psychology
Ghent University
Henri Dunantlaan 2
9000 Ghent
Belgium
sandra.verbeken@ugent.be

Silja Vocks
Department of Clinical Psychology and Psychotherapy
Osnabrück University
Lise-Meitner-Str. 3
49076 Osnabrück
Germany
silja.vocks@uni-osnabrueck.de

Claus Vögele
Department of Behavioural and Cognitive Sciences
University of Luxembourg
11, Porte des Sciences
4366 Esch-sur-Alzette
Luxembourg
claus.voegele@uni.lu

Jennifer E. Wildes
Department of Psychiatry & Behavioral Neuroscience
University of Chicago
5841 S. Maryland Ave.
Rm M-340A, MC3077
Chicago, IL 60637
USA
jwildes@uchicago.edu

Diana Zhang
Department of Population and Public Health Sciences
Keck School of Medicine
University of Southern California
1845 N Soto St
Los Angeles, CA 90032
USA

Melanie J. Zimmer-Gembeck
School of Applied Psychology
Griffith University
Parklands Dr., G40_7.86
Southport QLD 4222
Australia
m.zimmer-gembeck@griffith.edu.au

Peer Commentaries

"Eating is hot. Eating is cool. Many people are conscious of it, some are obsessively concerned with time-restricted eating, vegan diets, healthy supplements, or muscle growth. Others struggle with their weight and are disgusted by their bodies. Many eat more than they need, some feel addicted to food. When are these behaviors, cognitions, and emotions healthy and when do they become unhealthy? Adrian Meule edited this excellent book describing various types of eating behaviors and eating disorders, and how they can be assessed and measured. The book is an indispensable contribution to our knowledge about healthy and unhealthy eating behaviors."

Anita Jansen, Professor of Clinical Psychology, Maastricht University, The Netherlands

"As the prevalence of unhealthy eating behaviors and their consequences continue to grow, the arrival of Meule's edited book could not be more timely. Its 20 chapters provide coverage of 'eating behavior domains' (e.g., restrained eating, craving, bulimia nervosa), 'adjacent domains' (e.g., body image, weight-related stigmatization), and 'assessment methods' (e.g., ecological momentary assessment, psychophysiological measures). Each chapter is co-authored by a world-renowned expert. Further, it covers not only various eating behavior patterns but also the domains that influence eating behavior (e.g., physical activity, body composition) and that eating behavior in turn influences."

Michael R. Lowe, Professor of Psychological and Brain Sciences, Drexel University, Philadelphia, PA, USA

"For students, researchers, and clinicians aiming to understand eating behaviors in their broadest sense this book provides a comprehensive resource. In a biological sense, eating behavior is driven by energy and nutrient requirements, but human food intake is further complicated by socio-cultural, emotional, cognitive, and physiological influences. The short title of this book belies the complex array of measures available to investigate diverse aspects of eating disorders, body image, body composition, physical activity, and momentary influences on food choice and intake. Here, internationally recognized experts provide detailed consideration of a wide array of instruments to explore varied, and sometimes controversial, aspects of eating behavior from addiction to weight-related stigma, and from self-reported aspects of eating traits to more objective, laboratory based measures of the drivers of food intake. This book is a one-stop shop and those interested in advancing knowledge of eating behavior need look no further."

Marion M. Hetherington, Professor Emerita, School of Psychology, University of Leeds, UK

Volumes in the series
Psychological Assessment – Science and Practice

Vol. 1
Tuulia M. Ortner, Fons J. R. van de Vijver (Eds.)
Behavior-Based Assessment in Psychology
Going Beyond Self-Report in the Personality, Affective, Motivation, and Social Domains
2015 (July), vi + 232 pages
ISBN 978-0-88937-437-9

Vol. 2
Yael Benyamini, Marie Johnston, Evangelos C. Karademas (Eds.)
Assessment in Health Psychology
2016 (February), vi + 345 pages
ISBN 978-0-88937-452-2

Vol. 3
Karl Schweizer, Christine DiStefano (Eds.)
Principles and Methods of Test Construction
Standards and Recent Advances
2016 (April), vi + 336 pages
ISBN 978-0-88937-449-2

Vol. 4
Peter Karl Jonason (Ed.)
Shining Light on the Dark Side of Personality
Measurement Properties and Theoretical Advances
2022 (July), viii + 320 pages
ISBN 978-0-88937-615-1

Vol. 5
Willibald Ruch, Arnold B. Bakker, Louis Tay, Fabian Gander (Eds.)
Handbook of Positive Psychology Assessment
2022 (November), vi + 464 pages
ISBN 978-0-88937-619-9

Vol. 6
Adrian Meule (Ed.)
Assessment of Eating Behavior
2023 (May), viii + 295 pages
ISBN 978-0-88937-616-8

For more information and further volumes, please see www.hogrefe.com